DARK
DAYS

DARK DAYS

~ THE STORY OF ~
FOUR CANADIANS
TORTURED
IN THE NAME OF
FIGHTING TERROR

Kerry Pither

Foreword by
MAHER ARAR

VIKING
CANADA

VIKING CANADA

Published by the Penguin Group

Penguin Group (Canada), 90 Eglinton Avenue East, Suite 700,
Toronto, Ontario, Canada M4P 2Y3 (a division of Pearson Canada Inc.)

Penguin Group (USA) Inc., 375 Hudson Street, New York, New York 10014, U.S.A.
Penguin Books Ltd, 80 Strand, London WC2R 0RL, England
Penguin Ireland, 25 St Stephen's Green, Dublin 2, Ireland (a division of Penguin Books Ltd)
Penguin Group (Australia), 250 Camberwell Road, Camberwell, Victoria 3124, Australia
(a division of Pearson Australia Group Pty Ltd)
Penguin Books India Pvt Ltd, 11 Community Centre, Panchsheel Park,
New Delhi – 110 017, India
Penguin Group (NZ), 67 Apollo Drive, Rosedale, North Shore 0632, New Zealand
(a division of Pearson New Zealand Ltd)
Penguin Books (South Africa) (Pty) Ltd, 24 Sturdee Avenue, Rosebank,
Johannesburg 2196, South Africa

Penguin Books Ltd, Registered Offices: 80 Strand, London WC2R 0RL, England

First published 2008

1 2 3 4 5 6 7 8 9 10   (RRD)

Copyright © Kerry Pither, 2008

Foreword copyright © Maher Arar, 2008

Author representation: Westwood Creative Artists
94 Harbord Street, Toronto, Ontario M5S 1G6

Manufactured in the U.S.A.

LIBRARY AND ARCHIVES CANADA CATALOGUING IN PUBLICATION

Pither, Kerry
Dark days : the story of four Canadians tortured in the name of fighting terror / Kerry Pither.

Includes index.

ISBN 978-0-670-06853-1

1. Almalki, Abdullah. 2. Arar, Maher. 3. El Maati, Ahmad. 4. Nureddin,
Muayyed. 5. Muslims—Civil rights—Canada. 6. Prisoners—Abuse of—Syria.
7. False imprisonment. 8. Terrorism—Prevention—Political aspects—Canada.
9. Civil rights—Canada. 10. National security—Canada. 11. Torture victims—
Biography. 12. Muslims—Canada—Biography. I. Title.

JC571.P575 2008   323.4'90971   C2008-902639-X

Visit the Penguin Group (Canada) website at **www.penguin.ca**

Special and corporate bulk purchase rates available; please see
www.penguin.ca/corporatesales or call 1-800-810-3104, ext. 477 or 474

IN MEMORY OF MY GRANDMOTHER,
LIU MING CHING (EYNSTONE),
WHOSE COURAGE AND TENACITY
WILL ALWAYS INSPIRE ME

Let us be clear:
Torture can never be an instrument
to fight terror,
for torture is an instrument of terror.

—FORMER UNITED NATIONS SECRETARY-GENERAL
KOFI ANNAN, MESSAGE FOR HUMAN RIGHTS DAY,
DECEMBER 10, 2005

CONTENTS

FOREWORD
BY MAHER ARAR

I FIRST MET KERRY PITHER at Dorval airport in Montreal on October 6, 2003. It was the day of my return to Canada, after having been released from 361 days in Syrian prisons where I endured physical and psychological tortures that I have often described as being beyond human imagination. I was extremely fragile, disoriented, and distrustful of people. I was met and greeted by my wife, Monia, who was accompanied by Alex Neve, secretary general of Amnesty International Canada; Riad Saloojee, the executive director of the Canadian Council on American Islamic Relations; and Kerry, among others. These three people were essentially complete strangers to me.

While we were still at the airport, Monia told me that I could trust them, at which point I felt comfortable giving them small snippets about what had happened to me. Monia explained to me later that the trio formed the core of a group of supporters who helped her in her struggle to get me back home. Weeks later, after having spent some time with Monia and my kids, I met with them again and told them exactly what had happened, down to the minutest details. Since then, they have become close friends of the family, and I respect them highly. During the entire four-year struggle that Monia and I waged, they have shared with us every moment of hope and despair, the good and the bad times.

Because of his extremely objective personality, Alex became my mentor, whom I frequently consulted on personal matters. As for Riad, I very much respected his integrity and his unique personality, which he combines in both the professional and spiritual aspects in his extremely challenging position. Kerry's numerous skills and talents, combined with her passion and her belief in justice, allowed her to play numerous important roles during our struggle: She advised the group on public relations and media strategy, coordinated media requests, and helped write some of my public speeches, among other things.

As I grew to know her better, I came to realize that Kerry was far from new to standing up for justice and advocating for the rights of vulnerable people and communities. Her human rights work in East Timor, for example, helped force the public's attention to the injustices being committed by the Suharto regime.

Winning my release from Syrian prison and eventually winning a call for a public inquiry was no easy task for Monia and me, considering the heightened post–9/11 security environment, the seriousness of the allegations against me, and the immense resources of the implicated agencies compared with our own—not to mention, of course, that it was against the wishes of all the governments involved. My release and return to Canada, where I can speak freely about what happened to me, was not in the interest of many powerful individuals and agencies, as it would open a can of worms that would put the spotlight on what has become known as "extraordinary rendition." Under that program, put into effect by the Bush administration, terrorist suspects are rendered by the U.S. government to torture chambers in various Middle Eastern and North African countries, such as Egypt, Morocco, Jordan, and Syria. It would also expose the direct or indirect complicity of other Western governments in such a program. Some of these governments perfected other "techniques" by which these suspects were harassed until they "voluntarily" left to countries where they could be detained based on information that could have originated only from the security agencies of the countries they had just departed. Indeed, only one day after I went public with my story, on November 4, 2003, Dana Priest, a renowned journalist with *The Washington Post*, wrote an article in which she referred to my case and also exposed the extent of the American extraordinary rendition program. On the Canadian side, the Arar Inquiry, led by Justice Dennis O'Connor, eventually exposed the role played by our security agencies. It also laid the groundwork for a follow-up inquiry, headed by Justice Iacobucci, into the role played by Canadian officials in the cases of three Canadian citizens: Abdullah Almalki, Ahmad El Maati, and Muayyed Nureddin. Their stories are described in full detail in this book.

The pattern of international complicity in torture became clear to me when I was still in Syria. Shortly after my arrival I found out that many terrorism suspects who were detained in the neighbouring underground cells were directly or indirectly rendered to Syria courtesy of the U.S. government and its allies in the so-called "war on terror." In this book, Kerry has drawn this pattern out of the shadows and into the light of day by pulling together the threads of the story through reliable sources such as the O'Connor report, as well as various reports published by Amnesty International and other trusted human rights organizations. She brings clarity to what is a very complicated and contentious matter, and her book will appeal to a wide range of people: academics, human rights activists, lawyers, and, perhaps most importantly, concerned citizens.

Kerry has also put a human face on the suffering of individuals and their family members. My experience in Syria tells me that, contrary to how many suspects were portrayed by some media through the eyes of security agencies, they were not violent, evil, or bad men, as we were led to believe. In fact, most of them have not been charged with any crime and some of them have since been released. It became clear to me that we were all sent to Syria for the sole purpose of extracting information through the use of techniques that were, and still are, strictly prohibited in a democracy.

This book comes at a critical time in Canadian history, where we have to make crucial choices as a society, and as civilized people. In this book, as the reader will soon find out, there are lessons for every one of us: politicians, security agencies, media, and Canadian Muslims.

Politicians need to ask themselves important questions, such as: Did they, by rushing to grant enhanced anti-terrorism powers to CSIS and the RCMP without also enhancing civilian oversight of those agencies, help foster an overzealous attitude to national security investigations? Have politicians assumed responsibility for the lack of political oversight during this period, especially those ministers responsible for these agencies? What about the important recommendation of Justice O'Connor regarding civilian oversight? Are they going to implement it in full in order to avoid a repeat of what happened?

The reputations of the RCMP and CSIS, as well as Canada as a country, have been tarnished as a result of what happened in these cases. I have no doubt that an overwhelming majority of the officers involved in national security investigations are honest and have a strong desire and commitment to protect our national security. But they must understand that good intentions alone are not sufficient. Whether there was a true threat, a perceived threat, or an exaggerated threat, their actions must remain guided by domestic law, international law, and the Canadian Charter of Rights and Freedoms. These officers have to be extremely careful when dealing with countries that do not share our standards of human rights. They have to remember that both torture and direct or indirect complicity in torture is an international crime. I invite each one of them to picture themselves for a minute spending just one day in one of the tiny underground cells where the Syrian torturers kept three Canadian citizens for periods ranging from 74 days in the case of El Maati to 482 days in the case of Almalki.

The role that some journalists played in these cases is also worth noting. Most journalists have written balanced articles and kept the stories alive. These journalists deserve respect and applause. Others, unfortunately, knowingly or unknowingly, became instruments in the hands of anonymous Canadian and American officials whose agenda was to prejudice public opinion. These officials leaked a damaging mixture of selective, inaccurate, and false information to these journalists, most of which was either extracted under torture or was a pure fabrication by the Syrian Military Intelligence. These journalists must know that the damage they have done to people's lives is beyond repair, and the stigma created by those leaks will follow the victims for the rest of their lives. These journalists must ask themselves how they would feel if they were publicly slandered in the eyes of all of society by a trusted authority. I am sure that an honest answer to this question is that, as sacred as it is, the principle of freedom of expression in the media is not absolute. It must be exercised responsibly, professionally, and within a framework of ethics that supports seeking the truth, as opposed to seeking to enhance one's reputation by destroying the reputation of another person. I found it extremely disappointing that the majority of journalists who wrote one-sided stories about these cases completely ignored the section of the O'Connor report that was most relevant and important to them: the section where he cites how unfair some media coverage was, and criticizes the obvious pattern of "anonymous" sources steering public opinion through the media. The Canadian public has trusted you, the media, with tremendous power, so please use it responsibly and wisely; and if you have to err, please err on the side of the vulnerable and the weak.

Most Canadian Muslims have understandably felt both marginalized and frightened since the attacks on the World Trade Center on September 11, 2001, when three thousand innocent civilians were killed. Most preferred to keep silent about the harassment they experienced: frequent and invasive visits from CSIS officers to interview them, often at odd times of the day, or unexpected visits at their workplace. These visits would often include the officer's advice that it would be better not to seek the professional help of a lawyer. There is no excuse for staying silent, and certainly no advantage, as this book will clearly show. Yes, speaking out can result in tremendous personal sacrifices, but Muslims have to remember that they have a duty to society to defend their rights, or risk the erosion of all Canadians' rights. Previous generations of Canadians, including immigrants and Aboriginal peoples, have struggled and sacrificed their lives and possessions to build a society in which people could live protected by human rights and freedoms. This book will show that this work is far from done, and that the "quiet diplomacy" approach recommended by the Canadian government in dealing with countries such as Egypt and Syria is not just fruitless but actually damaging to the framework of support for human rights that we have built over time.

Please, as you are reading through this book, remember that these stories are real; they happened to real people, people who have wives, children, parents, and friends. They all have been harmed in different ways, but the harm has been profound and lasting. Please remember that the individuals who you will be reading about in this book paid a price—they satisfied the need for a scapegoat, for some sort of proof that the "war on terror" was going well. The months and years of torture, captivity, and hopelessness in Syrian or Egyptian dungeons is only part of their suffering. They paid a further price, beyond their suffering and the loss of human dignity: They also lost their reputations, their employment, their self-respect and self-image. The effects of the physical and psychological harm they endured may never entirely fade.

Finally, we should all ask ourselves an important question: Do we, as a civilized nation, feel safer when the agencies we have tasked with protecting our well-being and security resort to tactics that violate our basic human rights? My own answer to that question lies in the epigraph to this book, the words of Kofi Annan, former secretary-general of the United Nations: "Let us be clear: Torture can never be an instrument to fight terror, for torture is an instrument of terror."

AUTHOR'S NOTE

WHEN MONIA MAZIGH walked into my office in May 2003 looking for support, she insisted that her husband, Maher Arar, was innocent. I told her I agreed with what she had been telling the public for months—that he had the right to be presumed innocent and that shipping anyone off to be tortured is a travesty. More than five and a half years later, Maher Arar has been exonerated and has become a household name in Canada.

The day after he first told the world his story on November 4, 2003, *The Globe and Mail* wrote an editorial saying, "Mr. Arar's case stands for nothing less than the presumption of innocence, and whether that presumption is to be a casualty of the world-wide war on terrorism."[1]

It is that question that is at the heart of this book.

I believe that the other men I write about in this book—Ahmad El Maati, Abdullah Almalki, and Muayyed Nureddin—like Maher Arar and everyone else, have the right to be presumed innocent.

To tell these four stories, I have relied on almost five years of first-hand interviews with the men and their families to reconstruct a narrative of events in Canada, Syria, Egypt, and points in between.

Of course Canadian officials have the right to be presumed innocent too. Describing their roles has not been easy, because so much of what happened on the official side has been cloaked in secrecy through claims of national security confidentiality. So I have relied on findings of fact from the Arar Inquiry's report, documents, and testimony presented at that inquiry, as well as other information in the public domain. Where information is lacking, I've posed questions.

Each of the men has asked me to keep the names of their children, some family members, and friends out of the book. "I'm sick of ruining other people's lives just by knowing them," one of them explained. I've complied with this. Being publicly identified as related to or an "associate" or "friend" of someone who has been labelled a terror suspect can lead to raised eyebrows and awkward questions from employers, colleagues, and friends or, worse, being ostracized in the community. This is especially true for Muslims in the post–9/11 world.

So at times I have either withheld a name or, as indicated in the Notes, used a pseudonym. Some of the people I have chosen not to name live in or still travel to countries where they could be at risk. Some have already endured the impact of being named in the media. Others haven't. None have been charged with a crime. Most were never under investigation at all.

I've also chosen to write my own role, as an advocate who has actively supported these men's quest for answers, out of the story. Where I was directly involved in something I describe, I describe my role in the Notes.

Memory is often a casualty of torture. The men have done their best to remember experiences that they are working, both subconsciously and consciously, to forget and overcome. As you will see, they could not be precise about the timing of everything that happened.

I have included as much reference material as possible in the Notes—for example, coordinates for the detention centres in which the men were held and web pages in which the Arar Report, transcripts of testimony, and other relevant information are available—and I encourage readers to explore.

Finally, there is one more important resource that I urge readers to seek out. After I began this project, Monia Mazigh took on a book of her own, entitled *Hope and Despair*, to be published by McClelland and Stewart in the fall of 2008. While I have not yet read it, I'm convinced that it will provide a compelling first-hand account essential to truly understanding what she and Maher Arar have endured.

ONE

The Man with the Map

Late dawn, Thursday, August 16, 2001
Queenston-Lewiston Bridge, Queenston, Ontario

IT WAS JUST PAST DAWN when Ahmad El Maati drove up to the Canada-U.S. border crossing on the Queenston-Lewiston bridge, near Buffalo. A long-haul truck driver for more than three years now, he had crossed the border hundreds of times before, and twice already just this week. This time, the paperwork for his cargo wasn't customs-ready, and without a Pre-arrival Processing System (PAPS) barcode on the bill of lading, he needed to stop and clear U.S. customs. When he did, a customs officer said he'd have to inspect his truck. This had happened only three or four times in the three years Ahmad had been delivering to the United States.

The officer watched as Ahmad backed his truck into the inspections area, then climbed into the trailer with three other officers and a dog and inspected every container. "Where are you taking these batteries?" one of them asked. His tone was gruff, almost hostile. Ahmad pointed to his paperwork, which showed that the load of used car batteries was supposed to be delivered by noon that day to the East Penn Manufacturing Company in Lyon Station, Philadelphia. That was at least six hours away. He began to worry he might be late. "Come with us," one of the men instructed, motioning toward the front of his truck. This was unusual. Ahmad had never had his truck cab searched before. He watched as the men rifled through his personal belongings and papers. One of them held up a boarding pass from his recent trip to Syria.

"So, you do lots of travelling?"

"My wife is in Syria," Ahmad said.

His mind raced—was this going to count against him?

Two men in civilian clothes joined in the search, then held up a letter-sized sheet of paper, asking what it was. Ahmad looked at the paper. It was a street map of a section of downtown Ottawa with handwritten numbers on buildings. Ahmad explained that he had never seen the map before. This wasn't the truck he usually drove, he told them, his truck was in for repairs. There had been some papers and a pair of reading glasses in the truck when he picked it up. The map must have been among those items, which he had assumed belonged to the other driver. He had no use for the map, Ahmad said, because he never made deliveries in Ottawa. The handwriting on the buildings was not his, and he did not use reading glasses.

His answers didn't satisfy the U.S. customs officials, who had noticed that among the named buildings on the map were the offices of Atomic Energy of Canada and virus control laboratories. They asked Ahmad to go into the customs building with them, then told him to sit and wait in a hallway, and assigned an armed guard to stand next to him. Over the next few hours, Ahmad could see the men coming and going and talking in hushed tones in the hall. Ahmad asked for permission to call his employer to report the delay. Permission granted, he got his delivery rescheduled to the next day.

He was eventually taken into a room, where he was told to stand with his back to the wall and hold a number plate to his chest. "They treated me like a criminal," says Ahmad. A customs official took his photograph, asked him to sign his name several times on different pieces of paper, then asked him to look into a retina scanner. He was then taken to a small room and grilled with questions about his family and where he was born and raised. The officials asked again about the map in his truck.

"Do you know why you are here?" one of the men asked. "You are a knucklehead."

Ahmad's English isn't strong—he'd never heard the expression before—but the man's contempt for him was obvious. Ahmad was angry now and spoke up.

"I'm a truck driver, and this is how I earn my living. I can't have this happen every time I cross the border."

"Oh, yes, it will," one of the men warned. "And next time, it will be longer."

They gave him back his belongings and the map, which they had photocopied.

Eight hours after arriving at the border, Ahmad climbed into his truck and continued across the bridge into the United States. He was badly shaken and worried. He wondered if CSIS had anything to do with the day's events. In April, two CSIS agents had visited his father and his cousin in Toronto. This was the first time anyone in his family had been contacted by someone from the police or a security agency. The CSIS agents said they were there because Ahmad's passport had been stolen, but Ahmad, who was with his mother in Syria at the time meeting his future wife, had his passport with him.

Ahmad didn't want trouble: He was looking forward to a new chapter in his life. He had fallen for the young Syrian woman, Rola, when he met her in Syria in April, and, after spending several days getting to know her and her family, had proposed marriage. She readily accepted, and the two families celebrated the engagement. In May, he had travelled back to Syria to legalize the marriage so he could initiate the immigration process to bring her to Canada. Ahmad remembers this time as the best in his life. The two were in love and talked about their future and starting a family, even choosing names for the children they hoped to have. For a boy, Ahmad wanted *Abdullah*, meaning "servant of God," and for a girl, *Mariam*, for Mary, mother of Jesus. The engagement was a turning point in Ahmad's life: It was a new page and a new responsibility, and he knew he would have to work hard. Ahmad had left Syria in June, promising to return in December in time to spend Ramadan with Rola, and to celebrate their marriage with a formal wedding ceremony.

Ahmad delivered the load of batteries in Philadelphia a day late, picked up new cargo, and drove back to Canada. When he returned to the depot he asked for some time off—he wanted to talk to his father about what had happened—but the dispatch manager told him he had another delivery, this time to the southernmost tip of Texas. Ahmad was very nervous as he crossed into the United States again, but this time it was at the Fort Erie crossing, his paperwork had the requisite PAPS barcode, and he was waved through without incident.

Back home in Canada, Ahmad filed a report about the incident at the border with Ann Armstrong, a manager at the trucking company he worked for, Highland Transport. He told her his concerns about the map and whether he would be able to continue driving to the United States. She wrote a letter he could carry with him saying he had reported the incident to the company. She also told him that it would be difficult to determine whom the map belonged to, as two other drivers had driven that truck before him, and one of them had stopped working for the company in July. "Ahmad is to be commended on the way he conducted himself during a trying time," she wrote in the letter. "He remained polite and professional all the while he was questioned and searched by customs."[1]

Ahmad crossed into the United States once more that August, again without incident. He carried his employer's letter with him everywhere but still felt very uneasy about crossing the border. His anxiety eventually got to him, and he reluctantly decided to quit Highland Transport and find work making local deliveries instead.

Just before 9 A.M., Tuesday, September 11, 2001
Dispatch office, Highland Transport, Markham, Ontario

AHMAD WAS FEELING A LITTLE DOWN. He had been a long-haul truck driver for more than three years and enjoyed life on the road. But now he was collecting his belongings from the cab of his truck and turning in the keys to Highland Transport. He remembers turning on the radio and hearing someone say an airplane had crashed into one of the Twin Towers at the World Trade Center in New York. When he walked into the dispatch office, he looked up at the television in the drivers' lounge across the hall. Three other drivers stood looking up at the CNN pictures of smoke billowing out of the building.

The dispatch manager, whom Ahmad hadn't seen for weeks, entered the office and told Ahmad how upset he had been when he heard about the incident with the map. He said he had investigated, learning from other drivers still at the company that one of the truck's previous drivers had probably got the map from a client in Ottawa. He was sorry to be losing Ahmad as a driver, he said—it had been an honour to work with him. As they talked, they heard the men in the lounge gasp. A second airplane had hit the south tower of the World Trade Center. It was clear now that the first crash had not been an accident.

Back at home, Ahmad's sister and mother told him that the World Trade Center towers had collapsed. Already there was speculation that the attacks had been perpetrated in the name of Islam. "I was sickened by the attacks—they were against the Muslim nation and humanity," Ahmad says. "And I knew there would be implications."

That afternoon he and his mother were in their suburban Toronto apartment when there was a knock at the door. Ahmad opened it to find two men standing there. They gave their names and said they were from CSIS. They asked if they could come in, but Ahmad told them that if they wanted to speak with him, they would have to do it outside. He led them to the elevator and went down to the lobby with them. "We were alone when they came, and I was very afraid," Ahmad's mother, Samira al-Shallash, recalls. "When they left I called Ahmad's father and told him some people came and took Ahmad. I still remember that when his father came, his face was white."

Ahmad and the two men sat on a bench outside the apartment building. They told him they were visiting lots of people because of the attacks that morning—a strategy that CSIS later referred to in news reports as "knock and talk." And then they began their questions. "We heard about the map and the incident at the border," one of the men said. "Tell us about the map." Ahmad showed them the letter from his employer. "I always had that letter in my upper-left shirt pocket. I carried it everywhere with me," he says. The men read the letter and said they wanted to talk about his travels and his life. Ahmad told them where he had grown up, and about his mother and father.

They asked him to walk with them to a doughnut shop at a nearby plaza, where they sat on the patio. Ahmad had answered all their questions so far, but as time went on, he started to worry. He wanted a lawyer, as he was afraid he would be misinterpreted. "I told them, 'If I have a lawyer present I will tell you anything you need to know.' They got angry, and told me this was not a court and I did not need a lawyer."

"Ahmad, you know that you have sponsored your wife to come to Canada, and you know that her application will go through us. We are going to stop that," said the man who seemed to be in charge. Ahmad was shocked and said again that he wanted a lawyer. The man leaned forward and said, "You know that we are called *Mukhabarat*," using the Arabic word for intelligence agency, a word synonymous with torture in Middle Eastern countries. Ahmad was surprised that he had used an Arabic word, especially this one. He felt threatened. "You know how the Mukhabarat in Canada deals with citizens, and you know how the Mukhabarat deals with their citizens over there," the man said, meaning in the Middle East.

Ahmad asked if they were threatening him. The man answered no, they just wanted him to cooperate. "I told them, 'I think you are threatening me and I insist I would like to have a lawyer.' I kept repeating that, even to the last moment. I kept saying I wanted a lawyer because I did not want to be misunderstood or misinterpreted. I said it to the point that they were repeating those words back to me like it was a joke." Before they left, Ahmad asked them to give him their names again. The man who had done most of the talking wrote his name, Adrian White, and phone number on a piece of paper in his notebook and tore it off for Ahmad.

Back at the apartment, Ahmad found his mother and father waiting for him, terrified. They talked about everything that had happened: the CSIS visit in April when Ahmad was in Syria, what had happened to him at the border, and the CSIS visit that day. They worried about what would happen next. Did CSIS believe Ahmad was somehow involved in terrorism? Would they really stand in the way of Ahmad's future with his wife?

AHMAD EL MAATI IS A BIG MAN with a friendly face and a broad smile. He is always warmly greeted by neighbours who share the elevator with him in his Toronto high-rise apartment building. In 2008, Ahmad is unable to work and lives with his mother. He is trying to organize women-only hours at the swimming pool for his mother and other Muslim women in the building.

Ahmad was seventeen when he immigrated to Canada in 1981 with his father and older brother, Amr. When his younger sister finished high school, his mother, a schoolteacher from Syria, followed with her. Although Ahmad was born in Kuwait, his citizenship is Egyptian, through his father. The family first settled in Toronto, then Montreal, where Ahmad took college courses in electronics before studying statistics for two years at Concordia University. Ahmad became a Canadian citizen in 1986 and worked odd jobs, including driving a taxi in London, Ontario, and factory work in Montreal.

Ahmad and his family say that soon after the attacks of September 11 they realized why CSIS was interested in him. It wasn't just that he was a devout Muslim. Ahmad had served with the mujahideen in Afghanistan in his twenties and, after returning to Canada, had taken five hours of flying lessons. Until 9/11, the flying lessons had seemed an inconsequential part of Ahmad's past. Now they had taken on a whole new meaning.

In the spring of 1999, after taking his first truck-driving job with Leger Trucking in Montreal, a friend told Ahmad about the money that could be made operating an air-taxi service in the Montreal-Ottawa-Toronto triangle. Being a pilot seemed more profitable and prestigious than driving trucks, so Ahmad signed up for lessons at the Buttonville Airport in Markham, Ontario. He began the lessons in a single-engine Cessna but found it too time-consuming, expensive, and terrifying and so gave it up after a total of only five hours of flying. He sounds a little embarrassed when he talks about it now. "I'm ashamed to say it ... I just couldn't do it. It was too terrifying for me. I couldn't stand the heights."

His time in Afghanistan, however, had changed him—in a good way, he stresses. Through the 1980s, Ahmad had watched what was happening there with interest. The Soviets had invaded, and thousands of young Muslim men from around the world were answering the call to help with the Afghan refugee crisis, and to join forces with the mujahideen fighting the Soviets. Ahmad's brother Amr went in 1988, but within two weeks of arriving contracted hepatitis C and malaria. He was very ill and spent four months in a Peshawar hospital recovering before returning home to Canada in 1989.

Ahmad had inherited a love of travel from his parents, and they travelled extensively as a family. At first, Ahmad's parents left the boys in school when they travelled. When Ahmad was three and Amr was four, their father put them in a Catholic boarding school in Beirut twice for four months at a time. "It was nice in a way because these were very expensive schools ... the nuns took us on trips into the mountains and other places," Ahmad says. But the boys would rather have been travelling with their parents, and after their second summer at the school, in 1969, the boys revolted, insisting they travel with their parents from then on.

And they did, going to Damascus every summer to see his mother's family, and from there they went to Europe. In 1972, his father brought a Chevrolet Impala, and every two years they went on months-long road trips, to Iraq, Syria, Turkey, Romania, Yugoslavia, Hungary, Austria, and Switzerland. In 1978, they went farther, starting in Iraq, then driving through Europe as far as Scotland, and eventually making their way back to Syria. Other trips, to Egypt, Greece, Italy, and Lebanon, followed.

Now, Ahmad's love of travel and adventure, as well as a sense of religious and humanitarian duty, were calling him to Afghanistan. "I finally made up my mind in 1991 to go. I felt by going there I would do something for humanity and Muslims and the Afghans." He thought he would go for three or four months. "I was a young man, very idealistic," he says.

Ahmad flew through New York to Peshawar, Pakistan, which was crowded with Afghan refugees. But within days, Ahmad had left the busy, dusty streets of Peshawar for the deserted landscape of war-torn Afghanistan. Of all the countries he'd travelled to in his youth, he says he had never seen a country so beautiful as Afghanistan. He immediately fell in love with the landscape and the people, who he says were as beautiful and tough as the terrain on which they lived. "They are the most proud, generous, coura-geous people I ever saw in my life ... if they want to do something they do it."

By this time Afghanistan was in ruins, and the people had suffered horrific losses in the war. Between one and two million Afghans, mostly civilians, had died. Their villages and way of life had been destroyed, and landmines, not crops, were planted everywhere. More than a third of Afghanistan's population was living in refugee camps in Pakistan and Iran. The Soviets had left Afghanistan in 1989. Nine years of occupation had cost them fifteen thousand lives and more than thirty thousand casualties.

But the Soviet-backed Communist party that had taken the country's capital, Kabul, at the beginning of the conflict remained, led by President Mohammad Najibullah. Now the mujahideen fought each other for control of Kabul.

Ahmad joined the well-organized, well-funded forces of Gulbuddin Hekmatyar, an Afghan warlord who had for several years received the bulk of millions of dollars in aid the U.S. and Saudi governments funnelled to the mujahideen through the Pakistani intelligence service. It was this faction that was most open to receiving Arab foreigners into its ranks. Ahmad soon decided that this was not going to be the three- or four-month-long adventure he had envisioned. "After I saw what was going on and saw the suffering of the people, and how brave and nice and proud they are, I said ... the least thing I can do is just stay with them and help in whatever way I can."

Ahmad completed a month of basic training with the mujahideen in Bari, south of Khost, to become a foot soldier. Most of the time was devoted to physical fitness, the rest to using a Kalashnikov and a rocket-propelled grenade launcher. In the end, though, he didn't see much of the front, and never fired a rifle in combat, held back by a knee injury during a wrestling try-out in high school. "I couldn't fight—I knew my limits." Instead, he drove ambulances, helped whenever he could with first aid, and cooked for the fighters.

In the spring of 1992, Ahmad was stationed in Logar province, south of Kabul. By this time, Afghanistan had been plunged into a period of lawlessness, especially in Kabul and the surrounding region, which had become the staging ground for a brutal civil war among the various mujahideen factions. Najibullah's government fell in April 1992, and a peace agreement signed between Hekmatyar and his rival, Ahmed Shah Massoud, in May made Hekmatyar interim prime minister. But the deal quickly fell apart as the factions attacked one another again. Together, they laid siege to Kabul, and tens of thousands of civilians lost their lives as the war raged on for the next four years.[2]

Hekmatyar, like all the other mujahideen leaders fighting for control of Kabul at the time, has since been accused of war crimes. Ahmad doesn't think Hekmatyar was any worse than his rivals. Ahmad was several miles south of Kabul in Logar province and says he didn't see any of the carnage first-hand. "I could hear bombardment from both sides, but I didn't hear of civilians being targeted." If he had seen that happening, he would not have stayed, he says.

By 1996, the Taliban had taken over Logar province from the south. Ahmad's group was stationed east of Kabul in Saroby. It was around this time that Ahmad's brother, Amr, returned to Afghanistan and came looking for him. He arrived in Saroby just as the Taliban reached Kabul and Ahmad's group was beginning its retreat north. Ahmad and his brother travelled with the group in a long convoy through the Salang tunnel high in the Hindu Kush mountains. "This was heartbreaking to me, to be driven out by the Taliban—a force that I believed was not sincere for the cause of Afghanistan," Ahmad says.

When they reached northern Afghanistan, Amr left for Pakistan. Hekmatyar had already fled into exile in Iran. Ahmad stayed with the men he'd been stationed with but longed to follow his brother into Pakistan so he could go home to Canada. The Taliban was slowly taking over the country, and Ahmad's group was now surrounded. With the Taliban standing in the way of Pakistan, the only way out was through Iran. Ahmad fled there in November 1997.

Once in Tehran, Ahmad telephoned his mother. She had separated from Ahmad's father and was in Saudi Arabia with Ahmad's sister. The two made plans to meet in Syria and visit her family before going home together to Canada. Ahmad travelled across the Iranian border to Pakistan, where he met up with his brother in Peshawar. Amr was working with a Canadian-based aid agency there called the Health and Education Project, a project set up by Ahmed Said Khadr.

The Khadr family, of course, would become infamous in Canada in the years following 9/11. At the time, Ahmad says neither he nor his brother knew that CSIS already had Khadr in its sights. Neither did Canadian prime minister Jean Chrétien, it would turn out. Until 1995, Khadr had worked in Peshawar as regional director for a Canadian-based aid organization called Human Concern International (HCI). In November of that year, the Egyptian Embassy in Islamabad was attacked by two suicide bombers. Khadr was detained the next month by the Pakistani intelligence and accused of helping to fund the attack. Khadr denied any connection to the attack, and his family appealed to Prime Minister Chrétien, who was in the region on a trade mission at the time, for help. Chrétien urged then-Pakistani prime minister Benazir Bhutto to ensure Khadr was treated fairly. The Pakistani intelligence had no evidence of his role in the bombing, so Khadr was released, without charge, after three months in detention. He returned to Canada and was dismissed by HCI.[3] When he returned to Pakistan, he set up his own charity, called the Health and Education Project.[4]

Amr and Ahmad stayed together for three months while Ahmad renewed his Canadian passport and obtained a visa to travel into Syria. Ahmad left for Syria in March 1998. He would be travelling by bus to Islamabad, then flying to Karachi and staying overnight before leaving for Damascus to meet up with his mother. The two brothers were in tears as they stood waiting for the bus. Amr asked Ahmad to stay with him, but Ahmad reminded him that their mother needed him. He said he knew that Amr was happy in Peshawar, and hoped he would marry soon and settle down. They spoke through the open window, and as the bus pulled away, Amr held on to the window frame for as long as he could. "It's as if he knew we would not meet again," Ahmad says.

He and his mother were reunited in Damascus, where they stayed with Ahmad's grandfather. Ahmad wanted to marry, and his mother wanted to help, but he was broke. He needed to get back to Canada and establish a career and earn some money first.

Ahmad returned to Canada in 1998, moving in with his father in Toronto. It had been twelve years since he had lived in Toronto. He had few connections and couldn't find work. He looked up a friend in Montreal, Ibrahym Adam, who was looking for someone to help with his family business, a garage, and went to work for him as a mechanic's assistant.[5] Ahmad had heard there was lots of work in the trucking business, and he longed to travel and see more of North America. So, after a couple of months, Ahmad used the money he had earned at the garage, plus a little borrowed from his father, to attend truck-driving school in Scarborough, Ontario. After two months of training, he earned a class AZ truck-driver's licence.

In March 1999, Ahmad travelled to Saudi Arabia to perform the hajj for the first time. (He went to Mecca a second time, in 2001, to accompany his mother, as women aren't permitted to perform the hajj alone.) Performing the hajj is the fifth pillar of Islam: Every Muslim who is physically and financially able must perform the pilgrimage to Mecca at least once in his or her lifetime. Up to two million pilgrims do the hajj each year, in the twelfth month of the lunar Islamic calendar. "This was a life-changing experience, spiritually, mentally, in every way," Ahmad says. When he returned, he got his first truck-driving job with Montreal's Leger Trucking. The company had a dedicated run between farms in Salinas, California, and a Montreal warehouse that supplied lettuce to Quebec's major supermarkets and the McDonald's restaurant chain. After a few months Ahmad decided to look for work elsewhere. Not only did he prefer driving alone, he also was earning only about $750 for every thirty-hour run. Driving solo meant triple the pay, so when he saw an advertisement for a Toronto-based company called Motion Supply, he applied. The company hired him in the spring of 2000, eventually assigning him to drive for Highland Transport.

Ahmad loved driving for Highland Transport and worked all the time, taking only a half-day off per week. "It's like a paid hobby, a paid vacation. You see different places every time you go. I went to all but three states, and almost every city and major town in the United States. I love driving, I loved working on my own, and the money was good."

"Your Name Is 'Number Five' Now"

Evening, Tuesday, September 11, 2001
Richmond Hill, Toronto

THE FIRST TIME Ahmad saw the man in the silver Toyota Camry was the evening of the CSIS visit on September 11. He and his mother, along with his sister and her husband and children, drove home from visiting friends. Ahmad had his mother and four of his nieces and nephews in his car. His sister and brother-in-law and their other children were following in another car. His sister's family lived in Richmond Hill, a community north of Toronto, at the end of a cul-de-sac. It was late, and the streets were quiet. Ahmad had noticed a car following them into the neighbour-hood. Now it drove behind them into the cul-de-sac. As they parked, Ahmad's sister remarked that she noticed the car, too. Ahmad wanted to know who it was and so got back in his car and drove after the silver Camry, which had exited the cul-de-sac. He pulled up beside the car, stopped at an intersection, and motioned to the driver to roll down his window. "Are you following us?" he asked. The man seemed taken aback and unprepared for the confrontation. He muttered something and sped away.

After that, the surveillance became even more obvious: They wanted Ahmad to know he was being followed. Ahmad swears that on some days more than a dozen cars followed him at the same time. Everywhere. They waited for him outside his building, followed him to pick up his truck, followed him from one end of the city to the other while he made his deliveries, followed him shopping and running errands, followed him to the mosque, and followed him back to his home at night, where they'd sit waiting for him to leave again. The man in the silver Camry was always there. Ahmad remembers him well, and guesses he was in his late forties, with dark hair and skin, maybe Middle Eastern or South American, and always wore glasses—dark ones when he was driving or outside during the day. The man would pull up beside Ahmad at intersections and just sit there staring at him.

Ahmad's aunt, Sana Wassef, remembers one evening when the man in the silver Camry came in handy. Ahmad and his mother were at her house and decided to go out for dinner. On the phone to Ahmad's father, Ahmad suggested they go to the Red Lobster in Scarborough. "His father said, 'Which Red Lobster?' and Ahmad told him which Red Lobster," Sana remembers. His father came to pick them up in his car. "We lost our way—we didn't know where the restaurant was, but then Ahmad suddenly said, 'Okay, okay, follow that car!'" He had seen the man in the silver Camry. "He was now in front of us, and he entered the Red Lobster, and we went behind him." By then, Ahmad had assumed his family's phones were being tapped.

"Another time we went to the country—to Terra Cotta—it is a beautiful area, and in the fall it is full of leaves. We were walking in the leaves. And then we said we'd have dinner in one of the restaurants, so, of course, they followed us. It was a remote area ... it was late fall, cold, and it was night. And we felt so bad that we were having dinner, and these people, at night time, they are sitting in their cars waiting ... we were thinking, 'Why don't we invite them to have dinner with us?' but, of course, we didn't."

Sana laughs about it now. But back then, it wasn't funny: Over time, it became nerve-racking for the whole family. Whenever they went for dinner, as a family or with friends, the cars followed; sometimes the men even came into the restaurant and sat at the next table, staring at them while they ate.

Sana also remembers Ahmad's visits. "Our house is on a corner ... we had big windows," she says. Ahmad felt uncomfortable and wanted to close the curtains. He felt as if they were on a stage. "I used to say, 'No leave it open, I want them to see that we are not doing any plotting or anything, that we are just normal people in our home.'"

The conspicuous surveillance continued through October and into November. Ahmad's father, an accountant and auditor, remembers sitting down one day to calculate how much the surveillance was costing taxpayers. "Each guy would take his salary twice because it is overtime, and there are two in a car—and so many cars.... It was a huge amount!"

Afternoon, Saturday, October 13, 2001
Home of Samira al-Shallash and Ahmad El Maati, Toronto

AHMAD ENJOYED HIS WEEKENDS OFF—that was the good thing about driving locally. Stretched out on the couch, he turned on the television to watch the news. His mother was in the kitchen preparing dinner. He read the news ticker scrolling across the bottom of the screen on CTV Newsnet and caught his breath. Had he read that right? The news scrolled across the screen again: A thirty-six-year-old Kuwaiti man had been stopped at the U.S. border with a map detailing nuclear facilities and virus control labs in Ottawa. Ahmad was not a Kuwaiti citizen, but he had been born there, was thirty-six, and it was clear this story was about the map he'd been stopped with.

CTV's story, it turned out, was based on a front-page story of that day's *Globe and Mail* titled "Kuwaiti found with papers on sensitive Ottawa sites." Journalist Peter Cheney wrote that "investigators probing the Sept. 11 terror attacks have been told that a Kuwaiti man was found with documents detailing Canadian atomic-energy facilities and disease-control labs." The FBI wouldn't comment, but the RCMP's spokesperson Corporal Eric Simard told Cheney that there was an ongoing "criminal investigation" and that "infiltration of nuclear facilities" was part of the RCMP's focus. The discovery of the documents, said the article, "adds weight to growing concerns that Canada may have been targeted by terrorists."[1] The report about the "Kuwaiti man" with a map prompted the Toronto-based nuclear safety group, Energy Probe, to call for the shutdown of nuclear plants. "A terrorist attack on a nuclear-power station, when operating, could kill tens of thousands," Tom Adams, executive director of Energy Probe, was quoted as saying in the article. "A reactor station that has been temporarily shut down eliminates the risk of a terrorist-induced meltdown."

The story had first appeared a day earlier on the front-page of the *Los Angeles Times*. Describing leads being investigated by the FBI, it said that "in Canada, U.S. agents were briefed on a 36-year-old Kuwaiti man in whose belongings were discovered documents that identified specific buildings in an Ottawa government complex—notably the atomic energy building and the virus and disease control labs."[2]

Ahmad was horrified. There was some mistake, and he needed to fix it fast. He remembered a lawyer who had come around to the mosque offering services to Muslims who were feeling harassed after 9/11. Ahmad and his father talked and decided to see this man, Rocco Galati, first thing on Monday. By the time they talked with him on Monday, Ahmad was apoplectic. The *National Post* had picked up the story; the sensational headline read "Terrorists eye nuclear plants, expert says: 'Ample evidence': Kuwaiti man had sensitive documents on N-plant, virus lab."[3] "Terrorists are clearly gathering information for their next move," read the first sentence "and the target could be Canada's nuclear facilities, a former official with the Canadian Security Intelligence Service says."

The former CSIS official, David Harris, said that he would "count on" nuclear material "being in the wrong hands" and warned that "people in the West don't fully understand the hatred extremists have for our society. Once you appreciate that it's an absolute obligation of honour and necessity for them to rid the world of as many of us as possible, then all of a sudden where's the surprise that people have been looking around in our nuclear secrets and sensibilities? Canada ... needs a radical improvement in its defence and security measures to protect against threats like this."

It was that morning, on October 15, 2001, that, as we shall see, Canada's new anti-terrorism legislation was tabled in Parliament.

Ahmad and his father told Galati about the day at the border and the map. They told him about the day CSIS agents came to Ahmad's apartment, and what they had said about stopping his wife from coming to Canada. They told him about Ahmad's time in Afghanistan, and the flying lessons. And that Ahmad was being followed, everywhere, all the time. Ahmad gave Galati the phone number Adrian White had given him at their meeting on September 11 and asked him to set up a meeting as soon as possible so they could clear things up. They wanted to set the record straight with CSIS and answer to their suspicions. What they didn't tell Galati, because they didn't know, was that their names, and that of Ahmad's brother, Amr, had appeared on a U.S. terrorist watch list.[4]

Galati called Adrian White several times, leaving messages, but White never returned the calls.

3 P.M., Sunday, November 11, 2001
Pearson International Airport, Toronto

AHMAD HAD PLANNED TO WAIT UNTIL DECEMBER to go back to Syria. But now he was feeling harassed, and he was worried that CSIS was going to stand in the way of his future with Rola. He wanted to see her as soon as possible, celebrate their marriage, and bring her home. His mother, Samira, wasn't happy with his decision. She had heard in news reports that the Americans and the Syrians had been working together since 9/11, and she was anxious that Ahmad might run into trouble there. She wanted him to postpone the wedding. They argued, but Ahmad was determined not to let CSIS stand in the way of this new chapter in his life.

He and his mother set out for Pearson International Airport at around three o'clock in the afternoon on Sunday, November 11. They were booked to travel together to Frankfurt on Air Canada flight 872, departing at 5:35 P.M., then to Vienna on Austrian Airlines. From there, he would travel to Damascus, and his mother would go to Cairo to visit family before joining him in Syria within a week.

Ahmad's cousin rented a minivan to get them to the airport, as they had lots of luggage, packed full of gifts for Rola's family. When they pulled up to the curb in front of the terminal, the man in the silver Toyota Camry sped into the spot behind them. Another car pulled in front of them. Four men, wearing dark suits and dark sunglasses, got out of the cars and stood watching as Ahmad and his cousin unloaded the van. Ahmad was angry and told his mother and cousin to ignore them. Ahmad wondered whether they were going to stop him from leaving.

Ahmad and his cousin loaded the heavy bags onto carts and rolled them up to the Air Canada check-in counter. They noticed three more men watching them.

"Your bags are both over the weight limit, sir," the ticket agent informed Ahmad. He was surprised—he had expected to pay extra but didn't know there was a weight limit for each bag. After some discussion, they realized the only solution was to buy another bag and spread the weight out. Ahmad's cousin ran to a store in the airport, returning with a new suitcase. The men standing to the side watched as Ahmad and his mother repacked all of their bags, distributing the weight among them. After some time, they were ready to check in. Running late now, they hurried to clear security. Ahmad went to embrace his cousin and bid him farewell. Just then, one of the men watching them interrupted and showed Ahmad his badge.

"Ahmad El Maati, I am from the O.P.P. [Ontario Provincial Police] and I need to talk to you."

"He was not laughing, but he had a sort of serious smile on his face, as if he was saying 'You know all about us and that we were following you and now we want to talk to you,'" Ahmad remembers.

Ahmad's cousin stepped in. "They have a flight to catch—are you going to stop them?"

The officer said no, they wouldn't.

"Do you promise?" Ahmad's cousin asked.

They said yes, they would make sure Ahmad and his mother didn't miss their flight. The men took Ahmad into an elevator, down into the basement of the airport, and into a small room. A woman opened the door for them. That woman and two men stayed in the room with him. One of them was the man with the O.P.P. badge. Ahmad remembers there was a camera in the room over the door.

"Where are you going?" one of the men asked.

"To Syria."

"Why are you going?"

"For my wedding."

"Where are you going to stay?"

"At my grandmother's house."

"How much money do you have?"

Ahmad had about $3500, and his mother had another $3500. This was for Rola's dowry, he explained (in the Arab world, it is customary for the groom's family to pay a dowry to the bride).

"Where is the map?"

"With Rocco Galati; he is my lawyer" Ahmad replied, passing them Galati's business card.

Ahmad asked if they were going to stop him from travelling. No, they replied, then left the room. A few minutes later the men came back and told Ahmad they would escort him to his flight. Ahmad was upset, and as they exited the elevator he asked them, "Are you going to do to the Muslim community here what you did to the Japanese in World War II?"

"This is not for us to decide, this is for the politicians to decide," one of the men answered.

His mother was waiting for him. She had been questioned too, after Ahmad was taken away. Asked why she and her son were travelling, she replied that they were going to Syria for Ahmad's wedding. One man asked how many children she had, where they were, and how much money she and Ahmad had on them. He was astonished to hear they were carrying $7000.

"I asked him, 'Why are you surprised? We are going to a wedding!'"

They asked why she was going to Cairo and not to Damascus with Ahmad. She explained that she was going to see family in Cairo and would be joining Ahmad in Syria for the wedding.

Then they asked, "Do you know any terrorists?"

Samira looked at him, incredulous, and asked how, at her age, and in her situation, she would know any terrorists.

When the men returned with Ahmad, Samira and Ahmad bid Ahmad's cousin goodbye and went through security, the men following closely behind. At the gate, the airline agent took their boarding passes and handed them new ones—their seats had been reassigned.

Ahmad and his mother walked down the passenger bridge to the airplane, the men following close behind. Ahmad looked behind him as he boarded. The men were standing just outside the door to the aircraft, watching them. As Ahmad and his mother hurried down the aisle to their newly assigned seats, many of the passengers stared up at them. The flight had been delayed just for them.

The aircraft was a Boeing 747, with a centre row four seats wide. Ahmad's mother sat next to the aisle, Ahmad sat to her left in the middle. Two men sat to his left. After the plane took off, the man beside him started speaking to Ahmad in Arabic.

"Where are you going?" he asked, with a Lebanese accent.

Ahmad told him he was going to his wedding. The man was talkative, asking lots of questions. Ahmad was tired and angry about what had happened in the airport and wished that the man would just stay quiet. But the man kept talking, telling Ahmad that he had a courier business in Mississauga on Dixie Road by Highway 401. He was a Christian Lebanese, he said, on his way to meet his brother in Vienna.

The plane landed in Frankfurt at 7 A.M. They had fifty minutes until their connecting flight to Vienna departed, so they walked to a café in the transit area for a coffee. When they had finished their coffee, they cleared German immigration and made their way to the gate for their connecting flight. It was then that Ahmad saw someone running toward them. It was the Lebanese man from the first flight. He was angry, and yelling at them.

"Where did you go? You are going to miss the plane!"

Ahmad asked him why he was so concerned. "When the man realized he had overreacted, he pulled back a little," Ahmad remembers. The man turned and ran back ahead of them to the gate.

When Ahmad and his mother reached the gate, the Lebanese man was standing by the desk with two men in civilian clothes. "He was their man," Ahmad says.

One of the men showed them his badge and said he was with the German border police. "Give me your passports," he instructed them.

Speaking in German, the man read out the information from their passports into his cellphone. Was something wrong? Ahmad asked. The man shook his head, signalling to Ahmad to be quiet—he was waiting for instructions. Then the man handed back their passports and told them to board their flight. The talkative Lebanese man was on the flight, too, but this time didn't sit with them.

A little over an hour later, the plane landed in Vienna. It was just after 9:30 A.M., and less than an hour before their flights departed for Cairo and Damascus. Ahmad went into the duty-free shop to buy more gifts for Rola's family. Samira, worried about her son, called her stepmother in Damascus to tell her that Ahmad would be there soon. Rola and her family would meet Ahmad at the airport and drive him to the house. The security checkpoint for Samira's flight was near Ahmad's, so she stood and watched as Ahmad went through to the waiting area for his flight. "He waved to me and I waved to him and he went through," she says.

When Ahmad entered the waiting area, all the passengers but one were seated. The man standing was talking loudly on his cellphone. He was speaking Arabic, and his accent suggested he was from Saudi Arabia or another Gulf state. When it came time to board, the man who had been on the cellphone took the seat next to Ahmad, despite the Airbus 320 being less than half full. As the plane took off he turned to Ahmad and said, "So, you are a Canadian?" Ahmad was shocked. How would this man know this? His Canadian passport was tucked out of sight in his pocket, and the man had been nowhere near him when he presented it at security. The man seemed to realize he had made a mistake and turned away from Ahmad. He seemed nervous and fidgety for the rest of the flight.

The plane had barely touched down in Damascus when the man undid his seatbelt, stood up, and started walking very quickly to the front of the airplane. Ahmad remembers he had no hand luggage. A flight attendant yelled at the man to sit down, as the plane was still coasting toward the gate. He reluctantly took a nearby seat, but as soon as the plane came to a stop, he jumped up again, jostling to get ahead of the other passengers. Ahmad reached for his bags and waited to disembark with the other passengers. As he entered the terminal, he could see the man: "There was a long hall, and I saw the guy running—not walking—running to get to the immigration desk." Ahmad lost sight of him when the man ran down the stairs.

It was now late afternoon in Damascus, and Ahmad had been travelling for more than sixteen hours. "I was feeling sick in my stomach—feeling that something was going to happen." There weren't many people waiting at immigration; only two or three people were ahead of him in line. When it was his turn, Ahmad handed his passport to the men in the booth. One of them typed his name into the computer, then turned to him and said there was a mix-up with his name. When Ahmad asked what he meant, the man pointed over Ahmad's left shoulder to an office. "You can find out about it over there," he said.

Ahmad walked over to the office and stood outside the closed door. The door opened and five burly men came out and surrounded Ahmad. "I knew that was it for me," he says. The one in charge repeated that there was a mix-up with his name and that Ahmad was to come with them. "I said, 'Come where?' and they said, 'Just come with us.'" Their tone was threatening. "They were talking to me like they wanted to punch me, but they couldn't do it yet." One of the men walked in front of Ahmad, leading the way. The others walked beside and behind him. Ahmad was told to pay for a baggage cart, then led to the baggage area. To the other passengers waiting for their bags, Ahmad says, he must have looked like a VIP surrounded by bodyguards—bodyguards who looked like they were expecting trouble. But he didn't feel like a VIP—he was their prisoner now.

When his bags arrived, the men led Ahmad to the immigration area. The customs officials seemed frightened when they caught sight of the men. "They were not scared of me, they were scared of the people [escorting] me." The customs officials nervously rushed them through, barely checking Ahmad's papers.

"I knew I was heading for something bad ... very bad," he says. "I thanked Allah thousands of times that my mother was not with me."

They walked through the doors leading outside, and then one of the men grabbed Ahmad's arms and handcuffed his hands behind him. A light-coloured car sped up to the curb, and Ahmad was pushed into the back. With a man planted on either side of him and the man in charge in the passenger seat, the car pulled away. As it sped off, the men in the backseat pulled a hood over Ahmad's head and pushed his head down to his knees. The man in the passenger seat asked Ahmad his name.

"Ahmad El Maati."

"No, no. Tell us your other name!" the man barked.

"He was mocking me," Ahmad says. When he gave his name again, one of the men punched him in the face.

After about thirty minutes, the car slowed to a stop. They seemed to be at an entrance point of some sort, and Ahmad thinks he heard soldiers stamping their boots in salute. The car drove a bit farther before stopping again. Ahmad was pulled out of the car and led into a building, up a flight of stairs, and into a room. He could smell smoke. He was presented to a man who appeared to be in charge.

"Tell us your story," the man demanded.

"What's going on? What story? What do you want?" Ahmad asked, bewildered.

"Don't worry, we will teach you how to speak," came the answer.

Ahmad knew the man's accent: He was an Alawite, a member of Syria's ruling minority religious sect, a sect with little tolerance for practising Sunni Islamists. Sunni Muslims account for more than 70 percent of the Syria's population of eighteen million, but the Alawites have controlled the country's armed forces, intelligence, and ruling Ba'ath party since 1970 when Hafez al-Assad took the presidency and established autocratic rule. He brutally crushed any sign of rebellion by Sunnis. His son, Bashar al-Assad, inherited the throne when his father died in June 2000. A British-trained eye doctor, Bashar was just thirty-four and had not expected to be head of state, but his brother's death made him the only surviving heir.

Syria has been an important player in East-West relations since it gained independence from the French in 1946. For the United States, the challenge has always been one of balancing its support for Israel with the need to support Arab nations to safeguard its economic interests. Like most of the world, Syria sought ways to appease the United States after 9/11—it wanted off the U.S. list of "state sponsors of terror," where it had been since 1979. Clamping down on so-called Islamic extremism was something the regime had been doing for decades. Now that lined up nicely with the U.S. agenda. So after 9/11 the Syrians shared intelligence on al-Qaeda with the United States, intelligence it had compiled because of alleged links between al-Qaeda and the Muslim Brotherhood. For decades, the Muslim Brotherhood had posed the biggest threat to Hafez al-Assad. Membership in the Muslim Brotherhood was, and still is, punishable by death. Now as far as George Tenet, head of the CIA, was concerned, Syria was fast becoming a valuable ally and source of intelligence.[5]

Of course, Ahmad didn't know this. All he knew was that people like this man hated practising Muslims like him.

Guards led Ahmad to another building, where they took off his hood. He found himself in an office with a big window, a second door across the room, and three beds pushed up against the walls. His bags were there. A man sat behind a desk in front of him. Ahmad would later learn this man was the prison manager.

The guards had taken Ahmad's passport and money pouch. Now they handed them to the manager, who counted the money—US$3500 and about five hundred Syrian liras—before putting it in a box in his desk. Then the men pushed Ahmad though the second door into a hallway. They put his bags into a room and told Ahmad to wait in the hallway and face the wall. His hands were still handcuffed behind his back. Then the men walked away.

As Ahmad stood there, waiting, his mind raced. He had spent many summers in Damascus with his family, especially in the late 1970s and early 1980s when the Muslim Brotherhood was rising up against the ruling Ba'ath regime. "We stayed in my grandfather's apartment. Every night we'd hear bombs. I tasted part of the oppression in Syria." It was then he'd heard about torture in Syria. "I knew what they did to practising Muslims, and I knew what they used to do with whomever they caught." He also learned about the 1980 massacre at Syria's Tadmur Prison: The day after an assassination attempt on the then-president Hafez al-Assad, al-Assad's brother led his forces into the prison and murdered an estimated one thousand inmates in their cells. The inmates, accused of belonging to the Muslim Brotherhood, were Syria's finest intellectuals: scholars, doctors, and engineers. He remembered stories told by his mother's aunt, who had lived in the Syrian city of Hama, a stronghold of the Muslim Brotherhood. In March 1982, in response to violent attacks against al-Assad's regime, Syrian troops levelled the ancient city and, according to the Syrian Human Rights Committee, massacred between thirty and forty thousand people. The people in charge here were ruthless.

Ahmad thought again about his mother and how relieved he was that she wasn't with him now.

The men came back, pushed him into the room where his bags were, and removed his handcuffs. They opened his bags and started distributing the contents among themselves. Ahmad had been thinking about torture, but he hadn't anticipated having to go through this indignity first. He watched as they pulled out the suit he'd bought for his wedding and an expensive pearl necklace his father had bought for Rola. They took the perfumes and other gifts Ahmad had bought for Rola, and the cologne he'd bought on the airplane for Rola's father. They took the children's toys that Ahmad's aunt had bought for Rola's niece. Ahmad says there must have been about $5000 worth of gifts in his bags. It was like a celebration for the guards, and they were laughing. When they were done, just a few items of clothing remained.

One of the men turned to Ahmad. "Where are the documents?" he asked.

What documents? Ahmad asked. One of the men swore at him and punched him in the face. His nose began to bleed. The others slapped him and hurled insults at him and, worse, against the prophets and Allah—the worst form of disrespect for any Muslim. Ahmad refuses to repeat the words they used. Then two of the men grabbed him and led him out of the room and through a doorway across the hall. Ahmad's legs were weak as he was led down a flight of stairs. As they reached a landing, Ahmad could see hanging on the wall in front of him a picture of the former president, Hafez al-Assad. Beside it, in a crude frame, was a phrase from the Qur'an: "And We did not do them injustice, but they were unjust to themselves."[6] It was a cruel joke, a mocking welcome message for the Muslim prisoners from their secular hosts.

They turned right on the landing, then descended the second flight of stairs. At the bottom, another door opened into a hallway leading to the right. It was about six feet wide, and eighty feet long, with grey iron doors on either side. Ahmad was surprised to hear the sound of several voices coming from behind them, from what could not have been very large cells, given how close the doors were to each other. They must be packed in there, he thought. He'd later learn that these were common cells. Nine of them, about fifteen by twenty feet in size each, held up to sixty prisoners at a time. Beyond those were smaller "double" cells, the last on the right holding women and children. He was led past those and through another doorway. In front of him were two tiny rooms with filthy pit toilets, essentially holes in the ground, and to either side a metal gate, beyond which he could make out very narrow, dark hallways less than three feet wide. On each side of the hallways were small iron doors that looked like closet doors. "I didn't know what they were," Ahmad says. "I didn't even imagine these could be for humans." The men led him to the right, down the narrow corridor, stopping in front of the last iron door on the right. One of the men slid the lock open. The sound was awful, metal grinding against metal. He peered into the dark space. It was more of a box than a cell, really, barely as high as he was tall, barely wider than his body, and only about seven feet deep. There were two ragged blankets on the floor, and the foul stench of urine and excrement in the air.

"Your name is number five now," one of the guards said. He then pushed Ahmad inside, pulled the door shut, and slid the lock into place.

THREE

The Ressam Effect

Morning, Tuesday, September 11, 2001
Somewhere over the Atlantic Ocean

ON THE MORNING OF THE 9/11 ATTACKS, Canada's Foreign Affairs minister, John Manley, was on a flight from Frankfurt to Toronto. He was summoned to the cockpit to hear the news on BBC Radio. "One of my first thoughts on board that Air Canada flight on 9/11 was of Ahmed Ressam," he says. "I was immediately aware that if these attacks on the U.S. had a Canadian connection, then we would face deep and lasting problems of profound significance to our economy and possibly our way of life."[1]

Ahmed Ressam was the man CSIS had let get away. Now better known as the "millennium bomber," Ressam, an Algerian refugee claimant, very nearly got away with his plan to mark the new millennium with an explosives attack on the Los Angeles International Airport.

Terrorism investigators in France and Italy had warned CSIS about Ressam's circle of friends several years earlier, and by 1996 CSIS had started watching them.[2] By this time, Ressam was living in Canada illegally: His bid for asylum had been refused and he had ignored an order to leave the country by July 1995. Living in Montreal, Ressam supported himself by drawing welfare and by robbing tourists and selling their passports and identification. Twice he had been convicted for theft, fined, and released, despite the immigration warrant. But CSIS considered him a secondary figure in its probe of his acquaintances, which included a man Ressam would later say was a recruiter for al-Qaeda, Abderraouf Hannachi.[3] CSIS had the apartment bugged, and listened in as Hannachi boasted about the paramilitary training he'd received in Afghanistan, encouraging his friends to follow his example. But CSIS discounted the threat the men posed, dubbing the apartment they used to meet in the "BOG"—"bunch of guys"—and their anti-Western rants and plotting as "terrorist Tupperware parties."[4]

When Ressam finally did leave the country in 1998, he says it was for terrorist training in Afghanistan, arranged by Hannachi. At the Khalden camp in Afghanistan, he says he trained in light weapons, handguns, small machine guns, rocket launchers, explosives, and sabotage—"how to blow up the infrastructure of a country." The targets were to include "electric plants, gas plants, airports, railroads, large corporations, gas installations and military installations," as well as hotel conferences. Through experiments on dogs, he learned about the effects of poisonous gases—cyanide being one—and how to release these gases near the intake vents of buildings. He also learned urban warfare, assassination tactics, and how to avoid detection by dressing like a tourist and staying away from mosques.[5] This wasn't about learning to fight as a foot soldier in a war in Afghanistan— Ressam says he was trained, and given instructions, to attack the United States.

CSIS agents knew where Ressam was going when he left Canada: They had overheard him boast about having a new Canadian-sounding name and, unbeknownst to him, had even taken his picture at the airport when he left. But, it seems, they never bothered to check the name he was travelling under. If they had, they would have learned he had obtained a Canadian passport using the name Benni Antoine Norris, and they could have put the name on Canadian and U.S. watch lists. But, it seems, they didn't. And so it was that in early 1999, after receiving instructions to launch an attack on the United States,

Ressam, still posing as Norris, was able to travel freely back through Los Angeles International Airport, and then into Canada, without being stopped.[6] If immigration officials in either country had known the name he had used to travel to and from Afghanistan, they might have discovered that when he returned, he was carrying instructions on how to assemble explosives, some of the chemicals he needed to assemble them, and US$12,000 to help fund an attack.[7]

Continuing to use the name Norris, Ressam rented a Montreal apartment and shopped for supplies. He bought electronic components to build timing devices and went to garden centres to purchase urea, which, when mixed with nitric acid, becomes highly explosive. He also stole nitric and sulphuric acid from agricultural fertilizer manufacturers.[8]

In April 1999, investigators in France put in an urgent formal request to Canada: They believed Ressam and his friends were sending false passports and funds to terrorists overseas, and wanted Ressam and the others questioned, and their apartment searched.[9] It took two months for the RCMP to assign Corporal David Gendron to the file, and another three before the force actually went to the apartment building where Ressam's group hung out. At 6:15 A.M. on October 4, 1999, RCMP officers rang the buzzer at the apartment building's entrance. Ressam was in his apartment but escaped through the unguarded back door when he heard the buzzer.[10]

Ressam recruited two other Algerian asylum seekers in Canada: Abdelmajid Dahoumane, to help him assemble the explosives, and Mokhtar Haouari, who provided Ressam with the funds to buy supplies—as well as an Algerian living in the United States, Abdelghani Meskini, who would help on the U.S. side. Ressam and Dahoumane travelled to Vancouver, rented a hotel (under the name Norris), and started assembling the explosives. On December 14, 1999, they loaded the explosives into the spare-tire compartment in the trunk of a rented green Chrysler sedan and drove to Victoria. There they parted. Ressam would cross alone by ferry into the United States, and Dahoumane would travel back to Montreal.

As the cars rolled off the ferry in Port Angeles, Washington, customs inspector Diana Dean did as she usually did, stopping each driver, asking a couple of questions, then wishing them a safe trip and motioning them on their way. When she came to Ressam, she noticed he seemed nervous and asked him to step out of the car. Her colleagues searched the trunk and found what they thought was a cache of drugs: green bags of white powder, four black boxes, and jars of brown liquid. Ressam bolted, but the customs officers caught up to him before he could hijack a car in a nearby parking lot. Two days later they learned that the man they were holding was Ahmed Ressam, and that his cargo was highly explosive components for a bomb. Without any advance warning, customs inspector Diana Dean had managed to do what CSIS and the RCMP hadn't, and stop Ressam.

Back in Canada, RCMP investigators searched Ressam's apartment, seizing several items, including a map of Los Angeles. The FBI asked the Canadians to look carefully for any marks on the map. They were worried that there might be others still planning an attack to mark the New Year, and were anxious for any clue about possible targets. The RCMP investigator told the FBI there were no marks on the map.[11]

The FBI and U.S. prosecutors travelled to Canada in May 2000 to examine CSIS and RCMP evidence they could use against Ressam. They learned for the first time that CSIS had recorded four hundred hours of conversation between Ressam and his friends but had destroyed the tapes; only summaries remained. Then they asked for the map of Los Angeles and soon noticed what the RCMP had somehow missed: circles in green ink around Los Angeles' three airports. Ressam later testified that the Los Angeles International Airport was his target.

As the trial approached, U.S. prosecutors were stunned to learn that the Canadian government didn't want CSIS agents to testify, saying it worried that intelligence secrets could be revealed in cross-examination.[12] They eventually gave in, and the trial went ahead, with CSIS testimony, in March 2001. But Canada would frustrate U.S. prosecutors and the judge overseeing the case again when it refused to allow the person who translated CSIS surveillance tapes from Arabic to testify in person about what those tapes revealed. CSIS argued that testifying would put the translator and his or her family in danger. CSIS offered to let the translator provide anonymous testimony, but the judge ruled against this idea as being unfair to Ressam and blasted CSIS for having destroyed the tapes in the first place.

In the end the jury found Ressam guilty on nine counts, including conspiracy to commit an act of international terrorism. He faced a sentence of up to 130 years in prison. Apparently impressed by the fairness of his trial, Ressam later agreed to confess all and testify against one of his Montreal accomplices, Mokhtar Haouari, in exchange for a lighter sentence. His chilling confession at Haouari's trial in July 2001 unleashed a storm of criticism over how Canadian investigators had bungled the case. With 9/11 just two months away, Ressam had become the poster boy for CSIS incompetence and lax passport controls, and the case inspired a range of new monikers for Canada, such as the Club Med for terrorists, an Islamic extremist aircraft carrier for launching attacks on the United States, a terrorist haven, and the weak link in North American security.[13]

So it was no surprise that John Manley and so many others recalled the Ressam case on the morning of the 9/11 attacks. Along with calls for more money and power for intelligence and security agencies, the possibility of a Canadian connection became a convenient diversion from the stunning security and intelligence failure that 9/11 represented for the United States. The questions came hard and fast. How was it possible that no one had advance warning of the attacks in a country with an intelligence budget of more than $30 billion and an almost unimaginable array of technology and tools at its disposal? The public would learn much later what the FBI learned the day after the attacks—that the CIA had withheld crucial information that could have led the FBI to two of the hijackers *before* the attacks.[14]

And so it was that within hours of the attacks in New York and Washington, politicians, journalists, news anchors, and lobby groups on both sides of the border were repeatedly citing the Ressam case and speculating that the hijackers had used Canada as a base. On September 12, unnamed U.S. officials told ABC News that at least some of the hijackers had come from Canada. The next day, the front pages of Canadian newspapers quoted Vincent Cannistraro, a former head of counterterrorism at the CIA, saying that U.S. investigators knew that one of the hijacking teams had entered the United States through Quebec and Nova Scotia. That story was picked up in *The Boston Globe* and, the next day, in *The Washington Post*, and the next, in the *New York Post*. Within a week of the attacks, this information turned out to be false—none of the hijackers entered the United States from Canada—but the myth persisted, fuelling the sense that Canada was, in part, to blame for the attacks.[15]

North of the border, John Manley says, the goal very quickly became to "minimize the effect of 9/11 on the Canadian economy."[16] "We have to make every effort to satisfy the United States as to the level of our border security," he said in a television interview five days after the attacks. "We have simply too much at stake economically ... over 1.3 billion dollars U.S. per day in trade. We can't have them build a wall around the United States and us be on the outside of it.... We'll need to satisfy them."[17]

By September 14, Canada, through Minister John Manley, made it clear that Canada would back a U.S. decision to launch attacks in retaliation for 9/11.[18] The United States and Britain launched the first bombardment of Kabul, Afghanistan, on October 10; a week later, Canada sent the HMCS *Charlottetown*, HMCS *Iroquois*, and the supply ship *Preserver* to join them. The first major wave of Canadian soldiers would follow in February 2002. This was a big step: Canadians weren't there as U.N.

peacekeepers, a role we've grown used to, but as "combat soldiers acting in concert with American forces."[19]

When President Bush gave his wartime address to the Joint Session of Congress on September 20 and thanked fifteen countries for the support they'd offered so far, he didn't mention Canada's scramble to welcome hundreds of U.S.-bound flights grounded after the attacks. This was interpreted as an intentional snub, a message to Canada that it had better work much harder to appease its southern neighbour. One of Bush's speechwriters later confirmed that Canada had been intentionally omitted from the speech.[20]

In October, President Bush appointed Governor Tom Ridge to advise on homeland security. In Canada, Prime Minister Chrétien asked Manley to serve as Ridge's counterpart, and chair the Cabinet Committee on Public Safety and Anti-Terrorism. Set up in October 2001, this ad hoc committee of heavy-hitting ministers, with direction from senior bureaucrats in the Privy Council Office, was mandated to oversee Canada's response to 9/11. Manley took RCMP commissioner Giuliano Zaccardelli with him to meet with Ridge in Washington, D.C., on October 24.[21] Two days later, the United States passed the Patriot Act, sweeping new anti-terrorism legislation that, in addition to implementing unprecedented surveillance powers, included a section called "Protecting the Northern Border," which threatened to triple resources at the border with Canada and worsen the gridlock already being experienced. In Canada, the Cabinet Committee on Public Safety and Anti-Terrorism had set to work on its own initiatives.

First up was more money for CSIS, the RCMP, and other agencies to carry out national security work. On October 12, the government gave the RCMP $59 million for anti-terrorism work. A week later CSIS got $10 million, and the Communications Security Establishment, the organization tasked with spying on phone and electronic communications, got $37 million. Much more would soon follow.

Next up was Bill C-36, the Anti-terrorism Act (ATA). Hastily drafted in just four weeks, the act—almost two hundred pages of bilingual text—was tabled in Parliament on October 15, 2001. According to the government, the legislation would "stop terrorists from getting into Canada and protect Canadians from terrorist acts," supply the tools "to identify, prosecute, convict and punish terrorists," stop the Canada–U.S. border from "being held hostage by terrorists and impacting on the Canadian economy," and help us "work with the international community to bring terrorists to justice and address the root causes of such hatred."[22] Justice Minister Anne McLellan argued that the ATA was about prevention, saying, "Our laws must reflect fully our intention to prevent terrorist activity, and, currently, they do not."[23]

According to critics—an army of eminent scholars; legal experts; anti-racism, human rights, civil liberties, Aboriginal, refugee, and immigration organizations; trade unions; and representatives of Canadian Arab and Muslim communities—the ATA was unnecessary. Existing laws and international agreements already provided an adequate legal framework for preventing terrorism, and the ATA would forfeit the very democratic values and freedoms we were trying to protect, values and freedoms that many Canadians believe set us apart from our neighbour to the south. Abusing and eroding respect for human rights and democratic values, they argued, would only increase the threat to human security and freedom.

Kent Roach, a University of Toronto law professor who has written extensively on the ATA and the response to it, says "the failure of September 11 was one of law enforcement, not of the criminal law."[24] The existing Criminal Code could have stopped the 9/11 hijackers before they got on the plane, he says; the ATA, which constituted "massive and permanent change to Canadian law with respect to terrorism," was less about legal necessity than its political and symbolic value.[25]

The new act contained a definition of terrorism, one that included an unprecedented reference to political, ideological, and religious motives, requiring prosecutors to show that the terrorist activity was committed "in whole or in part of a political, religious or ideological purpose, objective or cause."[26] The government argued then, and continues to argue today, that this is necessary to distinguish terrorism from other crimes. Roach points out that the definition made it a *legal duty* for police to investigate and collect evidence about a person's political and religious beliefs and practices, something the police know very little about.[27] Many warned about racial and religious profiling, saying that rather than addressing the root causes of hatred, as promised, the ATA would foment hate, leading to the use of race "as a crude proxy for criminality ... using the way a person looks, for example, persons of Arab origin or Middle Eastern appearance as a reason for targeting that person."[28]

The ATA also ramped up the national security mandate for the RCMP and other police forces by criminalizing knowingly joining, leading, funding, harbouring, recruiting, or facilitating terrorist groups. In addition to warning that the new offences left people and organizations vulnerable to guilt by association, many critics recalled the RCMP's scandals in the 1970s, when the force interpreted a government order to clamp down on Quebec nationalists as a mandate to break the law, resorting to barn burning, break-ins, and burglary. The scandal led to the creation of the McDonald Commission of Inquiry, which found the RCMP simply didn't have the training, sophistication, or analytical capacity for national security work. The RCMP was pulled out of much of its national security work, and the civilian spy agency, CSIS, and its independent watchdog, the Security Intelligence Review Committee (SIRC), was created in 1984 to focus on that work.

The Anti-terrorism Act gave the police sweeping new powers of preventative arrest and investigative hearings, too. Armed with a warrant, police could now detain someone they believed might be about to commit a terrorist offence, hold that person without charge for up to seventy-two hours, and impose strict bail conditions. Suspects could be compelled to answer questions in investigative hearings, losing the right to remain silent. Many felt this was the most dangerous element of the ATA.[29] John Manley, however, defended the need for the new powers, arguing that without the new laws, "we wouldn't be able to prevent a terrorist action from occurring, where we had some knowledge that something was about to happen but we had no basis on which to arrest or incarcerate somebody."[30]

CSIS wasn't without its faults, clearly, but what had changed at the RCMP to warrant such a robust national security mandate? Would the RCMP, armed with the new mandate and powers provided in the ATA, break the law again? And if it did, who would know? Justice Minister McLellan assured the Senate committee examining the ATA that there was sufficient oversight in place:

> Honourable senators, proper review and oversight of the powers provided under Bill C-36 will also help to ensure that the powers are applied appropriately. In this regard, I would emphasize that various accountability mechanisms already established under Canadian law will apply to the exercise of powers under the bill. This would include, for example, such mechanisms as the Commission for Public Complaints against the RCMP and the various complaint and review mechanisms that apply in respect of police forces under provincial jurisdiction. Significant powers under this bill are subject to judicial supervision and, in many cases, this is in addition to explicit, ministerial review and supervision powers.[31]

For these reasons, she argued, "the House of Commons believes that the establishment of any further review mechanism was not warranted."[32]

The head of the Commission for Public Complaints Against the RCMP, Commissioner Shirley Heafey, was very concerned about the new powers and mandate given to the RCMP. But at the time, she thought her agency would be given new powers, too. "I believed then that given the enormous changes this legislation meant for the RCMP, and given Minister McLellan's assurances that we could provide sufficient oversight, we would be getting more resources and more power, too. That never happened," Heafey says.[33]

The ATA also meant that for the first time, Canada's electronic spy agency, the Communications Security Establishment (CSE) could spy on the telephone and electronic communications of Canadians, as long as the other party to the communication was outside the country. Until the Anti-terrorism Act, the CSE was prohibited from spying on any communication involving a Canadian citizen. Claude Bisson, the retired judge charged with overseeing the CSE, warned this could contravene the Privacy Act.[34]

The privacy commissioner, George Radwanski, warned that his powers would be eroded by the ATA, as did Information Commissioner John Reid, the independent ombudsman appointed to oversee the Access to Information Act. They said ATA provisions would give the solicitor general the power to issue certificates to override access-to-information and privacy laws. According to Reid, this gave the minister the "unfettered right to cloak information for an indefinite period.... We are trying to understand what the department is trying to protect." Radwanski warned the provisions would allow government officials to create "a Big Brother file on every Canadian, with every piece of information collected."[35] Radwanski won some amendments to the bill before it passed, but he and his successors would continue to sound the alarm about privacy concerns and the security agenda.

The ATA meant the federal Cabinet could now designate organizations as terrorist groups without any means of appeal beforehand, and little means for appeal after the fact. Government could also now deprive groups of charitable status and seize their property, again, with limited grounds for appeal. As Roach points out, these after-the-fact appeals would come too late, *after* the group had been stigmatized as a terrorist entity, and after people had been scared off supporting the organization.[36] Moreover, the new law meant that the court could see secret evidence being used by intelligence or law enforcement agencies to argue that the group should be listed as a terrorist entity or deprived of its charitable status, evidence the group itself would not be permitted to see or challenge.

Keeping secrets was all the more important now, the government argued. And so the Security of Information Act, created under the ATA, replaced the World War II–era Official Secrets Act, the aim being to protect against leaks of information in the new "war on terrorism." The ATA expanded the definition of *secret* and made it a crime to disclose or illegally possess information the government deems sensitive. The media warned this could erode journalists' right to protect their sources.[37]

Keeping secrets became easier too: The ATA amended section 38 of the Canada Evidence Act so that information deemed "injurious to international relations or national defence or national security" could be kept secret.[38] The attorney general could now issue certificates to conceal information "obtained in confidence from or in relation to a foreign entity," even if a court had ordered the information be disclosed. This meant that if the RCMP took its new mandate and powers too far, and, for example, broke the law as it had in the 1970s, section 38 could be used to shield officials and agencies from political embarrassment and public accountability.[39]

The Liberals used their majority to cut off debate on the bill in the House of Commons. It passed with few amendments just over a month later, on November 29, 2001. Debate was cut short again at the Senate, and the act became law on December 24, 2001. On December 10, Finance Minister Paul Martin announced the "Security Budget," allocating $7.7 billion to security spending. Almost $1.6 billion was allocated to CSIS, the RCMP, and other security-related federal agencies. CSIS's overall budget was increased by 30 percent with $300 million, and funding the RCMP received in October was topped up to

$576 million. The budget also allocated just over $1 billion to immigration and refugee screening, $1.6 billion to emergency preparedness and military spending, $2.2 billion to air security, and $1.2 billion to border initiatives. Did all this spending make Canadians feel safer? That seemed beside the point—this budget, like the ATA, was about making the United States feel better about Canada.

Two days later, Governor Tom Ridge and John Manley signed the Smart Border Declaration and associated thirty-point Action Plan. Much of the thinking behind the Smart Border plan predated 9/11 in the form of a proposal Canada called the Canada–United States Partnership, or CUSP. But before 9/11, border issues weren't a priority for the United States—Manley remembers handing the CUSP proposal to Colin Powell, who "accepted it graciously" but paid little attention to it.[40] So for Canada, the attacks were an "opportunity" for Manley to push an agenda already on the books: "I wouldn't want to give the impression that we somehow were happy that the opportunity had been presented in this fashion ... but clearly we now had senior U.S. people, particularly Mr. Ridge, sitting in the White House, paying attention to the northern border. That was definitely an opportunity."[41]

Canadian business saw the opportunity, too—much of the rationale for the Smart Border Declaration and the Action Plan came from the Coalition for Secure and Trade-Efficient Borders, a powerful lobby group uniting the Canadian Manufacturers and Exporters, the Canadian Chamber of Commerce, the Canadian Council of Chief Executives, and more than forty other business associations and companies.[42]

The plan, according to Manley, wasn't just about security, the "prevailing worry in the United States"—Canada shared that objective—"but from the Canadian point of view, the primary objective was economic."[43] The plan meant more efficient movement of goods across the border, which almost everyone agreed was essential, given the Canadian economy's reliance on exports to the United States.

But the thirty-point Action Plan went further. Many argued it compromised Canadian sovereignty by, for example, integrating immigration policies and the work of Canadian and U.S. intelligence and law enforcement agencies and opening up information sharing in unprecedented ways. Others argued this loss of sovereignty was essential, just a sign of the times. "Canada will have to adopt US style immigration policies if it doesn't want the border between the two countries to become impossible to cross," commented Robert J. Ritchie, the CEO of Canadian Pacific. "We must make North America secure from the outside. We are going to lose increasingly our sovereignty, but necessarily so."[44]

Canada said that, under the plan, it would share data from its Advance Passenger Information (API) and Passenger Name Record (PNR) program for high-risk travellers, which allowed for the creation of Joint Passenger Analysis Units to help identify high-risk travellers. (Gathered by airlines when passengers reserve and check in for flights, API records include the passenger's name, date of birth, citizenship, and passport data. PNR data include more detailed information such as travel itineraries.) This meant privacy laws would have to be amended, which they were by the spring of 2003, permitting airlines to provide passengers' personal information to foreign governments, the RCMP, and CSIS.[45]

According to the twenty-seventh point in the thirty-point Action Plan, the United States and Canada would "continue to cooperate in removing individuals to source countries," and "to date, the United States and Canada have conducted 5 joint operations resulting in 313 removals." The government doesn't elaborate on whether the deportees' rights to counsel, defence, or to be safe from torture were violated.[46]

It allowed for the creation of the Integrated Border Enforcement Team, the Integrated Marine Enforcement Team, and Integrated National Security Enforcement Teams, effectively merging the FBI and RCMP, the CIA and CSIS, and American and Canadian border officials, and complicating any possibility for effective civilian oversight of their work.

The integration of policing and security work meant more information sharing, too—between American and Canadian border and immigration officials, and between American and Canadian law enforcement and security agencies. Speaking a few months later before the Standing Senate Committee on National Security and Defence, Ronald Bilodeau, the Privy Council Office's security and intelligence coordinator, described the progress being made in implementing the plan: "Under the 30-point Canada-U.S. border agreement, we have now integrated anti-terrorist teams with Canadian and American security agencies. We have them in fourteen places now. Information is exchanged readily and locally at these border points. Information is exchanged between the Canada Customs and Revenue Agency and its American counterpart, between the immigration department and its American counterpart."[47]

In just three months, in an atmosphere of crisis, the Security Budget, the Anti-terrorism Act, and the Smart Border Declaration and Action Plan had fundamentally shifted Canada's legislative and political framework. Was this, Canada's new security agenda, a proportionate response to the attacks on the United States? Was this new national security agenda consistent with the institutions and values so fundamental to public security, such as the Constitution, the Charter, the rule of law, and domestic and international human rights protections? In our rush to appease the United States, had we sacrificed the very principles so many Canadians feel set us apart, in a good way, from our southern neighbour?

And, importantly, how would this impact on the conduct of agencies and officials charged with implementing Canada's new security agenda?

Saturday, September 22, 2001
CSIS office, Toronto

WHILE THE NEW POLICY FRAMEWORK was being implemented, CSIS and the RCMP, equipped with more resources and anticipating their expanded mandates and powers, set out to make up for Ahmed Ressam in their own way. That meant demonstrating that, this time, they could get their man.

On September 22, 2001, Jack Hooper, then director general of CSIS's Toronto region, chaired a meeting of members of CSIS; the RCMP; and the Ontario, Toronto, and Peel police forces. Hooper says that at the time, CSIS was focused on preventing a second wave of attacks and had been following a group of suspects he said had the capacity to carry out a terrorist attack. Hooper says his agents had been working around the clock and were "exhausted, and at a breaking point."[48] He wanted help with the investigations, especially when it came to surveillance. After some discussion, the police suggested these cases be pursued as a criminal investigation; CSIS, as an intelligence-gathering agency, had taken the investigations as far as it could.[49] Hooper decided to hand over at least some of the investigations to the RCMP. He said he would send the RCMP a letter outlining what CSIS knew about the targets, along with a profile of what was known about al-Qaeda, so that it could make the comparisons.

Two advisory letters went from Hooper to the RCMP. The first, dated September 26, 2001, was about suspects in the Toronto area, declaring them an "imminent threat to public safety and the security of Canada."[50] Ahmad El Maati was likely one of the people named in the letter, which is still blocked from public release. The second came at the request of the RCMP. This one gave it primary responsibility for investigating another individual—likely Abdullah Almalki, a Muslim Canadian living in Ottawa. Hooper says the amount of information given to the RCMP was unprecedented; CSIS had never handed over so many investigations at once to the RCMP.[51]

On September 24, the RCMP's "O" Division in Toronto created a joint force investigative team called Project O Canada to handle the investigations. The government has carefully guarded information about who made up the Toronto team, but it is known that it included RCMP investigators and members of the Ontario, Peel, and Toronto police forces. Ontario Provincial Police sergeant Scott Mills was assigned to head up the investigation into Ahmad. Team members had little or no experience with national security investigations—that expertise simply didn't exist in the RCMP at the time.[52]

O Canada's first step was to take CSIS information about the men, and the "imminent threat" they posed, to the Ontario Crown attorney. The team wanted charges to be laid. But the Crown said no—the information was tainted (in what way isn't publicly known) and there wasn't enough evidence to file charges against anyone.[53]

Hooper says it was then that the investigation became a "disruption exercise": The goal was now to "diffuse and disrupt" the apparent threat.[54] RCMP commissioner Giuliano Zaccardelli later testified before a Senate committee about the shift in tactics: "The tendency is for the Crown and law enforcement to want to go to court and successfully prosecute the case ... CSIS would say that there may be another way of dealing with the matter. Particularly since 9/11, we have had to accept going to a disruptive mode, because prevention is the most important thing. The consequences of allowing an event to take place rather than doing everything possible to prevent it are unimaginable."[55]

"This represented something of a sea change for law enforcement agencies. Do not abandon the intelligence and the information simply because it cannot be used as evidence in a court of law," Hooper told the same committee. "At the end of the day," he said, "if prosecution is not viable, there are other techniques."[56]

FOUR

Squeezed Out of Canada

8:30 P.M., Tuesday, September 18, 2001
Home of Abdullah Almalki, Ottawa

ABDULLAH ALMALKI'S FAMILY was startled when the doorbell rang. It was getting on in the evening and they weren't expecting any visitors. It was a week after the 9/11 attacks, and as the only identifiably Muslim family in their suburban neighbourhood of Barhaven, they'd been feeling unwelcome. Abdullah's Malaysian wife, Khuzaimah, who wears the hijab, found that other mothers in the playground—mothers she used to talk to every day—now hurriedly rounded up their kids and left when Khuzaimah arrived with hers. She had stopped driving, after hearing stories of veiled women being forced off the road. Abdullah stopped using his credit cards: Most store clerks would be polite, until they read his name. "People smile and then they get the card and instead of just saying 'thank you' they freeze—their faces changed," he remembers.

The Almalki family wasn't alone. Police forces across the country reported that hate crimes against Muslims had risen sharply in the week since 9/11, with incidents ranging from "assaults, arson, death threats and bomb threats to slurs yelled out of passing cars, vandalism and venomous emails."[1] The police emphasized that this was just a snapshot of a bigger picture: Most incidents likely weren't being reported to them. Just that day the media reported that a female Muslim medical resident in Montreal had been grabbed by the throat and spat at in an elevator.[2] Later that week, a fifteen-year-old boy in Ottawa—who when asked if he was an Arab said yes—was beaten almost unconscious.[3] So, understandably, Abdullah was nervous when he went to answer the door. Would it be someone blaming his family for 9/11?

When he opened the door, the man standing on the doorstep showed him an identity card and said he was from CSIS. His name was Alexander Gelvan. He wanted to come in and ask Abdullah some questions. Why, Abdullah wondered, was CSIS coming at that time at night, and why not call first? Angry, Abdullah, said no. If Gelvan wanted to talk with him, he'd have to do it with a lawyer present. Gelvan persisted, saying he had just a couple of questions. He asked Abdullah about a Montreal friend of his, Ibrahym Adam, a Muslim who had a commercial pilot's licence and owned a Cessna. He seemed to be implying that Ibrahym was missing and was one of the 9/11 hijackers. Abdullah said Ibrahym would never do anything like that—the attacks weren't consistent with Muslim laws.

"If you look at Islamic law, you cannot do these things. Those attacks are totally against the teaching," Abdullah told Gelvan.

After Gelvan left, Abdullah called and left a message for Ibrahym. His friend called back the next day and told Abdullah that no, he was not missing, and that CSIS knew this. CSIS agents had been questioning him, too.

Abdullah had dealt with CSIS before; they had called on him twice in 1998, once in early summer and then again a few months later. Back then he didn't even know what CSIS was. If it was in the news, he wouldn't have known. "I'm not a news junkie—I open the newspaper to read about technology and cars, not politics." Early in the summer of 1998, a woman named Theresa Sullivan from CSIS had phoned Abdullah, asking if they could meet. Abdullah had never heard of CSIS before. He was curious and saw no reason not to meet, so agreed. They met a couple of days later at a coffee shop. Sullivan asked Abdullah about his family, his education, and his business. Abdullah was open and described much of his life to her. "I didn't feel there was anything to hide, and I didn't know they were not a reputable organization. It didn't cross my mind that they would be similar to Syrian intelligence, for example."

He told her he had immigrated to Canada from Syria in 1987, when he was sixteen years old, with his parents and three brothers, and had become a Canadian citizen in 1991. He had finished high school in Ottawa, graduating from Lisgar Collegiate Institute in 1989. He studied to become an electrical engineer at Carleton University. He didn't tell her he'd always been top of the class.

Abdullah's a talker, and Sullivan encouraged him, asking about his travels. He told her that he had travelled to Pakistan in the fall of 1992 for three months. He had sponsored an Afghan orphan there and was anxious to learn more about the situation in Afghanistan and Pakistan. Seeing the human impact of the war in Afghanistan inspired him to find a way to use his engineering skills to help. He returned the following summer for two months to work on a United Nations Development Programme reconstruction project that was being awarded to the Canadian-based aid agency Human Concern International.

That fall, back in Canada, Abdullah married Khuzaimah, whom he'd met at university where she was working on her Ph.D. in economics. With his mother's blessing, they married in October 1993 and went together to Pakistan that fall so Abdullah could continue his engineering work there.

Sullivan was intrigued. Had he worked with the HCI regional director, Ahmed Said Khadr? Yes—Abdullah told her he had found Khadr to be a bit of a micro-manager and difficult to work with. This was one of the reasons he and Khuzaimah returned home earlier than planned, in April 1994. That fall, HCI's chairman and executive director awarded Abdullah a Certificate of Appreciation, in recognition of his voluntary services. Abdullah's first son had been born that summer.

Then Sullivan asked if Abdullah had received military training in Afghanistan, and whether he knew any of the mujahideen there. Of course not, Abdullah told her. He was an engineer, and his work in Afghanistan had been on reconstruction projects.

Sullivan asked about Abdullah's business. Abdullah and Khuzaimah had started an electronic components export business when they returned to Canada, combining his expertise in electronics with hers in business administration and economics. In Pakistan, Abdullah had researched the market and knew there was money to be made supplying electronics to a company called Microelectronics International, Pakistan's largest privately owned military and government manufacturer and supplier. The company needed quality components and systems, such as hand-held two-way radios, and Abdullah knew he could supply them at a competitive price. The plan worked, and their company, Dawn Services, was doing well.

Sullivan asked if Dawn Services had sold equipment to the Taliban. Abdullah was surprised by the question and told her no, it had not. He emphasized that the equipment his company exported was not strategic or in any way related to weapons and did not require military export permits. After he and Sullivan had talked for three hours, he asked why she had come to talk with him. She told him CSIS did such interviews randomly.

Sullivan called again later that summer. This time she said the Canadian government was interested in how the Muslim community felt about the American's August 20 attack on a pharmaceutical factory in Sudan. Al-Qaeda had launched its debut attack on American targets: On August 7, suicide bombers attacked U.S. embassies in Kenya (killing 213—12 of whom were Americans—and wounding 4500) and Tanzania (killing 11 and wounding 85, all of them Africans). The attacks had outraged Muslims as much as they had Americans, but then the United States launched retaliatory attacks against the Sudanese government, the regime that had given bin Laden refuge. Citing intelligence reports claiming a pharmaceutical plant in Khartoum North was actually manufacturing chemical weapons, the Americans targeted it with thirteen Tomahawk missiles. The intelligence was wrong; Sudan lost the plant that manufactured half its medicines and employed three hundred people, and a night watchman was killed. But Sullivan moved on quickly from that subject.

"What was Khadr's relationship with bin Laden?" Sullivan asked Abdullah. He said he had no idea, he didn't know Khadr that well. Sullivan asked him to speculate. He could say only that it would be hard to imagine Khadr working for anyone because he liked to be his own boss, Abdullah said. Sullivan repeated the question she had asked at their first meeting. Had Abdullah ever sold equipment to the Taliban? No, he told her again. She also wanted to know if he had sold anything nuclear to Pakistan (Pakistan had recently performed nuclear tests). No, of course not, Abdullah said; he had never dealt with nuclear materials, nor was he a nuclear engineer.

This time, Sullivan's questions were bothering Abdullah. "I told her, 'If you have anything about me, I'd like to know, so I can clear it up.'" He warned her not to believe rumours, which spread easily in the Muslim community. All she would say was that if CSIS did have anything on him, she couldn't tell him what it was.

That was the last time Abdullah heard from Sullivan. But it wasn't long before he noticed other strange happenings. In late 1999, he and his employees noticed that all of Dawn Service's shipments had been opened then resealed with customs tape. This was highly unusual. Customs had done spot checks in the past, but nothing like this. He called Canadian customs to find out why this was happening and was told they were just random checks. That didn't make sense. If they were random, why was every shipment being inspected?

Then, in December, Abdullah was stopped and questioned at the Vancouver airport on his way back into Canada from a two-week business trip in Hong Kong. This was a busy time, as clients were worried about Y2K and wanted two-way radios on hand before December 31. Abdullah had travelled extensively for his work—to the United States, Asia, the Middle East, and Europe—

and had never been stopped before. Two officials, one in uniform, the other in civilian clothing, thoroughly searched his luggage. They were particularly interested in his invoices, suppliers' and clients' names, and other work-related documents, taking them into another room. The officials then asked him to name all the companies he dealt with, as well as all his shipping destinations. They wanted detailed information about how he conducted his business and seemed particularly interested how he transferred funds. Abdullah answered their questions but was infuriated—surely they had no right to ask all these questions?

When Abdullah finally arrived home, a Muslim taxi driver he knew told him he'd been asked by CSIS agents to find an excuse to visit Abdullah's home, then look for bomb-making equipment. He had refused, saying that he knew Abdullah and his business and that their suspicions were unfounded. Abdullah was shocked to learn this; his company didn't deal in weapons of any kind.

Then, in February 2000, Abdullah heard from CSIS again. This time, a woman named Violaine Pepin phoned his office, wanting to talk with him. He agreed to meet with her the next Friday, on the eleventh. When he arrived at the coffee shop, as arranged, she was with a man who would give only his first name, "Dave." They asked Abdullah about his trip to Hong Kong, and implied that he had said things he hadn't when he was stopped in Vancouver. "It was clear that they were twisting information and fishing," Abdullah remembers. When he got home, he described "Dave" to his wife. Khuzaimah said he fit the description of a man who had come to see their house twice, each time with a different real estate agency—the house they were renting was being sold—while Abdullah was in Hong Kong.

Abdullah thought about the CSIS questioning and about the questioning at the airport, what the taxi driver had told him, what had happened at customs with the business's shipments, and what his wife had told him. This wasn't just about people asking questions anymore; he had been treated like a criminal at the airport and he was being harassed. More importantly, his business was built on his reputation, and if CSIS was talking to people in the Muslim community about him, his business was going to suffer. "They could investigate me for ten thousand years, as long as I don't feel it and no one knows about it and they don't ruin my reputation," he says. "My biggest asset was my good reputation. If they start going around putting doubts in people's minds that there is something about me—just the fact that I was being investigated [means] I will lose business."

It was time to see a lawyer. He called the lawyer he used for his business, who recommended a criminal lawyer, Michael Neville. Neville told him he should never speak to CSIS without a lawyer and that, even when travelling, he had the right to remain silent. "There is no course in university telling you 'Your right when CSIS comes is this and this,'" Abdullah says. "It was good to know my rights." When Abdullah asked what he could do to protect his reputation, Neville warned that a defamation suit would likely just end up costing a lot of money and get him nowhere.

That spring, Abdullah received a strange phone call from an employee at Scotiabank, who told him that because, as he knew, he was under investigation, she needed information about a dormant account he had in his name. Abdullah was surprised and asked what she meant. She seemed to try to cover up her slip, saying that it was a routine check.

That July, Abdullah and his wife and kids were moving into a new home. The landlord told them that the previous tenant had been slow to get his things out and had left the town home in a mess—they would have to clean before moving in. Abdullah took some boxes over in the meantime. Then he decided to try something: He sprinkled baby powder in the front hall before leaving. "Anyone who has kids knows that if there is baby powder on the floor it goes everywhere," he says. He was curious, were the people investigating him going to bug his new home? The next morning, he returned and found footsteps in the powder. He called the Ottawa police to report a break and enter. The officer he spoke with took his name and the details but said the police could not take it any further if there was no sign of forced entry and nothing had been broken or stolen.

Abdullah's business did well from 1999 to 2000. He had been ahead of the game in 1999 and had expanded beyond exports to importing cellphone components. He leased office space in a business park and was able to keep four employees on the payroll.

All of Dawn Service's shipments were still being opened and inspected. His employees found the office doors unlocked one day, yet the alarm hadn't gone off. But Abdullah didn't hear again from CSIS—not until that evening on September 18, 2001.

ABDULLAH SAYS HE LEARNED a lot of his business skills from hearing how his uncles and grandfather ran their businesses. They taught him that business is all about reputation, building relationships and trust, and communicating with confidence.

He learned from his father, too. Now retired, Abdullah's father had built a solid reputation as a civil lawyer and businessman by working long hours. He was in court in the mornings, spent afternoons in his office, and on weekends took his sons with him while he took care of his businesses. He wanted them to watch and learn.

"He's someone who taught us to take responsibility," Abdullah says, noting that his parents chose not to hire servants like many of their relatives. His mother, who earned her master's in education after they moved to Canada, raised the children. They were four boys; Abdullah is the second oldest. They lived in an apartment in the upper-middle-class al-Muhajirin neighbourhood in the new part of Damascus, at the foot of Mount Qassioun, where the air and streets are cleaner than in the Old City below.

"Playing on the street was not an option [for us], even though most kids would go to the streets to play football," Abdullah remembers. His parents enrolled the boys in organized sports instead, hiring a driver to shuttle them back and forth to the gym for basketball. Abdullah and his older brother took to electronics at an early age, so their father enrolled them in an after-school electronics course and brought electronics kits home for them to play with. They were spoiled in other ways: "There was a mini-market where my brothers and I used to think that we got all the chocolate and candy we wanted for free—not realizing everything we got was recorded and my father paid the bill at the end of the month."

The whole family is well educated: All the men and women on both sides of Abdullah's family have university degrees. Most are lawyers, some are doctors, a few are engineers. Abdullah's father expected top marks from his sons and enrolled them in the best elementary school in Damascus. "We had to come first or second or third in school or privileges would be taken away," Abdullah says. They took English classes after school, too, which came in handy when they moved to Canada in 1987. Abdullah's father's exacting standards when it came to education were balanced by a certain amount of freedom and responsibility as the boys grew older. His father let Abdullah drive his brand-new Mazda whenever he asked.

Abdullah describes his father as "extremely protective." In Syria, especially given the political climate of the 1980s, that meant practising their religion in private and steering clear of politics. The family, like most in Syria, are Sunni Muslims. Abdullah and his brothers were brought up to fast and pray. His father went to the mosque on Fridays, taking his family only for the Muslim holidays of Eid-al-Fitr, marking the end of Ramadan, the Islamic holy month of fasting, and Eid al-Adha, the Festival of Sacrifice, held in memory of Abraham's willingness to sacrifice his son for God, and which occurred about seventy days after Eid-al-Fitr, at the end of the annual pilgrimage to Mecca. "We prayed at home because going to the mosque would be dangerous," Abdullah says. He remembers that a friend of the family used to

take his sons to the mosque for dawn prayers every day. For that,
they were detained for two years.

In the *Report of the Events Relating to Maher Arar*, more
commonly known as the Arar Report, Justice O'Connor, chair of
the Commission of Inquiry into the Actions of Canadian Officials
in Relation to Maher Arar, describes Abdullah as a "very
religious man, educated in the Koran, who was viewed as an
elder in the community."[4] Abdullah, who never spoke with Arar
Inquiry counsel, disagrees with the characterization. He says only
dedicated Islamic scholars deserve such as a description—he
doesn't have enough knowledge of the Arabic language, nor the
sciences. "I would still say, even though it is very risky now and
problematic [to say this after 9/11], that I am not as religious as
I should be."

Abdullah's studies in the Qur'an started when he moved to
Canada and could go to the mosque. His father followed the
Hanafi school of Islam but was happy to have his sons learn what
they could when they arrived in Canada. Abdullah learned the
Shafi'i school of Islam, which worked out well for Abdullah's
marriage, as it is the school almost all Malaysian Muslims follow,
including Khuzaimah's family. The Shafi'i school of Islam,
Abdullah says, "flies in the face of being a member of al-Qaeda."
Osama bin Laden follows the ultra-conservative Wahhabi school
of Islam.

8:30 A.M., Friday, October 5, 2001
"A" Division, RCMP headquarters, Ottawa

IT WAS STILL EARLY IN THE DAY when Inspector Michel Cabana
sat down with Inspector Garry Clement, criminal operations—
"CROPS"—officer at the RCMP's "A" Division in Ottawa.[5]
Clement was assigning Cabana to manage a new national
security investigation. Cabana had been with the force for twenty
years; he'd spent the first sixteen years with the force in New

Brunswick and had been with the Integrated Proceeds of Crime (IPOC) unit in Ottawa since 1997.[6]

It was a tumultuous time in the force after the attacks. "The impact was severe from a member's perspective ... life as we knew it for the investigators stopped on 9/11," Cabana says. "The priorities that everybody had been assigned to, or [were] working on, prior to 9/11 were basically put on the shelf and everybody was redirected to try to address the threat and the crisis that was ongoing with respect to terrorist attacks."[7]

For Cabana, like many others in the force, this meant his first-ever foray into a national security investigation. The RCMP's initial response to the attacks was to set up Project Shock. Based in headquarters, it was an attempt to coordinate the flood of tips coming in from the public.[8] Cabana was assigned to create a case management system for the vast amount of information.[9]

In a video conference in late September, members of IPOC units across the country had been told the RCMP was also setting up the Financial Intelligence Task Force to investigate terrorist funding. The goals of the task force, and of Project Shock, IPOC members were told, were prevention first, then intelligence gathering, and lastly, prosecution. This represented a fundamental shift in priorities for RCMP investigators, a change approved all the way up to the RCMP commissioner, Giuliano Zaccardelli.

Now Cabana was taking over management of a new investigation. Dubbed Project A-O Canada, it was being set up in response to a call for help from Toronto's Project O Canada. Clement told Cabana that Project O Canada needed a team in Ottawa to help with its investigation of an Ottawa man named Abdullah Almalki.

CSIS appears to have alleged (it isn't known for sure what CSIS told the RCMP) that Abdullah, through his international business dealings, was suspected of facilitating terrorist activities. Bill C-36, the Anti-terrorism Act, was just days away from being introduced in Parliament. Once passed into law, the act would

make facilitating terrorist activities a criminal offence. It would
be up to Project A-O Canada to investigate Abdullah's international business relationships.

Clement told Cabana it would be an "open book investigation." The team would be working closely with the FBI and CIA,
and Cabana's "marching orders" were to share all available
information with those agencies.[10] This was unusual. The information was to flow freely, without restriction, and the caveats—
the usual safeguards that imposed restrictions on how the
Americans could then use that information—would not apply. It
was a "caveats down" situation. It was all about prevention,
Cabana says. "In other words, you do everything you can to
make sure nothing happens anywhere. If at the end of the day we
are successful in prosecuting individuals or groups, that's fine.
But right now the priority is not to accumulate the information
in an admissible format; the priority is to make sure that nothing
blows up."[11]

The A-O Canada team would peak at forty members,
including twenty investigators and support staff. Investigators
came from the RCMP's commercial crime unit; "A" Division's
IPOC unit; the RCMP's National Security Investigations Branch
(NSIS); CSIS; the Ottawa, Gatineau, Hull, and Ontario
Provincial Police forces; the Sûreté du Québec; the Canadian
Border Services Agency; and the Canada Customs and Revenue
Agency, and had the support of lawyers from the Justice
Department. Like their counterparts in Toronto, team members
had little or no experience in anti-terrorism investigations or in
dealing with intelligence agencies. With a few exceptions, Cabana
and his team had no training in national security investigations,
information sharing in a national security investigation context,
analysis of terrorism-related information, Muslim cultural mores
and values, or human rights issues in the context of national
security investigations.[12] Cabana would later describe the investigation as a "learn as you go" experience.[13]

Cabana reported to Clement. Clement, in turn, reported to Chief Superintendent Antoine Couture, the officer in charge of "A" Division's CROPS unit, who received daily situation reports, or "sitreps," and occasional briefing notes. The daily sitreps and briefing notes were copied to headquarters and CSIS.

The team's work was guided by a sense of urgency: Intelligence agencies believed that 9/11 was just the first in a series of attacks. A second wave was imminent, the team was told, but no one knew where, or when, it could happen.[14]

Early afternoon, Friday, October 12, 2001
Mango's Café, Ottawa

ABDULLAH HAD NO IDEA he was being watched when he went for lunch with Maher Arar on Friday, October 12. But he was, by three separate surveillance teams: two from the RCMP and one from the Ottawa police. Maher had no idea that going for lunch that day would change his life forever. But it did. It was then that he first became a "person of interest" to the RCMP.[15]

Maher and Abdullah knew each other, but not well. Both had come to Canada from Syria as teenagers, and their families knew each other—not surprising given how small the Syrian community in Canada was at the time. Abdullah remembers meeting Maher for the first time sometime when he was still in high school in 1987 or 1988. Maher and his parents had just immigrated to Canada and settled in Montreal, and his family came to Ottawa to visit with Abdullah's family not long after they arrived. Much later, when Maher ran a company with his brother, Abdullah had bought computer equipment from them. Since then, Maher had moved to Ottawa, for a while working with one of Abdullah's brothers, so he and Abdullah saw each other occasionally.

Like Abdullah, Maher was a successful engineer fascinated with emerging wireless communications technologies. He went to high school in Montreal, going on to study computer engineering at McGill University. It was then that he met Monia Mazigh, who was finishing her master's degree at the University of Montreal's Hautes Etudes Commerciales and starting a Ph.D. in finance at McGill University. Monia had grown up in Tunisia and immigrated to Canada in 1991. Fluent in French, Arabic, and English, her dream was to have a family, continue her education, and eventually become a professor. They married in 1994, and Maher went on to complete his master's degree in telecommunications at the University of Quebec's Institut national de la recherche scientifique.

Maher and Monia had their first child, a daughter, in 1997. The following year they moved to Ottawa, where Maher took his first job as a digital signal processing designer at a small high-tech start-up called Nexlink Communications, and later went to work for SpaceBridge, another Ottawa-based high-tech firm. Abdullah's brother worked there, and he and Maher became friends. But his big break came in September 1999 when he was offered a position as a communications application engineer at The MathWorks, a high-tech company in Boston. Monia stayed in Montreal until she finished her Ph.D., later joining Maher in Boston. In early 2001, they decided to move back to Ottawa where Maher would start up his own company, SimComms Inc. The MathWorks became one of his biggest clients.

When Maher met up with Abdullah on October 12, things had been going well. His business was thriving, and he and Monia were expecting their second child. He had called Abdullah the day before to invite him for lunch. He needed a printer cartridge, and he'd been told that Abdullah knew someone at the Future Shop in South Ottawa who could get him a good deal. It was respectful and in keeping with their culture to invite Abdullah out to lunch before asking for a favour. They had agreed to meet the next afternoon at Mango's Café, a small Middle Eastern restaurant in a strip mall just across the street from the Future Shop.

Neither remembers exactly what they talked about that afternoon, but Maher says he remembers telling Abdullah that Monia was pregnant. Abdullah and Khuzaimah had four children, all born in Ottawa, and he wanted to know who they'd used as a midwife. Abdullah thinks they also discussed how unwelcome they'd felt as Muslims since 9/11. At any rate, the conversation, and the food, was pleasant enough. After the lunch, Abdullah suggested they walk off the meal together.

Both Maher and Abdullah remember it was damp but not raining when they went outside—Abdullah is certain about this because he was wearing his dark brown suede jacket and wouldn't have risked ruining it by walking in the rain. After a short walk they drove in Maher's car to a local prayer space in time for the sunset prayer, and then to the Future Shop. Then Maher took Abdullah back to his car at the restaurant, and they went their separate ways.

For Maher and Abdullah, the get-together wasn't a particularly significant event. They had eaten together, walked together, prayed together, and shopped together. But soon after that lunch, A-O Canada deemed Maher Arar a "person of interest" and assigned Corporal Robert Lemay and Sergeant Rock Fillion to investigate him. Members of A-O Canada conducted income tax and credit bureau checks on Maher and Monia. They went to local schools and asked about them. They asked about them at car rental companies at the Ottawa airport. They made enquires about them with U.S. Customs, the U.S. Immigration and Naturalization Service, and the FBI.

By the end of October they knew where he was born, when he had come to Canada, and that he had lived in Montreal and then moved to Ottawa. They learned that Abdullah was listed as an emergency contact on the rental lease for his apartment. They learned that he held two university degrees and that he had worked for The MathWorks Inc. in Boston and now had his own company, SimComms, which he operated out of his home in Ottawa. They learned that he had had two residences, one in Ottawa and one in Boston. They knew about his brothers and parents, and that he had a young daughter. They learned he had no criminal record and wasn't wanted on any charges.

Nothing they had learned pointed in any way to any evidence that Maher, or Monia, were a part of, associated with, or sympathetic to any terrorist organization. But by the end of October, A-O Canada had requested that both Canadian and U.S. customs issue "border lookouts" for Maher, Monia, and "other individuals"—almost certainly including Ahmad and Abdullah. The request to both Canada Customs and the United States characterized Maher, Monia, and the "other individuals" as "a group of Islamic Extremist individuals suspected of being linked to the Al Qaeda terrorist movement."[16]

Riad Saloojee, then-executive director of the Canadian Council on American Islamic Relations, was one of many speaking out against the increasing use of the term *Islamic extremist*. "It reductively ties an entire religion to violence, something that is rarely, if ever, employed with other faith groups," he says. "How often is violence adjectivized by [the words] *Jewish* or *Christian*? The constant repetition of the mantra 'Islamic violence' connotes that the faith's normative character condones, even sanctions, violence. We would never accept this crass bigotry about any other faith—but we turn a blind eye to its usage with Islam."[17]

Sometime in late October 2001
Merivale Road, Ottawa

IT WASN'T UNTIL SOMETIME IN LATE OCTOBER or early November that Abdullah realized he was being followed. He was driving with his brother and noticed that a man with a baseball cap in a dark blue Chevy Lumina had been behind them for a while. They slowed down. The Chevy slowed down. Then they *really* slowed down. The Chevy followed suit, then suddenly sped by them. A while later, on their way back home, the Chevy, with the same man behind the wheel, was following them again.

A few days later, Abdullah was on his way to bachelor party when he noticed he was being followed, this time by several cars.

To confirm his suspicions, he quickly took a turn, and then another, parked in between two cars on the side of the road, and turned off his lights. "I wanted to see what they'd do. You can know something, believe something, but you want to get to a point where you know for sure," he says. "I parked, turned off the lights, and I saw them zooming one after the other past me. They kept on circulating in the area—driving very fast in a residential neighbourhood, maybe eighty kilometres an hour. Then I drove off ... they lost me."

Soon after, he saw the cars again. For Abdullah, the surveillance was an affront, an insult, and he wanted to see if he could outsmart whoever was following him—to what lengths would they go to keep up with him? He started slowing down before traffic lights, then speeding through just as the lights turned yellow. "I wanted to see if they would go through a busy intersection on a red light, and they did." When a car was between them stopped at a light, he was shocked to see the cars following go up on the sidewalk and around the other car before driving through the red light to follow him. Did they know he saw them? "It was like, 'We know that you know we are here but we are trying to hide that we are here.'"

Then the men tailing him made themselves known. Abdullah remembers one man following him inside a Canadian Tire store, making it obvious he was watching to see what Abdullah bought. Every evening during Ramadan, as Abdullah went to the mosque to pray, he saw cars waiting for him at intersections along the way. "Whenever I left the house, the entourage would leave with me." Then one day he noticed a pole across the street from the house with a camera on top, in clear view.

His wife, Khuzaimah, and the children, were followed, too. Khuzaimah noticed it one day when she was driving with the kids to the public library. She had seen the cars before. When she went with Abdullah to the doctor and for groceries, men in cars had followed them to the doctor's office, and waited, then followed them to the grocery store, and waited, and then followed them home and camped out there. But this time was different: She was alone with the kids.

The man followed her van into the parking lot, then watched as she, five months pregnant, wrestled the kids—aged one, three, five, and seven—out of their car seats, strapped the youngest into her stroller, and shepherded them to the library entrance. "I didn't look at him ... I was a bit scared, just me with my kids," Khuzaimah says.

After a half hour of helping the kids pick out books, Khuzaimah took them upstairs to the check-out counter. The man, who had followed them inside, passed by them on his way to the exit. As he walked out, he set off the alarm. He fumbled a bit, embarrassed, then held his hands up in the air to show the clerk he wasn't sneaking books out of the library. Khuzaimah found him waiting in the hallway; he followed them outside, watched as Khuzaimah loaded the children into the van, then trailed them home.

Looking back, Khuzaimah remembers being very frightened, but she is incredulous now. "What is there in the children's section? Why this harassment? After this incident, how are you going to live a normal life?"

"It got to the point where we felt that every word we were saying was monitored. We wondered, are they filming us, do they have cameras in the house?" Abdullah says. "[Some] people think, well, what's the big deal with being taped? Well, imagine that now I give you a tape recorder, and you have this tape recorder turned on 24/7 everywhere you go, every person you talk to, every program you watch, everything you do, and I'm taping you—how long can you take it? I don't think many people can take it for three hours."

Before long, the family decided to get out of Canada for a while. They were feeling harassed and, since the attacks, unwelcome. They decided to travel to Malaysia to spend time with Khuzaimah's mother, who was ill and who they hadn't visited since 1996. Khuzaimah and Abdullah left the country separately:

Abdullah thought he'd be harassed at the airport and that he'd be delayed for several hours, if not a full day, so he left a day before Khuzaimah and the kids, on November 27. Expecting the worst, Abdullah went to the airport early, but nothing happened. He sailed through security and on to his flight without so much as a second look from officials. Now he thinks CSIS and the RCMP wanted nothing more than for him and his family to leave. "We were squeezed out of Canada. It is as if you have a cat and you keep annoying the cat until it jumps out the door and leaves the house," he says. "They really squeezed us out of Canada."

FIVE

"Tell Us About the Map"

1 P.M., Friday, November 16, 2001
Home of Sana Wassef, Toronto

AHMAD EL MAATI'S AUNT, SANA, was on the phone in her home in the Rosedale neighbourhood of Toronto when the police arrived. Ahmad had been missing now for four days. His mother, Samira, had phoned from Cairo to tell Sana the news. Sana and Ahmad's father, Badr, called the consular division of DFAIT (Department of Foreign Affairs and International Trade), but officials there hadn't been able to locate him yet. "At this time I didn't know what happened to Ahmad ... all I knew was that he didn't arrive there and I didn't know where he was ... I thought then that they were interrogating him and then he would be released and that's it," Sana says.

Sana answered the door to find two men outside. One was dark, the other was fair and red in the face. The fair one held out his identity card. His name was Scott Mills, and he was with the O.P.P. Sana couldn't have known, and Mills didn't tell her, that he had joined Project O Canada on September 25 and was leading the investigation into Ahmad's case.[1] She invited them in and offered them coffee or tea, which they declined. They asked if her husband was home, and she told them no, it was a Friday and he was at Friday prayer. "Of course they knew," she says now. They asked if Sana realized that the deed of her house was not in her name but in her son's. Yes, she said, but why was that an issue? "They wanted to show me that they knew everything about us," Sana says. They asked about her education, her husband's education, and about all of her brothers, including Ahmad's father, and their education and careers. They asked about Ahmad and his education. She told them he had studied statistics in Montreal. How religious was Ahmad? they wanted to know. "I said, 'We are all religious, he is just like us. We pray and we fast.'" Why did Ahmad go to Mecca twice? "I said, 'The first time he was making hajj for himself, the second time, because a woman cannot go for hajj alone, he went with his mother.'"

The men then asked why Ahmad had gone to Syria; they acted as though they didn't believe he had gone for his wedding. If it was a wedding, why hadn't his mother gone with him? Sana told them Samira had planned to join him after spending a few days in Cairo. Why hadn't his father also gone to Syria? Sana explained that there would be two ceremonies: one in Syria, and one at home in Canada when they returned. Sana thinks the men finally started to believe her about the wedding once she described all the shopping she, Samira, and Ahmad had done for gifts for Rola's family. The police should have known, she thought to herself. They'd been following them. Then Mills said something interesting.

"I can't remember his exact wording, but what he meant was that if he had known this he would have advised [Ahmad] not to go," Sana says. "I can't comment if it was a human moment or if it was just a slip of the tongue, but that is what he meant."

3 P.M., Monday, November 12, 2001
Cairo International Airport, Cairo, Egypt

WHEN AHMAD'S MOTHER, SAMIRA, collected her luggage at the Cairo airport after her flight, she found her suitcase bound with white security tape. The lock had been broken. Shortly after arriving at her daughter's home in the city, she got the phone call from Damascus. Ahmad's bride, Rola, was very upset. She had waited for hours at the airport, but Ahmad hadn't shown up. Samira caught her breath, then called her stepmother, who is well connected in Damascus. Her stepmother called her contacts in the Syrian government, but they just insisted that Ahmad hadn't arrived in Damascus. Samira says she was very distressed and began to scream and cry, while her daughter tried to calm her down. "I knew that they had detained him," she says. "And I knew what they would do with him."

Samira called Sana in Canada, and Ahmad's aunt called Foreign Affairs to report Ahmad missing and to ask for help. Myra Pastyr-Lupul, the case management officer for the Middle East region at DFAIT headquarters, took the call. She says the first step was getting confirmation from Austrian Airlines that Ahmad had been on the flight to Damascus. That took time; apparently it was difficult to access passenger lists because of heightened security after 9/11.[2] In the meantime, inquiries in Syria were turning up conflicting leads. Syrian officials told Rola's family that Ahmad had been sent to Cairo, likely to deter further inquiries. Badr reported this to Pastyr-Lupul at DFAIT.

Several days later, Ahmad's uncle in Vienna was able to confirm through Austrian Airlines that Ahmad had indeed been on the flight to Damascus. Officials at the Canadian Embassy in Syria continued to check with the Syrians, who would say only that they had no record of Ahmad being there. The Egyptian authorities said the same thing.

Then the family was given another reason to worry. *The New York Times* reported it first. Then the Canadian media jumped on the story. Journalist David Rohde had arrived in Kabul on November 17, soon after it fell to the Northern Alliance. Local Afghans tipped off reporters about a couple of homes Arabs were said to have been living in. It was there that Rohde found documents belonging to Ahmad's brother, Amr. Also found in the houses were anti-tank missiles; a flight simulator computer program; lists of U.S. flight schools; documents about chemical, biological, and nuclear warfare; copies of letters to and from Osama bin Laden; and other documents clearly linking the former residents to al-Qaeda. The *Times* reported that "The one individual clearly identified in the documents in the houses is a Canadian citizen. A July 1996 letter from the Canadian immigration service to an Amro Abouelmaati [Amr El Maati] in Toronto informs him that his Canadian citizenship certificate is enclosed. Near the letter was a patient card from Toronto General Hospital in Mr. Abouelmaati's name. It was not clear whether Mr. Abouelmaati was a member of the group or whether his identity was stolen, a tactic Al Qaeda members have used in the past."[3]

Reporters rushed to try to interview anyone they could find in the El Maati family. Badr, Ahmad's father, said then and says now that he has no idea why Amr's documents were in one of the houses. He and Amr's mother are adamant that Amr would not have condoned the violent tactics of al-Qaeda evidenced by the other items found in the houses. Samira wonders if the *Times* might be right—maybe Amr's things were stolen. Amr could be careless with papers, she says. They hadn't heard from Amr since 2000, when he sent pictures of a school he was working at. They hadn't thought much of the long silence until then. Now they were worried for his safety.

On the morning of November 26, as Ahmad's family waited anxiously for news on either of the sons, Badr got a call from an O.P.P. officer. The police wanted to meet with him, and Badr agreed. He met with Scott Mills and Dave Truax later that morning at the Second Cup coffee shop on Bayview Avenue, south of Eglinton Avenue, in northeast Toronto. The O.P.P. officers weren't in uniform, and their tone was friendly, but their questions weren't.

They asked Badr where Amr was, and Badr told them what he had told the media—that he didn't know where his son was—and the last time he'd heard from him was more than a year ago. Had Amr received military training? No, not to his knowledge; Amr had gone to Pakistan to do aid work. The last Badr had heard, Amr was working with a new charity called the Canadian Relief Foundation, which received CIDA (Canadian International Development Agency) funding from the Canadian government and provided aid to Afghan widows and orphans. Mills and Truax asked where Ahmad was, and Badr told them he left for his wedding but was missing. They asked Badr to rate how religious he was, from one to ten, compared with his sons, and how often he went to the mosque. They asked what he thought of 9/11. Eventually, the meeting ended, and Badr left, frustrated by the questions.

A few days later, in early December, two CSIS agents, Adrian White and Rob Cassolato, knocked on Badr's apartment door. They wore suits. Badr invited them in, and they asked him where his sons were. Badr told the agents the same thing he had told Mills and Truax. Badr was again frustrated by these enquiries; he believed CSIS already knew the answers, including where Ahmad was being held, something Badr desperately wanted to know.

Nighttime, Monday, November 12, 2001
Far' Falastin, Damascus, Syria

IT TOOK A WHILE before Ahmad, "number five," could make anything out after the guards locked him in the tiny cell. "This must be the last step before death," he thought as his eyes adjusted to the darkness and he could see his surroundings.

He reached for one of the blankets on the floor beneath him. It was thin and rough to the touch. There was a window in the metal door, but it was blocked. A few inches above his head was a small opening in the ceiling with metal bars across it. A faint shaft of light barely reached through to the back wall. The cell was only about a foot wider than he was. The walls and floor were cement, cold and wet.

Ahmad was shivering. He was scared and cold. He didn't know how long he had before the guards came back for him, so he prayed quietly, then sat on the floor to wait. He thinks it was a couple of hours later that he heard a guard's footsteps. The lock slid open and the door swung into the cell. Ahmad had to jump out of the way. The guard ordered him out and led him back upstairs into a room, where he tied a piece of rubber over his eyes.

Then the interrogation started. Someone said they'd received information about him and read out the names and addresses of his family in Toronto, the make and colour of his car, and its licence plate number. They knew his address, the man said, and read it out to him. He had the wrong apartment number so Ahmad corrected him.

Then the beating started. Ahmad was punched in the face and kicked at. The men in the room screamed insults at him, his family, and his faith. Finally, one of the men said, "Tell us about the map!"

Ahmad, guessing that his answers would be passed on to CSIS in Canada, wanted to prove he had nothing to hide. He told the men of how he had found the map in his truck—the letter from his employer that was in his bag would prove it. They just laughed at him. He told them he was likely suspected after 9/11 because he was a Muslim who had gone to Afghanistan and had taken flying lessons, but he had done nothing wrong.

One of the interrogators leaned in and told Ahmad that they were going to bring Rola in and rape her, there, in front of him. Ahmad was terrified—did they have Rola? He knew this kind of thing happened in Syria. He pleaded with them, saying that he had told them the truth.

"No," the man yelled. "We need to hear something new!"

"I can't invent something," said Ahmad.

"No," the man replied, "You can invent something."

Then things got worse. Ahmad was ordered to strip down to his shorts and lie on his stomach on the floor. In pain from the beating, he moved slowly. The men yelled at him to move faster as he struggled out of his shirt and pants. When Ahmad was lying down, the men grabbed his hands and handcuffed them behind his back, then lifted his feet up and tied his wrists to his ankles with a rope. He was like a sheep ready for slaughter, Ahmad says. Ice water was poured all over his body, then he was whipped on his feet, legs, knees, and back with a thick metal cable. The pain was sharp and fierce, but the first strokes were the worst. After a few lashings, Ahmad's feet and legs went numb, but that was what the dousing with ice water was for—to bring the feeling back. He could see the interrogators' shoes from under the blindfold. The ones without the cable kicked him in the face and his back and legs.

Ahmad begged the men to stop, asking why they were doing this to him. They just laughed. "They were asking me to repeat my story, and I kept repeating what happened, and they said that's not what we want to hear. They kept threatening me and mocking me and said they were going to inflict permanent injury—they said I wouldn't be able to have kids later on."

Ahmad lost track of how often he was taken down to his cell and back up for more torture but remembers that eventually he couldn't walk and had to be dragged up and down the stairs. In his cell, without the blindfold, he saw his legs were covered in blood. His feet were too swollen to fit into his shoes.

"After I just couldn't take it anymore, I told them, 'I'm willing to say whatever you want me to say,'" Ahmad recalls.

The men asked him about people he knew in Canada—including Abdullah Almalki and Maher Arar. Ahmad told them he knew Abdullah but not very well. They first met through Ibrahym Adam, he explained, the man who owned the garage he had worked at in Montreal. They'd probably talked three or four times. Ahmad knew that Abdullah and his family were well connected in Ottawa's Muslim community, and had consulted him about finding someone to marry. Ahmad had also stopped in to see Abdullah in Ottawa before going to the Syrian Embassy to apply for a visa to go meet Rola. Ahmad told his interrogators that he had met Maher at the garage too, but that he knew him even less than he knew Abdullah.

The interrogators wanted Ahmad to say he had seen both Abdullah and Maher in Afghanistan. Ahmad told them the truth: that he thought he had seen Abdullah in Afghanistan in an administration building with a group that was applying for a permit for a NGOs project, but that he hadn't spoken to him.

"They said, 'They were with you in Afghanistan.' I said no, I briefly saw Abdullah, and I knew Maher from the garage, but I didn't see Maher in Afghanistan.

"'No, you saw Maher in Afghanistan. You have to say that.'

"I said no, I didn't know Maher from Afghanistan. So they started punching and beating me. So later on, I said yes, I had seen him in Afghanistan."

The interrogators asked about Ibrahym Adam, too. They knew he had a pilot's licence. Ahmad told him that yes, he was Ibrahym's friend; he had worked for him at his garage. They asked about his brother, Amr. Ahmad said he'd last spoken to him when he'd called from the Canadian Relief Foundation's office in Kabul in 1999. They asked Ahmad if he had planned to seek asylum in Germany when he landed in Frankfurt. Ahmad thought of the man running in the Frankfurt airport, panicked and yelling at him and his mother. "No," he said, "I came to Syria for my wedding."

Then the men got to the heart of the interrogation: They wanted Ahmad to confess to a plot. "They said I had to say that when my brother called, he told me to take flying lessons and sent me the map for an attack," Ahmad says. He told the interrogators that the allegation didn't make sense. When Amr had called, he had already quit the lessons, and he hadn't spoken to him since.

"Okay, we will say that he told you to drive a truck and blow it up," one of the interrogators said. It was a team effort now, filling in the blanks together.

"Fine," Ahmad said.

"Now tell us the names of who helped you."

Ahmad didn't know how to respond—there were no names to tell. "Amr just told me to drive and he would take care of the rest," he offered.

"You wanted to blow up the U.S. Embassy in Ottawa!"

Ahmad thought quickly. He worried that if he agreed that the target was the U.S. Embassy, he would be sent to the United States, not back to Canada, so he changed the story slightly. "It wasn't the U.S. Embassy," he said. "It was the Canadian Parliament."

The interrogator seemed pleased. "He was feeling very happy now, like this new information was even juicier," Ahmad recalls.

Mission accomplished. Ahmad's blindfold was removed, and he was handed a pen and paper and told to write it all down. Ahmad started to write down the fabricated story but changed his mind and instead wrote the truth—he just couldn't implicate himself and his brother in writing. For that, he would suffer more abuse. He handed his interrogators the document and was taken back to the cell in the basement. A few hours later, guards came for him, kicking the cell door open so that it hit Ahmad, throwing him against the back wall.

"They were shouting at me, screaming, the whole dictionary of insults. Then they started kicking me while I was still inside [the cell], and grabbed me by my hair and beard, dragged me upstairs, handcuffed me from the back, and took me inside the room."

The man who'd been in charge of his interrogation was there. "You want to change your story now?" he yelled at Ahmad.

"He brought a cigarette out. I felt the heat of the cigarette on my cheek. They were kicking me and beating me and then they laid me down, and then he started burning my shins and I was screaming like crazy. And then he said, 'I am going to burn your eyes now.'

"I said I'd write down whatever they wanted." One of the men gave Ahmad a pen and paper, but his hands were shaking and he couldn't write. He suggested they do it. "Because we agree on everything, why don't you write it down?"

They did as Ahmad suggested. Ahmad thinks he finally signed the document about a week after the interrogations started. By then, he says, he had lost track of time. Ahmad wasn't permitted to read the document but was made to sign it and place his thumbprint on the bottom of the page.

Ahmad's shins are still scarred from the cigarette burns. He's glad his interrogators didn't burn his eyes. He says that by signing the false confession he traded his innocence for his eyes.

AFTER AHMAD SIGNED THE "CONFESSION" the interrogations were less frequent, sometimes accompanied by beatings, sometimes not. Ahmad spent more and more time just waiting, not knowing when the guards would come for him next. He obsessed over why this was happening to him. Who were the men who'd followed him on his flights? Had CSIS somehow arranged for this to happen to him? If CSIS had questions for him, why, he wondered, hadn't the agents just returned his lawyer's calls and talked to him in Canada? Why had his interrogators wanted him to implicate his brother too? Just because he had also been in Afghanistan? "I am a Muslim. I took flying lessons. I was in Afghanistan. I understood that they might be suspicious after 9/11. But I don't believe in al-Qaeda's views. Not then, and not now," he says. Day and night, he could hear other prisoners being tortured. First, he'd hear the footsteps and hope they weren't coming for him. Then he'd hear the lock on one of the other cells slide open. After a few minutes, the screaming would start.

At night, while the guards dozed, Ahmad could hear the prisoners in the other solitary confinement cells whispering to each other. Although separated by cement walls and iron doors, they were physically close to each other, since the cells were so small and the hallway so narrow—the ten cells in that corridor took up only about fifteen by fifteen feet.

The man in the cell across from Ahmad's whispered to him first. Initially, Ahmad was too frightened to respond but, after about two weeks, he dared to ask the man where he was.

"What is this place?"

"This is Far' Falastin, an intelligence branch for foreigners," the man answered.

The Syrian Military Intelligence, or Shu'bat al-Mukhabarat al-'Askariyya, like all of Syria's security services, is notorious for torturing detainees. According to the U.S. State Department report on human rights in Syria in 2001,

> former prisoners and detainees report that torture methods include administering electrical shocks; pulling out fingernails; forcing objects into the rectum; beating, sometimes while the victim is suspended from the ceiling; hyperextending the spine; and using a chair that bends backwards to asphyxiate the victim or fracture the victim's spine.... Torture is most likely to occur while detainees are being held at one of the many detention centers run by the various security services throughout the country, and particularly while the authorities are attempting to extract a confession or information regarding an alleged crime or alleged accomplices.[4]

The Palestine Branch, or Far' Falastin, Branch 235, is the most feared detention centre in Syria. Amnesty International's 2002 report for Syria singled out Far' Falastin as a particularly dangerous place, saying "torture and ill-treatment continued to be inflicted routinely on political prisoners, especially during incommunicado detention at the Palestine Branch and Military Interrogation Branch detention centres."[5] The notorious detention centre is situated within a larger security compound sprawling about three city blocks just west of downtown Damascus.[6] From the road the compound appears as a collection of concrete buildings behind a long, high wall cornered by watchtowers and guarded by machine gun–wielding soldiers. A sliding black metal gate and an enormous sign that reads, in English, "No

Photography" mark the entrance.[7] Less than a mile southwest of the crowded and bustling Omayad Square and the luxurious Sheraton Hotel, the road outside the security compound is always strangely quiet, avoided by locals.

Inside the black gate a road winds past several buildings, including the Syrian Military Intelligence headquarters, the Mahkama Alaskare (a military court), and at least three detention centres: Far' Tahkek Alaskare (military investigations branch); Far' Manteka (regional branch), and Far' Falastin. Far' Tahkek Alaskare is said to have an underground tunnel, thirty yards long, less than fifty inches wide, and about two yards high, holding between 100 and 150 detainees at a time.[8] Little is known about Far' Manteka now, though it once housed hundreds of detainees at a time.

First built when Hafez al-Assad seized power in the 1970s, Far' Falastin sits at the southwest corner of the compound, just over the wall from Damascus University. The main entrance to the compound is on Falastin Road—some believe this is where the detention centre gets its name. Others say that the name reflects its function within the counterterrorism division of the Syrian Military Intelligence. Its detainees are often foreigners, some accused of terrorism links, others of constituting a threat to state security.

Far' Falastin sits within its own walls within the compound, with a guardhouse at its gate. The entrance to the two-storey grey cement building is through the prison manager's office, which has a wall of windows facing north onto the parking lot. The detention centre, according to the Syrian Human Rights Committee, was designed to house less than 100 prisoners, but is always filled at many times its capacity with between 300 and 600 prisoners.[9] There are two other buildings within these walls—one, a redbrick building that houses one of the offices used by Major General Hassan Khalil, more often referred to as General Khalil, the powerful head of the Syrian Military Intelligence. The other contains the offices of some of the generals who report to him.

According to Franco Pillarella, Canada's ambassador to Syria from 2000 to 2003, Khalil is a man so feared by Syrians that his name is not spoken aloud.[10]

Ahmad would learn later that the man who'd been in charge of his interrogation—the one who'd burned him with the cigarette—was Colonel George Salloum. He was the head of the Far' Falastin's counterterrorism interrogation team. A Christian Arab, Salloum was about Ahmad's height, five foot nine inches tall, and in his late forties or early fifties. He was balding, his clean-shaven, round face surrounded by a fringe of black hair. He stands erect, strong, and with authority, other former detainees say, and is always well dressed in pressed pants and a golf shirt, his shoes well shined.

After 9/11, Far' Falastin was seeing a new wave of international prisoners—the detention centre and its interrogators were being pressed into service for the United States and its allies in the "war on terror." Ahmad was one of the first to arrive.

AHMAD EVENTUALLY LEARNED that the prisoners in his section were numbered, as he was, by the cell they were in. Starting on the right-hand side of the narrow corridor to the right of the toilets, the cells were numbered from one to five—Ahmad's, the last on the right, was number five—and then from six to ten across the hall and back toward the toilets. The man who first spoke to Ahmad from the cell across the hall was in number six. Ahmad later learned he was a Palestinian from Lebanon.

The cell next to Ahmad's, number four, was empty when he arrived. But before long, an Iraqi officer was brought in and put there; he had been detained with his mother-in-law at the border. His mother-in-law was being held with other women and children in one of the double cells leading from the bigger hallway. The man in cell number three was a Syrian from Aleppo, in the northern part of the country. Cell number two was empty at first, but later a Syrian man was brought in. He was very badly tortured; to Ahmad, his screams seemed louder than the others.

Cell number one was empty when Ahmad arrived but was later occupied by an Iranian who had been stopped crossing into Israel from the Syrian-controlled area of the Golan Heights. His screaming and crying drove the others crazy. Ahmad was able to calm him down by speaking to him in Farsi.

Over time, Ahmad grew to trust and admire the man in cell number ten the most. His nickname was "Abu Ahmad" (no one used their real names at Far' Falastin). A Syrian, he'd been stopped crossing the border into Turkey. An Islamic scholar had occupied Ahmad's cell before he arrived and had taught Abu Ahmad to recite the Qur'an, which he did whenever he could. He became a close friend to Ahmad. "He gave me courage and changed me from being emotionally destroyed to being very strong," Ahmad says. Ahmad told him that he wanted to take back his false confession. "He said, 'Don't do it. If you recant, they will kill you,' so I didn't."

Ahmad caught a glimpse of Abu Ahmad once. It was the only time he saw another detainee at Far' Falastin. He was in the toilet, and the door hadn't quite closed before the guard led another prisoner into the toilet beside him. He heard the man speak to the guard and realized he'd just seen Abu Ahmad. "He was a young man, blond, and his eyes were sunken, like he was blind." At the first chance, Ahmad asked him if he was blind. "He said, 'I'm not blind but because I've been two years in darkness I can't see very well." The man in cell number six was alarmed. "It is very dangerous to see other detainees," he warned.

The prisoners at Far' Falastin had a pact: They didn't tell newcomers how long they'd been there until those newcomers had been in for a while. Ahmad asked, but Abu Ahmad didn't tell him until much later that he had been there, in the grave, for two years. "If he had told me that at first, I would have broken completely," says Ahmad. "*El abbar*," the grave—that's what the guards and interrogators at Far' Falastin called each of the solitary cells, which made sense: Each of the tiny cells off the narrow hallway was seven feet high, six feet deep, and three feet wide. And all were several feet underground.

Ahmad didn't know then that he was just one of the first to be delivered to Far' Falastin courtesy of Western intelligence agencies. Not long after he arrived, a man in his early forties named Mohammed Haydar Zammar, a German businessman from Hamburg, was locked into cell number thirteen. A father of five children, Zammar was six feet tall and weighed more than three hundred pounds when he was first detained. He would have barely fit in his cell.[11] Ahmad didn't know Zammar and never knew he was there, as there was no way of communicating with the detainees in the cells in the left-hand corridor.

Ahmad found it difficult to keep track of the days as they passed. But it was a major preoccupation. Each morning when he woke up, he'd remind himself of that day's date, the previous day's date, and the next day's date. If he wasn't sure, and if it seemed safe to communicate, he'd confer with the other detainees. Sometimes they'd agree and sometimes they'd disagree. Keeping track of the time of day, so they'd know when it was time to pray, was even more of a preoccupation for the detainees, who were all observant Muslims. They took turns reciting the *azan* (call to prayer), because if they were caught they'd be beaten.

The detainees were given barely enough food to survive, and what they got was often rotten and gave them diarrhea, yet they were allowed out of their cell to use the toilet only once or twice a day. They each had a bottle in their cells for urine but had to use a food container for emergencies in between toilet trips.

The guard would take one prisoner to the toilet at a time. Once that man was inside with the door closed, the guard would bring another prisoner, to the second toilet. When his door closed, the first would be forced out, whether he was done or not. The prisoners each had two minutes, exactly. The routine was designed to prevent the prisoners from seeing each other. The time limit was just about making conditions all the more unbearable.

The washrooms were each about an arm's-length deep and wide, six feet high, with a door that opened inward. The filth and the stench from the pit toilets were unimaginable, Ahmad says. There was a tap on the wall, about a foot and a half from the floor. Beneath it was an old sixteen-litre tin once used for olive oil. The top had been cut away so that the rim was jagged and sharp. Detainees used the tin as a bucket, but because they were so rushed they would inevitably cut their hands on the sharp edges. They weren't allowed to use the sinks outside the washrooms.

Ahmad remembers one day he was so sick of his own stench that he used his two minutes to try to wash. But the water was freezing cold. "I was sick for several days after that," he recalls. It was an unusually cold winter in Damascus that year—Ahmad remembers two of the guards remarking on how much snow had fallen—but there is no heat in Far' Falastin. He remembers Abu Ahmad breaking down and crying one day because he was so cold. There were two blankets in Ahmad's cell, which he slept between, using his jacket rolled up on his shoes as a pillow.

After he'd been there for a couple of weeks, the guards pulled him out of his cell to shave his head and beard. When he tried to stop them from shaving his beard—Ahmad, like most Muslims, believes a beard is required by his faith—they beat him.

Ahmad remembers the first time the electricity went out during his detention. The light in the hallway, kept on at all times, shut off, and everything went pitch black, and very quiet. After a few seconds, he heard something scurrying on the floor outside his cell. It was the rats. They lived in the pipes and had come out of the toilets to look for food. "Thank God they didn't come to me, but they went next door." The Iraqi soldier in cell number four started screaming and kicking at the rats—he couldn't see them so it was like kicking at ghosts, Ahmad says.

"We learned then that when the light goes out, the first thing you do is block the space under the door—with your clothes or anything, just block it!" Ahmad says.

There were cats, too. They'd walk over the bars overhead, occasionally stopping to mark their territory by spraying urine, hitting the prisoners below. They were scared of the bigger rats, too. "At one point I heard a cat screaming like crazy ... the cat saw a big rat and it couldn't attack it, so it was sort of scared of it [being so big] ... that's why it was screaming like crazy."

Ahmad is still haunted by the story of one of the women being kept in the double cell behind his. "There were two young women who were very, very brave," Ahmad recalls. They were two sisters, detained with their husbands and their father. One of them would stand by the door of the cell, reciting the Qur'an for the other prisoners down the hall to hear. "She knew that when they heard a young girl reading the Qur'an, it would boost their morale. She was just seventeen."

She tried communicating with others by tapping on the wall that backed on to the solitary cells. Although the others didn't dare talk with her, Ahmad did. They could hear each other by pressing their ears against the wall. She had been at Far' Falastin for more than a year. At one point, her husband had been kept in Ahmad's cell, but he had been taken somewhere else some time ago, she didn't know where. She told Ahmad they had been detained just forty days after her wedding. Pregnant at the time, she'd been tortured until she lost the baby.

SIX

Seven Searches

Monday, December 31, 2001
Canadian Embassy, Damascus

IT HAD BEEN SIX WEEKS since Ahmad disappeared, and diplomatic notes from the Canadian Embassy to the Syrians were going nowhere. The Syrians were refusing to confirm he was in detention. Gar Pardy, the director general of DFAIT's Consular Affairs Bureau, asked Ambassador Pillarella to see if he could get an answer out of someone higher up. That seemed to work. On Monday, December 31, a full seven weeks after Ahmad was first detained, the office of Syria's deputy foreign minister, Suleiman Haddad, confirmed that Ahmad was in Syrian custody. It added, however, that Canadian officials needn't concern themselves with the case because Ahmad was a Syrian citizen—consular access would be denied.[1] No, Ahmad isn't a Syrian citizen, the Canadians clarified, he's a dual national of Canada and Egypt. The Canadian Embassy pushed Syria for more information: Where was Ahmad being kept? Could they have consular access? The Syrians ignored the requests.

Pillarella had been the ambassador to Syria since November 2000, just over a year. At the embassy he oversaw the work of about a hundred staff; twenty-seven were from Canada, the rest locally employed Syrians. Pillarella had competing responsibilities—ambassadors don't just represent the interests of the consular division, they also represent all Canadian agencies in the country they are accredited to—but he saw no conflict between representing the RCMP and CSIS on the one hand and Consular

Affairs on the other when it came to Canadian citizens in detention.[2]

No stranger to intelligence work, Pillarella had been director of the Foreign Intelligence Division at DFAIT from 1992 to 1997 before being stationed as ambassador to Algeria and then Syria, which might explain why he felt compelled to keep the RCMP informed on Ahmad's status. Two days after hearing from Haddad's office, Pillarella called Steve Covey, the RCMP's liaison officer for the Middle East, stationed in Rome, to let him know that Syria had confirmed it had Ahmad in custody, and that the embassy would be pursuing consular access.[3]

Henry Garfield "Gar" Pardy was no stranger to intelligence issues either. A native Newfoundlander who says he never should have left home, he describes himself as a maverick.[4] He joined Foreign Affairs in 1967 after studying political science at Acadia University. His posts included working in New Delhi in 1969 through to 1972, at what was once called the National Security Section. There he helped negotiate a memorandum of understanding on RCMP work overseas. He also worked in Washington as an intelligence liaison officer to the CIA for four years. During the Soviet occupation of Afghanistan, Pardy worked on prisoner-of-war issues and developed a strong interest in the politics of the region. Pardy served as ambassador to various countries, including Costa Rica and El Salvador, before becoming the director general of the consular division in 1995. Although he loved his work, he was looking forward to his retirement in the summer of 2003.

Pardy says he didn't know that Pillarella passed that information on to the RCMP. "Pillarella shouldn't have done that," Pardy says. His responsibility to the RCMP doesn't involve passing on consular information. For Pardy, the first priority was the consular duty—to offer protection and assistance to Canadians abroad. "It wasn't a decision for Franco to make. Franco should have come to me and said there's something else going on here. That would have given me an edge on the case. Can I get more from the

RCMP by giving them something they already know, to see if they can give anything to us to help him? The point [is] that two parts of the Canadian government are working at cross-purposes here, and the primary [purpose] must be the well-being of the Canadian."[5]

OF COURSE, THE RCMP ALREADY KNEW where Ahmad was and was seeking a very different kind of access. Before Ahmad left Canada, the RCMP, likely Project O Canada in Toronto, provided information about him to the Americans, which, the Arar Inquiry says, it is reasonable to assume, was provided to the Syrians and led to his detention.[6] It's not clear who the men who followed Ahmad to Damascus worked for. Nor is it clear what CSIS's role was in Ahmad's detention.

Now Inspector Clement, the man Cabana and A-O Canada reported to at RCMP headquarters, wanted the Syrians to let them interview Ahmad. He had already asked the Americans for help.[7] Clement says whether or not Ahmad had been tortured wasn't the issue; the RCMP's concern was getting a statement it could use in the Canadian courts.[8]

The Syrians weren't biting. The Syrian Military Intelligence, and General Khalil in particular, didn't like working with the police; Khalil preferred to deal with other intelligence agencies, such as the CIA and CSIS. No matter—by the end of November, Project A-O Canada had the answers, having learned from "confidential sources" about the plot Ahmad had "confessed" to.[9] Until then, he had been a target of O Canada in Toronto. Now he became a target of A-O Canada.[10]

Like everything else related to CSIS's relationship with the Syrians, whether CSIS provided the Syrian interrogators with the information or the outline of the plot that the Syrians wanted Ahmad to confess to, is a secret. Whether CSIS then got Ahmad's "confession" from the Syrians, with or without the assistance of the Americans, and provided it to Project A-O Canada is also a secret. As is whether, if CSIS did provide the so-called confession to the RCMP, CSIS analyzed the information for reliability to determine whether it might be the product of torture, in light of Syria's human rights record.[11]

Either way, when A-O Canada learned about the plot from the "confidential sources," the team conducted a threat assessment of the information and concluded that the threat was high but, nonetheless, not imminent, likely because the man believed to pose the threat was in detention. It was unlikely that he'd be able to launch any kind of attack on Ottawa from there.[12]

It was in the following January that Corporal Randy Walsh, the lead investigator and affiant for A-O Canada, filed an affidavit to justify search warrants on seven locations in order to further "an investigation into an Al Qaida terrorist 'sleeper cell' in Canada."[13] The RCMP wanted to search three locations in Ottawa—the home Abdullah's family shared with his parents, his sales manager's home, and his younger brother's home; two locations in Toronto—the apartment Ahmad shared with his father and the Khadrs' residence; and two in Montreal—the home and business of Ibrahym Adam. The RCMP would later tell the media that none of the people they would question during the searches was actually a suspect.

Walsh asked that the application be sealed, in part because "information and material was obtained by the RCMP in confidence from CSIS and from several institutions of foreign states, such as the FBI...."[14] Years later, the Arar Inquiry revealed that the application relied on "information received from a country with a poor human rights record." Walsh named the country the information came from but didn't mention that the information might have been obtained through torture. Moreover, says the Arar Inquiry report, "no assessment was made of the reliability of the information."[15]

What the Arar Inquiry report doesn't say is whether sealing the order, which remains in effect today, was requested because Walsh used Ahmad's "confession" to justify the search warrant. Nor does it say whether it was CSIS or the FBI that provided the "confession" to the RCMP.

In addition to the information that may have been the product of torture, Walsh relied on tips received by two anonymous callers. One described the suspects as "strong Muslims." The names in the document in Walsh's affidavit are blacked out, but it's clear that Walsh was referring to Abdullah when he described "counter intrusion/surveillance techniques such as his use of baby powder to mark a doorway," and "tactics that included pulling over the side of the road, shutting off his lights, and the driving via a side street with his lights off."[16] Walsh also wrote in his affidavit that as a result of the "intensive investigation," he believed one suspect "fled Canada as he had become aware of law enforcement and/or intelligence community efforts to monitor his actions."[17] Abdullah laughs at the assertion now; the people following him were being so obvious, he couldn't help but become aware of them.

Early morning, Tuesday, January 22, 2002
Home of Badr El Maati, Toronto

AHMAD'S FATHER WAS UP EARLY that morning. He didn't sleep much these days, since Ahmad had gone missing. It was a Tuesday, and he had to meet with Scott Mills of the O.P.P. Mills had called a few days earlier, asking Badr to meet him for coffee again. These meetings were proving frustrating for Badr. He had nothing more to say, but maybe this time the police had news about Ahmad, so he had agreed to meet Mills at the Second Cup. Badr put on his coat, opened the door of his apartment, stepped into the hallway, and locked the door. Then he turned, and jumped. "I saw two guys and an army of men behind them."

It was Mills and another officer. Behind them, in the stairwell, were a dozen or so men and one woman, all in bulletproof vests.

"Let's go inside," Mills suggested.

It took Badr a few minutes to pull himself together, and he doesn't remember if they showed him a warrant. He unlocked the door and the police all followed him into the apartment. Mills told Badr to sit at the dining room table while the others started rummaging through everything in his apartment. As in the past, Mills was polite, but now Badr felt like he was being held prisoner in his own home. Struggling to regain his dignity, he was the consummate host. "I had a cake in the kitchen, so I brought it and offered it to him." Meanwhile, the police rummaged through his things, packing them into boxes and taking them out of the apartment. They went through Badr's papers, then found Ahmad's papers. They took his trucking logbooks and the will he'd prepared before performing the hajj. "They took everything, and then they took my computer," he says. He shakes as he thinks back to that day.

Badr's apartment was on the fifth floor of a six-floor building. He doesn't know if the police were using the elevator to carry out his belongings, but they were making a lot of noise. He wondered what the neighbours were saying. A couple of hours later, Mills told Badr that an officer would be back with a receipt for what they'd taken, and they all left.

Badr sat on the couch, stunned. "The way they tell me 'I am meeting you at the Second Cup' and then I open the door and he is in front of me ... why didn't they just tell me they were coming? I know I'm a good person, why come and search and take things from my house, like I was a criminal? If I wasn't a Muslim, things wouldn't have happened that way. After that I lost faith in everything ... they breached my trust."

It was a busy day for Projects O and A-O Canada—in addition to Badr's home, the RCMP-led teams raided another in Toronto, that belonging to the Khadr family. In Ottawa, A-O Canada searched the home Abdullah and his family shared with his parents, his younger brother's home, and his sales manager's home.

Still in Malaysia with his wife and kids, Abdullah had no idea what was going on, but, wondering why his sales manager wasn't answering his emails, he phoned. The man's wife answered. She seemed reluctant to talk to Abdullah, eventually saying her husband had gone to see a lawyer. When he pressed, she told him a little about what had happened to them on Tuesday morning. He learned the rest later.

More than a dozen officers in civilian clothes had banged on their door at seven o'clock in the morning, yelling that if it wasn't opened immediately they were going to break it down. They had a warrant and were there to search the home and the cars. The couple had two daughters, one three years old, the other eighteen months. The police told the sales manager and his wife that they would have to send their children away while the police finished the search. When their grandmother arrived to take them, the RCMP searched the children's bags, boots, and clothing before they were allowed to leave. The girls had been crying since the police banged on the door; now they were screaming.

Once the children were out of the way, the police separated the couple and grilled them for hours, saying they were there because of Abdullah, who was "a very bad man." They told her husband that they had a chart of al-Qaeda and that Abdullah was "at the very top." The officers apparently spent a lot of time sitting and listening to the family's audiotapes of Islamic children's stories. Six hours later they left, having confiscated numerous things, including the computer used for the business, phone records, and religious books.

Then Abdullah heard from his brothers. A team of officers had also banged on his younger brother's door at seven o'clock in the morning, threatening to break it down. His brother and his brother's wife had no children, but she was four months pregnant and had morning sickness, but still the officers wouldn't let her use the washroom for hours. Abdullah's brother refused to answer their questions without a lawyer present. He ran a consulting business from his home, and the police took his computers. They told him they'd already been to his parents' home and that there would be a news conference later to announce what they found in the searches.

Abdullah's parents were in Syria when the police searched their home. Their sons found it ransacked. "As if a thief went through it and [was] just looking for anything," is how one of Abdullah's brothers later described the scene. "It was just chilling, you know, you walk into your house and you've been violated."[18] In the bedrooms, dresser drawers had been emptied, the contents strewn on the floor. Lighting fixtures had been dismantled, and picture frames lay smashed on the floor. The police had almost completely emptied Abdullah's office in the basement, confiscating his business records as well as personal items such as his high school notebooks.

Before leaving for Malaysia, Abdullah had clipped an article from *The Globe and Mail* titled "Review slams CSIS treatment of refugees: Spy agency has too much latitude to brand newcomers as terrorists, committee says." It was one of the few items the search party left in his office, placing it prominently in the middle of his desk.

The RCMP also visited Abdullah's youngest brother, Youssef, a medical student at the University of Western Ontario. Two officers knocked on his door at 7:30 A.M. and told him they were from the anti-terrorism squad. They wanted him to go with them for an interview. Youssef protested that he had to be at the hospital. They said he was lucky they didn't drag him out of his classes in front of his peers, then offered to drive him to the hospital and wait for him there. But Youssef wanted advice before doing anything, so he said he'd drive himself. The officers said they would meet up with him later. Youssef went straight to the dean's office. The staff there were supportive and advised him to get a lawyer. He did, and went with his lawyer to meet with the RCMP that evening.

The meeting lasted forty-five minutes. The police started by saying they were going to tape the interview. On the desk were two binders with Youssef's name on them. One of the officers had papers in front of him on the desk, and Youssef could see they contained his personal information, including "what kind of car I drove, what my credit card numbers were, driver licence, who my brothers were, my parents, just personal information."[19]

When Youssef's lawyer asked what the RCMP wanted, the officers said they suspected Abdullah had sent computer equipment to companies that in turn sold it to other companies, the equipment eventually making its way to terrorists. When pressed about the absurdity of the allegation, the officers admitted they didn't have any evidence.

The RCMP also questioned members of Abdullah's extended family and acquaintances that day, telling some of them that they did have evidence that Abdullah had knowingly sent equipment to terrorists. One officer, RCMP captain Erika Sheridan, told Abdullah's cousin that the police had confirmed that Abdullah was a member of al-Qaeda. Then Sheridan asked his cousin if she thought Abdullah would be making his way to Syria (from Malaysia). Abdullah's cousin told Sheridan she didn't know.

The RCMP had also searched Ibrahym Adam's home and business in Montreal. Abdullah says Ibrahym later told him that police squads cordoned off the city block surrounding their home, then hammered on the door until they opened it. When they did, the police stormed in with their dogs. Ibrahym's children were apparently terrified to wake up to the sight of police dogs in their bedrooms. The house was turned upside down, and the children were left traumatized by the experience.

The more Abdullah heard about what had happened in Canada, the angrier he got. Another friend of Abdullah's was pulled over while driving and questioned about Abdullah. Abdullah's reputation was being systematically destroyed in the community, and now his family was being targeted, too. His office had been emptied of all its records, and his sales manager couldn't work without his computer, as it contained the business information.

There never was a news conference about the searches. It seems the RCMP found nothing worth announcing publicly. The Walsh affidavit says the RCMP hoped to find "materials related to the production of and preparation of explosive materials," information exposing possible "money stashes" to finance terrorists operations, "various manuals, documents, photographs, designs, logs, illustrations, maps, letters and data files related to potential targets."[20] Instead, the RCMP seized twenty-six hard drives (with about 120 gigabytes of potential storage space), about forty VHS tapes that included family videos, about a hundred computer discs, two boxes of shredded documents, and about twenty thousand pages of documents.[21] The RCMP now claims some of the items it seized had been hidden in walls and rafters, but it refuses to say which items and where. Abdullah says no one in his family noticed that the RCMP had searched inside the walls or rafters of their homes.

The only news about the searches that did surface surfaced because Abdullah's sales manager, outraged by how he, his wife, and his children had been treated, talked to the head of the Canadian Islamic Congress. The family was afraid of being named but wanted the public to know what happened. The president of the congress talked to the media for them. The RCMP, forced to respond to charges that the searches were an example of racial profiling, said that "the people being questioned aren't suspects themselves. They're removed by one or two layers and they're not under arrest or charged."[22]

Abdullah's parents and brothers didn't go to the media. They were petrified, Youssef said. "We were all scared. There was this new terrorism bill where you could be taken away for no reason. I mean, when I went down and was interviewed, my lawyer said if it wasn't for this bill I wouldn't even let him talk to you guys ... so it was just an aura of fear ... being remotely associated as a terrorist.... Some friends told me people were calling me names behind my back like al-Qaeda, things like that. Just because they heard I was being investigated."[23]

Shirley Heafey, then head of the RCMP's watchdog, the Commission for Public Complaints Against the RCMP, responded to the news by warning that this was an example of why the commission had insufficient power to impose checks and balances on the force since it had acquired new powers under the

Anti-terrorism Act.[24] "I remember reading about what happened in that search and being so upset. But the people who were most affected weren't registering complaints. They'd call our office but they refused to register complaints. They were too scared," Heafey says. She doesn't blame them; a complaint with the commission could just end up further stigmatizing the person in his or her community, especially as most investigations by the commission began with an interview by the RCMP itself. "Even if one of my staff did the initial interviews, the RCMP would know who lodged the complaint," she says.[25]

Justice Minister McLellan's earlier assurances that the commission would provide sufficient oversight for the RCMP weren't playing out: The commission hadn't seen any changes to its resources or powers. The commission had no power to compel the RCMP to provide documents to show what it was doing with its new powers. "I couldn't pry a sheet of paper loose from the RCMP. I paid a lot of attention to the media reports, because I couldn't find anything out from the RCMP, so the media was the best source of information for me about what they were doing," Heafey says. "I couldn't look at files or initiate a complaint without implications for the people most affected. And forcing someone to file their own complaint was not an option. What I needed, and never got, was audit power."

The RCMP's Canadian investigation had reached into Malaysia. Abdullah learned there that people he knew had been questioned by Malaysian officials about him. Then Abdullah was questioned.

Abdullah's wife, Khuzaimah, had developed symptoms of gestational diabetes and was anaemic, and a doctor advised her not to travel before giving birth: She needed to rest. So, instead of returning to Canada in December as planned, the family decided to stay in Malaysia until after the baby was born in February. Abdullah's visa was about to expire, so in early January he travelled over the border into Singapore to renew it. Returning to Malaysia, he was pulled aside by Malaysian immigration officials. They asked him to go in a car with them to the local police station to answer a few questions. At the station, a police chief named Tan asked him about his business and shared the answers with whomever he was speaking to on the phone. He asked if Abdullah would be returning to Canada. Yes, he had a return ticket, he said. Unlike the men who had brought Abdullah to the station, Tan was polite and professional and seemed to sense Abdullah's frustration. He told him not to blame the Malaysian government; it was the Canadian government that had asked them to do this. He was apologetic and gave Abdullah his passport with a three-month visa, then directed his staff to help Abdullah find his way back to a bus station so he could get back to his family in Kuala Lumpur.

Back in the city, Abdullah asked a friend in the newspaper business to work his contacts with Malaysian intelligence. They told him that Canada had been pressing for Abdullah's arrest. The Malaysians, despite having shown little reluctance to use their powers of preventative arrest against so many others alleged to have terror ties since 9/11, had refused Canada's requests.[26]

All this occurred at a busy time for Abdullah's company, Dawn Services, whose sales were up because of what it sold and who it sold it to. The company's biggest client, Microelectronics, was the main supplier of two-way radios to the Pakistani army and border police. The United States was pumping money into Pakistan so that Pakistan's army and police could beef up security at its border with Afghanistan. The fear, of course, was that key al-Qaeda players, including bin Laden himself, could cross over undetected and disappear. The United States had just announced new funding for Pakistan, including, among other initiatives, $73 million to "improve Pakistani border security by providing helicopters, vehicles, fuel, night vision goggles, communications equipment, training, and border post communications; and $7.5 million to replace existing outdated secure phones."[27] Abdullah had spent years building his reputation with Microelectronics. Now those years were paying off: He was its most trusted supplier.

What this amounted to was the U.S. government giving money to the Pakistani government, whose army used it to buy equipment from Microelectronics, which then bought components and equipment from Abdullah. Or, put another way, Abdullah was selling equipment and components to Microelectronics, which was then selling them to the Pakistani army to outfit the frontline border guards tasked with helping the United States by stopping al-Qaeda from crossing into Pakistan.

For this, the RCMP could have found evidence, if it cared to look for it. The funding for the Pakistani government had been announced publicly. The RCMP had seized all the waybills and purchase papers and other documents about Abdullah's clients in its searches. A quick call to Microelectronics would have helped settle matters. But that wouldn't happen for several more years. And when it did, it was a journalist, not an RCMP investigator, who made the call.

"We have never been questioned by any local or foreign intelligence agency about the imports in question," Munawar Ali, a retired air force officer and international marketing manager at Microelectronics, told *Globe and Mail* reporter Colin Freeze in 2007. "You are the first one who has asked for such information."[28]

THE RCMP ALSO WENT TO MAHER ARAR'S HOME Tuesday, January 22—at 7:30 A.M. It couldn't justify a search warrant for his home, so it wanted an interview instead. Monia was surprised to hear a knock at her apartment door so early. Maher was in Tunisia visiting her father, who was ill. Monia hadn't gone because she was pregnant and due in less than a month. She opened the door to find two men standing there: RCMP corporals Buffam and McKinnon. They told her they wanted to speak with Maher. She explained that he was in Tunisia and would be back in a few days. Buffam gave her his card, asking her to have Maher call. Monia was alarmed by the visit. What did the RCMP want with her husband? She called Maher in Tunisia. Maher had never had police come his door before and thought this was very strange, so he called Buffam and left a message for him the same day with the phone number where he could be reached in Tunis.

Buffam later claimed he called Maher back between two and three o'clock in the morning Tunis time and there was no answer. Maher is sure that he or his father-in-law would have heard the phone ringing if it had.

The two finally spoke three days later, after Maher had returned home. Buffam called, and Maher answered. Maher asked why the RCMP had come to his home, without notice, so early in the morning and disturbed his wife. Buffam explained that he hadn't realized that Maher was away, and asked if they could meet. Maher said he wanted to rest from his travel first and suggested they talk on the following Monday, January 28. Buffam insisted they meet the next day instead, on Saturday. He says Maher agreed, but Maher remembers it differently—he wanted to speak to a lawyer before meeting.

Maher wondered now if the RCMP's visit was connected to an earlier incident. He had been pulled aside by customs officials at the Ottawa airport after a business trip to the United States. Of course, he didn't know then that there was a "terrorist lookout" attached to his name, which might also explain why officials were so rude with him that day. They searched his luggage and his wallet, then insisted on seizing his computer and Palm Pilot for twenty-four hours, claiming he had to pay duty on them. This didn't make sense, as it was obvious the computer and Palm Pilot weren't new, and Maher told them that his employer had supplied the computer. The next day, when he returned to claim the computer and Palm Pilot, the officials accused him of having bought them in the United States and made him pay $231 to reclaim them. Maher was frustrated, since his employer had supplied him with the computer years earlier, but decided it would be easier to pay than to argue. He had decided then that this was harassment related to heightened security after 9/11, and if it happened again he would go to a lawyer. When he got home and turned on his computer, he noticed that someone had logged in to his computer that day.

So now, after talking to Buffam, Maher called lawyer Michael Edelson and made an appointment to see him on January 30. In the meantime, Edelson called the RCMP to say that if officers wanted to meet Maher, they would have to go through him.

That afternoon at Friday prayers, Maher ran into Abdullah's brother, who told him about the searches, and the questions the RCMP asked. One officer, he said, had asked him if Maher had "extreme views" about the United States. This Maher found ridiculous; he had always admired the United States, especially its business community.

Maher met Edelson on January 30, and while, as a criminal lawyer, Edelson would normally advise against any interview with the RCMP, Maher insisted he had nothing to hide. Edelson sent a letter to the RCMP saying his client would come in for an interview but only if the police agreed to some basic conditions: Edelson would be present, Maher would not provide a sworn statement, and the interview could not be videotaped, although it could be audio-taped. They wanted to be able to read, and correct, if necessary, any transcript of the interview. He didn't want anything Maher said to be used as evidence, and he wanted the right to instruct his client to refuse to answer questions he didn't think Maher should answer. In addition, he wanted the right for Maher to leave at any time. Edelson thought these were pretty standard conditions, given the RCMP's refusal to tell him anything about the investigation or to explain whether it regarded Maher as a witness, or a target.

A-O Canada decided to give up. Cabana had concluded that the fact that anything Maher said "could not be used in relation to any prosecution against anybody, anywhere, basically rendered the interview, for all intents and purposes, useless."[29] A-O Canada also concluded that the fact that the Almalki family and Maher were using the same lawyer was further evidence that they were part of a group. Criminal organizations, Cabana said,

are often represented by one lawyer. He wasn't aware that the
Imams in local mosques had recommended three lawyers to
Muslims who were feeling harassed. Edelson was one of them.[30]
Edelson was also particularly well known in the Muslim commu-
nity because he represented Liban Hussein, a Somali Canadian
wrongly accused of terrorist financing.[31]

SEVEN

Damascus to Cairo

Sometime after midnight, Friday, January 25, 2002
Far' Falastin, Damascus

AHMAD ISN'T SURE ABOUT THE DATE but thinks it was January 25, just after midnight, when the guard came to get him from his cell at Far' Falastin. A few hours earlier, Abu Ahmad had asked him if the Syrians had taken Ahmad's photograph. No, why? Abu Ahmad explained that he'd had a dream that someone had come to take their pictures, then released them all. Abu Ahmad often told the others about his dreams, believing that dreams could predict the future.

Whenever Ahmad heard the guard sliding the lock open on his door, he braced himself for another interrogation and more torture—the guards usually came to take prisoners for torture after midnight. This time, though, the guard ordered him to bring his jacket, then stopped him in front of the toilets to shave his head and beard. When they got to the interrogation room upstairs, the guard brought in his bags. He ordered Ahmad to change his clothes. When he did, he had to force a new hole into his belt to hold his pants up. He had lost seven inches around his waist.

Where was he going? Was he being released like in Abu Ahmad's dream? The guard just kept saying he didn't know.

The guard took him into the prison manager's office, where the manager pulled out Ahmad's passport and money. It was all there, except for the small amount Ahmad had spent to buy rations from the guards. But the deerskin pouch in which he had carried the money wasn't among the items returned to him. The pouch had been a gift from his brother and was very special to him. He was upset but didn't dare ask where it was.

Ahmad was taken outside and put in the backseat of a station wagon, his bags loaded into the back. The guards then brought out several boxes, which they fussed over, carefully positioning them on top of Ahmad's bags. Ahmad could smell that the boxes were full of baklava, the sublime Middle Eastern delicacy of ground nuts and spices, layered between paper-thin sheets of phyllo pastry, swimming in sweet orange blossom syrup. "Syria has the best baklava in the world," Ahmad overheard them say. It was a gift, they said. Wherever Ahmad was going, the baklava was going with him.

The general arrived and climbed into the front seat, then ordered the guards to switch Ahmad's handcuffs from the front to the back and hood him. They drove off.

When the car came to a stop, the general got out to talk with someone. Eventually, the guards took Ahmad out of the car and pulled off the hood. He was standing at the bottom of steps leading up to an airplane. His bags and the boxes of baklava were on the ground beside him.

Am I being handed over to a country in Europe, or to the United States? Ahmad wondered.

The general looked at the picture in Ahmad's passport, then at Ahmad. Putting the hood back over Ahmad's head, he led him up the steps and into the plane. The guards followed, carrying his bags and the boxes of baklava.

The passenger plane seated at least a hundred people, but as Ahmad was led down the aisle, he could see from under the hood that all the seats were empty. He and his new escorts—he thinks there were at least ten—were the only passengers. He was buckled into a seat, still handcuffed and hooded, and the plane took off. Ahmad listened hard for sounds of any crew but heard no one except his escorts, barely: They spoke rarely, and when they did, in very hushed tones, so low he couldn't make out what language they were speaking. Later, when he asked to use the washroom, one of the men just signalled no with his finger, which Ahmad could make out from under the hood.

After about an hour and a half, the plane started its descent. He guessed it was around 3 A.M. when they landed. Hooded and not able to see where he was going, Ahmad missed his footing at the door of the airplane, at the top of the stairway. He screamed as he stumbled forward. Someone caught him from behind just in time to stop him from tumbling down to the tarmac.

Once on solid ground again, Ahmad noticed the air was different; it was drier than in Syria.

Someone spoke as he pushed him onto the floor of a van. "*Khosh!*"

Ahmad realized he was in Egypt—*khosh* is "enter" in the Egyptian dialect. Ahmad had been to Egypt three times as a boy, the last time when he was fifteen. He had flown from Damascus to Cairo with his father and sister to visit his aunt and remembers swimming in the Mediterranean Sea and playing on the beach in Alexandria. He had come from Damascus this time, too, but this time he was going to see a very different side of Egypt.

The CIA had used Egypt to torture terror suspects since as early as the mid-1990s; the country was an "obvious choice" according to one former CIA agent, because it was the largest recipient, after Israel, of U.S. foreign aid, and, he said, because its security agencies were known for their brutality.[1] That was before 9/11. After 9/11, when the "extraordinary rendition" program really took off, that brutality was being used more and more. Robert Baer, a former CIA case officer in the Middle East, explained to *Guardian* reporters Adrian Levy and Cathy Scott-Clark how rendition works: "We pick up a suspect or we arrange for one of our partner countries to do it. Then the suspect is placed on civilian transport to a third country where, let's make no bones about it, they use torture. If you want a good interrogation, you send someone to Jordan. If you want them to be killed, you send them to Egypt or Syria."[2]

Amnesty International reported in 2002 that Egypt's emergency laws, in effect since 1981, provided the president with "wide-ranging powers including the censorship, confiscation and closing of newspapers on the grounds of 'public safety' and 'national security'" and the power to "order the prolonged detention without charge or trial of anyone suspected of being 'a threat to national security and public order.'"[3]

The organization also reported that the "vast majority of political detainees who have been tortured report that they were tortured while held in incommunicado detention at premises of the SSI [State Security Intelligence]," and that "the number of reported cases of death in custody remains alarmingly high."[4]

The U.S. State Department report for the same year noted that people accused of being associated with terrorism were especially targeted:

> The security forces continued to arrest and detain suspected members of terrorist groups. In combating terrorism, the security forces continued to mistreat and torture prisoners, arbitrarily arrest and detain persons, held detainees in prolonged pretrial detention, and occasionally engaged in mass arrests.[5]

The State Department reported that "torture and abuse of detainees by police, security personnel, and prison guards was common and persistent":

> Principal methods of torture reportedly employed by the police included: Being stripped and blindfolded; suspended from a ceiling or doorframe with feet just touching the floor; beaten with fists, whips, metal rods, or other objects; subjected to electrical shocks; and doused with cold water. Victims frequently reported being subjected to threats and forced to sign blank papers to be used against the victim or the victim's family in the future should the victim complain of abuse. Some victims, including male and female detainees, reported that they were sexually assaulted or threatened with the rape of themselves or family members.[6]

Ahmad winced when the van started moving. His arms and shoulders were in a lot of pain because his wrists had been handcuffed behind his back for so long.

The van eventually pulled into what he later learned was the Mukhabarat al-Aama, the General Intelligence headquarters, in the Abdeen area of Cairo. His hood was removed briefly so he could be photographed. When he saw the camera, Ahmad thought of the dream Abu Ahmad had had. He smiled just as the camera snapped his picture. "If you find that photo, you'll see a big smile," he says, laughing about it now.

His bags were there, but the boxes of baklava were gone.

He was given a prisoner's uniform and his handcuffs were removed so he could change. Then his arms were cuffed behind his back again and the hood was shoved back over his head. A man checked his pulse and blood pressure—Ahmad guessed that he was checking to see if he could survive torture—and then he was led into to another, smoke-filled, room. He guesses there were about five or six men there.

"Tell us your story!"

Ahmad took a chance. He told them that what he had told the Syrians was false.

The men were on him within seconds, but this time, the blows were carefully aimed, not haphazard like in Syria. "It was as if they were trained in some kind of martial art," Ahmad says. His hands still cuffed behind his back, Ahmad was knocked all over the room. They forced him to crouch. Pain shot through his knee, but if he leaned or fell forward he was beaten even harder. They screamed insults at him against his mother, father, sister, and brother, and against Allah. They had lots of questions about his sister, who was living in Egypt.

"You know your sister is in Cairo. She is in the next room," one of the men said. Then he shouted, as if to someone in the next room, "Take off her clothes, I am coming to rape her!"

Ahmad, screaming, he says, "like never before in my life,"

collapsed on the floor, broken. He'd heard stories about family members being used that way in Egypt.

"Okay, it's true, I was going to attack the Parliament in Ottawa," Ahmad said. He repeated the false confession about the map, and the plot, because he thought it was what they wanted to hear. One of the men claimed they had a lie detector and could tell he was lying. Ahmad didn't know what to say then.

He was led out of the interrogation room to a cell, where his hood was removed, though his hands remained cuffed behind his back.

The cell was cleaner and a bit larger than "the grave" at Far' Falastin. It had a steel door with a small, locked window. The floor and walls were concrete, and there was a light in the ceiling several feet above his head. There was a cement bench and two or three blankets.

Ahmad was left in the cell for about an hour before being taken to see another official, who seemed of high ranking. There was no beating this time. "He was speaking in a soft tone and saying 'Ahmad, I only want you to tell us exactly what happened.' So I jumped, I said this is the truth, and told him about the letter from my employer." The man sent for the letter from Ahmad's things.

As the man read the letter, Ahmad urged him to contact Canada and verify it; "I told him, you can kill me if you find out I'm lying." The man seemed to believe what Ahmad was saying and cursed the Syrians for their inferior interrogation, but said he would verify the story. Leaning into Ahmad's face, he said, "If I learn you are lying, I will cut you to pieces."

Over the next few hours, Ahmad was taken from one office to another, eventually talking with four different men. They seemed to be checking for inconsistencies in his statements. He was then taken back to his cell, where a guard told him they'd be keeping him awake. Over the next twenty-four hours, he was taken for more interrogations. He was exhausted, and his arms and shoulders were hurting even more now from being handcuffed. Finally, his cuffs were removed, he was brought food, and allowed to sleep.

The interrogations continued for a month. Ahmad was questioned almost every day and subjected to constant verbal abuse. The questions here focused on his time in Afghanistan, and whom he knew there. "They showed me lots of pictures, but I didn't know anyone in them," he says. "Most of the people with me in Afghanistan were killed, so they weren't in those pictures," he says.

The only human contact he had at the Mukhabarat al-Aama was with the interrogators and the guard, who he would ask to take him to the toilet. He was handcuffed and blindfolded whenever being moved. "I never saw or heard any other detainee," he says.

Ahmad's only connection to the outside world was the sound of the call to prayer from a nearby mosque and the sound of passing trains. "It saved me, and I knew when to pray, which I didn't in Syria. I knew the time." Ahmad didn't know he was in Cairo; he thought that he could smell the sea and so was in Alexandria, and he thought what he was hearing were ships, rather than trains.

This place was very different from Far' Falastin. The interrogation rooms were clean, and the cells were hosed down once a week. The prisoners were taken to shower on Fridays, too.

Ahmad begged for a Qur'an but was refused one until, after being there about a month, he was finally given one. "Seeing the Qur'an in my hand gave me the strength to keep living," Ahmad says.

The guard was friendly with him and seemed to know his story. One day he told Ahmad that he knew that information had come from Canada. "Our countries are like boots that do anything the West wants," he said.

Saturday, February 2, 2002
"A" Division, RCMP headquarters, Ottawa

IT'S NOT CLEAR why Ahmad was moved from Damascus to
Cairo, or if the transfer was suggested, or arranged, by CSIS or
the RCMP. One thing is certain: It would now be much harder to
work for his release. Ahmad's mother is Syrian, but Ahmad is
not. He holds automatic dual Canadian-Egyptian citizenship
because his father is Egyptian. As Justice O'Connor would later
note in his report, "all of the countries to which the United States
has rendered terrorism suspects impose significant bars to renun-
ciation of citizenship."[7] At least in Syria, the government couldn't
claim he was their citizen, and the Vienna Convention would
have applied.

Inspector Clement, the man A-O Canada reported to at RCMP
headquarters, says he learned on February 11 that Ahmad was in
Egypt. It's not clear whether Clement or anyone else in the
RCMP or CSIS knew ahead of time Ahmad would be sent there.

After the searches in January, the RCMP felt it was even more
important to get an interview with Ahmad. Indeed, it appears
that on the same day Ahmad was sent to Egypt, Cabana was
discussing it with the Americans.[8] A-O Canada went elsewhere
for help, too: Team members talked about it with senior officers
at "A" Division, with the Criminal Intelligence Directorate at
RCMP headquarters, with the RCMP's Middle East liaison
officer in Rome, with CSIS, and even with DFAIT.

A-O Canada's dealings with the FBI and CIA after the searches
had become "more frequent" and "less formal"; the "open book
investigation" had opened its books to the FBI and CIA.[9] By early
February, one or two FBI agents had their own pass card to get
into the RCMP headquarters, though they still needed an escort
to get into "A" Division, where A-O Canada's offices were
housed. Most of their time was spent in the office shared by Staff
Sergeant Patrick Callaghan, seconded to A-O Canada from the
Ottawa Police Service, and Sergeant Kevin Corcoran, recruited to

the team from the O.P.P.[10] A-O Canada let them see anything they wanted to see, and the FBI spent days poring over the materials seized in the searches.[11]

On February 19, a FBI team arrived to work out of Project A-O Canada's offices, and for the next three days, "engaged in a rigorous review" of all of A-O Canada's files, not just the items seized in the searches.[12] By February 21, the FBI had walked away with a portion of the paper documents seized in the searches, as well as with copies of the seized hard drives, and a summary of the Walsh ITO (Information to Obtain) used for the searches.[13] The information the RCMP shared with the FBI had no caveats attached, nor was it screened for relevance, reliability, or personal information, all conditions required by RCMP policy.

Meanwhile, A-O Canada continued its efforts to interview Ahmad. Team members had raised it again in a meeting on February 5 with the FBI, then again on February 28, when Assistant Commissioner Proulx took the issue all the way to the RCMP's deputy commissioner Garry Loeppky. It seems Proulx was looking for Loeppky's input on one option being offered, perhaps by the Americans or the Egyptians. "I advised we need to have questions asked and if [REDACTED] has access and can do that with our questions and [provide] verification that it is he being interviewed[,] it might suffice," Loeppky wrote in his personal notes that day.[14]

Late February–early March 2002
Mukhabarat al-Aama (General Intelligence headquarters), Cairo

THE QUESTIONS CHANGED about a month after he was taken to Egypt, Ahmad says.

A guard came to Ahmad's cell, handcuffed and blindfolded him, then took him to an interrogation room. He removed the handcuffs and instructed Ahmad to sit in a chair. The guard sat in another chair behind him.

A voice on an intercom ordered the guard to remove Ahmad's blindfold. There was a television in front of Ahmad. The power came on, and he could see a diagram on the screen. The voice on the loudspeaker asked Ahmad if he recognized the diagram. No, Ahmad answered, he didn't know what it was. He was worried he'd be beaten.

The man began to yell, accusing him of lying. Ahmad was desperate—what should he do? Should he lie? He asked that the document be brought to him so he could see it up close on paper.

The man ordered the guard to replace Ahmad's blindfold. Once it was on, someone came into the room, then left. Again over the intercom, the man ordered the guard to remove Ahmad's blindfold. On the desk was the map of Ottawa, the one the American officials had found in his truck. The one he'd told the officers at the airport was with his lawyer, Rocco Galati. Ahmad didn't know that Galati had given the map to the RCMP.

"I thought they were trying to implicate me in something different. So when I saw it was the map I was so relieved. I told them, 'This is the map I told you about!'" Ahmad says.

Ahmad thinks the man had zoomed in on a certain part of the map when showing Ahmad it on the screen, which is why he hadn't recognized it.

The guard replaced Ahmad's blindfold and led him back to his cell. A few days later, Ahmad was taken from his cell again. This time the questions were about a remote control he had bought for his television in Toronto. Ahmad explained that he had gone to buy a remote for a television his sister had given to him and his mother. For three days, he drove all over Toronto looking for one that would work with that particular TV set, finally ending up at the Sony Store on Gordon Baker Road in North York. He remembers the quest well. It was after 9/11, and he had been followed to all the stores by several cars. He ended up returning the remote control because it didn't work. The cars had also followed him when he took it back.

Ahmad was taken back to his cell.

A few days later, he was interrogated yet again. This time it was about the Canadian passport he had been issued before leaving Pakistan in 1998. The Egyptians wanted him to confess that he had deliberately washed it.

Ahmad had accidentally left his passport in his pants when they went through the laundry during his preparations to perform the hajj in 1999. He took the damaged passport to the passport office to have it replaced for his trip. The passport office kept his old one and issued him a new one. Now his interrogators were accusing him of having washed the passport on purpose.

This interrogation was particularly harsh. Ahmad was beaten and kicked until he signed a "confession" saying he had deliberately destroyed his passport. This was the first time he was forced to sign anything in Egypt.

Back in his cell, doubled over in pain, Ahmad thought back to the questions about his passport. He was mystified, and wonders now if the Canadians thought he'd tried to conceal the customs stamps showing he had been in Pakistan. But this didn't make sense: He had applied for that passport at the Canadian Embassy in Islamabad. Why would he have done this if he had been hiding his travel?

BY APRIL, the FBI and CIA already had a lot of A-O Canada's information, but they wanted more. After the FBI agents finished their three-day review of the search information, they put in a formal request for the information in a February 22 letter to the RCMP's Commissioner Zaccardelli.[15] Headquarters passed the letter on to A-O Canada without any direction as to how the request should be answered. The CIA put in its own request, too.

By then, according to Cabana, everyone had agreed at an all-agency meeting on January 31 that any and all information would be shared with the Americans, not just the information obtained through the searches. So that's what A-O Canada investigators did: They prepared two CDs containing 3337 files— essentially every single document Project A-O Canada's investigation had generated or received—and gave them to the FBI and CIA sometime in late March or early April. But, again, none of the information, in what would come to be known as the "data dump," had been screened for relevance, reliability, or personal information, and none, not even the information from CSIS, had caveats attached.[16] RCMP policy on information sharing had been disregarded entirely. The Arar Inquiry later revealed that much of the information was inaccurate, irrelevant, unreliable, and very personal indeed.

Government secrecy stymied any possibility of the Arar Inquiry commenting in its report on the accuracy of the information shared about the other Canadians targeted by the investigation, but Justice O'Connor did note numerous errors in the information about Maher, information that painted him as much more than a "person of interest" to the investigation. For instance, it had taken Maher less than twenty minutes to get from his west-end Ottawa home to Mango's Café to meet Abdullah for lunch back in October 2001, but, according to A-O Canada's information, he had driven all the way from Montreal—making the get-together seem all the more important. Maher, too, was noted as having refused an interview with the RCMP, rather than having offered an interview subject to conditions stipulated by his lawyer. The information included names and addresses retrieved from Maher's Palm Pilot, along with speculation on the part of A-O Canada that some of the people "might have links to extremist activity."[17]

One of the documents on the CD was an analytical diagram titled "Bin Laden's associates: Al-Qaeda Organization in Ottawa." The diagram had Abdullah's name at the centre, directly connected to Maher. Ahmad's name was almost certainly among the others on the chart, which, while never released publicly, was described in the Arar Report.[18]

EIGHT

The Prevention Side of the Mandate

Between 3 and 4 P.M., Friday, May 3, 2002
On board Saudi Arabian Airlines, approaching Damascus

IT HAD BEEN A ROUGH FEW MONTHS for Abdullah and his family. First there had been the news about complications with Khuzaimah's pregnancy and the need to stay on in Malaysia until after the birth. Then questions at the Malaysan border, and the bad news from Canada about the searches, and their aftermath. It was a busy time for Dawn Services, and the logistics had been complicated when the company's computer and records were seized.

The birth of Abdullah and Khuzaimah's fifth child, a boy, in February had been very difficult. Khuzaimah couldn't walk for a full month afterward. Abdullah worked with her mother to care for her, the new baby, and the other four children while she recovered. After a few weeks, he was able to devote more time to his business. He set up meetings with clients in Singapore and Saudi Arabia.

It was on April 3 that Abdullah left his wife and five children in Kuala Lumpur with her mother. Khuzaimah was up and walking, and his fifth and youngest son, was thriving at one and a half months old. Abdullah was worried about his business: A shipment to his biggest client, Microelectronics, had disappeared. Microelectronics needed connectors for an order of high-frequency radio systems it was assembling for the Pakistani Rangers patrolling the Pakistani borders. Abdullah found a company in Texas that could manufacture the connectors, but it would take time. Time, for Microelectronics, meant money. It would pay a penalty for each day it was late delivering the radios. Abdullah worked hard to make sure that as soon as the manufacturer had the order ready, it would ship to his New York warehouse space for processing, before being shipped to Pakistan the quickest way possible. He had to track things from Malaysia; his sales manager back in Ottawa wasn't able to do much without his computer and the business records.

Abdullah had contracted the company that ran the warehouse to process the shipment. As soon as the connectors arrived from the manufacturer, the company's staff counted them, then removed all the labels that would identify the supplier and repackaged them—a critical step for any import/export business to prevent clients from dealing directly with suppliers—readying them for shipment to Pakistan by FedEx. FedEx picked them up on February 21. If all went well, Microelectronics would have its connectors within a week.[1]

But all didn't go well. Abdullah checked the tracking system the next day and learned that on the same day FedEx faxed a copy of the airway bill to his Ottawa office, the shipment had been pulled from the airplane for an unspecified export-control process. Abdullah called the manufacturer in Texas to ensure that there wasn't an export-control requirement for the connectors that he hadn't been aware of. The manufacturer assured him that there wasn't. In the meantime, his sales manager had called the export-control office, only to be told that the authorities there had never seen the shipment. He called Abdullah and told him the shipment seemed to have disappeared. FedEx didn't have it, and neither did the American export-control facility.

Two months later, the shipment was still missing, and Dawn Services was out hundreds of thousands of dollars. Microelectronics, the company's biggest client, was losing money, too, and wasn't happy. Looking back now, Abdullah wonders if CSIS or the RCMP asked the FBI to seize the shipment, and if it did, what recourse he has for getting the money back.

Despite the continuing uncertainty around the missing shipment, Abdullah's meetings in Saudi Arabia had gone well. But then he'd learned from his parents that his grandmother was ill, and that the family thought it was serious. His grandmother had eight sons and one daughter, Abdullah's mother, and many of them were travelling from around the world to see her now.

Abdullah and his brothers had spent a lot of time with his grandmother when they were kids. "She was extremely close to us," Abdullah says. She had a big, beautiful home in Damascus, and kept toys and pyjamas there for her grandchildren, for their frequent visits. Once Abdullah's family moved to Canada she had come twice to visit, but he hadn't seen her in years.

Abdullah hadn't been in Syria for fifteen years, and a flight to Damascus from Jeddah would take only a couple hours, so he booked a flight on Saudi Arabian Airlines, then called to tell his parents he'd be there at about 4 P.M. on Friday, May 3.

Now, as his flight approached Damascus International Airport, Abdullah could see the lush greenbelt to the east and south of the ancient city. Called the Ghouta, it is often referred to as the Damascus oasis. His family owns land in the Ghouta, and his favourite childhood memories are of playing with his brothers and cousins among flowering fruit trees in the area's lush orchards.

Abdullah's parents had arranged a special welcome for Abdullah in Syria: A woman was waiting at the door of the airplane to take him to the airport's ornate VIP lounge, where his mother was waiting for him. They embraced, and she introduced him to his cousin, whom he'd not met before. While Abdullah sipped lemonade with his mother, his cousin handed his passport to the VIP lounge staff, who took it to the immigration officials. When one of the officials came to say that airport security wanted to speak with Abdullah, he walked over with his cousin to see what they wanted. They were asked to go into an office.

In the office were three men. Abdullah asked if this had anything to do with his military service. By law, every male in Syria must serve thirty months of military service when they turn eighteen. Abdullah had left Syria when he was sixteen, and his father had since ensured that all of his sons' military service deferrals were in order so that they could return to Syria without trouble whenever they wanted. That had to be done every five years, and Abdullah's deferral did not expire until March 2003.

It had nothing to do with military service, the man replied. Abdullah's cousin started to get angry and asked what was going on. One of the men asked him to leave. He did so, reluctantly.

Another man pulled out a book. "It is recent," he said. "The report was received from the embassy on April 22, 2002." Then he led Abdullah into another room. There, two other officials asked him about his family and why he hadn't been in Syria for so long.

"He is wanted for Branch 235," one of the officials said.

Abdullah asked what that was.

"Far' Falastin."

Abdullah had heard of Far' Falastin but didn't know its reputation as a house of torture.

Not to worry, the man assured him, it wouldn't take long.

They asked Abdullah to empty his pockets. Seeing that Abdullah didn't have any Syrian money, the men suggested he go to the currency exchange booth and get some so he'd have money for a cab when he was done at Far' Falastin. While all this was happening Abdullah's luggage and laptop bag had been brought in. He didn't know it then, but when an officer had gone to get the bags from the lounge, he'd told Abdullah's mother and cousin to leave without him. The two men who went with Abdullah to the currency exchange counter offered to carry his bags for him.

"They told us to chain you from head to toe, but you don't look dangerous," one of them said.

But Abdullah didn't take him seriously. "They weren't armed and were being so polite with me. I didn't think he was serious. I didn't feel that there was any misunderstanding that I couldn't resolve," he says.

Abdullah got the money and then followed the men out the door to a waiting minibus. It was the shuttle bus that brought the immigration officers to the airport; there were about ten workers on the bus. Abdullah looked out the window and chatted casually with the two men as the bus made its way from the airport into the city. They reassured him again that he wouldn't be held up for long.

After about thirty minutes, the minibus drove into a compound and stopped outside a gate. Once off the bus, Abdullah's escorts told him that he'd have to carry his own bags now. Abdullah tipped them anyway for carrying his bags until then, giving them each five hundred liras. As they went through the gates and into a building, Abdullah saw a blindfolded man in the office ahead of them. That's when he realized Far' Falastin wasn't a friendly place. That made him nervous. But he kept his concern to himself, still certain matters would be sorted out soon.

By the time it was Abdullah's turn to go into the office, the blindfolded man had gone. A man behind the desk stood up.

"You are spoiling him," he said to his escorts.

"Yes, they are," Abdullah said, smiling.

Looking back now, he says this was the worst way he could have responded. But the old Abdullah—the man standing in that room, smiling—had lived his entire life learning and expecting that as long as he had never done anything wrong and treated others with respect, he would receive that respect in return. All of his memories and experiences of Syria had been good ones. Of course, he says now, like everyone in Syria, he'd heard stories about oppression and torture. But those stories were far removed from his own experience of a childhood entirely devoid of politics. He was a young, successful businessman, brimming with confidence in his ability to resolve problems and negotiate solutions.

"I am an engineer—a problem solver," Abdullah says. "As the owner of a company that dealt all over the world with people of many cultures, I was used to solving major problems. In my life I dealt with people of all levels of status and power, from poor refugees to United Nations directors to some of the richest of European businessmen. I knew it was pointless to argue with someone who only knew to follow orders. I was focused on speaking with someone in power, hoping to sort things out, like I'd been able to do in Malaysia."

A guard took him through a door inside the office and into another room with a desk and lockers. He asked Abdullah to empty his pockets, then took Abdullah's wallet, Palm Pilot, and laptop, writing in a ledger how much money Abdullah had and stamping the entry with Abdullah's thumbprint.

Abdullah saw out the window that it was just before sunset.

The guard told him to take what he needed from his bag.

"For how long?" Abdullah asked.

He was surprised when the guard told him three days but still believed that once he was able to speak with someone in charge, they would let him go. He asked if it was cold in Damascus at this time of year and the guard seemed surprised and told him yes, he had better assume it would be.

Abdullah took out a pair of pants, a pair of underwear, a sarong, socks, a fleece vest, his toothbrush, toothpaste, a handkerchief, and his Tums and Tylenol. The guard was in a hurry. Abdullah wanted to take a towel but couldn't find it quickly enough.

The guard pulled a rubber blindfold over Abdullah's eyes.

"That made me very worried. But I didn't let it show. I just wanted to speak to someone in a position of higher authority. There was no sense getting angry with this guard," Abdullah says. The guard took him into another room. After a few minutes, Abdullah heard many people enter the room.

"You're here in Syria, you're not in Canada, you don't have a lawyer, and you have to speak," a man said. "Which way would you prefer to be dealt with? The friendly way or the other way?"

"The friendly way," Abdullah replied.

The man asked someone to get him a chair, then asked Abdullah to explain what he had been planning in Canada, and why the Canadians, Americans, the British, and the whole world were interested in him.

Abdullah started to talk but was interrupted with more questions. Does he know Ibrahym Adam? Does he know Ahmad El Maati? They asked about a third man Abdullah didn't know.

Yes, Abdullah said, he knew Ibrahym; he was asked about him in Canada and thinks he was of interest to investigators because he is a Muslim, and a pilot. Abdullah didn't recognize the second name at first. Abdullah didn't know Ahmad well. He had met him once in Ottawa, and maybe once more in Montreal, through Ibrahym. He had talked to him on the phone about a bride for a friend of his.

"You must prefer the non-friendly treatment!" the man yelled.

Then it came. A slap, hard, across the face.

Abdullah's whole world shifted at that moment. For the first time in his adult life, he had no control. His skills, his confidence, his upbringing couldn't help him now. There was no negotiating with these people. This was a totally different world. "That slap changed everything. He took away my humanity and crushed my dignity," he says. Now he was shaking, and his heart raced. "My heart felt like it was going to jump out of my chest."

The interrogator insisted Abdullah knew Ahmad, so Abdullah asked him to describe him. He was a big man, an Egyptian, the interrogator said. Abdullah realized he was referring to Ahmad, and said yes, now he realized who was meant. His voice faltered now, not confident, like it had been before the slap. The interrogator ordered Abdullah to take off his jacket, shoes, and socks and to lie on the floor on his stomach. His knees were bent, with his feet in the air. Two or three men started whipping the soles of his feet with cables. "It was like people pouring lava on the soles of my feet," Abdullah remembers. The men without cables were kicking him. When Abdullah flipped onto his back, he was ordered to lie back on his stomach. Then one of his assailants stood on his head, the other on his back, and took turns whipping his feet and kicking him.

The questions came as hard and fast as the lashings. What was his relationship with Ahmed Said Khadr? Had he sold equipment to al-Qaeda or the Taliban? Had he dealt with Osama bin Laden or al-Qaeda? What computer equipment had he sold to them?

Abdullah replied that he had not sold to them or dealt with them in any way. "I was still trying to answer in logical ways. I said, 'Go to my computer and you'll see what I sell, I don't sell computers.'"

Every few minutes the men would stop the whipping, pour cold water on his feet and legs, and tell him to stand and jog on the spot. Then they ordered him to the floor again to resume the whipping. "At that time, I had no idea why they did that. Later, the other prisoners told me it was to keep the blood circulating so I could feel the torture. The worst lashes with the cables are the first five or ten, after that the pain gets a bit duller. That's why they wanted the water and circulation in the feet so I would feel the pain all the time," Abdullah says.

Abdullah saw from under his blindfold what they were beating him with. It was a black, double-folded twisted cable.

"I told them the truthful answers to the questions, but it didn't work. Eventually, I got to a point where I broke down and couldn't take it anymore," he says.

They asked what his position was in al-Qaeda, then insisted Abdullah was bin Laden's right-hand man. Abdullah told the interrogators this didn't make sense: Everyone knew bin Laden's right-hand man was al-Zawahiri. The interrogators agreed; they had meant to say that he was his left-hand man. To that, Abdullah said yes. He lied, telling them what he knew they wanted to hear—that he knew bin Laden. When asked from when and where, Abdullah said from when he worked on United Nations Development Programme projects in Pakistan and Afghanistan.

The beating stopped and the men left the room. But before long, they came back and accused him of lying: bin Laden had been in the Sudan when Abdullah was in Pakistan and Afghanistan. Abdullah told them that he had never met bin Laden and had only said it to stop the torture. But the beating started again, the interrogators saying that now it was *falaka* (beating on the soles), next it would be *dulab* (the tire), and then the chair, electric shock, and nail pulling. They continued torturing and questioning him all night about his family, his brothers, and why he had not been in Syria for so long. They threatened to bring in his parents to be interrogated. After a while, Abdullah was no longer able to speak—his mouth wasn't working. He lost consciousness. He woke up to find someone taking his blood pressure.

They were done with the torture for the day.

He was dragged back to the room where his belongings were. When the blindfold was pulled off, he looked down. His feet and ankles were covered in blood. The skin was ripped off the inside of his right ankle. The big toenail on his right foot had turned sideways.

The men ordered him to strip. They searched him, then let him dress. They took the shoelaces and insoles out of his shoes. His feet were so swollen it took a long time to get his feet into the shoes, even without the insoles and laces. Abdullah was then made to pick up the things he'd taken from his bags and carry them down a flight of stairs. Every step was painful, and Abdullah moved very slowly. In shock, he didn't notice the pictures or the phrase from the Qur'an on the wall on the way downstairs, or the doors on either side of the hall at the bottom of the stairs, or the toilets at the end of the hall, or the how small the doors were on either side of the narrower hallway when they turned right.

One of the men pushed him into a small cell. "You don't talk. If you want something, knock on the door. No one should hear your voice or know you are here," he said, closing the door and sliding the lock shut.

Abdullah pried off his shoes. His bloodied feet stuck to the blanket. He wrapped himself in his suit jacket and curled up on his side on the floor. He thought he could hear someone reciting verses from the Qur'an. What he didn't notice was how small, or dark, or cold, or dirty the space was, which is odd, given that he is usually claustrophobic. He just didn't want the door to open.

But it did.

In a few hours, his interrogators came back and dragged him upstairs for more interrogation. This time, they told him, they were giving him a break from the torture, but if he didn't talk, tomorrow they'd use the *dulab* (tire) and then the chair and electric shock. They wanted him to talk about his relationship to Khadr, to say Khadr was his link to al-Qaeda. That interrogation lasted about eighteen hours.

They came for him again on the morning of the third day. He was taken from his cell to an interrogation room, blindfolded, and told to strip down to his underwear. They brought the *dulab* into the room—the car tire used to completely immobilize victims for torture—and told Abdullah to sit on the floor. They pulled his legs through the centre of the tire so that the backs of his knees were against the inside rim—they bent his upper body forward and forced his head through the tire—now his head and lower legs protruded out of one side of the tire, his shoulders, arms, and torso out the other side. He was wedged in so tightly that the inside of the tire pressed hard against the back of his neck and knees. The men kicked him until the tire was parallel to the floor, his head and lower legs forced upward, all his weight pressing on his lower spine. The idea, Abdullah says, is to completely restrain the victim with their body parts exposed and vulnerable. They started whipping him with the cable, aiming for the soles of his feet, his head, and his genitals.

While some of the men lashed at him, another asked the questions and wrote down his answers. He was questioned again about Khadr and asked about all the Muslims he knew in Canada. "You must be hiding something because we were told you are wanted in Canada. Authorities everywhere are looking for you!"

Again he was questioned about Ibrahym and told that his friend had been plotting another 9/11.

"I told them he would never do such a thing. If he wanted to crash a plane into a building he would not have worked so hard to get his licence. Check with the Canadians, [I said,] as far as I know he has never been arrested, or charged with anything. But I finally broke down and lied and told them what they wanted to hear, that he had a *jihadi* spirit."

The interrogators asked for Abdullah and Khuzaimah's email addresses, the passwords to their email. Abdullah gave them his password, but he didn't know Khuzaimah's.

Abdullah tried to reason with the men, arguing that if he had been wanted in Canada, he would have been detained there, or the Malaysian authorities would have extradited him. "But it didn't matter what I said. Nothing would stop the beating. If I lied, they beat me. If I told the truth, they beat me. So I was telling the truth after because it didn't matter what I was saying. Whenever I lied or confessed to something, I did tell them after that I lied because they were torturing me."

After several hours, the beating stopped, but Abdullah was kept in the tire for about an hour before he was taken out and had his blood pressure checked.

He wasn't able to eat much of the food he was brought. He was shivering uncontrollably and didn't have much control of his body from the waist down. He could barely move his arms and hands. "They asked me to eat an orange, but it burned the top of my mouth where I think the skin was gone from screaming."

Abdullah lay there until the late afternoon or evening, when he was questioned again. Later that night the main interrogator came back, told Abdullah to pull off the blindfold, and Abdullah saw his assailants for the first time. Their names, he'd later learn from other detainees, were Abdallah and Haitham, and they were members of the Far' Falastin's counterterrorism interrogation team. The main interrogator, Haitham, was from the Alawite sect, and known to detainees as the most ruthless of the team. He would later tell Abdullah that he'd tortured Ahmad, too.

Haitham started moving Abdullah's legs, helped him to slowly stand, then ordered the guards to take him to his cell.

"You are number three," he said. "You will never forget that number."

Abdullah soon learned that this was his cell number. The Syrian from Aleppo who'd been in cell number two when Ahmad was there was gone, and now the grave-like cell was his. It was just two doors away from where Ahmad had been three months earlier.

Thursday, May 13, 2002
Damascus

AT THE CENTRE OF ADNAN AL-MALKI SQUARE, in the Abou Roumaneh district of Damascus, is a statue cast by Syrian artist Fathi Mohammad. There's a museum, too. Like the statue, the square, a road leading from the square, and a neighbourhood close by, the museum memorializes the man who was a leading Ba'athist and popular leader of the Syrian army in the 1950s.

That man, Lieutenant Colonel Adnan al-Malki, along with many other senior army officials, was stripped of his rank and thrown into Al-Maza Prison in May 1953. They had been deemed a threat to the iron-fisted rule of Adib al-Shishakli, who, after seizing power in a 1949 coup, had consolidated power by dissolving parliament, establishing a military dictatorship, and staging a referendum to make himself Syrian president. The U.S. Truman administration approved of al-Shishakli, largely because he backed the extension of the Arabian American Oil Company (Aramco) Trans-Arabian Pipeline through Syria. His pro-Western policies had earned the promise of significant U.S. military and financial aid.[2]

The prisoners at Al-Maza revered al-Malki. He is said to have always been well dressed "in a dark, carefully pressed suit, his blond hair neatly combed and his thick beard well-groomed." He would march, "stiff as a ramrod with an expressionless face" around the prison courtyard, inciting mutiny among the prisoners. His jailers, however, treated him with respect, too, for they knew that in tumultuous times, today's prisoner could be tomorrow's ruler."[3]

They were right to be cautious. Al-Shishakli was overthrown in 1954 by another coup, and with a new regime in place, Adnan al-Malki became the head of the Syrian army. Syrian voters had thrown their support behind the Ba'ath and left-leaning parties that al-Shishakli had repressed. The United States wasn't happy with the change. The CIA warned the situation "was the worst of all the countries in that area."[4] They especially didn't like al-Malki, who opposed Syrian participation in the Baghdad Pact, a NATO-like defence alliance proposed for the region by the West, and who worked to help undermine Iraq's pro-Western premier. The United States feared the possibility of al-Malki seizing power and formalizing an alliance with Egypt.[5]

Then one Friday afternoon, on April 22, 1955, al-Malki sat among other dignitaries and military leaders in the VIP section of the Damascus municipal stadium. They were there on their day off to cheer on the Syrian army's football team in a match against the Egyptian coastguard team. At 4:40 in the afternoon, a military police sergeant stood behind al-Malki, drew his gun, and fired. The popular colonel was killed instantly, his blood staining the jacket of the man sitting next to him. The Russian and Egyptian ambassadors and other dignitaries bolted in the panic.

The ensuing investigation revealed that the assassin was a member of the Syrian Social Nationalist Party, whose plans, it seems, had the backing of the CIA. The assassination, it turned out, was supposed to have been just the first in a series of incidents designed, with the backing of Britain and the United States, to destabilize the regime.[6] Adnan al-Malki is buried beneath the one-room museum in Adnan al-Malki Square where the slain hero's blood-stained shirt, and the gun used to assassinate him, are displayed.

History, of course, is full of coincidences. Adnan al-Malki was Abdullah Almalki's father's cousin. The man sitting next to him when he was killed was a friend, and another prominent military leader of the times. He had been the head of the military school in Homs, then deputy chief of staff under al-Shishakli. His name was Mohammad Amir al-Shallash. His daughter is Samira al-Shallash and her son is Ahmad El Maati.[7]

ABOUT A MILE SOUTH OF ADNAN AL-MALKI SQUARE and several yards underground was Abdullah Almalki's cell at Far' Falastin. It was his tenth day there, and one of the other prisoners was trying to get him to talk. The man had been calling out to him for days but, so far, Abdullah hadn't answered. He was disoriented, exhausted, and scared, and the screaming from upstairs was a constant reminder of the guard's order to stay quiet.

"Sneeze. Cough. Do something to show you are okay," the voice whispered. After about ten days, Abdullah coughed. The man answered by reciting a Hadith:

> Be mindful of Allah, and Allah will protect you. Be mindful of Allah, and you will find Him in front of you. If you ask, ask of Allah; if you seek help, seek help of Allah. Know that if the Nation were to gather together to benefit you with anything, it would benefit you only with something that Allah had already prescribed for you, and that if they gather together to harm you with anything, they would harm you only with something Allah had already prescribed for you. The pens have been lifted and the pages have dried.[8]

"I had known this Hadith by heart since I was in school, but the meaning had never clicked until then," Abdullah says. He'd later get to know the man. It was Abu Ahmad, the man who had been there for more than two years and who'd been a friend to Ahmad El Maati. He was still locked in cell number ten.

Abdullah's interrogations had been continuing by day. At night he'd be put back in the tiny cell. Abdullah asked to be sent to Canada. They would see, he told them, that the intelligence agencies and police there would have no reason to hold him.

"Canada doesn't want you to be free. And you are a Syrian and we don't hand over Syrians to other countries," was always the response. He asked how long he would be there. A month or two, Haitham told him. The horror of staying even one day longer hit Abdullah hard. "I told him my cell was like a grave and I would rather have a real grave than be kept there."

The beating had stopped on Abdullah's fourth day at Far' Falastin. Even the verbal abuse had been toned down. Abdullah had asked for some clothes and other items from his bags. That would be difficult, the interrogator had said, but not much later Abdullah was able to buy soap and clothing through the guards, and the guard let him wash.

Shorter interrogations meant more time in the cell. Abdullah couldn't see much but he could feel that the walls were cement and the floor cut stone. Condensation seeped down the back wall onto the floor. He could smell mould in the cell, and the stench of excrement and urine from the toilets. Over time he got used to the smell of the mould and didn't notice it as much. But he never got used to the smell from the toilet. There were two empty *halva* containers, which he used to hold the food that was doled out, and three blankets. The blankets on the floor were wet from the condensation. He wasn't given a water bottle until the second week of his detention. In the meantime, he had to drink when he could from tap on the wall in the washroom.

The sound of the guard's footsteps terrified him. The guard was either coming to take someone for more interrogation and torture or to let someone out of his cell to use the washroom. Things had improved somewhat since Ahmad had been there, months earlier. Now the prisoners were allowed to use the washrooms three times a day. When Abdullah arrived, in the spring, the cockroaches were enormous, crawling over each other in a constant battle for space on the narrow ledge over the washroom door. They didn't seem to mind, or scatter, when the door opened or closed, but sometimes they'd fall from the ledge.

Abdullah found the two-minute toilet time limit especially harsh. It was always a struggle to use the toilet, empty his urine bottle, wash out his food containers, and fill his water bottle before the guard started yelling and kicking in the door. Most of the time the pipe over the toilet just dripped cold water but occasionally it would be running, non-stop, with scalding hot water, making it impossible to use the toilet. "These were the worst times I had ... desperately needing to use the washroom and then getting there and not being able to use it."

On Fridays, the prisoners were given ten minutes each in the washroom. They would use the extra time to wash themselves and their clothes, leaving the clothes to dry on the gate opening into the narrow hallway. If one prisoner didn't have enough clothes, another would leave something on the rack for him. They had to keep track of the guards' shifts, though, to ensure that the guards didn't notice different people taking the same clothes. Eventually, Abdullah stopped hanging his clothes there because of the rats, which came up from the toilet and tracked raw sewage all over them. "The rats owned the place and they owned the washrooms. Remember, these washrooms are empty except for twenty minutes in the morning and twenty minutes in the afternoon and twenty minutes in the evening," Abdullah says—and so the rats were used to having the run of them. He remembers feeling the rats walking over his legs at night and knocking over his food containers. Fortunately, though, they didn't bite him.

The guards at Far' Falastin seemed to try to outdo one another's cruelty. They worked in three shifts, each with three men led by a chief. Detainees were forced to refer to them as *mouallem*—master. "The men in solitary confinement are at the guards' mercy. They can make your life easier, or hell," says Abdullah. "Constantly you would hear them pulling people out of the cell and whipping them with the cable and then putting them back in. One guy was beaten all the time on his way into and out of the washroom." Some guards seemed to enjoy torturing the detainees, others didn't.

The guards used the detainees from common cell number seven as servants. These prisoners were usually men who had deserted the military or failed to show up for their military service. Whenever they were needed, the guards would call out for sab'a—seven. "They were treated like dirt, they had to do all the work in the jail, from cleaning the jail and interrogation floor to carrying and distributing food. The guards basically are like masters and these guys are their servants," says Abdullah. They were often ordered to wash and iron the guards' clothes.

These were the men who fed the solitary confinement detainees, who got just enough food to keep them alive. In the morning they were given tea, a few olives, and either a spoon of yogurt, a spoon of jam, a piece of halva, or a boiled egg. "The tea used to be dirty and in most cases cold with different 'flavours' such as diesel and soap. Once I actually took a cockroach out of it and [then] drank it, as the tea was hot and I was extremely cold," says Abdullah. For lunch they were given rice or bulgur, some vegetable in tomato sauce, and a piece of fruit. Sometimes they got chicken or red meat. At night, they received pita bread, a boiled potato, lentil soup, and a small piece of salad vegetable such as cucumber, green pepper, or tomato.

The food didn't smell right, but Abdullah was hungry and in the beginning ate whatever he was given. He eventually had to stop eating the meat, olives, and lentil soup because they gave him diarrhea. When that happened, the guards usually refused to let him out of his cell to use the washroom, either completely ignoring his requests or mocking him. Like other detainees, he often had to use one of his food containers as a toilet.

Over time Abdullah learned how long Abu Ahmad had been at Far' Falastin and that he'd been detained when Hafez al-Assad was still Syria's president. "His existence made my existence easier, I guess, because I felt sorry for him. He would say to us, 'What we have now is paradise compared to when I came.'" As the most senior detainee among them, it was Abu Ahmad who knew when it was safe to start, and stop, whispering. The talk was never about politics or interrogations because they always assumed that one of the prisoners might inform on them. The man in cell number one, two doors down, had been accused of being a spy. He was around forty years old and illiterate. He didn't know how to pray, so they taught him.

Over time Abdullah came to know others being held there, too. Far' Falastin was fast becoming a destination of choice for those detained courtesy of the United States and its allies as part of the "war on terror."

Two doors down from Abdullah, in number five, the cell Ahmad had once occupied, was a man in his thirties, a student named Abdel Halim Dahak. He said he had been detained in Pakistan, held there for six months, then flown with two others to Syria by the Americans on May 14. Author Stephen Grey would later find indications that these prisoners were transferred in a CIA-owned jet.[9] Abdullah remembers that Abdel was especially badly tortured and once had to be carried back to his cell because he was unable to walk.

The two other men flown in from Pakistan were among more than a dozen people captured alongside Abu Zubayda, a man who the United States, at the time, believed to be a senior leader of al-Qaeda, in a raid by U.S. and Pakistani agents in Faisalabad, Pakistan, on March 27, 2002. One was named Omar Ghramesh. He was locked in number eight, across from Abdullah. The other, a teenager, was locked in cell number twelve, to the left of the washrooms. Abdullah never learned his name. His brother was apparently being held in U.S. detention at Guantánamo. Nearby him, Zammar, the giant German man in custody thanks to German intelligence, was still stuffed into cell number thirteen. A man named Barah Abdul Latif was kept in cell number seventeen on that side, too. He'd been interrogated by Americans in Pakistan before being sent to Far' Falastin.

Bahaa Mustafa Jaghel, twenty-nine years old, was locked in cell number seven across the hall and one over from Abdullah. He'd arrived the day after Abdullah, on May 4, after being detained in Pakistan and interrogated by the Americans. Abdullah got to know him well and learned that he was a computer designer who had used the internet to speak out against the Taliban and al-Qaeda.

The other detainees told Abdullah that his torture had been especially harsh: People are usually restrained in the tire for only thirty minutes at a time and are usually whipped fifty to a hundred times, not hundreds of times, like he, Abdullah, was on the first day alone. The other detainees had heard it all.

Unlike Ahmad, Abdullah was able to keep track of time. He had hid a pen in the seam of his pants, and some tissue, which he used for a makeshift calendar. So he knows that it was on June 12 that he was taken upstairs, blindfolded, put in an interrogation room, and first heard the voice of a new lead interrogator, with new questions. The questions were specific. They concerned his knowledge of twenty or so people in Canada, some of whom he knew, including Maher Arar. At one point he was asked about an organization whose name he didn't recognize. When his blindfold was removed so he could see the name of the organization in writing, he saw the new interrogator's face. This man, he would later learn, was Colonel George Salloum, the head of the counterterrorism interrogation team at Far' Falastin—the same man who'd burned Ahmad's shins with a cigarette.

Salloum asked Abdullah about his family's Canadian bank accounts, and if he had any in Switzerland, which he didn't. Salloum asked him to describe, in detail, every step his company took to make a sale, from providing a price quote to delivering the product. Then Salloum asked about trade names Abdullah had registered in Ontario, and which he had unsuccessfully tried to register as corporate names with Industry Canada. Abdullah knew this information could have come only from the company records the RCMP seized in the January searches. The interrogators kept referring to his brother's company as his, and Abdullah kept correcting them. Salloum was friendly with Abdullah, saying at one point that he wanted to finish so Abdullah could leave.

"People like you don't belong here," he said.

When Abdullah asked what they had against him, an interrogator showed him the first lines of a report. It stated that he wasn't just a regular member of al-Qaeda but an "active member." Abdullah told them again that this was a lie. Neither he nor anyone he knew had ever had anything to do with al-Qaeda.

On June 15, Salloum came downstairs to get Abdullah. He seemed to be in a hurry, asking him questions even as they climbed the stairs to the interrogation floor. He wrote Abdullah's answers down quickly, then sent him back to his cell. The next day another interrogator asked how long Abdullah had been there. Abdullah told him it had been forty-five days. He'd see the summer sunshine, the interrogator said.

"Which summer?" Abdullah asked.

"This summer."

Friday, May 31, 2002
FBI headquarters, Washington, D.C.

APRIL AND MAY HAD BEEN A BUSY TIME for the A-O Canada team. It had become "very popular" and had pulled together a road show of sorts, a PowerPoint presentation on the genesis of their investigation, the targets, the search results, and, in the more recent versions, Abdullah's departure from Canada.[10] The show, presented at RCMP headquarters and to numerous government agencies—the Canadian Department of Justice among them—was variously called "The Pursuit of Terrorism: A Canadian Response" and "The Pursuit of Terrorism: A Global Response" and included about thirty slides.[11] Abdullah and Ahmad were among those named, and Ahmad's brother, Amr, was mentioned. Three slides contained information about Maher, and at least one officer who saw the show concluded he was a target, not just a "person of interest." One slide noted that Maher had refused an interview with the RCMP and was a business associate of the main target, Abdullah. Neither of these assertions was accurate. It's unclear how much of the information about the others was also wrong, because none of this documentation has been publicly released.

One of the concluding slides, titled "Project A-O Canada: What's Next," noted that the team hoped to compel Maher and three others, likely the others whose homes had been searched in January, to appear as witnesses at an investigative hearing. This would have been a first. There hadn't been such a hearing since the Anti-terrorism Act was passed. Because Maher and the others were referred to as "witnesses," it meant that the RCMP didn't anticipate charging Maher, or any of the others, at that time.[12] On May 31, 2002, Inspector Cabana and staff sergeants Callaghan and Corcoran flew to Washington, D.C., to present a slide show at FBI headquarters.[13] The goal of the trip was to convince U.S. prosecutors to launch a criminal investigation into Abdullah and his associates in the United States. Among those who gathered for the presentation were officials from the U.S. Department of Justice, the FBI, and other agencies, likely including the CIA. The show was pretty much identical to the one shown to Canadian agencies and included the same inaccurate information. The Americans didn't make any decisions on the spot, and Cabana, Callaghan, and Corcoran came away not knowing if they'd succeeded in persuading the Americans to launch a criminal investigation into Abdullah. Corcoran talked to the FBI the following week. The FBI agent said the Canadians had been well received and asked for a copy of the presentation they had given in Washington.

The RCMP later claimed it didn't know Abdullah would be travelling to Syria and didn't know until May 31 that he was in detention.[14] It also claimed it had expected him to return to Canada in December as planned, and when he didn't, it had lost track of him.

Which raises an important question: If the RCMP didn't already know, who had given the Syrians the information that led to Abdullah's detention, and the initial report and questions? It was likely CSIS. The CSIS watchdog, SIRC, would later examine the agency's relations with foreign agencies. It found that sometime between January 1, 2002, and December 31, 2004, CSIS provided information to a foreign agency that "could have contributed to that agency's decision to detain a Canadian citizen (who was also a CSIS target) upon arrival in that foreign country."[15] This could refer to Abdullah. Of course, the Syrians had already asked Ahmad about Abdullah on November 2001, so they had at least some information about Abdullah then.

SIRC also says "questions provided by CSIS to this agency via a third party [perhaps the CIA?] may have been used in interrogating a Canadian citizen in a manner which violated his human rights," and that "information the Service received and used from a foreign agency may have been obtained under duress."[16]

Abdullah hadn't noticed anyone following him to Damascus, or in Malaysia, but wonders now if that sense of freedom was artificial. "Did they want me to feel like I was under a microscope in Canada so I'd leave? Did they want me to feel everything was fine in Malaysia so I could go to a country like Syria or Jordan or Egypt?" He also wonders now if that's why, back in January at the time of the searches, the RCMP asked his cousin whether she thought he'd be going to Syria.

Was this what CSIS deputy director Jack Hooper and RCMP commissioner Zaccardelli meant by the "new paradigm for operations between CSIS and the RCMP" used in these cases—the "diffuse and disrupt" strategy?[17]

Friday afternoon, June 21, 2002
"A" Division, RCMP headquarters, Ottawa

WHILE A-O CANADA WAITED FOR NEWS from the Americans, other news came in from Syria. It was just five days after Far'

Falastin's lead interrogator had rushed to finish his report on Abdullah's interrogation that Corporal Rick Flewelling, the man at RCMP's headquarters assigned to watch over Project A-O Canada, went to meet with the team in the "A" Division building to discuss Abdullah's interrogation. He recorded some of the discussion in his notes, which were censored before being released at the Arar Inquiry:

> [REDACTED]: Assessment completed and proceed with the next step in the process in order to have [REDACTED] brought back.

> [REDACTED] or solicit the assistance of CSIS, L.O. Rome + DFAIT to apply the necessary pressure in an effort to gain access.

> Questions:
> • intel versus criminal
> • do we want him back
> • do we have enough to charge

> "A" Division would really like him back for the purposes of laying charges under Bill C-36.

> The question is really how is Syria going to play.

Later that afternoon there was another discussion, and Flewelling added to his notes:

> We may have to take and be satisfied with the prevention side of the mandate and hope additional information can be gleaned with respect to
> • his plan
> • other plans we are not aware of
> • other individuals + or groups
> • etc.[18]

The "prevention side of the mandate" appeared to be the only option at the time. CSIS wanted the RCMP to lay charges against Abdullah. If it did, according to the RCMP, CSIS could have him returned to Canada.[19] But that was just the thing. A-O Canada didn't have anything to charge Abdullah with. So, until it did, it seems, it saw no other choice but to make sure Abdullah stayed where he was.

Sunday, July 7, 2002
Far' Falastin, Damascus

AFTER ABDULLAH'S FAMILY had been told to leave the airport
without him, they contacted the authorities. They started with
the Syrian Military Intelligence, wondering if this was a misunderstanding about his military service deferral. Syrian intelligence
officials told them they had information from abroad they had
had to act on but that things would be resolved soon. Hearing
that, Abdullah's family decided against calling anyone in the
Canadian government for help right away. It was because of
Canadian officials that Abdullah had been detained—they were
sure of it—and they believed that contacting Canadian officials
would just make matters worse. Abdullah's parents waited as
long as they could before telling Khuzaimah, still in Malaysia
with the children, what had happened. When they finally did, a
few weeks later, they urged her to focus on taking care of herself,
the new baby, and the children, while they worked to help
Abdullah in Syria.

The family's efforts in Syria finally paid off in July, when they
were able to secure a visit with Abdullah. It was a Sunday, a busy
day in Syria, where, like other countries in the Middle East,
Fridays mark the start of the weekend and Sundays the first day
of the workweek.

A guard came for Abdullah. He assumed he was being taken
for more interrogation but was less anxious than he had been in
the past. Things had been getting friendlier, and he sensed that
the Syrians had come to distrust the allegations against him and
would release him soon. But instead of being taken into an interrogation room, this time he was taken into the prison manager's
office. He was very surprised to find his cousin there. That his
family had managed to arrange a visit was something unheard of
for detainees in solitary confinement at Far' Falastin. Clearly, the
family had influence in Syria.

The prison manager remained in the room while Abdullah
visited with his cousin. Abdullah asked about his wife and

children. He was very worried that they might come to Syria, where they could be detained, too. His cousin asked how he was being treated, and Abdullah responded that he was being treated well; he didn't want to jeopardize his chances of release. His cousin told Abdullah to be patient: His case was taking time to sort out because it was an international one. Abdullah asked his cousin to ask his family to push the Syrians to hand him back to Canada. He'd done nothing wrong, he said, and could prove that in Canada. His cousin informed Abdullah that he'd been told that the Canadians were pushing for him to be sent to a U.S. base in Guantánamo, Cuba. That worried Abdullah. He needed to get to Canada, where he could get some kind of fair process.

The meeting lasted about fifteen minutes. When they were done, Abdullah was taken back to his cell. He believed that the visit was another good sign. "I was very happy. It was the first time [since being at Far' Falastin] I had seen someone who wasn't a stranger, and who wasn't there to hurt me."

The next day another good thing happened. A guard came and told Abdullah he would be allowed outside for some air and sun. Abdullah grabbed his blankets to air out and was taken up the stairs and into an outdoor courtyard. This was the first time Abdullah had seen the sun since he'd arrived at Far' Falastin more than two months earlier. Initially, he couldn't open his eyes completely because of the glare. Once his eyes had adjusted, he looked up at the sky and saw a jasmine tree above the fence. He remembers marvelling at its beauty. But he was shocked when he looked down and saw that his skin was yellowish and covered in the red dots of lice bites. "I could not believe how much my body had deteriorated," he says. Abdullah lay his blankets on the ground in the sun. He'd never seen them in the light before. "There was yellow and black mould growing on them."

Abdullah began to walk, then tried to run, around the yard, but he kept stumbling. There was a guard with him, keeping watch. Abdullah told him he'd seen his cousin. The guard remarked that it was very unusual for someone in solitary confinement to receive a visit—this meant the investigation was over and things were going well. After about twenty minutes, the guard took Abdullah back downstairs. It took about an hour for Abdullah's eyes to adjust once again to the darkness.

That evening Abdullah was taken upstairs for more interrogation. This time, Haitham and another senior interrogator whose name, Abdullah would later learn, was Abu Elnour, were there. They had a printout of his interrogation report. There were comments and questions on it, written in pencil. One of the questions was whether his friend, Ibrahym Adam, had taken terrorism training or been to Afghanistan. Abdullah had already told them, as he'd told CSIS, that Ibrahym would never associate himself with the ideology of terrorism or al-Qaeda. "I kept on telling them he doesn't have that ideology. I think the reports they were getting were saying he did." They emphasized they were just trying to finish the report so he could get out of there, and their boss wanted it by 9:30 P.M.

Back in his cell, Abdullah asked the other prisoners what it all meant. Abu Ahmad said that the printed report would be sent to the branch director and that it could take up to two weeks for it to come back from the military intelligence headquarters. After that, the prisoner was usually released.

Abdullah was even more hopeful now. But he didn't know then that his cousin hadn't been the only unusual visitor to Far' Falastin that week. The RCMP's liaison officer for the Middle East, Steve Covey, had been there too, on July 4. This was the RCMP's first visit with General Khalil, of the Syrian Military Intelligence, and setting it up hadn't been easy. But Ambassador Pillarella, apparently eager to help the RCMP and had set up the meeting for Covey. He didn't, however, inform the people who could help Abdullah—DFAIT's consular division—that Abdullah was in detention. Foreign Affairs' consular services wouldn't learn until much later that month that Abdullah was there.

NINE

Extreme Treatment

Mid-June 2002
Mabahith Amn al-Dawla al-'Ulya (State Security
Investigations services) facility, Cairo

AHMAD HAD LOST TRACK OF THE DAYS but thinks it was in mid-June that he was moved from the Mukhabarat al-Aama, Egypt's General Intelligence headquarters. The guards came to his cell with some clothes and told him to change into them. They handcuffed and blindfolded him, then put him in a van, where they made him lie on the floor under a blanket. Ahmad says about five guards were in the van with him. After driving for less than a half hour, they arrived at their destination. If Ahmad could have seen out the window, he would have seen a massive iron gate of sharp interlocking spears, like teeth, open to let them through, then close behind them. He would have seen the ramp leading down under a building—a sort of loading dock—before the guards opened the van doors and pulled him out. He would later learn that he had been taken to the Mabahith Amn al-Dawla al-'Ulya (State Security Investigations services) central base for interrogations in Nasr City, a district of Cairo.[1]

As soon as he was led into the building, Ahmad heard a buzzing sound—the sound of an electric current—punctuated by screams. The screams were intense, "like someone was dying," Ahmad says.

The officers inside seemed to be expecting him. His handcuffs and blindfold were removed, and Ahmad found himself standing before a desk in a large room. The man who had removed the blindfold and cuffs took the seat behind it. He looked mean. Ahmad was flanked on either side by the guards who had brought him there, and by others. His bags were there, too. To the right Ahmad could see a long, wide hallway and prisoners, some standing, some sitting on the floor leaning against the wall. Some were in civilian clothes, others in uniforms. They were all blindfolded and handcuffed with their hands behind their backs.

The man behind the desk ordered Ahmad to strip to his boxer shorts, then handed him a blue prison uniform and ordered him to put it on and take off his shoes. His hands were cuffed behind his back again and the blindfold replaced—it would remain on for all of his time at the Mabahith Amn al-Dawla al-'Ulya facility, even when he was in his cell. Then he was led barefoot toward the hallway where he had seen the prisoners. He expected to join them, but instead they turned left at the room where the screaming was coming from and went down another, narrower hall. Ahmad could see from under his blindfold men standing or sitting on the floor in the middle of that hallway. "It was so crowded, which means the cells were crowded, but they had reserved one for me, especially," Ahmad says. They led him to the last cell on the left side. He thinks it was cell number fourteen.

The blindfold, an old piece of rotten blanket, was tied so tightly it hurt Ahmad's eyes and caused a rash on his face. From under it he could see the floor and the bottom part of the cell. It was all cement, about four feet wide and ten feet deep, with a long cement bench along the left side. At the back of the cell, on the right, was a pit toilet.

Ahmad's hands remained cuffed behind his back except for ten minutes each day when the guards cuffed his hands in front so that he could relieve himself and eat. "Those ten minutes were like the whole world for me," he says. When the position was switched, it usually took several minutes just to get his arms to move forward—they'd locked in position. Sometimes it took so long he didn't have time to use the toilet. Sleeping with his hands behind his back was near-impossible: "If I lay on my stomach I couldn't breathe, if I lay on my side it hurt my shoulders, and I couldn't lie on my back because the handcuffs were eating my hands, which were bleeding and infected. So I couldn't sleep, which is what broke me down to pieces. On top of that, the screams."

Occasionally Ahmad passed out from the pain. Over time, his right shoulder felt as if it were coming away from his body. He begged and begged for the cuffs to be moved to the front or taken off, but the guards just scoffed at him. The pain was so intense, Ahmad says, that eventually he couldn't help but scream and cry out.

Even drinking water from the tap on the wall by the toilet was difficult. "If I wanted to drink, because I was handcuffed from the back, first I had to open the tap, so I put my feet on the tap and turned it. The water goes on the floor. Then I have to kneel on my knees and put my mouth to the tap to suck the water."

Ahmad wasn't given much food; just enough to keep him alive, he says. The food came once or twice a day, usually a piece of pita bread, with rice or beans on top. The guard would throw the food through the bars onto the floor of the cell. Unless the food happened to be delivered during the ten minutes his handcuffs were switched to the front, Ahmad had to kneel and eat off the floor like an animal. Rats the size of his hand would come out from the toilet and sometimes beat him to the food. The toilet was home to huge cockroaches, too. "Whenever I had the strength I would kick at them and try to scare them."

The flusher for the toilet never stopped running. "It was constant, like a stream of constant water, non-stop. Like an angry flush that went on and on. I think they did it on purpose to break me down," Ahmad says. The sound of prisoners being electrocuted didn't stop, either. "[They were] only a few feet away and across the hall. And what scared me most was I [knew] that maybe my turn was next. I was living constantly with this fear that I would be next, I would be next, I would be next."

After being there for about ten days, it *was* his turn.

Ahmad was led into an interrogation room where four or five men were waiting.

"Whether you tell us the truth or not, we are going to torture you anyway," said a man whose voice Ahmad would come to know well.

Hit from behind, Ahmad was forced to his knees, then grabbed by the hair and his head yanked back as the men slapped and kicked him. Then the electric shocks started. The men stood behind him, prodding him with a rod. "It's difficult to describe the feeling," Ahmad says. "You feel your soul is coming out of your body, and your heart's going to stop and you lose control of yourself and screams come out unconsciously."

This time they started with his hands, shoulders, legs, and stomach. Later they aimed for his genitals. Afterward, Ahmad saw the device being used: a black rod, about a foot long, with a handle on one end and a point on the other.

These sessions sometimes lasted for several hours at a time. The questions weren't about anyone in Canada, though the Egyptians had detailed information about Ahmad's life in Toronto. They mentioned Ahmed Said Khadr, but only once. He didn't seem important to them, Ahmad says. The lead interrogator wanted to know anything Ahmad could tell him about Egyptians he had known in Afghanistan. What was incredible, says Ahmad, is what he already knew: "That man knew everything about my time in Afghanistan ... my friends who died, where I was when, things that happened in general to me, everything." The man wasn't trying to get him to confess to anything. The torture and interrogation was just about getting information and focused on his time in Afghanistan. "But they knew everything. They knew I only went there to help the Afghans." What was even more incredible was that the interrogator told Ahmad he'd known him in Toronto.

"Don't you know me, Ahmad? I was praying right beside you in the Salaheddin mosque in Toronto." Ahmad was shocked. He didn't recognize the man's voice and has no idea if he was making it up. Regardless, the man's English was fluent. And he was the one who wrote down whatever Ahmad said. Was this man with a Western intelligence agency? That may never be known. But one thing is certain: that man had higher standards than most of the others at the prison—he would later insist the guards clean Ahmad up before they brought him in.

After a few weeks at the Mabahith Amn al-Dawla al-'Ulya facility, Ahmad's clothes were beginning to fall apart. It was very hot and humid, and there was no air circulation in his cell. "I was rotting away, literally. My clothes, or whatever was left of them, were all dirty ... sometimes I would pee on myself because ten minutes [in the toilet] is not enough, plus the sweat. I was stinking, stinking. I don't know how I could stand myself." It was the interrogator in charge of his file who drew the line. When the guards took Ahmad in to see him for more torture and interrogation, he started yelling at them.

"Take this filthy pig out of here and wash him!"

The guards didn't heed the man's orders at first, taking Ahmad to his cell and then back again without washing him. This happened three times. The third time, the man told the guards he'd kill them unless they washed Ahmad before bringing him again. They took Ahmad to a big washroom with showers, removed his handcuffs, and told him to wash. It was the first human thing that had happened to him since he arrived there weeks before. "I felt like my soul was coming back to me," he says.

10 A.M., Tuesday, July 16, 2002
"A" Division, RCMP headquarters, Ottawa

IT HAD BEEN A MONTH since RCMP corporal Rick Flewelling had written in his notes about the possibility of A-O Canada having to be satisfied with the "prevention" side of its mandate. Steve Covey, the RCMP's liaison officer for the Middle East, had been reassigned, and that day he was in Ottawa to brief Cabana, other A-O Canada team members, and representatives from the Justice Department. Covey was there to report on the meeting that Franco Pillarella, the Canadian ambassador to Syria, had arranged for him with General Khalil in Damascus on July 4. It's not clear if Covey had been to see the Egyptians about Ahmad as well. Either way, he was there to talk about how the RCMP might get access to Abdullah, or get access to information from the Syrian interrogators. Cabana's superiors at RCMP headquarters had already suggested sharing information with the Syrians in order to "further the investigation."[2]

Cabana's notes from the meeting indicate that the necessary arrangements for the "prevention side of the mandate" were in place: "Mr. Covey provided a brief overview of the situation [REDACTED] and his efforts to broker a deal. Mr. Covey advised that in his view [REDACTED] will never be returning to Canada. We subsequently discussed protocol for sharing of project info with Syrians to reciprocate."[3]

Because of the blacked-out names, it's not clear whether Covey was referring only to Abdullah or to Ahmad too. Nevertheless, a deal had been made, and it was time to "reciprocate."

Two days after Covey's briefing, Superintendent Wayne Pilgrim, the officer in charge of the RCMP's National Security Investigations Branch, sent a briefing note to RCMP commissioner Zaccardelli saying that there were indications that Ahmad had been exposed to "extreme treatment" in Egyptian detention.[4] Despite this and subsequent briefings, there's no evidence in the public record that Commissioner Zaccardelli tried to help Ahmad or tried to stop the officers under his command from making things worse for him. The same can be said of Abdullah's case.

Zaccardelli had met with FBI director Robert Mueller on July 15.[5] Did he discuss either Ahmad or Abdullah's cases? Whether he did or not, the RCMP had not succeeded in convincing the FBI to open a criminal investigation into Abdullah or his associates in the United States.[6]

Canada's top spy, Jack Hooper, was being briefed about torture in Syria at this time, too. In July he received a memo about the Syrian authorities' use of torture, especially in detention centres run by security services, and especially when the goal was to extract a confession. In fact, the memo reported information identical to that in the U.S. State Department and Amnesty International reports on the subject.[7] It's not clear who sent the memo to Hooper or why. But it was most probably about Abdullah, as he was the only Canadian in Syrian custody at the time.

Meanwhile, the Consular Affairs division of Foreign Affairs had received word on Ahmad. A couple of weeks earlier, on July 2, the Syrian Ministry of Foreign Affairs had finally replied to the numerous diplomatic notes from DFAIT's Consular Affairs Bureau. The reply said: "The Ministry would like to inform you that Mr. Abou Al-Ma'ati [Ahmad El Maati] declared he will leave the country to Egypt, and they don't have any information about how he left as there are different borders. Also, he did not declare the date of his departure." This wasn't true: Ahmad hadn't been allowed to "declare" anything before he'd been loaded onto the flight that carried him to Cairo.[8]

On July 16, Gar Pardy, director general of DFAIT's Consular Affairs Bureau, instructed the Canadian Embassy in Cairo to send another diplomatic note to the Egyptians and, this time, to attach the note from the Syrians, ask for consular access, and let them know the RCMP would like to interview Ahmad. The embassy's diplomatic note, sent the next day, stated: "Canadian authorities have reason to believe Mr. Abou El Maati entered Egypt sometime after the 29th of December 2001 and is currently in the custody of Egyptian Police authorities." The note included Ahmad's passport number, birthdate, and place of birth. It stated that his family members "strongly believe he is in Egypt" and requested consular access. And then, to conclude: "Furthermore, the Royal Canadian Mounted Police Liaison Officer resident in Rome is planning to request access to Mr. El Maati in order to further a major investigation in Canada. Changes are underway in the staffing of the Liaison Office in Rome and as soon as these have been resolved a request for access from the RCMP to the Egyptian police will be made."[9]

Pardy didn't draft the note but says he hoped that by indicating the RCMP's interest, the Egyptians, who until now had been refusing to confirm they were holding Ahmad, might take the RCMP more seriously. "This was about applying pressure on the Egyptians to acknowledge they had him. Within two weeks of this [note] going in to them, they acknowledged the fact that he was there for the first time."[10]

Pardy didn't think at the time that telling the Egyptians that Ahmad was the subject of a major investigation could hurt him. They already knew that, he says, and this was about trying to get the Egyptians to take the RCMP's attempts to locate him more seriously. "Conceivably it might be of some value for El Maati to talk to the RCMP. We didn't know any of the background at this point. We didn't know [then] that the RCMP were the ones that were probably instrumental in making sure that the poor bugger ended up in this situation," he says now.

Wednesday, July 17, 2002
Far' Falastin, Damascus

ABDULLAH WAS WORRIED. Everything had been going well—the friendlier interrogations, the visit from his cousin, the twenty minutes in the outdoor courtyard—but the previous night everything seemed to have suddenly changed. He'd been taken upstairs, and an interrogator had been violent again, calling him names, slapping him and accusing him of having lied to them.

Now he was back in the interrogation room, with two or three interrogators. They called him names and slapped his face, then ordered him to stand on one leg with his hands up. Every time he lost his balance they beat him. It went on for hours. Then Colonel Salloum entered the room with five or six other interrogators. Salloum slapped Abdullah across the face and asked why he had lied. He hadn't lied, Abdullah protested. Salloum left the room.

The interrogators blindfolded Abdullah and the beating began this time with a man named Khaled in charge. For several hours it would be the same relentless cycle of ruthless torture and futile pleas for mercy—the beating and whipping with the cable until Abdullah couldn't talk anymore. One of the men beating him told the others that Salloum would be back at seven o'clock that evening and wanted to see blood. They asked him about funding bin Laden terrorist camps and training in Afghanistan, who had trained him there, even supplying a name. Abdullah told them that he'd say he trained in Afghanistan—anything to stop the torture.

Hours later, Salloum came back into the room. "I've got orders to beat you until you have to be hospitalized!" he yelled.

Khaled told Salloum that Abdullah had confessed to the training but that he claimed to have said that only to stop the beating. He wouldn't be allowed to sleep or rest for three days, they warned him: They would torture him until he told them the truth. Later that night, Abdullah was left alone for a couple of hours. "I felt like an animal waiting to be slaughtered," he recalls. He lay on the floor, trying to make up a list of names to give if asked again who was with him at the camp.

The beating started again the next morning. The interrogation room had a cement ledge, perhaps part of the foundation, running along the bottom of the wall. It was about a foot high and less than half a foot deep. Near the top of the wall was a window with a metal frame. The interrogators ordered Abdullah to stand on the ledge, his back to the wall, and reach over his head to hold on to the window frame. Then they pushed his feet out from under him, leaving him hanging. When he let go and fell, they beat him. The more they beat him, the less able he was to hold on. "It reached the point where they would prop me up, but as soon as they let go of my legs I would fall again."

So they tied him up instead, using a rag to bind his wrists to the metal frame. This technique of suspending a victim by the wrists is known as *shabah*. And Abdullah was suspended now as they fired the questions at him, this time about Ahmed Said Khadr. But Abdullah couldn't even move his lips. When he was finally untied, he fell to the floor and blacked out while they were beating his back. The next thing he remembers is sitting on the floor and realizing he couldn't move or feel his hands. He would later notice that one of his back teeth had been broken at some point during this interrogation session.

Abdullah's interrogators told him they had planned to release him, until they had received a new report. The beatings continued, with a belt, and the cable, for another two days. After that, he was brought up from his cell every second or third day for more. The physical torture lessened but the tone was still intense. Now, in addition to threats of more torture against him, the interrogators said they would be bringing his parents to the prison.

Not much later, Abdullah saw the report they'd received. A search of his parents' home, it read, had turned up weapons and proof that he was an aide to bin Laden and a high-ranking member of al-Qaeda. Had the RCMP or CSIS told the Syrians this? There were, in fact, no weapons found in the searches; the RCMP was still saying it had nothing it could charge him with; and the FBI, which had seen everything related to the searches, was still refusing to launch a criminal investigation into Abdullah.

TEN

"I Was Tortured"

Sometime in July 2002
Mabahith Amn al-Dawla al-'Ulya (State Security Investigations services) facility, Cairo

THE GUARDS CAME TO AHMAD'S CELL with some of his clothes and removed his handcuffs so he could change. Ahmad could barely bring his arms forward, as they'd been handcuffed behind his back almost constantly for about six weeks now. Getting dressed was next to impossible. The guards put the cuffs back on him and walked him down the hall, past the torture room, past the desk, and out the door. Shoved into a van, he was again made to lie on the floor; blankets and a tire were piled on top of him.

Ahmad was driven to another facility. Instead of being put in a cell, he was left in a hallway with other prisoners. The guards had told him to stand against the wall. Although he was still blindfolded, he could tell that there were many prisoners seated or standing against the wall. Ahmad stood with them, waiting, for hours. His legs were tired but he didn't dare sit down. Off the hallway were interrogation rooms. Occasionally, he'd hear prisoners being taken in and questioned, and sometimes tortured with electric shock. But the buzz of the electrical current and the screaming wasn't constant here, as it had been at the Mabahith Amn al-Dawla al-'Ulya facility. When the guards eventually took Ahmad into an interrogation room, he said he had nothing new to say. The interrogators threatened him and seemed frustrated but didn't beat him, instead just instructing a guard to take him back out into the hall. "By this point I had been subjected to everything, and there was nothing more they could do to me," says Ahmad.

After a few more hours, he was allowed to sit on the floor. The prisoners were whispering among themselves. This was the first time Ahmad was able to communicate with anyone except guards and interrogators since he had been in Syria. But they had to be very careful: If the guards caught them, they were beaten with a stick or kicked. Prisoners there seemed to be locals who had been rounded up on the streets, not accused of links to terrorism, like Admad. One of them told Ahmad they were at the State Security Investigations (SSI) services headquarters in Lazoughli Square in Cario.[1]

A while later, a guard came and moved Ahmad's handcuffs to the front. He didn't wait for Ahmad's arms to inch forward but just yanked them. "It was always torture on top of torture," Ahmad says. But that pain was worth the relief of having his arms in front again. It was difficult to sleep because the prisoners were not allowed to lie down. If one of them started to lean to the side, the guards beat him. Ahmad was beaten just for trying to adjust his blindfold.

He was kept in the hallway for about two weeks. Many of the prisoners complained of anal hemorrhaging. Not much later, Ahmad developed the same symptom. He thinks this was caused by sitting for so long on the cold tile floor. Ahmad was told not to speak about his case, then taken downstairs and put in a common cell, about fifteen by twenty feet, with a small room containing a toilet and a tap to drink from and wash with. He could use the washroom whenever it was free. It was a freedom he hadn't experienced for months.

"This was like heaven. It was the first time in eight months that I could freely see and speak with other people." The others in the cell were mostly political prisoners and all were Muslims, so they prayed together. The stronger prisoners helped the weaker ones, sharing their food and clothes. They gave Ahmad clothes to replace the rotting ones he was wearing. They were especially nice to him because he was considered a foreigner.

Talking with the others, Ahmad learned more about the detention centre he'd been transferred from. He learned it was the
Mabahith Amn al-Dawla al-'Ulya facility, the State Security
Investigations services. He'd been kept on the highest underground floor; prisoners there are tortured, but not as severely as
on the floors below. The lowest level, the prisoners told him, is
where they rape family members, and where they take prisoners
they are going to torture to death. Ahmad remembered the elevators he'd passed there, and shuddered.

As the days went by, the cell became more crowded, forcing
the prisoners to take turns lying down to sleep—about forty
people could sleep at a time while the other twenty or so stood.
The guards kept bringing in more prisoners. There was just one
small window in the door leading out into the hall. "The cell was
like an oven, and I couldn't breathe," Ahmad says. He started
blacking out and had a severe asthma attack; the first severe
attack he'd had in his life. The other prisoners screamed to the
guards for help. He wasn't the only one—other prisoners were
collapsing, too. After a few panicked minutes, the guards opened
the door to the hallway. The space was still very crowded and
hot, but it helped just enough that Ahmad's attack subsided.

Ahmad didn't know it then but his case had been transferred
from Egypt's security service to the Ministry of the Interior. He
thinks it was July 31 that he was handcuffed and led outside
without a hood or blindfold, into the blazing Egyptian sun.
Barely able to open his eyes, he felt "reborn," he says. It had been
eight months since he'd been in the sun.

The guards helped Ahmad into a prison truck, then loaded his
bags. Ahmad stared out the window as they drove out into
Lazoughli Square, busy with cars and trucks and people, then
west to the Kornish al-Nil, the highway that runs along the east
bank of the Nile River. He felt almost normal.

After a long drive they arrived at Istiqbal Tora prison, in south
Cairo, an enormous facility housing thousands of prisoners.
Conditions were relatively better there.[2] Ahmad was allowed to

dress in his own white *galabi*, the traditional Arabic long white shirt, worn over white pants with sandals. He was assigned to a common cell with about nine other people. During the day, the cells were opened and prisoners could walk around the facility.

It was there that Ahmad met an Egyptian-Canadian prisoner, who told Ahmad that he had been detained for three years but would soon be released. Ahmad quickly asked if he ever got consular visits. Yes, he said, and so Ahmad gave him his name, passport number, and his father's name and phone numbers. The man, as far as Ahmad knew, hadn't been detained for anything related to terrorism.

Wednesday, July 31, 2002
DFAIT headquarters, Ottawa

IT WAS AT THE END OF JULY, three months after Abdullah was detained, that the consular division first learned through DFAIT's Security and Intelligence Bureau that he was in Syrian detention.

There are, it turns out, two intelligence divisions at DFAIT: one, the Security and Intelligence Bureau, led by Director Scott Heatherington, and the other, the Foreign Intelligence Division, overseen by Director General Dan Livermore and Deputy Director Jim Gould. (Until the Arar Inquiry many years later, little was publicly known about DFAIT's intelligence divisions.) Myra Pastyr-Lupul, the case management officer for the Middle East region, asked the passport office for Abdullah's records, and got them two weeks later. She put in a request to the Canadian Embassy in Damascus to send a diplomatic note asking the Syrian Foreign Ministry about Abdullah. With no answer two weeks later, another note was sent. Despite repeated requests for information, there'd be no official reply until the end of April 2003, almost a year after Abdullah was detained.

Monday, August 12, 2002
Istiqbal Tora prison, Cairo

"CLEAN YOURSELF UP. You have a visitor."

The guard's order caught Ahmad by surprise. He washed, wondering who was here for a "visit." Was it another interrogator? A few minutes later, the guard led him to an office. Two men and a woman greeted him and explained they were from the Canadian Embassy: Stuart Bale, the consul; Jean Ducharme, the vice-consul; and Mira Wassef, a locally employed consular officer who spoke Arabic and occasionally interpreted what the Egyptian officials said for the sake of the other Canadians. Four Egyptian officials were also in the room. One sat behind the desk; the others, wearing big, dark sunglasses, stood. Ahmad thinks they were with the security service.

Ahmad was shocked by this unexpected visit, but looked straight at the Canadians, took a breath, and spoke. "I was badly tortured in Syria, I was beaten with an electric cable, and I was forced to give a false confession."

The Canadians, writing furiously in their notebooks, were visibly stunned. Ahmad didn't look at the Egyptians; he just wanted to say his piece before they stopped him. "I don't know how the courage came to me to say it. I didn't even think of the consequences. The first thing that came to my mind was to clear my name. I just wanted to say I was tortured and was forced to say a false confession," he says.

Ahmad told the Canadians that he'd been questioned by CSIS in Toronto on September 11, 2001, and had asked for a lawyer. He told them he was followed to the airport in Toronto and questioned there about where he was going, then followed on his flights to Damascus, where he was detained upon arrival. He told them CSIS knew everything about him.

Bale asked Ahmad what he had confessed to. Worried it could be used against him, Ahmad didn't want to tell Bale what he'd falsely confessed to; he didn't want to tell Bale anything about his confession unless he could tell him everything, and he couldn't talk about how he'd been tortured in Egypt in front of the Egyptians. Bale asked whether Ahmad would tell a Canadian intelligence official if one came to speak with him. Ahmad was appalled by the suggestion. "I told him I would only talk to Canadian security officials on Canadian soil." Bale told him the consular division had been looking for him everywhere. That made Ahmad angry.

"That's not true," he said. "CSIS has known about everything that has happened to me, from A to Z." He asked them to tell his family he was okay and not to worry, then stood up. He didn't trust the Canadian visitors anymore and wanted the meeting to end.

The consular officials came again on September 1. Ahmad remembers telling them this time that he hadn't been outside for fresh air or sunlight for months. He remembers one of the Egyptian officials saying things would improve after the "renovations." Ahmad gave the consular officers a letter for his sister, hoping she'd be permitted to come see him soon.

A few days later, the guards took all the prisoners in Ahmad's wing into an outdoor courtyard for thirty minutes. One of the guards told Ahmad this was because he had complained to the Canadians about the lack of fresh air and sunlight. To the other prisoners, Ahmad was a hero. Many hadn't been in the sunshine for years.

Tuesday, August 13, 2002
"A" Division, RCMP headquarters, Ottawa

A-O CANADA GOT THE NEWS THE NEXT DAY. It received a fax saying that consular officers had seen Ahmad El Maati and he reported that he had been tortured in Syria. The news led to a flurry of activity. A-O Canada's primary concern, however, wasn't whether their targets, Canadian citizens, had been tortured or how that affected the reliability of his "confession." Its concern was now that DFAIT was arranging for the family to get in to see Ahmad, and he'd likely tell them about the torture too. What if the family went to the media?[3]

A series of urgent meetings were called, first with the Department of Justice, officials from RCMP headquarters, A-O Canada team members, and RCMP media relations. Then with CSIS and DFAIT. The minutes for that meeting, held at 1:30 in the afternoon on August 15, say the gathering was "a proactive measure to discuss media lines," should Ahmad's allegations of torture become public. According to the minutes, "The media attention is expected to be intense." Everyone at the meetings agreed that "minimal information will be put out due to the ongoing police investigation."[4]

DFAIT officials asked whether, if Ahmad returned to Canada, the RCMP would lay charges. No, said A-O Canada team members, they didn't have anything to charge him with. Which is curious, given that the RCMP had received Ahmad's "confession" before the end of November 2001, almost nine months earlier, and a few days later would use it to justify applications for telephone warrants in Canada. Sometime in September 2002, the RCMP filed an application for a telephone warrant that referred to the "confession" Ahmad had made in Syria—that his brother had asked him to take flying lessons, and that Ahmad had accepted instructions to launch an attack on the Parliament Buildings with a truck bomb.[5] According to the RCMP application, the confession had been corroborated and "is still accurate and continues to be true."[6] The RCMP didn't tell the presiding judge about Syria's human rights record or that at the time Ahmad "confessed," he was being held incommunicado by the Syrian Military Intelligence at Far' Falastin, a detention centre notoriously used to obtain "confessions" through torture. The RCMP did say that DFAIT officials had visited Ahmad and that he appeared to be in good health, with no signs or bruising or scars. It neglected to mention that the consular visit had taken place nine months after Ahmad had given the "confession." Instead, the officer who signed the application speculated that

Ahmad had recanted his confession to consular officers in an effort at "damage control."[7]

It was likely Corporal Randy Walsh who signed the application, as he was the affiant for A-O Canada at the time. Upon hearing Ahmad's allegation of torture, A-O Canada's primary concern wasn't that Ahmad had been tortured. Instead, the team worried that if Ahmad was released and returned to Canada, he'd be a national security threat because of the plot he confessed to. That the confession was now even more likely the product of torture didn't seem to change A-O Canada's analysis of the threat.[8]

DFAIT told Ahmad's father about the visit but not that he reported he'd been tortured. The family had assumed this anyway. They were just comforted to finally know for sure where Ahmad was.

Sunday, August 25, 2002
Far' Falastin, Damascus

IT WAS SUNDAY when the guard came to tell Abdullah to clean himself up because he was going to be released. Abdullah didn't believe him. The day before he'd been taken upstairs and whipped with the cable again, and asked about his time in Malaysia, his wife, and her family.

After Abdullah had washed, Colonel Salloum came to look him over. He ordered a guard to take Abdullah to his cell to put on better pants. "They were huge on me," he says. After so long in detention, Abdullah could count his ribs—he'd lost between forty and fifty pounds. Salloum told the guard to get Abdullah laces for his shoes and a belt. The guards then took him outside, handcuffed, and put him in a car with Salloum and the prison manager. Abdullah couldn't believe it. They'd forgotten to blind-fold him.

Abdullah gazed out the window as they drove out of the compound and onto Falastin Street. It was incredible to see cars, people, life, but he was still in pain and scared, uncertain about what was to come. From there they turned left onto Addakhel Street, merging into busy Omayad Square then turning onto Adnan al-Malki Street. As they drove north toward Adnan al-Malki Square, Abdullah noticed how much the trees had grown since he'd last been there as a teenager. Circling Adnan al-Malki's statue, they passed the street leading to Abdullah's grandmother's home, just one block away, then the street where Abdullah had grown up. Abdullah wondered if he'd ever see his grandmother again. Finally, they turned into Far' Ma'aloumat, Branch 111 of the Syrian Military Intelligence. Once inside the building, Abdullah was made to stand, blindfolded once again, in a hallway for about an hour before being taken into an office. Several other people entered the room. Abdullah could see from under his blindfold that Salloum was writing.

One of the men began questioning Abdullah in English. A Syrian interpreter translated the questions into Arabic, and the general from Far' Falastin instructed Abdullah to answer in Arabic. The interrogator asked Abdullah about his wife and her postgraduate studies, when he had been in Malaysia, and where he had stayed and gone while he was there. He asked Abdullah who he knew in Malaysia and why Abdullah and his family didn't live in Malaysia. Abdullah told them that he liked to visit but that his family's life was in Canada. Abdullah could tell by his accent that the man was from Malaysia.

Abdullah was taken out of the room, then brought back in. The questions this time were about his business and the period when he had worked in Pakistan. Abdullah could see from under his blindfold that there were two reports on the table, one in English marked "Secret" and the other in Malay. It was obvious to Abdullah that the man questioning him believed Abdullah was a member of al-Qaeda. Abdullah spoke up, saying that he wasn't a member and didn't share the ideology. The man seemed surprised. As the meeting drew to a close, Abdullah asked the man why they had not interrogated him while he was in

Malaysia. He answered that they hadn't been interested in him until after the Syrians detained him.

Once back at Far' Falastin, Abdullah told an interrogator that he believes that the Malaysians were sent by the Canadians to question him. The interrogator replied that the Canadians had been asking to interrogate him directly but that headquarters had so far refused their request.

It was around this time that Abdullah remembers being on the interrogation floor and seeing a young boy, maybe seven or eight years old, taking his sister to the washroom. "It broke my heart to see children in this place," he says. He'd heard the voices of women and children coming from the cell behind his. He'd heard the women coming back from being tortured, and crying, and had been able to tell from the guards' questions that the children were as young as his own. But actually seeing the children was different. The presence of these young children in such a horrible place, with their exhausted and drained mothers, still haunts Abdullah. He always listened very carefully to their voices, constantly worried that his wife and children had been lured into coming to Syria, or that his interrogators had carried through on their threat and detained his mother.

11 A.M., Tuesday, September 10, 2002
DFAIT headquarters, Ottawa

A-O CANADA WANTED HELP from the Department of Foreign Affairs. The team wanted to interview Abdullah in Syria. If it couldn't do that, it wanted the Syrians to interrogate him on its behalf.[9] Chief Superintendent Couture, Inspector Cabana, and staff sergeants Callaghan and Corcoran, all from team A-O Canada, and the RCMP's liaison officer to DFAIT, Richard Roy, were meeting with Dan Livermore, Scott Heatherington, Jim Gould, Don Saunders, and Jonathan Solomon from DFAIT's intelligence divisions. Inspector McDougal from RCMP headquarters arrived late. Ambassador Pillarella was in Ottawa on holidays but attended anyway. Others were there, too—perhaps from CSIS—but their identities are a secret.[10] Nobody from DFAIT's consular division was invited to the meeting. And it's no wonder. It had been less than three weeks since Ahmad told consular officials he'd been tortured in Syria—it's unlikely the consular division would have endorsed A-O Canada's plans for Abdullah, who was still in Syrian custody.

A-O Canada members explained why they were interested in Abdullah. Pillarella explained what he knew about how the Syrian Military Intelligence worked, and informed the group that General Khalil had finally admitted Abdullah was in Syrian custody. The RCMP asked about sending the Syrians questions to ask Abdullah. Cabana's personal notes describe how the meeting went from there: "Mr. Pillarella suggested that the Syrian authorities would likely be expecting us to share with them. We explained our intentions to share any of our project information relevant to whatever investigation Syria is conducting with them. We explained that packages have already been prepared to this end."[11]

"If you are going to send questions, would you ask them not to torture him?"[12] It was DFAIT's Jonathan Solomon, the junior officer in the room, who spoke up. He knew Syria's record on human rights and about Canada's obligations under the United Nations Convention against Torture, and was surprised this was even being suggested. Things got awkward after that. Scott Heatherington appears to have backed up Solomon, pointing out that Ahmad had just reported he had been tortured in Syria. Cabana noted that it was possible that Ahmad had lied about the torture.[13]

Who else said what at the meeting and what else was said is still classified. What is clear, however, is that Cabana and the rest of the A-O Canada team were undeterred by what Ahmad had reported about torture in Syria. Later that day, Cabana sent a fax to Staff Sergeant Dennis Fiorido, the RCMP's new liaison officer for the Middle East. The fax cover letter read:

It is our understanding that the Syrians are prepared to question ALMALKI on our behalf. While their offer is appreciated, it obviously would be in our best interests to interview ourselves.

We would request that you approach your Syrian contact to see if they will grant us access to conduct our own inter-view of this individual. The Syrians have been most cooper-ative with our earlier requests and we are hoping that our requests will meet with favourable review. In the alternative, we are contemplating providing the Syrian officials with questions for ALMALKI.

The Syrian authorities have expressed an interest in infor-mation we have on ALMALKI and we are lead [sic] to believe that they would like access to our information to assist them in their inquiries. I would propose that the Syrians be approached and advised that we would like to extend an invitation for their investigators to come to Canada and meet with our team to share information of common interest.[14]

The same day, Fiorido was also asked to "get further informa-tion from the Syrian authorities in preparation for their proposed interview of Mr. El Maati in Egypt."[15] Asked later about his thoughts on Ahmad's allegation of torture, Fiorido said he'd just assumed that Ahmad had been "looking for some leverage to gain whatever he was intending to gain" and it was up to others to think about torture and human rights.[16]

Wednesday, September 11, 2002
Istiqbal Tora prison, Cairo

AHMAD EL MAATI HADN'T SEEN ANYONE IN HIS FAMILY since he'd left his mother at the airport in Vienna ten months earlier. He hadn't imagined they'd be able to visit, so he was very surprised to see his sister and her husband when he walked into the office. There were two consular officials there, too—the vice-consul, Jean Ducharme, and Mira Wassef, consular officer.

"I couldn't believe it when I walked into the office and saw my sister and my brother-in-law," Ahmad says. "It was a huge surprise. We were so happy. We hugged and we were crying like babies." Ahmad says his sister noticed that Ducharme was crying, too.

Ahmad didn't tell them about the torture, but they knew, he says. "I didn't want to hurt them, even though I knew, deep down, that they already knew I was tortured. When we sat down they were looking at me strangely, as if they could see what I had gone through."

Their conversation was strained, of course, with Egyptian officials looking on.

Ahmad asked about his mother. They explained that she was in Canada but was returning the next week. They'd brought him dry foods, not realizing they could bring in cooked food. They brought halva, tea, underwear, and T-shirts. They'd hired a lawyer, they told him, and were working on obtaining a release order.

When the visit was over, Ahmad's spirits were lifted. He shared the food with his cellmates.

About two weeks later, the guards came into the wing and called out the names of fifty or so prisoners. Ahmad's name was on the list. The guards ordered the prisoners to get ready for transfer. Ahmad noticed that the other prisoners looked very worried—they seemed to know this wasn't good news. Ahmad wondered if he was being punished, because, during the second consular visit, he'd said he hadn't had access to fresh air and sun.

Loaded onto a truck, the prisoners were driven north of Cairo. One of the guards said they were being transferred to the Abu Za'abal prison. The prison is notorious. Referred to by the Egyptian government as a "prison area," it is located on a vast swath of land about twenty miles northeast of Cairo on the Al-Ismalia Highway, which runs alongside the northwest side of the Al-Ismalia Canal. An industrial area, the air is thick with smog from surrounding factories. As the truck neared the prison compound, the prisoners could see the canal on the right of the highway. Animal corpses were floating in the water.

The truck turned left off the highway and stopped outside a fort-like entrance guarded by soldiers armed with machine guns. They drove another hundred yards or so. Ahmad could see a very old-looking prison on the right, surrounded by trees. That's the Leman Abu Za'abal prison, someone said.

Up ahead, on the left, Ahmad could see what was obviously the maximum-security prison, surrounded by high walls topped with barbed wire, security cameras, and several watchtowers. The truck turned left and drove through a gate and parked alongside a long, narrow rectangular cage-like structure with a brown roof and metal fencing for walls. The guards ordered the prisoners out of the truck and into the cage, where they were searched, and some beaten. But they didn't touch Ahmad. Instead, someone came out from a nearby administration building and took him out of the cage and behind the administration building. There were three long prison wings on the left—the official led Ahmad into the middle one and walked him to a cell on the west end.[17]

The cell was about four by six feet, with a pit toilet in the back. A blanket was hung from the wall in front of the toilet for privacy. There was a tap too, and a bucket.

"There was water most of the time but sometimes it was cut off, so we had to keep the bucket full for washing ourselves and our dishes. At the end of the day I would see a green film on the bottom, and sometimes tadpoles." Ahmad later learned that this was the only water prisoners had access to, not just for washing but also for drinking. It flowed directly, untreated, from the canal.

Ahmad noticed that the heavy metal door leading into his cell was marked with a Chubb Security logo. There was a small rectangular slit in the door, about one inch high and eight inches wide. There used to be glass in the opening, but it had been broken by former detainees desperate for air. The other prisoners were allowed out of their cells between ten o'clock in the morning and three o'clock in the afternoon. Ahmad would wash his clothes, then stuff them through the hole in the door so that the others could hang them to dry in the courtyard.

The cell was meant for solitary confinement prisoners, but Ahmad had been assigned a cellmate. "Right away, I knew he was an informer," Ahmad says. "He kept asking me questions, and finally I told him that I'd been told by the security officials not to talk to anyone about my story. He was so angry!" Ahmad made it very clear he didn't like him, and the two barely spoke again.

In the mornings, the guards called out the names of prisoners for whom the Ministry of the Interior had issued "release orders." On October 15, a release order was issued for Ahmad. He was excited, but not because he thought he was really about to be released. He knew by then that in Egypt, although release orders are issued all the time, new detention orders are issued within days. The order meant prisoners would be transferred to the State Security Investigations (SSI) services headquarters in Lazoughli Square in Cairo. There, they'd be put in a common cell where they could mingle with other prisoners before a new detention order was issued and they were transferred back to Abu Za'abal. This was purely an administrative process but meant a break from the routine. "We could go for a drive and see the outside world, then meet new people and get news," Ahmad remembers. "That's why we liked those release orders, even though we knew we wouldn't be released." Ahmad spent five or six days at SSI headquarters before being sent back to Abu Za'abal and once again locked into his cell.

ELEVEN

Tunis to New York

Wednesday, September 25, 2002
Tunis, Tunisia

MAHER ARAR HAD BEEN WITH HIS FAMILY IN TUNISIA since late June. His wife, Monia, his five-year-old daughter, and four-month-old son had travelled there ahead of him in early June. The family wanted to be close to Monia's father, who was ill, and they knew they might have to stay for a while. Maher had remained in Ottawa for work before joining them. For Maher, who says he was very much a workaholic in those days, this was a chance for a much-needed break: "This was the first time in years that it wasn't about work, but beaches, fun, and family time; it was a way for me to get away from my stressful work life."

By September, Maher felt rested and refreshed, but now he had to return home for business. His former employer, MathWorks, had emailed him about a potential contract. Monia would stay on in Tunisia with the children to spend more time with her father. Maher bid his family farewell and waved goodbye from the taxi taking him to the Tunis airport.

Maher had used his air-miles to book his flight. He would fly to Zurich first, stay overnight in the airport, then continue on to New York and, finally, Montreal. He had left his car in Montreal and would stay there a couple of days with his mother before driving home to Ottawa. It would be a long trip, but he was used to travelling, and he could work on the plane.

12:55 P.M., Thursday, September 26, 2002
"A" Division, RCMP headquarters, Ottawa

STAFF SERGEANT CALLAGHAN got the call at 12:55 in the afternoon. An FBI agent told him Maher Arar was flying into New York at 2 P.M. and that the Americans were going to refuse him entry, interrogate him, and send him back to Zurich. Did the RCMP have any questions it would like asked on its behalf? Callaghan said he'd get back to them.

Callaghan told Corcoran, and they asked Walsh to pull together the questions for the FBI. Walsh went to the questions prepared for the interview with Maher back in January that never happened. He made a few quick edits and tagged on a concluding paragraph. Callaghan reviewed the questions, then told Walsh to get Cabana's approval and send them to the RCMP's National Operation Centre to pass on to the FBI. Cabana wasn't around, and Walsh understood the FBI's request to be urgent so sent the questions off, without Cabana's approval, just before 2 P.M.

The fax cover memo noted that the list of questions "was one prepared earlier this year prior to Arar's sudden departure from Canada."[1] The concluding paragraph tagged on by Walsh read: "ARAR kept a low profile while in Canada but seemed to be connected to many of the targets of our investigation. ARAR had been asked by our members for an interview as a potential witness but ARAR sought legal counsel and declined. ARAR soon after departed the country rather suddenly for Tunisia."[2]

The RCMP had already told the Americans that Maher and his wife were members of a "group of Islamic Extremist individuals suspected of being linked to [the] Al Qaeda terrorist movement." An allegation for which, the Arar Inquiry would determine, the RCMP had no basis. And despite being peripheral to the investigation, the information the RCMP had already shared with the Americans variously referred to Maher as a suspect, principal subject, target, or important figure. The RCMP had also already told the Americans that Maher had refused an interview, and now it was saying that again. Which didn't make it any more true. Now the RCMP was telling the Americans that Maher's departure for Tunisia had happened "suddenly" after he "declined" the interview. That was wrong, too. Maher hadn't left for Tunisia until nearly five months after his lawyer had been in touch with the RCMP to say yes, subject to conditions, he would consent to an interview.

The RCMP fax also claimed that Maher had been in Washington, D.C., on September 11, 2001, the day of the attack on the Pentagon. In fact, Maher had been in San Diego on a business trip with a colleague from The MathWorks.

No one in A-O Canada thought to attach caveats to the information they shared that day. Like all the other written information they had shared with the Americans so far, it could be used by the Americans in any way they wanted, without seeking anyone's permission.[3]

2 P.M., Friday, September 26, 2002
John F. Kennedy International Airport, New York

JUST AS WALSH WAS FAXING THE FBI, Maher's American Airlines flight touched down at John F. Kennedy International Airport. He wasn't expecting trouble when he lined up at the American immigration counter. The RCMP had never responded to the letter about the interview request, sent by his lawyer, Michael Edelson, back in February. Having travelled frequently in the United States before, he was used to navigating through its airports. He'd never experienced problems, even after 9/11.

This time, however, after the immigration official entered Maher's name in the computer, he asked Maher to step aside, then escorted him to another area. At first, Maher wasn't worried, thinking it was just a routine check. But after an hour and a half of just sitting and waiting, he started to wonder what was going on. Then another official came to take his fingerprints and photograph. Maher asked why he'd been pulled aside. "Just regular procedure," he was told.

Before long, other officials arrived. Maher thought they were the airport police. They searched through his bags and his wallet, then photocopied his passport. They asked him to turn on his laptop and leave it on the counter. Maher kept asking what was going on, but the men refused to answer. He asked several times if he could make a phone call but that too was refused.

More men arrived, from the New York Police Department (NYPD) and from the FBI. It was now about 4 P.M., but Maher still had time to catch his flight to Montreal. The authorities said they had some questions for him, then they'd let him go. One of the men asked the questions, another just watched Maher, making sure he could see the gun strapped to his leg. "I was scared and did not know what was going on. I told them I wanted a lawyer," Maher says. "They told me I had no right to a lawyer because I was not an American citizen."[4]

Maher was asked where he worked and how much he earned, and about his travel in the United States. Maher explained about his work permits and the business he'd done in America. He was asked about a recent business trip to Japan. "They were consulting a report while questioning me, and the information they had was so private I thought, this must be from Canada," Maher says. The officials asked if they could see information on his computer; he agreed, saying he had nothing to hide.

Maher was then asked about several people, some who Maher knew, most who he'd never heard of. One was Ahmad El Maati. Yes, Maher knew him, but not well, he said. He had met Ahmad a couple of years ago in Montreal at a garage where Maher got his car fixed while visiting family. He was asked if he knew Abdullah. Yes, Maher replied, he knew Abdullah but knew his brother better, having worked with him at high-tech firms in Ottawa. Maher told the officials that the Almalki family had moved to Canada from Syria around the same time his did. He was asked about times he'd seen Abdullah. Maher described what he could remember.

The more Maher answered the questions, the more he was treated as if he were lying, and the ruder the officials got. The questions were coming fast, and the officials wanted the answers fast. Any hesitation on Maher's part was unacceptable. Both men were yelling at him now, hurling insults, swearing and accusing him of having a selective memory. The officials acted as though they were sure Maher knew much more about Abdullah than he was letting on. Maher just kept telling them everything he knew about everything they wanted to know.

Then one of men pulled out a rental application Maher had signed for his apartment in Ottawa in 1997. "I could not believe they had this. I was completely shocked," he says. The official pointed out that Abdullah's name was on the application. Maher had forgotten he had put Abdullah's name down—not knowing many people in Ottawa when he moved there from Montreal, Maher had listed Abdullah as an emergency contact. His interrogators seemed convinced that he was intentionally downplaying his relationship with Abdullah.

Why were they being so rude? Maher wondered. Why did they think he was lying? "I told them the truth. I had nothing to hide. I had never had problems in the United States before, and I could not believe what was happening to me." The questioning continued for five hours. By now, he had missed his flight to Montreal. When the two officials were done, another official questioned him until midnight. "I was very, very worried and asked for a lawyer again and again. They just ignored me ... they would not tell me what was happening," Maher says.

His wrists and ankles were chained and shackled, and he was taken to a waiting van and driven to another building, where his bags were waiting. Maher was made to sit with other detainees before being put in a cell. It was now around 1 A.M. The guards removed the shackles from his ankles but left the handcuffs on, then searched him, took his shoelaces, and locked him in the cell.

Maher waited. After about a half hour, he knocked on the door, telling the official who came that he needed to sleep. The official brought him a blanket but left the light in the cell on. Maher lay on one of the metal benches in the cell but was too disoriented, too scared, and too worried to sleep. At about six o'clock in the morning, he knocked on the door again, this time to ask for food. He hadn't eaten since his flight from Zurich. No one responded.

A little while later, two FBI agents took Maher to a room, where they had his Palm Pilot and asked him to open it. Maher did, entering his password. He had nothing to hide, he kept telling them, and would show them whatever they wanted to see.

After a few hours, they broke for lunch. Maher wouldn't be eating, though. Instead, he was taken back to his cell, his ankles again shackled. At around five o'clock in the evening, two men came and removed the shackles.

"We want you to voluntarily go back to Syria," one said.

"No way, send me to Canada where I was going."

"You are a special interest, okay!" the man replied angrily.

"Then send me back to Switzerland or Tunisia."

The man left the room without answering but returned ten minutes later to lead Maher to an office. There, he sat at a computer, asking Maher questions and typing in his answers; he then printed out a form for Maher to sign. "They would not let me read it, but I just signed it. I was exhausted and confused and disoriented. I had not slept or eaten since I was on the plane." He was then taken back to the cell.

At about six o'clock that evening, he was brought food from McDonald's. It was cold, but Maher was hungry so he ate it, still handcuffed. A couple of hours later, three armed FBI agents entered the cell, shackled Maher's ankles again, and led him outside to a waiting SUV. When the SUV pulled into a prison, Maher's handcuffs and ankle shackles were removed and he was told to undress for a strip search. Maher was uncomfortable undressing in front of the men and protested, but they insisted.

They gave him underwear and a bright orange prison uniform, then shackled his ankles and wrists again.

Maher was taken to a doctor, who gave him a shot—"I asked what it was, and they would not tell me. My arm was red for almost two weeks from that." As Maher was led to his cell he was videotaped, as he had been upon his arrival at the prison and would be at other times during his detention. "I had never seen a prison before in my life, and I was terrified. I asked again for a phone call, and a lawyer. They just ignored me," Maher says.

Maher was led into a cell, where his handcuffs and shackles were removed, and the door then locked. Maher asked again for a lawyer, as well as for toothpaste and a toothbrush. His requests were ignored and he was left there, alone.

Friday, September 27, 2002
Tunis, Tunisia

MONIA WAS WORRIED. Maher was supposed to call when he reached Montreal and hadn't. She called her mother-in-law in Montreal and learned he hadn't arrived. His brothers said they would check with the airlines and call the police in New York, while Monia contacted the Canadian Embassy in Tunis. The woman she spoke to there promised to pass the information on to DFAIT's consular services in Ottawa.

For the next two days, Maher's brothers called a number of places looking for help. They eventually learned from American Airlines that Maher hadn't been on the flight to Montreal. Then they called the RCMP, who told them to call the local police. They called the Montreal police, who told them to call the New York police. The New York police said they couldn't help either, so his brothers called the RCMP again. This time whoever they spoke to told them to call DFAIT, which they did, on the morning of September 29.

Tuesday, October 1, 2002
Metropolitan Detention Center, New York

MAHER HIMSELF DIDN'T KNOW WHERE HE WAS—his queries had been ignored. He had been detained for five days now, and he was scared. Very scared. He hadn't slept much at all, and he was being kept apart from the other prisoners. He still didn't have toothpaste or a toothbrush.

On the fifth day, an official had come to his cell and handed him a document stating that the U.S. Immigration and Naturalization Service had found him inadmissible to the United States because he belonged to al-Qaeda. Maher was devastated. "This was such a serious allegation, with no basis whatsoever," he says.

But the next day, on Tuesday, October 1, Maher finally got the phone call he'd been asking for. He had two minutes, they said. Maher called his mother-in-law in Ottawa. Maher told his mother-in-law where he was, that he wasn't being treated well, that he was scared because the Americans might send him to Syria, and that he needed a lawyer. Then his time was up and he was taken back to his cell.

Wednesday passed with no more news. Then, on Thursday, officials came and took Maher into a cell-like room with a table and chairs. A woman stood when he entered, introducing herself as Maureen Girvan, the manager of consular services at the Canadian Consulate General in New York. His family had been looking for him, she said. The call to his mother-in-law had helped them track him down.

Maher was in tears now thinking of his family. He told Girvan what had happened to him each day thus far and showed her the document he'd been given that accused him of being a member of al-Qaeda and declared him inadmissible to the United States. He told her he was innocent, that he had always admired the United States and had never had trouble there before. He told her he was scared he'd be sent to Syria.

Girvan told him that wouldn't happen. He was a Canadian citizen travelling on his Canadian passport. The Americans had recognized his citizenship by allowing a Canadian consul to visit. He was in the system now, and his family had arranged for a lawyer to come see him.

When the meeting was over, Maher, unconvinced by Girvan's assurances, was still very worried.

TWELVE

New York to Damascus

Tuesday, October 3, 2002
Far' Falastin, Damascus

THIS WAS THE THIRD DAY THAT WEEK Abdullah had been taken up from his cell to be questioned about Maher Arar. The first time was in the evening of September 30. He'd been taken up to see Colonel Salloum, Khaled, and four or so other interrogators. They wanted him to tell them everything he knew about Maher. They told Abdullah they were going to beat him because he hadn't already told them about Maher. He reminded them that they had asked him about Maher back in June. They asked Abdullah to write, in detail, everything he knew about Maher, and then sent him back to his cell, warning that he'd better not have lied. Abdullah didn't know that Maher had been in U.S. detention for four days.

Abdullah was called up and asked about Maher twice again the next day.

Now it was Tuesday and there were more questions. Salloum wanted to know if Maher had been to Pakistan or Afghanistan. Abdullah said no, not to his knowledge. Salloum wanted Abdullah to say Maher was with al-Qaeda. Abdullah said he didn't know anyone connected to al-Qaeda. Salloum threatened him, saying he was lying. Abdullah repeated that he didn't know anyone in al-Qaeda.

Salloum ordered an interrogator to send a report about these questions to headquarters so it could be faxed by noon. Then he turned to Abdullah. Maher will be here soon, he said. And if he found out Abdullah had lied, he'd put Abdullah in a barrel of human excrement, cut his food rations, and torture him with "the chair" until he was paralyzed.

Abdullah said he had told Salloum everything he knew. If he wanted more, he should give him a blank paper to sign and fill it himself. Salloum left the room, after ordering the other inter- rogator to torture Abdullah and to be ruthless. The interrogator looked at Abdullah and remarked that they knew more about him now than his own family did, and they didn't understand why the Canadians kept insisting he was guilty.

It hasn't been determined who was behind the questions asked of Abdullah during this particular interrogation. Or who was being faxed the answers. Was it the Americans who were holding Maher? Or were CSIS or the RCMP somehow involved, with or without help from the Americans?

Tuesday, October 3, 2002
Canadian Consulate General, New York

GIRVAN HAD HEARD ABOUT THE CONCERN that Maher would be sent to Syria from two sources now. Nancy Collins, the case manager for U.S. files at headquarters in Ottawa, had sent an October 1 note saying that Maher's brother had called "in a panic" about the possibility that Maher would be deported to Syria. Girvan then heard it from Maher at the consular visit.

But Girvan didn't think Syria was a possibility. It had never happened to a Canadian in the United States before, and she thought the threat of deportation to Syria was simply being used as leverage in the Americans' interrogation of Maher. Nor did she consider the concern to be related to an unusual event that had occurred on October 1. A high-ranking official at the public affairs office of the U.S. Immigration and Naturalization Service (INS) had offered to check on Maher's case with officials at John F. Kennedy Airport. Within minutes, he'd called Girvan back with an eerie warning. This case, he warned, "was of a seriousness that should be taken to the highest level," and he suggested she arrange for the Canadian ambassador in Washington to call the U.S. Department of Justice.[1] This, of course, was highly unusual, so Girvan had called DFAIT headquarters in Ottawa. Pardy was away, so she spoke to the person filling in for him. They decided high-level diplomatic intervention didn't made sense at this stage; instead they would keep working with the officials at the Metropolitan Detention Center for now.

Early morning, Wednesday, October 4, 2002
"A" Division, RCMP headquarters, Ottawa

STAFF SERGEANT CALLAGHAN got the CIA's questions about Maher Arar from RCMP corporal Rick Flewelling on Wednesday morning. Flewelling's fax noted that the CIA had contacted headquarters the night before, looking for A-O Canada's help with questions for Maher Arar. CIA agents wanted any evidence that would help them press criminal charges. Flewelling's fax cover read: "Find attached request forwarded by the CIA with a list of questions. They would be most appreciative of any additional information you can supply on this subject. They further request that any response be channelled through the FBI for evidentiary purposes."[2]

The fax also noted the investigators were facing time restrictions and that the INS was processing Maher for removal from the United States. There were seven questions, all about Maher's connections with other people, sleeper cell members or known terrorists. A-O Canada prepared its response and sent it out on Friday, October 4, at 5:05 P.M. It contained information obtained when Maher's computer and Palm Pilot had been seized in December 2001, and also discussed his meeting with Abdullah at Mango's Café in October 2001.

In A-O Canada's October 4 reply, it was admitted that the RCMP had not been able to establish that Maher was linked to al-Qaeda. Ironically, this was also the first time that A-O Canada ever complied with RCMP policy by attaching a caveat to written information shared with the Americans. The caveat clearly stated that the document was RCMP property, loaned "in confidence and is not to be reclassified, distributed or acted upon without the prior authorization of the originator."[3]

6:10 P.M., Saturday, October 5, 2002
Home of Corporal Rick Flewelling, Ottawa

CORPORAL FLEWELLING WAS AT HOME when the call came in from the FBI on Saturday evening. The agent told him that the FBI was concerned it didn't have enough evidence to charge Maher, so they were going to remove him from the United States. He noted that Maher was a dual citizen and had asked to come to Canada. The agent said that "Washington" wanted to know if the RCMP could charge him if he was sent there. Flewelling explained that the RCMP didn't have enough evidence to charge him with anything either. "Washington" also wanted to know whether, if Maher was sent to Canada, the Canadians could deny him entry. Probably not, said Flewelling, since Arar was a Canadian citizen.

Flewelling says it didn't occur to him that the Americans were considering sending Maher to Syria. He says that, at the time, he had no knowledge of the American practice of sending terror suspects to countries such as Syria.[4]

7 or 8 P.M., Saturday, October 5, 2002
Special Housing Unit, Metropolitan Detention Center, New York

SINCE THE CONSULAR VISIT TWO DAYS EARLIER, the only news Maher had had was when two immigration officers came to see him. The officers asked him to designate the country he wanted to be sent to: Canada or Syria. Maher designated Canada.

He had been detained for nine days. Now the guards had come to take him from his cell again. This time it was to see the lawyer his family had found for him. On the other side of a wall of glass and speaking through a handset, the lawyer introduced herself as Amal Oummih and said that she'd been in touch with his family but wasn't yet formally retained. Maher broke down again. He told her that the Americans wanted to send him to Syria. Oummih tried to reassure him, saying that he would be able to choose where he went and would have a hearing where he could argue his case. Maher wasn't convinced. He pleaded with her to do all she could. She'd be back soon, she promised.

Oummih would later describe the meeting to a reporter. Maher "was in very, very bad shape," she said, and "very emotional, very scared ... I was very concerned about him.... He didn't seem to know what was going on. He was very disoriented. He seemed very confused. He was very, very emotional. It wouldn't be an exaggeration to say that about half the time I just had to let him sob and cry."[5]

At around nine o'clock the next evening, on Sunday, the guards came to take Maher from his cell yet again, saying his lawyer was there to see him. Maher thought it was a strange time for his lawyer to be visiting but was glad to hear she was there. Maybe this meant there was good news. But when he was led into a room, he saw seven or eight people there but no lawyer.

"Where is my lawyer?"

"We called, but he refused to come," one of the men said.

Maher's mind was racing. Why "he"? Amal Oummih is a woman. Had his lawyer declined to come? Or were they misleading him?

Then the questions started. Why was he so opposed to going to Syria? "I told them I would be tortured there. I told them I had not done my military service; I am a Sunni Muslim; my mother's cousin had been accused of being a member of the Muslim Brotherhood and was put in prison for nine years." If the officials interrogating him cared about what he said, they didn't show it. The questions continued. Maher, desperate, asked for his lawyer again and again. They told him again that they had informed his lawyer but "he" chose not to come.

The questioning lasted for six hours. On numerous occasions, the officials claimed to be in discussions with "Washington." Eventually, they produced a form, which appeared to be a typed transcript of the interrogation, and asked Maher to sign it. Maher refused.

By the time Maher was led back to his cell, it was early morning. For the next few hours, Maher just sat, worried, and waited.

WHEN AMAL OUMMIH ARRIVED AT HER OFFICE on Monday morning, there was a message waiting for her from Edward J. McElroy, the district director for the INS in New York City: There would be a hearing for Maher Arar at 7 P.M. Not realizing the message had been left on Sunday, Oummih assumed the hearing was that coming evening. She spoke to another INS official, who told her that Maher had been taken to the INS's Varick Street facility for "processing" en route to another facility in New Jersey. Later that day, the INS again said that Maher had arrived at the New Jersey facility and that Oummih should call back the next day, on October 8, for details about his location.[6]

Meanwhile, the FBI called Staff Sergeant Callaghan the same day. The agent wanted to know again if A-O Canada "could link Mr. Arar to Al-Qaida or any other terrorist group."[7] Callaghan said that the only possible link was through Abdullah Almalki. Callaghan asked if an A-O Canada team member could come to New York to question Maher. The FBI agent said he'd look into it.

4 A.M., Tuesday, October 8, 2002
Special Housing Unit, Metropolitan Detention Center, New York

THEY CAME TO GET MAHER at three or four o'clock in the morning on Tuesday. They woke him up and said he was leaving but wouldn't tell him where he was going. They led him into a room, removed his handcuffs and shackles, and strip-searched him. Then they put the handcuffs and shackles back on and led him into another room. There, a woman read aloud to him from a document, which she said was the "decision of the Regional Director":

> In accordance with my responsibilities as Regional Director ... I have concluded on the basis of classified information that Arar is unequivocally inadmissible to the United States ... in that he is a member of an organization that has been designated by the Secretary of State as a Foreign Terrorist Organization, to wit: Al-Qaeda.
>
> The Commissioner of the Immigration and Naturalization Service has determined that your removal to Syria would be consistent with Article 3 of the United Nation's Convention Against Torture and other Cruel, Inhuman or Degrading Treatment or Punishment.[8]

If Maher had been able to read the document, he would have seen that page two said that "upon secondary inspection," it was determined that he was "the subject of a TECS/NAILS [Treasury Enforcement Communications System/National Automated Immigration Lookout System]—the border lookout A-O Canada had asked for. If he'd been able to read page four, he would have seen that the "unclassified" reasons for the Americans sending him to Syria were that he "was friendly" with Abdullah and his brother, and "Ahman" El Maati. According to the document, Maher had told them "Al-Malki exports radios and one of his customers was the Pakistani military," and that he'd had "three business meetings with Al-Malki," and "admitted to the FBI about meeting Abdullah Al-Malki at the restaurant where he and Al-Malki went outside and walked in the rain in October 2001."[9]

And, if he'd seen page three, he would have seen that it said that "as of October 7, 2002 Arar failed to provide a written statement and any additional information in response to the charge."[10]

But Maher wasn't allowed to read the document. He broke down and pleaded with the Americans not to send him to be tortured. They weren't moved. Instead, they made him change out of his orange prisoner's jumpsuit and into a brown one, then led him down into the garage of the Metropolitan Detention Center, still handcuffed and shackled, and loaded him into the back of a waiting van. By 5 A.M., the van had pulled into Teterboro Airport in New Jersey, across the Hudson River from New York, where Maher was led up a flight of steps and into a private jet.

2 P.M., Wednesday, October 9, 2002
Canadian Embassy, Washington, D.C.

GAR PARDY, of DFAIT's Consular Affairs Bureau, was at the Canadian Embassy in Washington, along with Nancy Collins, his case manager for U.S. files. They were there for a two-day conference starting the next day for Canadian consular officers working in the United States, and for officials from headquarters and the passport and immigration department in Ottawa. They would discuss issues and problems they were facing in the field, which had become particularly important in the United States since 9/11. U.S. policies were still changing, and deportation cases were on the rise.

It had been a busy few weeks for Pardy. He had just returned from a trip to London, where he'd been coordinating with the British in efforts to help William Sampson, a Canadian detained in Saudi Arabia and threatened with execution. Pardy first heard about Maher's case on October 3, the day after he flew in from London. He'd kept an eye on it since, though nothing he'd seen had especially alarmed him. Maher had been granted consular access, so his case seemed more positive than a couple of other security-related cases the bureau had dealt with since 9/11. Two men, one with landed-immigrant status in Canada and the other a dual Pakistani-Canadian, had been detained at the Metropolitan Detention Center in September 2001. Both were suspected of links to terrorism. Both had eventually been deported to Canada.

This afternoon, Pardy sat down with Collins and Robert Archambault, who worked in consular affairs in Washington, for a conference call with Girvan, still in New York. Girvan had heard from Monia the day before, who said Maher hadn't called her, as planned, from the Metropolitan Detention Center. Girvan had set up the call, so she contacted the detention centre to follow up. That's when she was told that Maher had been removed from the facility between three and four o'clock that morning. The timing of the move hadn't worried Girvan. She'd had numerous complaints from other detainees about being moved at odd hours. Girvan had continued calling around to try to find Maher. Eventually, someone at the INS public affairs office said there was no record of Maher being held in any INS facility and suggested she call INS headquarters in Washington. This was unusual; Girvan had never been referred to INS headquarters before. She immediately called and left a message.

During the conference call, Girvan explained to Pardy that she finally spoke with the counsel at INS headquarters earlier that day, who said he'd look into the matter. Girvan also told her colleagues that she'd heard from Monia again that morning. Monia had told her she was very worried Maher would be sent to Syria. A friend of the family had called the consular division yesterday to express the same fear. And Maher's brother had been calling to say the same thing since Maher had called his mother-in-law on October 1. Pardy, Collins, Girvan, and Archambault still thought there was no chance that would happen so decided to give it twenty-four hours, then figure out the next step.

That night, they all attended a reception to kick off the conference. Hosted at the Canadian Embassy on the terrace overlooking Pennsylvania Avenue and Capitol Hill, it was a fancy affair, with canapés and cocktails. But, Collins would later say, as the night went on, they started to question why several officials from the U.S. State Department who'd confirmed they would be at the event didn't show up.[11] Did this have something to do with Maher Arar's case? they wondered.

2 P.M., Thursday, October 10, 2002
Canadian Embassy, Washington, D.C.

GAR PARDY WAS CHAIRING THE CONFERENCE. It had just resumed after the lunch break when Collins and another consular officer, Hélène Bouchard, pulled him out of the room. They'd just had a disturbing conversation with an INS official. They had asked the INS official to phone on their behalf to try to locate Maher. They were in the room when she put in the call. Suddenly her "face became white," they said, and she hung up the phone.[12]

Collins and Bouchard had asked her where he'd been sent. The INS official answered that she just couldn't say. "And we then asked ... if it would be okay if we asked questions and if she can answer with a yes and a no without breaching any—well, I guess she was still breaching it ..." Collins would later say. Was he sent to Jordan? they asked—Collins knew that Jordan was sometimes used as a transit point on the way to Guantánamo. The woman nodded.

Girvan had bad news, too. She'd been in and out of the conference all day making calls and trying to reach the INS counsel. He had finally called her back and confirmed that Maher had been removed, and not to Canada. He wouldn't say more. She'd already told Pardy.

Pardy called Scott Heatherington, the director of DFAIT's Security and Intelligence Bureau in Ottawa. Heatherington told Pardy that a contact at the U.S. Embassy in Ottawa had informed him that Maher had been sent to Syria.

A-O Canada and CSIS already knew, too. A-O Canada had confirmed by two o'clock in the afternoon on October 9, through American sources, that Maher had been sent to Syria. RCMP headquarters learned sometime on the eighth or the ninth. A briefing note to Commissioner Zaccardelli dated October 9 and signed by Superintendent Wayne Pilgrim, the officer in charge of the RCMP's National Security Investigations Branch, said the RCMP learned that "ARAR was deported and subsequently escorted to Syria, by U.S. authorities at an undetermined time on October 8, 2002."[13] CSIS officials say they learned on October 9 that Arar had been sent to Syria.[14] On October 10, CSIS deputy director Jack Hooper wrote about what was happening to Maher Arar in a memo, saying, "I think the U.S. would like to get Arar to Jordan where they can have their way with him."[15]

Mid-morning, Tuesday, October 8, 2002
Somewhere over the Atlantic Ocean

PRESIDENTIAL AVIATION OF FLORIDA boasts a "fleet of superior corporate jets" and "personal attention to detail" that mirrors "the exceptional quality and grace of the lifestyle" that their "cultivated clientele expect and enjoy." Their goal is to "deliver sumptuous, discriminating travel experiences aboard impeccably maintained late model aircraft." "From take-off to touchdown," they say, "your Presidential experience promises a new spirit of sophisticated, distinctive jet travel."[16] Among its fleet is the Gulfstream III, a luxury jet that seats ten to fourteen, the wide, plush seats upholstered in butter-soft leather, the colour, of course, a tasteful off-white to complement the rest of the neutral decor. The lighting is ambient, the video and audio systems state-of-the-art.

Investigative journalist Stephen Grey would later determine that this cultivated client, the U.S. Department of Justice, would have paid about $120,000 to charter the Gulfstream for the flight it would take that day. The CIA's global prisoner transfer program was in full swing by now, and the agency didn't have enough of its own airplanes to transfer prisoners.[17]

For Maher, his wrists and ankles still shackled, this travel experience would hardly be sumptuous. He was seated at the back of the jet and had been tracking their route on a large video screen. They'd flown from Teterboro, New Jersey, to Dulles International Airport in Washington. There, everyone but the pilot and flight attendant had disembarked and a new team of agents had boarded.

While the plane sat on the tarmac at Dulles, Maher overheard some of the men on the team speaking on their phone, saying that the Syrians had refused to take Maher directly but that the Jordanians would take him. The flight left Dulles at 7:46 A.M. and stopped to refuel in Bangor, Maine, before taking off again at 9:36 A.M. and setting out over the Atlantic Ocean.[18]

The men escorting him sat down to lunch, offering some to Maher. Someone asked him if he'd like to watch a movie, so they watched two action movies. But he wasn't paying much attention. All he could think of was what was waiting for him at the end of the flight.

After about eight hours, the flight landed in Rome. After a short stop, they took off for Amman, Jordan. Once the plane was in the air again, the head of the team removed Maher's shackles and invited him to dine with the others at the front of the plane. He introduced himself as Mr. Kouri—a Christian-Arab name— and said his family was from Syria, too.

"There's a tradition in the Muslim world called Eid," Maher later told Stephen Grey, "and before they slaughter the animal they feed him, and that's exactly what I thought when I was on the plane. I was always thinking [about] how I could avoid torture, because at that point I realized that the only reason why they were sending me [to Jordan] was to be tortured for them to get information."[19]

Maher sensed that Kouri felt sorry for him. He told Kouri he was innocent and in no way connected to terrorism. Kouri suggested he ask the Jordanians to keep him in Jordan. He described Kouri's apparent sympathy to journalist Grey: "He was very sympathetic. I could tell in his eyes; he didn't tell me directly but I could tell in his eyes. I knew if I continued talking to him for another fifteen minutes, he would just cry. You could tell."[20]

Maher was still wearing the brown prison jumpsuit. As they neared their destination, Kouri gave him a pair of jeans and a turquoise polo shirt to wear. Maher still has that shirt. The label says it was made in Canada.

They landed in Amman at around two or three o'clock Wednesday morning, October 9. The men led Maher off the airplane to the six or seven Jordanian officials waiting at the bottom of the steps. They blindfolded and shackled him, then loaded him into the backseat of a van and told him to put his head down. As the van drove off, the Jordanians beat him on the face and the back of the head. "Every time I tried to talk they beat me. For the first few minutes it was very intense."

About thirty minutes later, the van stopped, and he was taken inside a building and made to stand against a wall. Then he was taken in an elevator up to another floor and put in a room. Someone removed his blindfold. He found himself facing two men. They asked him questions about himself and his family, then searched his bag, which had also been brought up. At around four-thirty in the morning, Maher was put in a small cell with a mattress. Maher was exhausted. He hadn't slept since he was woken up the previous day at the Metropolitan Detention Center, but he still couldn't sleep.

All the while Maher kept thinking that at any moment, the Canadian government would somehow find him and intervene. But it didn't. About two or three hours later, Maher was taken to see a doctor, who checked his heart and asked if he had any health problems. An hour after that, he was taken to see an investigator, who told him he was being taken to Syria to complete his military service. He was photographed and fingerprinted, then told he was leaving. The men seemed to be in a hurry.

Maher was blindfolded and handcuffed and taken outside. He heard the same voices he heard when he was brought from the airport. His escorts told him they were putting his wallet in his bag, and lifted his blindfold so he could check that everything was still there, then put him in a van. On the road, they didn't beat him this time. After nearly an hour of highway driving, Maher was transferred to a car, which then sped off again down the highway. It was very hot in the car, but every time Maher tried to wipe the sweat from his brow, his new escorts beat him.

His neck hurt from being forced to hunch over with his head down. The handcuffs around his wrists were very tight and cut into his wrists. The pain was excruciating, he says. About an hour and a half later, he was handed over to yet another team and put into yet another vehicle. Maher thinks this was at the Syrian border.

Two or three hours later, he heard the sound of the call to prayer and guessed they were in a city, likely Damascus. The car stopped and he was pulled from it and led into a building, where his blindfold was removed. Maher saw pictures of the Syrian president on the wall. The two men in the room rifled through his bag and took his watch, cologne, and some of the chocolate he'd bought in Tunisia to bring to his mother. Maher kept asking where he was, but no one would tell him. "They behaved like thieves." Maher was put in another room to wait. A man came in and asked Maher for chocolate. Maher promised to give him chocolate if he told Maher where he was. At Far' Falastin, the man said.

As evening fell, Maher was taken into another room and told to sit on a chair. The man Maher would later learn was Colonel George Salloum, the head of Far' Falastin's interrogation team, was there. He was pacing and asking the questions. The other two men present took notes. Maher was exhausted and terrified; tears streamed down his face. The first questions were about his family and when and why they had moved to Canada. Salloum had the name of Maher's brother, the one who had been calling DFAIT for help. Maher answered every question as quickly as he could, but if he hesitated, even for a moment, Salloum would point to a metal chair in the room.

"Do you want me to use this?" he asked. At the time, Maher didn't know how the chair worked, but he knew it had something to do with torture, and he wanted to put it off as long as he could. He asked Salloum what he wanted to hear. The questions, all about his travel and his family, went on into the night. At around one o'clock in the morning, Salloum ordered the guards to take Maher downstairs. And then, Maher, like two Canadian citizens before him, was led into the basement of Far' Falastin. Maher says he never noticed the pictures of the president or the phrase from the Qur'an on the wall in the stairwell. He kept his head down, he says. The guards led him along the wider hallway past the common cells and then turned right down the narrow hallway, stopping at the second tiny door on the right—cell number two.

"What's this?" Maher asked, incredulous, when they opened the door. He couldn't believe this tiny, smelly, filthy space was for a human being.

"This is your cell."

"How long will I stay here?"

They didn't answer but pushed him into the darkness, closed the door, and slid the lock into place.

THIRTEEN

"Tell Us You Went to Afghanistan"

8 A.M., Thursday, October 10, 2002
Far' Falastin, Damascus

MAHER WAS LEFT IN THE DARK for about seven hours. When the guards came to get him in the morning, he hadn't yet slept. Instead, he'd sat on the floor with his head in his hands through the night, his mind racing, tears streaming down his face. The fear of torture was torture in and of itself, he says. "All I could think about was how to escape torture."

The guards ordered Maher out of the cell, then led him up the stairs into an interrogation room; Maher kept his head down as ordered. Colonel Salloum came in and told Maher to stand. Salloum held a two-inch-thick, two-foot-long black twisted metal cable. Maher was crying and trembling with fear.

"Do you know what this is?" Salloum yelled at Maher. "Open your hand!"

Maher stretched out his right arm and opened his hand, palm up. The cable came down hard. The sharp, intense pain caused Maher to jump. The pain was worsened by the humiliation Maher felt; his dignity was shattered. He felt like a "bad Syrian schoolboy." And fear had overcome him completely.

"Open your other hand!"

This time the cable missed Maher's palm, coming down on his wrist instead. The whipping got more intense—on his palms, his wrists, then his hips and lower back. There hadn't been any questions yet, just yelling and insults. Like Ahmad and Abdullah,

Maher refuses to repeat the words the men used. All he will say is that they were "dirty, bad words."

Salloum questioned Maher about his family and other people he knew, but Maher's answers were never good enough. Salloum kept calling Maher a liar.

Maher pleaded with the men to tell him what they wanted. "I was ready to say anything to stop the torture. Anything." They would whip him three or four times, stop, then whip him again. Salloum warned him that next it would be the *dulab*—the tire— and the *kursee*—the chair and electric shock.

The session went on for about ten hours. Before ordering the guards to take Maher to his cell, Salloum warned Maher that the next day he would beat him to death. Maher didn't sleep that night either.

The guards came for him at around eight the next morning, Friday, and took Maher upstairs. Almost immediately they started whipping him with the cable. Maher screamed out in pain, pleading for them to stop. "By the end of the day I started to think they just wanted anything they could get to please the Americans. I told them I had nothing to hide."

"Tell us you went to Afghanistan!"

Maher was surprised. He hadn't been asked about Afghanistan in the United States. He told them he had not been, but as the beating intensified, he just wanted to stop the torture. "Yes, if that's what you want, I've been to Afghanistan," he said. Salloum seemed pleased by this and asked if Maher had received military training in Afghanistan. "I confessed that I had been to a training camp in Afghanistan. That was the only effective thing to do to stop the torture," says Maher. As with Ahmad and Abdullah, the answers his interrogator wanted were contained in his questions, so Maher just agreed to whatever Salloum said. The interrogators read him a list of names of training camps, and Maher randomly chose one of the names as the one he had been at. *That's what they wanted.*

"How did you go there?"

Maher didn't know how to answer. He had never been to Afghanistan and had no idea where the camp was.

The questions now turned to Abdullah and how Maher knew him, and about Maher's relationships with other people, about his family, his salary, and his bank accounts. "They accused me of lying when I told them what I did for a living. They didn't understand what I do," he says. The whipping and beating and insults went on for about eighteen hours that day. At one point Maher offered to kiss Salloum's hand to try to make him stop the torture.

Every few hours the men stopped beating him and moved him into the "waiting room," where prisoners were left to listen to other people being tortured. "They were screaming like crazy. When I heard that, I felt my heart was going to come out of my chest," Maher says. He remembers hearing one man's head being slammed on a metal table over and over again. After several thuds and screaming there was an eerie silence. "When you hear that, you have mixed feelings. One is selfish—is this going to happen to me the next time? The other is for the people. You say, 'My God, how could they do that to people?'"

The "waiting room" was empty. Messages scribbled on the walls belied the suffering that had occurred in that room. "Your rats will not scare me," one prisoner had written. Maher suspects the prisoner had been locked in with rats.

After a few hours, Maher was taken back for more beating in the interrogation room. Then, late at night, he was taken downstairs to his cell. "At the end of each day, they would always say, 'Tomorrow will be harder for you.' So I didn't sleep for the first four days," Maher recalls.

By Saturday his interrogators resorted to beating him with their fists, aiming for his stomach. There were more questions about Abdullah. Every time Maher gave an answer, the men yelled at him, "You are a liar!" Maher told them the names of everyone he knew, but the beating continued.

"Who do you know from the Syrian community?"

"I know Abdullah."

The men punched him in the stomach repeatedly, and kicked him, then slapped him in the face.

"You saw Abdullah in Afghanistan!"

"This is not true, but if that is what you want me to say, I will say it."

By Maher's eighth day there, the beatings had subsided. The interrogations were less intense, lasting about five or six hours a day instead of more than ten hours at a time. By then, though, Maher was so sleep deprived and disoriented, he was starting to doubt his own sanity. "Their next tactic was to take me in a room, blindfolded, and people would talk about me. I could hear them saying, 'He knows lots of people who are terrorists,' and 'We will get their numbers,' and 'He is a liar.' Then they would say, 'Let's be frank, let's be friends, tell us the truth,' and come around the desk and slap me on the face. They played lots of mind games."

After a few more days, Maher could tell by the nature of the questions that his interrogators seemed to be trying to verify information in a written report. They were in a rush, trying to finalize it. It was around this time that Abdullah remembers being hauled upstairs and questioned about Maher again. "I think they were questioning me from Maher's interrogation report," he says. "And I think I heard him shouting from another room."

Twice on Saturday, October 19, the Syrians took Maher to an interrogation room just to ask if he had been travelling to Ottawa or Montreal when he was detained. Although they didn't squeeze him into the tire, he was made to sit on it for hours, "just to scare me. Just the fear was enough," Maher says.

He'd later learn that like Abdullah, the men who'd interrogated him included Khaled, Haitham, and Abdallah.

MAHER'S DISAPPEARANCE was making news back home. On October 11, his wife, Monia, and his brother Bassam had started talking to the media. They'd also sought the support of Riad Saloojee, the executive director of the Canadian Council on American Islamic Relations. They felt the government hadn't done enough to prevent Maher's removal to Syria and hoped that media coverage would help motivate it to do more to help him now.

The New York Times and *The Globe and Mail* ran the first stories on October 12. Both reported that Maher had been accused of terrorist ties, and in both, Monia firmly dismissed the allegations. "The whole thing is insane. My husband is a father. He works. He isn't a terrorist," Monia told *The Globe and Mail*. She also spoke about the broader consequences. "It's not just my husband. It's the consequences for everyone else. I can't believe that the U.S. is prepared to deport people to Syria when they are citizens of another country."[1] But whereas the *Globe* story described Maher as a "respected Canadian engineer" and focused on a woman's efforts to find her missing husband, the *National Post* took a different angle: Its headline described Maher as a suspected terrorist.[2] These early days of media coverage marked the beginning of what would become a constant struggle for Monia, trying to get the public to see Maher as a husband, father, and professional instead of a faceless, dehumanized terror suspect.

The New York Times quoted Saloojee highlighting the same thing—Maher's removal from the United States was a breach of Canadian sovereignty. Saloojee also emphasized that Maher was at risk of torture because he had left Syria as a teenager and therefore hadn't fulfilled his military service. The article noted that, in the past, Canada had filed formal diplomatic notes to protest how its citizens were caught up in terrorism investigations and that, this time, Canada had not filed such a protest.[3]

9:30 A.M., Wednesday, October 16, 2002
Foreign Intelligence Division boardroom,
DFAIT headquarters, Ottawa

GAR PARDY, the director general of DFAIT's Consular Affairs Bureau, was angry and wanted answers about Maher Arar from the RCMP and CSIS. He'd called a meeting and made sure the right people were there. Wayne Pilgrim from RCMP headquarters attended, along with Richard Roy, the RCMP's liaison officer to DFAIT. Someone from CSIS was there also. Scott Heatherington, Don Saunders, and Jonathan Solomon from DFAIT's intelligence division were there. Nancy Collins from the consular division came with Pardy.

Pardy wasn't the only one who was upset. He says Bill Graham, the minister of Foreign Affairs, was "livid."[4] He had raised Maher's case over lunch with U.S. ambassador Paul Cellucci the day before. Cellucci had told Graham that the information that had landed Maher on an American watch list had come from Canada.[5] The American ambassador, it seemed, knew more about what was going on in Canada than the minister did. And journalists were calling Foreign Affairs asking why they were getting more information from the Americans than Canada.

Pardy, chairing the meeting, opened by saying that neither Syria nor Jordan would confirm it had Maher in custody. He noted that it had taken three months to get confirmation they had held Ahmad El Maati. Now, he said, he wanted to know what the RCMP's interest was in Maher Arar.

The RCMP had an interest in Maher but he wasn't the primary focus of RCMP investigations, Pilgrim replied. Instead, it was Maher's association with Abdullah Almalki and Ahmad El Maati that had sparked the RCMP's interest in him.[6] "That was a surprising element," Pardy says. "We'd had no communications with the RCMP or CSIS until this moment."[7] Now he knew that all three men were linked in some way, and all were detained in relation to a Canadian investigation.

"The tone of the meeting was more formal than usual," recalls Pardy. "Neither the RCMP nor CSIS would provide details on why Maher was a person of interest or confirm why the American ambassador would say that Canadian security officials knew why the Americans had acted as they did."[8]

Pardy left the meeting frustrated. He sat down to write a list of questions for Pilgrim. He wanted to know what Canadian investigators had told American officials about Maher, how the Americans had become interested in him, and whether the Americans had approached them about his removal. He also wanted to know whether there was any basis for considering Maher a threat. Pilgrim promised to provide answers by the end of the day.

Later that day, the U.S. ambassador gave a keynote address at a business luncheon in Toronto. A reporter asked him why the United States had sent a Canadian citizen to Syria. "I think you may want to check with your local people on that," the ambassador said.

Pardy didn't get the answers from Pilgrim until 1 P.M. on October 18. In the letter, Pilgrim noted that the RCMP had openly shared information with the Americans, which is how they'd learned about Maher. But, he emphasized, this didn't rule out the possibility that the Americans had their own information. The Americans had asked whether the RCMP could refuse Maher's entry to Canada, and the RCMP had said no, because he is a Canadian citizen. Finally, Pilgrim stated, the RCMP had no information concerning any threat posed by Maher Arar.[9] The letter didn't reveal the extent of the information sharing between the two countries. Nor did it disclose that the RCMP had given the United States information that labelled Maher and his wife, Monia, as "Islamic Extremist individuals suspected of being linked to the Al Qaeda terrorist movement."[10]

On the same day the *Toronto Star* ran a story saying Cellucci had made it clear to Foreign Affairs Minister Bill Graham that "Arar was known to Canadian police."[11] An "American diplomatic source, speaking on condition of anonymity," pointed out that Canada hadn't formally protested Maher's removal, suggesting "the Canadian reaction has been muted for a reason and that is because Canadian police are fully aware of the case against Arar."

Early morning, Tuesday, October 22, 2002
Canadian Embassy, Damascus

"MR. AMBASSADOR, General Khalil will see you in a half hour."[12]

The call to Canada's ambassador to Syria, Franco Pillarella, came from his contact in the Syrian Ministry of Foreign Affairs early Tuesday morning.

The Syrians had confirmed on Monday that they were detaining Maher. Given how uncooperative the Syrians had been in Ahmad and Abdullah's cases, Pardy hadn't been entirely optimistic that this would ever happen. Pillarella had met with Syrian deputy Foreign minister Suleiman Haddad on October 20 to raise both Maher and Abdullah's cases. On October 21, Haddad confirmed that Maher was in Syrian custody and that he would arrange for Pillarella to meet with General Hassan Khalil, the head of the Syrian Military Intelligence, to discuss consular access. "In a case that had many surprises, this was one of the better ones," Pardy says.[13] What Haddad had to say about Abdullah has never been revealed in public.

This would be Pillarella's second meeting with General Khalil at Far' Falastin. The procedure for getting to the facility was like something out of a spy movie. Pillarella's driver was instructed to drive to a designated rendezvous point. Cars were switched. Then an unidentified official from the Syrian Military Intelligence led the way.

They drove up to the walled security compound with watchtowers on each corner, past the guards armed with machine guns, and through the black metal sliding gate with the sign saying, in

English, "No Photography." Then they wound through the maze
of concrete buildings in the compound to the one housing Khalil's
quarters. The ambassador was shown into a living room. There
was a dining room, too, with a table and chairs for entertaining.[14]
Pillarella says he never asked if he was at Far' Falastin. It isn't
publicly known if he'd been there before and already knew.

The meeting lasted forty-five minutes. In addition to General
Khalil, Colonel Majed Saleh, another high-ranking Syrian
Military Intelligence official, was there. Khalil told Pillarella that
Maher "had appeared at the Jordan/Syria border yesterday
without warning, escorted by Jordanian officials who handed
him over."[15] Pillarella asked whether the Americans hadn't
warned the Syrians that Maher would be coming. It has never
been publicly revealed how the general replied to this question.
Khalil told Pillarella that Maher had already admitted ties to
terrorist organizations and that the Syrians would be continuing
their interrogations. Maher would be allowed to return to
Canada only if it were proven that he wasn't connected to
terrorism, which was unlikely, said Khalil, given his confessions.

As instructed by Pardy, Pillarella raised the issue of media
coverage in Canada, hoping this would provide leverage for
gaining consular access. It worked. Khalil said he would arrange
for Maher to receive a consular visit as early as the next day—as
Pillarella wrote in his report, Khalil said he was doing this
because he "did not wish to mar Canada/Syria relations on the
account of an alleged terrorist."[16]

10 A.M., Wednesday, October 23, 2002
Far' Falastin, Damascus

THE GUARD CAME FOR MAHER in the morning, this time
stopping him in front of the washrooms to shave his beard, then
ordering him to wash his face. He wouldn't say what for. "They
never tell prisoners what is happening or why they are doing

anything, so prisoners never know what will happen next. It's part of the psychological torture," says Maher.

The guard escorted Maher to a nearby building where Colonel Salloum was waiting for him, along with four or five other men. "They all seemed nervous and agitated," Maher recalls.

"Someone from the Canadian Embassy is here to see you," Salloum said. He pointed his finger at Maher. "Don't say anything about what happened."

Salloum led Maher into his office. An older man, short, pale, and bald, with glasses, stood up and shook Maher's hand, introducing himself as Leo Martel, the Canadian consul. Salloum directed Maher to sit in a chair, several feet from Martel. Two other Syrian officials were in the room, an interpreter and a note-taker. The interpreter was Colonel Saleh, the man who'd been at the meeting with Pillarella. He'd driven with Martel to Far' Falastin, warning him not to ask unpleasant questions.[17] Coffee was served to everyone, including Maher.

"How long have you been here?" Martel asked Maher. Saleh translated the question into Arabic. Maher started to answer in English but Salloum stopped him. Maher looked at Martel, trying to indicate with his eyes that he wasn't being treated well and couldn't speak freely. "I could not say anything about the torture. I thought if I did, I would not get any more visits, or I might be beaten again."

In Arabic, he told Martel he had been detained in the United States for two weeks before being put on a private plane to Jordan. Saleh translated. Martel asked why Maher had been brought to Jordan. Maher responded that there had been some last-minute problems—referring to the conversation he had overheard on the airplane about Syria not taking him—and the United States had chosen Jordan. Martel asked why. Salloum instructed Maher not to answer that question. "After a few tries, I was able to say I had only been in Jordan for a couple of hours before being taken to the Syrian border."

Maher remembers Martel saying that Maher's dual citizenship was complicating matters. Martel referred to a DFAIT publication warning that dual citizens travel at their own risk. "This was shocking," Maher says. "I did not end up in Syria in a natural way."

Maher, crying now, asked about Monia and the children. They were still in Tunis, Martel told him, and promised to convey Maher's message that he was very concerned about them. Was there anything the Canadian Embassy could bring him? Martel asked. Salloum stepped in again now, instructing Maher in Arabic how to answer the question. Maher turned to Martel: "I am Syrian and I obey the law of Syria," Martel's report would later describe Maher as saying. "I am proud of my country of origin and I am also proud of Canada, my country of adoption. I have been respected by my Syrian brothers and I am happy to have come back to Syria. The authorities have not exercised any pressure on me. You can see I feel well. Anything I ask for I receive."[18]

Martel told Maher that the Canadian media was very interested in his case. "The newspapers say he is being tortured, but look at him. He can stand up," Salloum said. Maher did has he was told and stood up. "They were not stupid to do that. I was not beaten on the soles of my feet. It was their way to show I was not tortured. Clearly they had beaten me in areas that were hard to detect." It had been more than ten days since he'd been whipped with the cable, but Maher remembers that his wrists were still bruised. Martel later said he hadn't noticed.

Salloum stood up, signalling that the meeting was over. The visit had lasted only ten minutes. Martel asked Maher to thank the Syrians for allowing the visit, and again Maher did as he was told. Maher thought that because of the visit, it might take two, maybe three weeks, but he'd be released.

Martel was right about the media. Maher's story had been big news for almost two weeks. A DFAIT spokesperson had told journalists what the RCMP had told DFAIT, that there was no evidence of Maher being linked to al-Qaeda.[19] Amnesty

International had issued an Urgent Action about Maher's case the same day Syria confirmed it was holding him. NDP leader Alexa McDonough had spoken out too, calling on the government to do more.[20]

On the same day as Maher's first consular visit, the *Ottawa Citizen* ran the first story linking the RCMP to Maher's detention. Monia had told journalist Mike Trickey that she thought Maher's problems had started with the RCMP. She described the January 2002 visit to their home by Corporal Randy Buffam and said she thought the RCMP may have "betrayed" Maher by passing information to the United States.[21] Trickey called Buffam looking for more information, but Buffam "refused to discuss the case."[22]

10:30 A.M., Tuesday, October 29, 2002
Far' Falastin, Damascus

MAHER GOT A SECOND CONSULAR VISIT six days after the first. Salloum gave Maher instructions before the meeting: "The consul is here again. Don't talk about the beatings. Don't tell him you are innocent. Don't talk about information you've given [us]. Show him you are happy and don't cry. You are a brave man."

The second meeting went much like the first: Ambassador Martel would ask a question in English, Colonel Saleh would translate it into Arabic, then Maher was expected to answer in Arabic. Salloum watched Maher while the note-taker wrote everything down. Martel handed Maher a letter from Monia. Maher broke down as he read it. After he regained his composure, he dictated a reply for Monia in Arabic. Saleh translated it into English, and Martel wrote it down: "My family is all my life. They are everything. Thank my wife for sending me the letter. I feel very proud of her.... She knows me best. By God's will I will be released because she knows me best. I will be released soon because I am innocent and she knows this. I would be happy if she could keep me informed on her situation as much as she can. I am in good health. Salaam to everyone."

Martel asked Maher how he was faring. Salloum answered for him, saying, "You can see he is well."

When Maher asked that the Canadian prime minister intervene, Martel said that it would be difficult because of Maher's dual citizenship.

Martel's notes describe the meeting as lasting half an hour, but Maher says that the visits were never longer than ten minutes. "The Syrians would never let a visit last for thirty minutes. Never," Maher says.

A couple of days later, Maher was back upstairs, being asked to sign and place his thumbprint on a handwritten document. He was not permitted to read it. Another document, this one about three pages long, contained questions, Maher recalls: "Who are your friends? How long have you been out of the country?" The Syrians wrote down the answers themselves, and Maher couldn't see what they wrote. On the last page, however, Maher was forced to write that he had been to Afghanistan.

Maher had become "number two." He was locked in the cell next to Abdullah's. He doesn't remember if the guards explicitly warned him to be quiet. "They don't have to tell you. You hear one guy being taken out and beaten and you understand what that means."

Maher doesn't remember when he first heard the other prisoners whispering to each other. "On the first day, or first two days, I heard someone reading the Qur'an, in a very faint voice." It was a sign there were other humans around him. "The first four or five days for me was about survival. I couldn't think of anything else. I started feeling a little bit safer after the consular visits. Maybe three weeks after I got there, I started talking with the others." He doesn't remember who spoke to him first. "I think everyone tried, but I didn't answer."

When Abdullah first whispered to Maher, he didn't know whether to believe it was really Abdullah. "I suspected everything about everyone at the beginning. I couldn't see anyone's faces. I didn't trust anyone. Is this really him? Eventually I figured it out through questions only he could ask."

The others helped orient Maher, giving him tips on how to survive. But the most important aspect of the whispering was that it helped the prisoners survive psychologically, Maher says, by boosting each other's morale. "The good thing is none of us was in a deep depression at the same time. The people who were in good shape would help the people in bad shape." The hushed exchanges were so risky that they were brief and rare.

Like the others, Maher didn't find out until about six weeks after arriving at Far' Falastin that he might be locked in the grave for a long time.

Sunday, November 3, 2002
Office of General Hassan Khalil, Far' Falastin, Damascus

AMBASSADOR PILLARELLA met with General Khalil again on November 3, the day before Pillarella was booked to fly to Ottawa. They talked for an hour, then Pillarella returned to the embassy, wrote up his report, and emailed it to DFAIT's Foreign Intelligence Division in Ottawa. Scott Heatherington, the head of the division, immediately sent it on to Pilgrim at RCMP headquarters and Cabana at A-O Canada, and to CSIS the next day.

Pillarella's report, marked "secret," said that Khalil was "absolutely positive" that Maher was linked to al-Qaeda and that Maher "had been recruited with the specific purpose of recruiting others in Canada." Further, according to the report, Khalil said that Maher had "clearly identified" Ahmad and Abdullah as his "sleeper cell" members and had admitted to training in Afghanistan. Pillarella reported that he had asked Khalil whether he could get a summary of "information obtained so far from Arar" to take to Canada, and Khalil had promised to get it to him before he left. "But Khalil promised much more,"

Pillarella wrote, including that he would allow a CSIS representative to come to Syria to review information "obtained so far
from Arar" and that officials "would be welcome to attend the
interrogation sessions," a privilege Khalil emphasized had not
been granted, despite repeated requests, to the Americans,
Germans, and the French.[23] Nowhere in his report did Pillarella
indicate that Maher's "admissions" were likely the product of
torture. Pillarella raised Abdullah's case too, saying that Khalil
now "seemed disposed to accept that he could meet with a
Canadian official." But Pillarella wasn't talking about a consular
official here who would be looking into Abdullah's health and
well-being. Instead, Pillarella's report shows that he'd raised this
for the RCMP, which had asked to have direct access to
Abdullah. Pillarella warned that Khalil preferred to deal with
other intelligence agents, not police officers. Khalil's invitation
was for CSIS, not the RCMP.[24]

The evening before Pillarella left for Canada, a report from
General Khalil was delivered to the ambassador's residence in
Damascus.[25] But Khalil hadn't sent over the documents Maher
was forced to sign and thumbprint, it seems. Instead, his report
was a summary of Maher's supposed confession. Back in Ottawa,
Pillarella turned over Khalil's report to DFAIT's intelligence
division, which passed it on to CSIS for translation. The one-
page, three-paragraph document was translated on November 7
and shared with CSIS, the RCMP, and the consular division. The
Foreign Affairs officials who passed on the "confession" information didn't conduct any kind of analysis of its reliability or
attach a note saying it was likely the product of torture.[26] The
result was that the RCMP became even more suspicious about
Maher after reading the summary of his so-called confession.[27]

Pillarella, who refused to assume or conclude that Maher had
been tortured, claims he accepted the document from General
Khalil because he thought it would help to know what evidence
the Syrians had against Maher.[28] Asked why he thought his
colleagues then shared it with CSIS and the RCMP, Pillarella said

it was shared so they could help Maher too, by disproving or verifying the information.[29] The RCMP and CSIS had a very different view. Indeed, Cabana would later say that he didn't think that either DFAIT or Pillarella were under "any illusion" that the RCMP would use the information to help Maher.[30]

It isn't clear how Pillarella thought his conversation with Khalil would hurt, or help, Abdullah, still in the basement of Far' Falastin in the cell next to Maher's, or Ahmad, who was still in Egyptian detention.[31]

4:15 P.M., Wednesday, November 6, 2002
DFAIT headquarters, Ottawa

AMBASSADOR PILLARELLA was due to brief interested parties on what the Syrian general had told him about Maher, with the notable exception of officials from the consular division, who weren't invited. Pillarella had briefed Gar Pardy, who was overseas in Beirut at the time, about his meeting with Khalil but hadn't informed him of this meeting. Unlike the consular division, the RCMP was well represented at the meeting: Inspector Cabana, the head of A-O Canada, and Chief Superintendent Couture and Superintendent Pilgrim from RCMP headquarters were in attendance. Inspector Roy, the RCMP's liaison officer to DFAIT, was also present. Representatives from the counterterrorism branch at CSIS were there, as were Scott Heatherington, Jonathan Solomon, and possibly others from DFAIT's intelligence division.

Pillarella's summary described the Syrians as very receptive, and although they'd acknowledged that Maher is a Canadian citizen, he would not be sent back to Canada soon. Khalil had invited the Canadian intelligence officials to observe interrogations, though he hadn't guaranteed a direct interview. Clearly, the Syrians were hoping to improve their image and build better relations with Canada.[32]

The CSIS officials at the meeting noted that the information that he had trained in Afghanistan, even if true, wasn't damning evidence against Maher. They wanted more information about what the Syrians had learned from Maher, and from Ahmad and Abdullah.[33] And they wanted to take Khalil up on his offer and send a delegation to Syria.

The DFAIT officials said they were happy to see CSIS agents go. The RCMP warned that CSIS representatives had better not interview Maher directly, as it could "taint any possible future evidence" in their cases against Abdullah and Ahmad.[34] No one mentioned the possibility that the information had been obtained using torture. Nor, it seems, did they explore how a CSIS trip to Syria might make matters worse for Maher or Abdullah by signalling to the Syrians that their interrogations were considered useful to Canadian agencies.

Not much later, CSIS's deputy director, Jack Hooper, "strongly supported" the request to go to Syria and approved it.[35]

Wednesday, November 6, 2002
Far' Falastin, Damascus

MEANWHILE, IN DAMASCUS, November 6 was the first day of Ramadan, and the first day Abdullah's cousin had been able to get permission to visit Abdullah since July. Abdullah had been living in the dark for more than six months. His cousin took one look at how thin Abdullah was and turned to the prison manager. "Are you not feeding him?"

Abdullah asked after his family. His parents were in Canada, his cousin said; Khuzaimah and the children were still in Malaysia.

"How are you doing?" Abdullah's cousin asked.

"I have been tortured, a lot."

The prison manager jumped up immediately. "This talk is off limits. This visit is over!" he exclaimed.

Abdullah's cousin did his best to calm the prison manager. He told him that he'd been shown Abdullah's file. He already knew. Abdullah thinks the Syrians showed his family the file to try to convince them his was an international issue rather than a domestic one.

When Abdullah asked his cousin for blankets and clothing, the prison manager interrupted. "We provide him with all he needs," he said.

"Send them to me anyway, please," Abdullah said as he was led out of the office, "and tell my family to pray for me, and not to worry."

FOURTEEN

"Your Guys Knew"

Mid- to late November 2002
Second Cup coffee shop, Bayview Avenue, Toronto

It appears CSIS agents may have been thinking about travelling to meet with Ahmad's interrogators, too. It had been one year since Ahmad's arrest in Syria and very little progress had been made on his case. Heeding the advice of the Canadian consular division, Ahmad's family had stayed away from the media. Myra Pastyr-Lupul, the case management officer for the Middle East region at DFAIT, had told Ahmad's father, Badr, on more than one occasion that the family should keep quiet and let diplomatic efforts play out. Canada has a better relationship with Egypt than with Syria, she'd said. Talking to the media might do more harm than good.

Badr thinks that it was in November that Adrian White from CSIS, the same agent Badr had spoken with the previous December, requested another meeting. Badr arrived at the Second Cup for the meeting to find White and another agent who would give only his first name, "Steve." The CSIS agents wanted to know if Ahmad had somewhere to stay in Egypt. "Yes, of course," Badr told them. "My ex-wife has a house in Cairo where Ahmad can stay, and we have other relatives there. His sister is there, and I have family there."

White told Badr that CSIS agents might be travelling to Egypt and that they would work to persuade the Egyptian authorities to release Ahmad. There was a catch though: They wanted Ahmad to promise to stay in Egypt rather than return to Canada. When Badr asked if Ahmad would have to stay in Egypt indefinitely, they didn't answer. Badr remembers they seemed concerned about Ahmad's story getting into the news. "I told them I wasn't going to risk hurting him by talking to reporters," Badr says. "I was still thinking [that not talking to the media] was the best thing to do."

10:30 A.M., Tuesday, November 12, 2002
Far' Falastin, Damascus

IT HAD BEEN MORE THAN TWO WEEKS since Maher's last consular visit and he'd started to worry that Martel wasn't coming back.

It was Ramadan now, and Maher, like the others, was fasting from what they guessed was dawn until sundown. At least he could pray more easily than the others. "I could pray because the door of my cell would only open if I pushed it from the inside, unlike the other cells. Others would be beaten if the guards opened the door and caught them praying. But I could pray without being caught," Maher says.

Over the first days and weeks at Far' Falastin, Maher had been forced to face the reality of his surroundings. He'd never get used to the horrors of the grave, he says. "I don't know if *cell* is the right word for the place. I would never have imagined in my life that a place like this exists." Maher gradually learned the routine. He learned that he would be let out to use the washroom three times a day. He learned that he'd be ignored, or screamed at, if he asked to be let out to use the washroom at any other time. He learned how to use the plastic bottles in his cell: One he took with him to the washroom to fill with water for drinking and washing before praying, and the other was for urinating in. He'd been allowed to take with him into the cell his carry-on bag, which he used as a pillow. He had long ago eaten the Tunisian pastries in them, and now used one of the empty pastry tins for prayer water. He would come to accept, over time, that he would have to use the other tin for his own excrement, especially when he had diarrhea. He had a plastic container for food and had to get used to eating with his hands.

He learned to endure the weekly beard shaving. This was meant to be humiliating and an insult to his faith. He learned that every Friday the prisoners had a few extra minutes to wash. The hot water in the washroom never worked while he was there. He found the filth in the washrooms and the cell particularly hard to take. Maher says he grew up in a culture of cleanliness. His hair, usually meticulously combed, grew long and straggly. "I [must] have looked like a monster," he says. Maher is tall and his hair often brushed against the filth on the washroom ceiling.

But the hardest thing to bear in the cells was the sound of prisoners being tortured, crying out to Allah, and begging for the torture to stop. The torture was often conducted directly overhead the prisoners' cells. They could tell by the sound which techniques were being used. "Above the cells ... in [the] washroom, they used to also torture people in the water," Maher remembers. "There were openings in the floor that let the voices in. It was so close. When we heard that, for three or four days, we all stopped talking. That's how powerful it is. People would stop talking."

Martel finally returned to see Maher on November 12. Once again, Maher was warned not to say anything before being escorted into the office. Martel handed Maher another letter from Monia, in which she wrote that she and the children would be travelling back to Canada. In tears, Maher dictated a response for Monia, saying he was glad she was returning to Canada and asking her to keep sending letters. "With God's will we will be reunited," he ended.

Martel had brought Canadian newspapers and magazines for Maher, but the Syrians said they would need to read them first. When Maher asked again whether the Canadian prime minister was going to intervene on his behalf, Martel said

Canada was doing all it could but reminded Maher of his dual citizenship. Martel would later explain that he hadn't wanted to give Maher "false hope."[1] The visit was over in less than ten minutes. Maher wondered why there had been such a delay between visits. He was losing what little hope he had left.

If only he could have seen the media coverage in Canada. Much of it had been sympathetic. Monia's unwavering defence of her husband's innocence and her outrage that the United States would treat a Canadian citizen this way had stuck a chord with many Canadians already uneasy about President Bush's so-called war on terror. Maher's colleagues at The MathWorks had been defending him, too, describing him as a brilliant and serious engineer.[2]

For the RCMP, however, the media coverage must have been bad news. Monia, journalists, and Canadian citizens in general were asking why the United States had abducted Maher and shipped him to Syria. U.S. ambassador Cellucci's public comments had fuelled speculation about Canada's role. Worse yet, Monia was due to arrive back in Canada on November 14. She'd been an effective voice on the phone from Tunisia; imagine how effective she was going to be in person.

Monia wasn't the only one arriving in Canada on the fourteenth. U.S. secretary of state Colin Powell was set to make his first official visit to Canada that same day and was scheduled to meet with Minister Graham. It was just before this visit that the media coverage started to shift. And it's clear that the shift was carefully orchestrated by officials on both sides of the border.

11:50 A.M., Thursday, November 14, 2002
Ninth-floor dining room, Tower A, DFAIT headquarters

"BY THE WAY, your guys knew what we were doing all along."[3]

That's how Foreign Affairs Minister Bill Graham would later describe what U.S. secretary of state Colin Powell said about Maher's case on his first official visit to Canada. National security issues were high on the agenda. Two days earlier, the Al Jazeera television network had aired a recording of what was purported to be Osama bin Laden's voice threatening a new wave of attacks on American targets. For the first time, the voice on tape named Canada, asking why it and others were aligning themselves with the United States in Afghanistan. The authenticity of this recording would later be challenged.

Graham asked Powell why Canada hadn't been consulted on the decision to send Maher to Syria. Powell encouraged Graham to ask Canadian officials, saying that they'd given their blessing for Maher's removal to Syria. The decision, Powell insisted, was based on information Canada provided.[4]

"Bill, you don't know what's going on, and I do because I've talked to the people that know," Powell said.[5]

Graham wanted specifics: "Okay, if somebody, by a wink or a nod explicitly said something, tell us who it is ... if you've got a name, give us the name."[6] But Powell, despite being well briefed on Maher's and other consular cases,[7] didn't give Graham any names.

It's likely that at least part of the discussion between Powell and Graham referred to Abdullah, Ahmad, and his brother, Amr. Two days before Powell's visit, Robert Mueller, the director of the FBI, issued an alert stating that Amr El Maati was "being sought in connection with possible terrorist threats in the United States."[8] The alert described him as armed and dangerous. When journalists asked what had prompted the alert, FBI spokesperson Paul Bresson referred to the documents bearing Amr's name found a year earlier in the house in Kabul. When asked why it had taken a full year to issue the alert, Bresson would say only that "information continues to pour in and, over time, it becomes more specific, corroborated, and substantiated."[9] Asked about the alert at a news conference the next day, Mueller said simply that "he's an individual we believe has associations with al-Qaeda, and we're looking to find him."[10] Both the CBC and CTV national news broadcast Amr's photograph on their news programs on the eve of Powell's Canadian visit, and the story ran in several newspapers across the country the day he arrived.

While Graham was meeting with Powell, the next day's news story was being generated. Now that the FBI had issued its alert, someone in Ottawa was trying to build suspicion around Maher, first, by publicly linking him to Amr El Maati but also by labelling Abdullah and Ahmad. The unnamed official spoke with Canadian Press journalist Stephen Thorne, who, to his credit, agreed to withhold Abdullah's name after speaking with Abdullah's brother. He did name Ahmad, however.

Referring to what the official source, "who spoke on condition of anonymity," had told him about Abdullah, Thorne wrote that another Canadian man in Syrian detention "is a suspected member of Osama bin Laden's al-Qaida terrorist network" and had "been linked with two other Canadian citizens now in Middle East jails while under investigation for suspected al-Qaida connections." One of those was Maher, he wrote, the other was Amr's brother, "28-year-old Ahmad Al Maati, also known as Ahmad Abou Elmaati [who] is in prison in Egypt."[11] (Thorne's source got Ahmad and Amr's ages wrong by ten years. Ahmad at that time was thirty-eight; Amr thirty-nine.)

That was the first time Ahmad's name had been published and publicly linked to al-Qaeda. Looking back, Thorne says he realizes he was being used to smear the men. "I don't want to leave the impression that I take what I can get. Obviously, we try to get at the truth. That's why I spoke to the family—to get their side of the story. But now, believing that they are innocent, which is the conventional wisdom anyway, I have no doubt I was used. We [the press] are used all the time. That's Ottawa. Everybody uses everybody."[12]

The next leak came just three days later. Headlines in several papers across the country, and on the front page of the *Ottawa Citizen*, declared that Powell had told Graham that the United States had provided the RCMP with evidence that Maher was linked to al-Qaeda. According to the *Ottawa Citizen* article, by reporter Mike Trickey, Foreign Affairs officials had been embarrassed to learn from Powell that the FBI had provided the RCMP with the evidence weeks ago.[13] Although this may have dovetailed very nicely with the previous leak that linked Maher and the others to the FBI alert on Amr, the claim simply wasn't true. First, Powell had emphasized that the information that had led to their decision to remove Maher had come from Canada. And, despite repeated requests by the RCMP, the FBI, even as late as 2005, did not provide the RCMP with any information about Maher. It had been the other way round, and the RCMP just hadn't owned up to it yet. But the unnamed official who had contacted the *Citizen*'s Mike Trickey had repeated the previous week's allegations, again publicly labelling Maher, Ahmad, and Amr as terror suspects linked to al-Qaeda.

Trickey can't remember if the official named Abdullah Almalki too, but either way, he didn't name Abdullah in his article. Interestingly, the official told Trickey that "the unidentified 31-year-old businessman [Abdullah] was apparently arrested on information provided by the RCMP who raided the house he was living in last spring,"[14] something the Canadian government has denied.

The news prompted debate in the House of Commons question period that afternoon. Opposition leader Stephen Harper cornered Deputy Prime Minister John Manley. "While the minister participated in high level consultations to defend a suspected terrorist," Harper said, "it apparently took a trip by the U.S. Secretary of State for the minister to admit what he really knew." It was clear now, Harper continued, that officials had had evidence on Maher's "activities" for weeks.[15]

Manley replied that it was important not to confuse the right to consular support with the issue of "whether there was substantive information that concerned this particular individual in the possession of U.S. officials." "In the former," Manley said, "of course we will intervene in order to ensure that consular rights are respected. In the latter, we will not be prepared to comment."

Calgary MP Diane Ablonzy stepped in to say that the Liberals "were asleep at the switch": "Mr. Speaker, it is time the Liberals told the truth: that their system of screening and security checks is pathetic. Arar was given dual Syrian and Canadian citizenship by the government. It did not pick up on his terrorist links and the U.S. had to clue it in. How is it that the U.S. could uncover this man's background so quickly when the government's screening system failed to find his al-Qaeda links?"

That night and the next day, the media interpreted Manley's comments as a sign that the government was distancing itself from Maher's case. CTV's national television news reported that the Canadian government had suddenly done an about-face and that while Maher was "first portrayed as a victim of U.S. injustice, now he's fingered as an alleged terrorist who slipped through Canadian hands."[16] CBC's *The National* reported that the government's refusal to comment signalled a change in opinion about Maher's innocence.[17]

The next day, MP Stockwell Day raised the case again during question period, accusing Manley of having been evasive the day before about Maher and his possible terrorist ties. Graham, he pointed out, had "proudly announced that there was no reason to deport Mr. Arar," and now there was information that the RCMP "had received warnings about Mr. Arar weeks, perhaps months ago."[18] Graham responded by saying, "We do not discuss in the House specific cases with respect to criminal activity" but that he wanted to assure everyone that the government is "vigilant when it comes both to repressing terrorism and to protecting the rights of Canadian citizens when necessary."[19]

James Bissett, a former ambassador to Yugoslavia, Albania, and Bulgaria, and former head of the Canadian Immigration Service, chimed in with an op-ed in the *Ottawa Citizen*, blasting the media and parliamentarians for their "deplorable" and "righteous sniping at our southern neighbour's sensible efforts to prevent another horrific terrorist onslaught." The moral outrage at what happened to Maher, he argued, was unwarranted, because, after all, he is an alleged terrorist. Bissett also took aim at Maher's dual citizenship. "Dual or multiple citizenship is permitted under Canadian law," he wrote. "Thousands of Canadians frequently travel on two passports, using the one that at any particular time is more convenient. There can be advantages to this arrangement but also disadvantages, as Mr. Arar has found out." Maher, of course, had been travelling on the only passport he'd used since becoming a Canadian citizen—his Canadian one. But that's beside the point. Despite having been the head of Canada's immigration service for five years, Bissett didn't appear to realize that most dictatorial regimes don't allow their citizens to renounce their citizenship. Dual citizenship for Canadians like Maher, Abdullah, and Ahmad is not a choice. Bissett also argued there hadn't been enough information sharing, which was "symptomatic of Canada's present state of denial that the terrorist threat is real,"[20] which was ironic, given how freely information had been shared.

One official, however, did speak out in Maher's defence, telling the *Toronto Star*'s Allan Thompson that Foreign Affairs officials had seen no evidence linking Maher to terrorism, and doubted the United States had either. "We are 99 per cent sure they have nothing on him, we think he's a victim of circumstance," the unnamed source said. "We are ready to go to the wall on this case. Ask yourself, if the U.S. really had something on him, why would they let him leave the country?"[21]

That week, the RCMP appears to have been trying to supply information to appear on the Fox Television network's *America's Most Wanted* a few weeks later, on December 7. On November 21, Corporal Rick Flewelling, the man at RCMP headquarters tasked with overseeing A-O Canada's work, wrote in his personal notes about "Cabana's refusal to supply information" requested by Superintendent Wayne Pilgrim, saying "the delay could have an adverse effect on what takes place with the American T.V. program." In his notes for the next day, he refers specifically to a meeting with RCMP assistant commissioner Proulx, in which they discuss Amr El Maati, and *America's Most Wanted*. The December 7 episode reported that Amr El Maati was an airline pilot who may have "snuck back into the U.S." to work with al-Qaeda sleeper cells. It's not known if the allegation had come from the RCMP.

Monday, November 18, 2002
Abu Za'abal prison, northeast of Cairo

AHMAD EL MAATI WAS STILL LOCKED in the same four-by-six-foot cell at the Abu Za'abal prison and had no way of knowing that he and his brother were in the news. He had now been in detention for more than a year and was just focusing on surviving day to day. The man he and other prisoners believed was an informer was gone. Ahmad had decided to refuse to eat until the man was removed from his cell. "When the guards got angry, I told them the only thing I want is either you take this guy out, or take me out." On the sixth day of his hunger strike the man was removed and Ahmad had the cell to himself.

On November 19, consular officers Stuart Bale and Mira Wassef came to Abu Za'abal for another consular visit. Ahmad told them he thought the release order had been a good sign. Again, Bale pressed Ahmad to agree to meet with an RCMP or CSIS official and, again, Ahmad told him that he would do that only once he was back in Canada. Bale would later report that they made a point of telling the state security official who monitored the visit that they were anticipating media coverage of Ahmad's case.[22] It isn't clear if the RCMP informed Bale about the upcoming *America's Most Wanted* show, or if they were just expecting Ahmad's family to speak out in response to that week's leaks.

In late November, Ahmad was transferred back to Cairo's Istiqbal Tora prison. He had only been there for a few hours when, in the middle of the night, he was pulled out of his cell, handcuffed and blindfolded, and forced to lie, covered, on the floor in the back of a van. Ahmad knew this meant he was being handed over to the State Security Service. "To be hidden like this again wasn't a good sign. I thought this meant I was going to be taken somewhere and tortured."

After a few minutes, Ahmad felt the van drive down a ramp and stop. He guessed he was back at Mabahith Amn al-Dawla al-'Ulya, the State Security Investigations services facility in Nasr City, where he'd been subjected to electric shock months ago. He was taken directly to a cell one row over from where he'd been kept the last time. "I was devastated to be back in this place," Ahmad says, "but this time, when they locked the door, they left the handcuffs in front." This meant less pain and that he could eat and relieve himself with some semblance of human dignity. Although he was blindfolded, he sensed that the facility was less crowded than it had been before. He hadn't seen other prisoners on the floor in the hall as he was led to his cell. And this time, the sound of the electric shock torture and screaming wasn't continuous.

Ahmad recalls the despair he felt at being back at the Mabahith Amn al-Dawla al-'Ulya facility. "My mindset was starting to change. To think in this way just kills you—that there is no end in sight. Like being in a long tunnel, with no light. When you start thinking this way, you are finished. If it wasn't for my faith in Allah, I would have gone crazy, or killed myself."

The next day Ahmad was taken out of his cell for interrogation. He can't remember exactly what the interrogators asked him but thinks the questions were about Canada again and that his interrogators were reviewing past interrogations. "I was expecting to be tortured, but this time there was no physical torture. Just the questions, and the constant fear of being tortured," he says.

Ahmad was kept at the Mabahith Amn al-Dawla al-'Ulya facility for about a week before being transferred back to Istiqbal Tora prison for a couple of days, and then back to Abu Za'abal, where he was put back in the same four-by-six-foot cell he'd left about two weeks earlier.

Monday, November 18, 2002
Ottawa

MONIA'S TRIP HOME WITH THE CHILDREN hadn't been easy. Before she could leave Tunisia she faced questioning by Tunisian officials—it has never been determined whether those questions were asked on behalf of CSIS or the RCMP. And, because the RCMP had requested a border lookout in her name, she and the children were pulled aside for secondary inspection when they arrived at the airport in Montreal. Customs officers photocopied their passport information, airline ticket stubs, and Monia's customs declaration information.

Over the weekend Monia had read the negative reports that had run in the newspapers that week. Then, on Monday morning, she saw the front-page article in the *Ottawa Citizen* about the Powell-Graham meeting. The leaks had very successfully diverted attention from questions about what role Canadian agencies may have played in Maher's detention to questions about Maher's innocence. But if they had hoped to deter Monia, it didn't work. That day she did an interview with Jacques Bourbeau, Global TV's Ottawa bureau chief, on *Global National*. The next morning she appeared on CTV's *Canada AM* before going to her first face-to-face meeting with Gar Pardy. What she remembers most about that meeting is that Pardy assured her that DFAIT had no evidence linking Maher to terrorism. Monia shared that assurance with a CBC radio reporter the next day, who then contacted DFAIT's communication branch. A flurry of emails warned the reporter that it should be clarified that Pardy's statement wasn't made on behalf of DFAIT as a whole, but consular affairs only. Clearly, the minister's office was worried. Gar Pardy clarified that what he said to Monia was that "we, the Consular Affairs Bureau, have no information linking her husband with terrorist organizations."[23]

Global's Jacques Bourbeau remembers being impressed by how "articulate" and "very logical" Monia was when he first met her. "There was just something about her situation and the way she was reacting to it, you just couldn't help but feel for the woman. I remember talking to my wife about it, saying, 'Can you imagine, your husband has disappeared, and no one will tell you anything?'"[24] He was also impressed by her argument about Canadian civil liberties and how her husband had been denied due process: "'Civilized governments don't do this,' she said. 'They don't kidnap somebody in the middle of the night and not tell the family for a couple of weeks. If my husband is guilty of anything then he should be brought to Canada.' For me, especially in the early days, that was the important issue. It wasn't about guilt or innocence."

Bourbeau said he realized early on that when it came to this story, he had to be skeptical of the government, not just of Maher and Monia. "I had discussions with journalists over time, and they really fixated on 'Is he a terrorist?' There was a lot of skepticism among my colleagues, [they thought] that he was. In my view, it was immaterial to the story. Especially when you look at Syria's human rights record, it was pretty evident what was happening to him. You have to ask what were the procedures that led to this guy rotting in a Syrian jail. That's what Monia put forward."[25]

FIFTEEN

"Dark Days"

IT MUST HAVE BEEN A NICE WAY for the A-O Canada team to end the day—with applause for their work from the RCMP's senior management. The accolades came from Deputy Commissioner Garry Loeppky; Assistant Commissioner Richard Proulx; Assistant Criminal Operations (CROPS) Officer for "A" Division, Inspector Garry Clement; and CSIS's deputy director, Jack Hooper, in response to A-O Canada's PowerPoint presentation on investigations into Ahmad, Abdullah, and Maher, and the alleged plot to attack the U.S. Embassy or the Parliament Buildings in Ottawa—the one that Ahmad had "confessed" to under torture.[1] It was much like the one they'd given the Americans back in May. All three men were now in detention in Syria and Egypt. Abdullah had been living in the underground cell at Far' Falastin for six months, without any consular access or even a formal acknowledgment by the Syrians that he was there. The RCMP's liaison officer in Rome had already indicated that, in his opinion, Abdullah would never be returning to Canada.[2] Pillarella had updated A-O Canada on Maher's situation, and although Maher was getting consular visits and there was media attention on his case, A-O Canada believed that because he'd "confessed" to links with al-Qaeda, it was unlikely that he'd be returning to Canada either.[3] Ahmad had been in detention for a full year now; there was no end in sight when it came to his incarceration, either.

Hence the applause. It was A-O Canada's moment to shine. Both of the main targets of A-O Canada's investigation were in detention. And now Maher was, too. Although he had only been of peripheral interest in the past, A-O Canada was more interested in Maher now because of what the Americans had done. Given that it was A-O Canada's information that had been behind the American decision, the irony is both tragic and absurd.[4]

Although the November 2 meeting had gone well, tensions between RCMP headquarters and A-O Canada were simmering. Headquarters wanted better briefings from A-O Canada, and more control over the project. Corporal Rick Flewelling had been brought in as file coordinator in June 2002 to ensure that information sharing was carried out in line with pre-9/11 policies. The problem with that, of course, is that the A-O Canada team believed that they were just following orders. They had been told it was an "open book investigation" and that "caveats were down."[5] Justice O'Connor would later conclude in his report of the Arar Inquiry that senior management was to blame for the way information was shared with the Americans. Senior management's direction to investigators had been "unclear and misleading" after 9/11.[6] He singled out Assistant Commissioner Proulx in particular, saying that it had been his responsibility to ensure that the limits to which A-O Canada could share information with other agencies be clearly set out in writing. The RCMP may have been under pressure after 9/11, but that was no excuse, he said, for the lack of direction from senior officers. O'Connor stressed that A-O Canada seriously misunderstood how information should be shared with the United States, and that, he concluded, played an important role in what unfolded for Maher.[7] It likely played an important role in what happened to Ahmad and Abdullah as well.

Headquarters wasn't happy with how much direct interaction there was between A-O Canada and American agencies either, and wanted it to stop, or at least be closely supervised. Flewelling was soon tasked with overseeing that, too. For Cabana, who was used to less-centralized criminal investigations, this was all about unnecessary interference in A-O Canada's work. By November, he was so frustrated he was talking about leaving the project and suggested it be incorporated into "A" Division's Integrated National Security Enforcement Team. By early 2003 Cabana had left the project, and Inspector Warren Coons took over as officer in charge of A-O Canada. The last straw for Cabana seems to have been when RCMP headquarters refused to let A-O Canada team members travel to the U.S. detention centre at Guantánamo to interrogate detainees—likely including the only Canadian there, the son of Ahmed Said Khadr, Omar Khadr, who'd been just fifteen when captured by American forces in Afghanistan in July 2002. Later, *Toronto Star* reporter Michelle Shephard revealed that it was CSIS and Jim Gould of DFAIT's Foreign Intelligence Division who went to Guantánamo that February to interrogate the then sixteen-year-old detainee.[8]

Saturday, November 23, 2002
Office of General Khalil, Far' Falastin, Damascus

THE CSIS DELEGATION had arrived in Damascus on Wednesday. Their meetings with the Syrian Military Intelligence (SMI) began on Saturday. The first was with General Khalil and four other SMI officials. CSIS says that discussion focused on general issues such as the war on terrorism, security politics, and the Middle East.[9] The Canadians then met with two SMI officials who provided detailed briefings on information they'd obtained from Ahmad, Abdullah, and Maher. Maher's case was discussed first, for an hour and a half, the process apparently hindered by interpretation. According to CSIS, the Syrians didn't view Maher's case as a major one, "and seemed to look upon the matter as more of a nuisance than anything else."[10]

Syrian deputy minister Haddad later told Pillarella that the CSIS delegation had left the Syrians with the clear impression that CSIS didn't want Maher back in Canada. The same would be said by Syrian ambassador Arnous to DFAIT officials in Ottawa and in subsequent meetings with other Canadian officials. CSIS later denied it said anything that would have left this impression.[11] What impression, one wonders, might CSIS have left about Abdullah?

Jack Hooper, the deputy director of CSIS, says the purpose of the meeting when it came to Maher's case was to "elicit information," not "exchange information."[12] What isn't publicly known, however, is what information was elicited or exchanged about Ahmad or Abdullah, or whether CSIS officials continued their meetings with the SMI the next morning.

Either way, something prompted a new round of questions for Abdullah early the next afternoon. An interrogator referred to handwritten papers and questioned him about Ahmed Said Khadr. Abdullah told the interrogator what he had told those before him: Khadr had been Human Concern International's regional director in Afghanistan and Pakistan when Abdullah had volunteered for the organization in the early 1990s. He repeated that he hadn't liked the way Khadr had managed the relief and reconstruction projects he worked on, which was one of the reasons he and his wife had returned home to Canada earlier than planned.

Interrogators, including Abdallah and Abu Elnour, also had new and detailed information about Ibrahym Adam and his family—the names of his relatives and details about relationships that even people close to the family wouldn't know.

Four days later, on November 28, Abdullah was taken up to the interrogation floor again. Based on the new questions they asked, Abdullah thinks Salloum and Abu Elnour had a new report from Canada. They asked Abdullah for detailed information about how his import/export business operated—step-by-step details starting from when a customer requested a price quote to when the product was delivered. They wanted to know how Abdullah's company shipped from one country to another without the goods passing through Canada. The Syrians appeared convinced that this was illegal. Abdullah explained it wasn't illegal, that corporations big and small operated this way, and that he always filed the necessary documents.

"You are lying. We received this information from the Canadian consul," Abu Elnour yelled at him. "It was very tense, and they were threatening to torture me," Abdullah recalls. Later he wondered whether the "consul" was Martel, the same consul who Maher had told him about after the visit just two days earlier. "I told them that the consul couldn't know very much about international trade if he was making these allegations. I suggested they get a book on exporting from Canada, which would demonstrate I was telling the truth."

Then the interrogators made a new allegation: Serial numbers on equipment that had been found in Afghanistan had provided "proof" that the equipment had come from Abdullah's company. "I stressed again that I never sold equipment to anyone in Afghanistan, and I asked them to describe the equipment," says Abdullah. "They said they didn't know that information. They didn't have the actual serial numbers either. I told them, 'Ask the Canadian government for the details so I could see whether I sold the equipment and to who.' I don't know if they ever did."

The new report also had questions about telephone calls he'd made in Canada. What internet café had he used in Ottawa? Could he list the internet cafés he knew? Abdullah said he didn't use internet cafés, as he had internet access at home.[13]

Abdullah couldn't have known then that in the RCMP's application for the search warrants executed in January 2002, Corporal Randy Walsh, drawing on his experience with drug traffickers, had described Abdullah's use of a computer at a Chapters bookstore as "suspicious."[14] "I didn't remember during the interrogation that I had used a terminal at Chapters, but I think I told them I used the library once when my connection at home was down," Abdullah says now. It had never occurred to him that this would be considered suspicious to anyone.

"When I told them that they should ask the Canadians for proof of what they were claiming about me, they told me I wasn't supposed to know the report had come from Canada, and I told them, 'It is obvious from the questions that this report comes from Canada.'"

The next questions made very little sense. The report appears to have alleged that Abdullah had recently shipped something to terrorists by sea, and that this shipment would provide proof of his connection to terrorism. "I told them, 'I've been in detention for seven months now. How could I ship anything? If the report says that this will be their proof, it means they have no proof and I must be innocent.'" Abdullah sensed that the Syrian interrogators were beginning to question the credibility of the Canadians' allegations against him.

The rounds of interrogations stretched on into December. At one point, Abdullah saw that the cover of the report read, in Arabic, "Meeting with Canadian delegation on November 24, 2002." Abdullah remembers a comment one of the interrogators made to him at the end of this round of questions: "We were the first people who faced terrorism in the '80s. We fought it with iron and fire, and everyone in the West criticized us. But now when they are faced with terrorism, they come to us for help."

Thursday, November 28, 2002
Foreign Intelligence Division boardroom,
DFAIT headquarters, Ottawa

GAR PARDY DIDN'T LEARN about the CSIS trip to Syria until after the agents returned. The delegation debriefed officials from Foreign Affairs on November 28, and this time, they invited Pardy. He was "floored," he says, that there hadn't been any consultation with the consular division before the trip.[15] It was at this meeting that a member of the CSIS delegation said he didn't believe Maher had been tortured. He wasn't an expert on torture, he admitted, but if Maher had been tortured, "there would have been a lot more damning information."[16]

This is indicative of a deeply disturbing mindset on the part of CSIS, according to Alex Neve, the secretary general of Amnesty International Canada: That CSIS seems to think that torture serves a purpose and is effective is "morally repugnant, in total contravention of international legal standards and quite simply wrong-headed," Neve says. "People will break under torture and will say anything about anyone or any topic, simply to bring the torture to an end. Or people will withstand torture and fail to divulge information because they know nothing, or refuse to divulge information in defiance."[17]

CSIS reported that the Syrians were accusing Maher of being a member of the Muslim Brotherhood and would likely charge him, though the death penalty wasn't likely. CSIS officials also said that it was unlikely that Maher would be released soon.[18] Maher notes that he was never questioned once about the Muslim Brotherhood in Syria. "It's not something they ever mentioned to me," he says. Looking back now, Maher wonders whether the allegation originated with CSIS—it would have helped ease pressure for his release if this were seen as an internal issue to Syria. There is no indication that the Syrians ever said publicly, or in any documented meetings with Canadian officials, that they believed Maher was linked to the Muslim Brotherhood.

Morning, Tuesday, November 26, 2002
Far' Falastin, Damascus

THE CANADIAN CONSUL, LEO MARTEL, had been to visit Maher on Tuesday. This time, before entering the office, Maher told Salloum that he needed to ask Martel for a sleeping bag and clothes. He was freezing, he said.

Martel had another letter for Maher from Monia. It was impossible for Maher to read these letters—his only connection with his family—without breaking down. When he finished reading he dictated a message for Monia.

Martel told Maher that he looked better than the first time he had seen him. Maher took a breath and tried to hint at what had happened to him. "Of course, because during the first two weeks there was a very intensive interrogation," he dared to say in English. He desperately wanted to communicate, somehow, that he had been tortured, and was being kept in unimaginable conditions. But he knew he had to be careful, with Salloum listening to his every word. He had pain in his knee, he said, but then added that it was from before his detention, hoping Martel would understand he was covering up. He asked for medicine for diarrhea and constipation. Martel asked if this condition was related to Maher's detention. But again Maher said that it had nothing to do with his detention but was a pre-existing problem. Martel said he would speak to the nurse at the embassy but that she was away for two weeks. The Syrian officials asked Maher to stand up and walk for Martel.

"You see, he is well and healthy and can walk."

Salloum turned to Maher and told him, in Arabic, what to say to Martel.

"You can see, my brothers are treating me very well," Maher said, as instructed.

When the meeting was over, Salloum led Maher out of the office. "I need to have a talk with you," Salloum said, looking upset.

A while later, guards came to Maher's cell and pulled him out, yelling, "We are taking care of you! Why did you complain?" Maher apologized, saying that he hadn't meant to make them angry. They shoved him back into his cell and pushed the door shut.

10:30 A.M., Tuesday, December 10, 2002
Far' Falastin, Damascus

MARTEL CAME TO SEE MAHER for the fifth time on December 10. He brought Maher money, which he handed over to the Syrians, as well as more reading materials, a letter from Monia, and photos of the children. The meeting took place in a different office than usual, and Salloum wasn't present. When Maher saw the photos, he broke down completely. Once again he dictated a response.

Maher wondered if Martel had noticed that he was wearing the same clothes as last time. He'd been wearing the jeans and shirt that the American agent had given him on the airplane for more than two months and they were filthy.

Maher asked Martel about the media coverage of his case. He knew that the Syrians would be concerned about publicity. But Martel told him that the media stories were becoming less frequent but that the consular division was still working hard on his case. Maher's heart sank. The guards took Maher, with the letter and photos from Monia, back down into the dark.

Maher was finding the visits more and more frustrating. The absurdity of being in a room talking to a Canadian government official one minute, then being back in the dark cell the next, was taking its toll. "After the visits, I would be very depressed, and hit my head and fists on the wall and go very quiet for three or four days. The mental toll was considerable." Maher thought that Martel now seemed less engaged than he had been, and that the Syrians had noticed this. "At the beginning, the Syrians seemed very worried about the visits, and would bring me coffee, and be very nice. But they saw the Canadians did not care, and became less concerned."

Maher pressed the guards to bring him clean clothes. They finally did, but not until the end of December. In the meantime, he spent hours looking at the photographs and reading the letters over and over again. "I could only see them by holding them up to the light that came in through the hole in the ceiling onto the back wall."

4 P.M., Monday, December 16, 2002
Eternal flame, Parliament Hill, Ottawa

IT WAS MINUS FIFTEEN CELSIUS with the wind chill, but about forty people huddled around the eternal flame in front of Parliament Hill to show their support for Monia and her children. It had been seventy-six days since Monia last saw Maher, and the initial flurry of media attention had slowed. The goal of the vigil was to help spark interest again.

Monia warned that what was happening didn't involve just her husband, and that all Canadians should be worried. "By keeping Maher in Syria[,] Canadians are losing a little bit of their freedom and democracy," she told her supporters, juggling a candle and her ten-month-old son in her arms. "I want the Canadian government to bring my husband home. I want more than words. I want my husband back."[19]

NDP leader Alexa McDonough, the parliamentarian who'd been the most outspoken on the case to that point, addressed the small crowd. "We're living in dangerous times. Maher Arar was detained, imprisoned, interrogated, and deported without the benefit of legal counsel, without consular access, without any explanation to his family. With no explanation to government. This should be a concern to every Canadian."[20]

Marlene Catterall, the Member of Parliament for the Arars' West Ottawa riding, was there also. She first heard from Monia three days after Maher disappeared and had been talking with Gar Pardy and Minister Graham's office about how to help.

McDonough had sent invitations to all MPs and was disappointed more hadn't turned out. She was most disappointed, though, with the terse response she received from Canadian Alliance MP John Cummins's office. The emailed reply, written by Cummins's researcher, Bryan Derha, had just three words: "Get a life." Once the response was publicized, Cummins sent an apology to the Canadian Council on American Islamic Relations, the organization that had originally emailed the invitation to the vigil.[21]

Late December 2002
Far' Falastin, Damascus

AS THE END OF THE YEAR APPROACHED, Maher entered a phase he would later refer to as the "dark days." Several weeks had passed with no news from the outside, and Maher was sinking into depression. The guards had finally brought him a Qur'an, which, along with the letters and photos from his family, helped a little. But soon Maher became what he calls "selfish" and started to think less and less about his family. He needed to focus very hard on surviving. "Life didn't mean anything for me anymore, without my kids, without knowing how Monia was. Life wasn't worth living anymore."

In the beginning, the cell had seemed like a refuge for him. Now it was another form of torture. Each day that passed felt like a year. The worst thing, he says, was not knowing what would happen next. "Were they going to kill me? Were they going to torture me?" Finally, he had what he calls a nervous crisis: "I got to a point where memories would crowd my mind, one after the other, one after the other, very quickly, and then I'd just scream. I would lose control and scream for ten seconds. My heart would start beating wildly. After that I could not breathe well and felt dizzy. This happened a few times ... and no one responded," Maher says. When it happened again, at around 7 P.M., a guard came and told him to go wash his face. Maher asked to see a doctor but one never came.

Those were the days when he believed he might never be released, Maher says.

Martel finally returned on January 7. Maher had been right—the Syrians had been less and less responsive to calls from the embassy. This time Martel brought an Eid card from Maher's daughter. Maher dictated two responses for his family. The first was to Monia, the second to his daughter, thanking her for the Eid card she had sent him.

He learned nothing from Martel about his case. Life in the grave was growing more and more unbearable. The winter was a very cold one and there was still no hot water. Maher and Abdullah noticed that in January and February, the cold even killed off the giant cockroaches. "Cockroaches were everywhere, in the cell and in layers over each other above the washroom door. There were big ones until winter, when I remember going into the washroom at noon and they were falling off dead. It was an extremely cold day and the guard told me that they did not spray anything, but it was because of the cold," Abdullah remembers. A few months later, he says, newer, smaller cockroaches appeared in massive numbers.

Sometime between January 12 and 14, 2003
Canadian Embassy, Damascus

WHEN STAFF SERGEANT FIORIDO handed the sealed envelope to Pillarella, the ambassador didn't have to open it—he knew what was inside. It contained the list of questions the RCMP wanted Syrian interrogators to ask Abdullah. Attached to the questions was a cover letter addressed to General Hassan Khalil:

> Depending on his [Abdullah's] willingness to answer truthfully and depending on the answers he provides to you, a second series of questions has been prepared for him ... we cannot disclose this second set of questions to him until we favourably assess the quality and accuracy of his answers.... The police unit investigating this matter in Canada is an integrated team composed of personnel from both the law enforcement community and from our intelligence community, the Canadian Security Intelligence Service.... I would like to propose that during my next visit to Damascus ... I meet with personnel from your agency in order to further

discuss this matter.... Also be aware that we are in possession of large volumes of highly sensitive documents and
information, seized during investigative efforts or obtained
from confidential informants associated to terrorist cells
operating in Canada. Our Service is readily willing to share
this information with your Service....[22]

Fiorido says he included the language about "large volumes of
highly sensitive documents and information" as a carrot to tempt
the Syrians and help encourage them to comply with the RCMP's
request.[23] Neither the RCMP, nor any other agency in Canada or
abroad, has ever produced any evidence linking Abdullah to any
terrorist cell, so it's not clear what justified the reference to
multiple "terrorist cells operating in Canada" or who the "confidential informants" were.

A-O Canada had prepared the questions in December and
January, after Pillarella had advised Fiorido that the Syrians
weren't going to let the RCMP interview Abdullah directly.
Fiorido drafted the cover letter, and CSIS and Cabana approved
it. The questions were copied to Corporal Flewelling and the
International Liaison and Protective Operations branch at RCMP
headquarters. Chief Superintendent Couture and his superior,
Superintendent Pilgrim approved the questions, though Pilgrim
would later say he hadn't known they'd been sent to General
Khalil.

Question number sixteen was: "What is your relationship with
Maher Arar?" The rest of the questions are still the subject of a
national security confidentiality claim by the Canadian government, but the Arar Report would reveal that the RCMP asked
about "heavy hitters" in al-Qaeda, people who Justice O'Connor,
the commissioner of the Arar Inquiry, says "by anyone's assessment, were serious terrorist threats."[24] The questions, and the cover
letter, were translated into Arabic for the Syrian interrogators.

Pillarella didn't check in with DFAIT in Ottawa, or the
Consular Affairs division, about the propriety of delivering the
questions. He was, it seems, always eager to help the RCMP, and

pleased to deliver the questions for them. Fiorido later described how "unprecedented" it was for an ambassador to "even show an interest in assisting us at this level."[25] Fiorido and Pillarella didn't talk about the likelihood that Abdullah would be tortured to get the answers to the questions. Yet, it should have been a working assumption. They both knew that Abdullah had been detained at Far' Falastin, without consular access, for eight months now. Pillarella knew that, officially, the Syrians hadn't yet confirmed they even had him in custody; they still hadn't responded to the diplomatic note sent by the embassy back in August.[26]

Fiorido knew that Ahmad El Maati had told Canadian consular officials in Egypt that he'd been tortured in Syria. He'd learned that from Staff Sergeant Callaghan just a couple of days earlier. Asked about it later, however, Fiorido would only say "it [torture] was never a concern because it was never considered."[27] He was, it seems, indifferent.

As for Pillarella, he says he didn't think the questions put Abdullah in jeopardy because there had been no sign during the consular visits that Maher had been mistreated, so there was no reason to assume that Abdullah would be.[28] Justice O'Connor would later point out how flawed this reasoning was, given the circumstances—the ambassador should have assumed that Maher had been tortured when he was questioned.[29]

Cabana had apparently discussed "difficulties that Mr. Almalki could face in these questions being asked" with Staff Sergeants Callaghan and Corcoran.[30] He later testified that sharing the questions with the Syrians was "troubling" but "appropriate" because Canada was still facing an "imminent threat."[31] Setting aside the fact that international law prohibits any justification for torture, the idea that the threat that they were investigating was imminent in January 2003 is ludicrous. Both of the main targets—Ahmad and Abdullah—had been in detention for months. The threat they had been investigating—a plot to blow up the Parliament buildings—was itself the product of torture and was more than a year old.[32]

Despite the fact that the questions named Maher in the context of "heavy hitters" and terrorist cells, Cabana said he didn't see how sending the questions could cause problems for Maher—the question that named him was merely about his relationship with Abdullah.[33] Nor apparently did Pillarella and Fiorido consider the issue of whether the list of questions would send mixed messages to the Syrians about Maher.

"These were troubling decisions to make," Cabana says, but he wasn't the only one who had made them. He'd consulted with other agencies and "experts" he says.[34]

And the "experts" Cabana says made the decision with him? They say they didn't know the questions were actually sent to Syria. The idea of sending questions for Abdullah had first been discussed in the September 10, 2002, meeting at DFAIT. A follow-up meeting had been held on October 25. Jonathan Solomon, the junior DFAIT official, had raised the issue of torture at the first meeting, and it came up in the second meeting also. Solomon and other officials from DFAIT's intelligence branch had left the October 25 meeting "displeased." They decided to draft a "fairly strict" letter to go from the assistant deputy minister to RCMP assistant commissioner Richard Proulx. Solomon drafted a memo about the initiative on October 30: "The RCMP are seeking either to directly interview [Almalki] or to send their Syrian counterparts a request that [Almalki] be asked questions provided by the RCMP," Solomon wrote. He proposed a letter to Proulx saying that "DFAIT will not support or assist in this matter if there is any risk of a Canadian citizen being question[ed] under duress at the behest of the Government of Canada."[35]

But the letter Solomon proposed, unlike the questions, was never sent. Dan Livermore, the director general of DFAIT's intelligence division, says it was his understanding that "the RCMP eventually agreed with us that they would not send the questions to the Syrians."[36] He had never seen anything in writing to confirm that, though, and had assumed the matter had been resolved at the level of Scott Heatherington, the director of DFAIT's Foreign Intelligence Division. Heatherington claims he never saw anything in writing either, but he also says that he understood that the RCMP had heeded the division's advice and weren't going to send the questions. All this was news to Cabana, who claims he doesn't remember ever being told at any meeting that torture was a credible risk and that the questions shouldn't be sent. The RCMP, both at the level of Project A-O Canada and at headquarters, claims its understanding was that it had the go-ahead from DFAIT. It pointed out that Pillarella, as ambassador, had the final say and had even agreed to play an instrumental role by seeing to it that the questions were delivered. Pillarella claims he believed that DFAIT supported sending the questions. Referring to this "startling breakdown in communication" as a "sorry state of affairs," Justice O'Connor noted that, "incredibly, there was virtually no written record of the communications among the various parties involved."[37] Incredible indeed. As for Gar Pardy, the man whose job it was to help Maher and Abdullah, he says Pillarella should have checked with Ottawa. If Pillarella had consulted him, he would have said "no bloody way. This is not a zero sum game here. We can't get in to see him, and you are sending questions to a man they won't even let us talk to."[38]

SIXTEEN

One-Way Window

Wednesday morning, January 15, 2003
Damascus

WHEN AMBASSADOR FRANCO PILLARELLA and Consul Leo Martel met with Suleiman Haddad, one of the two Syrian deputy Foreign ministers, Haddad told them that Maher didn't want to return to Canada. Martel pointed out that Maher's letters to his wife, and statements at the visits, showed quite the opposite. Haddad reiterated that CSIS had told the Syrians that "they have no wish to see Arar return to Canada and they were quite content with the way things were."[1]

Pillarella described the "curious" statements in the report he wrote up later that day. His report didn't mention anything about how he, the ambassador, had responded to the statement about CSIS.[2] On the stand at the Arar Inquiry many years later, Pillarella would say that Syrian deputy Foreign minister Walid Mouallem and General Khalil told him the same thing, and that every time he heard it, his reply was that Canada wanted Maher back as long as Syria had nothing against him.[3]

The questions for Abdullah were delivered to the Syrian Military Intelligence the afternoon of that meeting. Pillarella asked Martel to call Colonel Saleh to make the arrangements. That afternoon, Martel met Saleh at the Carlton Hotel in Damascus and handed him the sealed envelope. Martel claims no one told him what was inside and he just assumed it was something to help Maher. But, on the contrary, the contents of that envelope would not help Maher at all.

The day after the questions were handed to the Syrians, Minister Graham spoke with his Syrian counterpart, Foreign Minister Farouk Shara'a. The phone call, scheduled to take place on November 19, 2002, had been delayed pending a report from the CSIS trip to Syria.[4]

The American invasion of Iraq was looming, and this was a far more important matter for Syria at the time, so Graham began the conversation by discussing that. When they turned to Maher's case, Graham pointed out that it had a high profile in Canada, and Canadians were upset with the way in which the United States had sent Maher to Syria. He made it clear that Canada very much wanted Maher returned. The alternative was for the Syrians to charge him, Graham said, so he could defend himself. Graham reminded Shara'a that Maher was a Canadian. Shara'a assured Graham that if it was determined that Maher was linked to al-Qaeda, he would have a fair trial in Syria.[5]

That same day, an official from DFAIT's Middle East division spoke with the Syrian ambassador to Canada, Ahmad Arnous. Arnous was pleased to hear that the call had been made but pointed out that he'd been told that Canadian intelligence officials had said Canada did not wish to see Maher returned.[6]

Thursday, January 16, 2003
Far' Falastin, Damascus

ABDULLAH WAS HAULED UP for more interrogation the day after the RCMP's questions were delivered. "They didn't bother to hide anymore that the reports had been coming from Canada," he says. Abdullah saw that the new report had two pages of questions. They were about phone calls made from his home and seemed to imply that Abdullah was linked to al-Qaeda through Ahmad, and their mutual friend Ibrahym Adam. "I pointed out this contradicted what they had said before," Abdullah says. "The previous reports had said that I was their link to al-Qaeda, now they were claiming the opposite." The report also claimed that Abdullah had been to a military training camp in Afghanistan. Again Abdullah told them he hadn't.

Haitham told Abdullah that the Canadians had described him as very smart and had implied that he'd been deceiving them. "If I find out you've been lying to me, you and others here will suffer," he threatened. Haitham didn't physically torture Abdullah this time. Instead, other prisoners were brought up for torture in the nearby rooms. "I could hear them screaming and begging for mercy. It was awful. I think they were torturing the other people just to terrorize me, because normally Thursdays and Fridays are relatively quiet days. With every sound of a whip and a scream, my heart was sinking further and my fear jumping higher." Abdullah later wondered if his interrogators chose not to whip him because he was so obviously weak.

Maher was brought up and questioned in mid-January too, but he doesn't remember the date. He was asked about a man named Ra'ed Hijazi, a Boston cab driver. Had Maher known him when he lived in Boston? Maher told them no.

Abdullah remembers being asked about a Boston cab driver as well, though he thinks that was back in December. Like Maher, he didn't know him, and had said so. Neither men knew at the time that Hijazi had been accused of plotting a terrorist attack. Was Hijazi one of the "heavy hitters" the Arar report says some of the RCMP questions were about? If he was, the label "heavy hitter" may have been inappropriate. It turns out that if there ever was legitimate evidence that Hijazi, a dual American-Jordanian citizen, was a terrorist, it had been tainted by torture. Amnesty International reports that Hijazi was detained and tortured in Syria before being extradited to Jordan in October 2000, where he was tortured and forced to "confess" to having plotted an attack to mark the millennium, a confession he later recanted.[7] Maher later learned from other prisoners that Hijazi had been held and tortured at Far' Falastin, too.

Sunday, January 5, 2003
Abu Za'abal prison, northeast of Cairo

AHMAD'S MOTHER, SAMIRA, was given permission to visit her son in January, thirteen months after she'd last seen him at the airport in Vienna. She was nervous and scared during the two-hour drive to Abu Za'abal. "It was the first time in my life I had been to any prison. And I'd heard terrible things about this prison when I was young." After walking by the guards armed with machine guns at the prison gates and signing in, she was directed to take a seat in one of a row of carts hooked up to a tractor. In time, other prisoners' family members took their seats, and they were driven to the maximum security complex.

Samira remembers being shocked at Ahmad's appearance when she saw him. He had lost a lot of weight and his colouring was off. "He was wearing sandals, and I could see his legs and feet were blue. His feet looked terrible. And his face was blue. Maybe from a lack of sun?" For Ahmad, seeing his mother again was a cause for jubilation. "I entered the prison manager's office and saw my mother sitting there. I couldn't believe it. I rushed over and hugged her. I was so happy to see her. It was very emotional."

Samira had brought some of Ahmad's favourite food, including stuffed zucchini and sweet pastries. The officials in the room watched them closely. After twenty minutes, one announced that the visit was over. The time had gone too quickly for Samira, and she struggled not to show her anger as she was led away from her son. Before Ahmad could take the food back to his cell, one of the guards lifted the covers off the food trays. "He squeezed all the food, crushing it with his bare hands, as if he was looking for something hidden. I don't think he believed that. He just did it as an insult."

Later in January, the consular officials came to Abu Za'abal to visit Ahmad again. Frustrated, Ahmad explained that while he'd been told by his family that he had a lawyer, he hadn't seen him. He asked if the officials knew any more about

Samira al-Shallash, Badr El Maati, and their children—Ahmad (left), Amr (right), and their sister—in Kuwait, 1969. (COURTESY AHMAD EL MAATI'S FAMILY)

Ahmad El Maati (right), six years old, and his brother Amr El Maati (left), seven years old, in Kuwait, 1970. (COURTESY AHMAD EL MAATI'S FAMILY)

Ahmad El Maati in Damascus in spring 2001. Ahmad left this photograph with his fiancée Rola before returning to Canada. (COURTESY AHMAD EL MAATI'S FAMILY)

Abdullah Almalki in Malaysia about two months before he was detained at the airport in Damascus on May 3, 2002. (COURTESY OF ABDULLAH ALMALKI)

Maher Arar with his wife, Monia Mazigh, by his side, tells the world his story for the first time in the National Press Theatre in Ottawa on November 4, 2003. (CP PHOTO/TOM HANSON)

Muayyed Nureddin, on January 15, 2004, the day after his release from Syrian detention, in a crush of media as he arrives at Pearson International Airport in Toronto. (PHOTO: TOBIN GRIMSHAW)

Jack Hooper, former deputy director of CSIS, in the witness stand at the Arar Inquiry on August 25, 2005.
(CP PHOTO/JONATHAN HAYWARD)

The Arar Inquiry's lead counsel, Paul Cavalluzzo, at a press conference in Ottawa in December 2004. He is showing reporters how much the government censored the Arar Inquiry's summary of CSIS' involvement in Maher Arar's case.
(ROD MACIVOR/THE OTTAWA CITIZEN. REPRINTED BY PERMISSION)

Inspector Michel Cabana, former officer in charge of the RCMP's Project A-O Canada, takes the stand at the Arar Inquiry, August 2005.
(CP PHOTO/FRED CHARTRAND)

Ambassador Franco Pillarella, former Canadian ambassador to Syria, about to be cross-examined at the Arar Inquiry in June 2005. (PHOTO: BILL GRIMSHAW)

Leo Martel, the consular official who visited Maher Arar and turned Abdullah Almalki away from the Canadian embassy in Damascus, seen here stepping down from the witness stand at the Arar Inquiry in August 2005. (CP PHOTO/FRED CHARTRAND)

Gar Pardy, the now-retired director general of the Consular Affairs Division at Foreign Affairs, on the stand at the Arar Inquiry in the summer of 2005. (CP PHOTO/ JONATHAN HAYWARD)

Justice Dennis O'Connor, commissioner at the Arar Inquiry in Ottawa, holding the Arar Report on the day it was publicly released on September 18, 2006.
(CP PHOTO/FRED CHARTRAND)

Former RCMP commissioner Giuliano Zaccardelli walks away from the media following his appearance before the Commons public safety committee on Parliament Hill in Ottawa, December 5, 2006. He resigned the following day.
(CP PHOTO/TOM HANSON)

Back at home, Ahmad El Maati and his mother, Samira Al-Shallash, in Toronto, August 2005. (COURTESY AHMAD EL MAATI'S FAMILY)

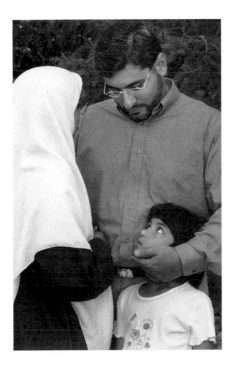

Back at home, Abdullah, his pregnant wife, Khuzaimah, and his youngest daughter in Ottawa in August 2005. (PHOTO: BILL GRIMSHAW)

*Ahmad El Maati (centre), Abdullah Almalki (left), and Muayyed Nureddin
(right) at a press conference on Parliament Hill on October 12, 2007. Ahmad
is holding up the September 6, 2005,* Globe and Mail *story by Jeff Sallot that
revealed the origin of the map that Ahmad was interrogated about in Syria and
Egypt.* (REUTERS/CHRIS WATTIE)

*Muayyed Nureddin attending one
of just four days of public hearings
at the Iacobucci Inquiry in Ottawa
on April 17, 2007.* (CP PHOTO/TOM
HANSON)

why he was being detained, and noted that he had been questioned on a regular basis at first but less lately. Once again, Ahmad says, Stuart Bale seemed preoccupied with getting him to agree to meet with CSIS or the RCMP, in Egyptian custody. And once again, Ahmad told them bluntly that he would be happy to meet with them, "but on Canadian soil."

The visit, like the others, had been monitored by a senior state security officer named Walid. This time, when the visit was over, Walid took Ahmad back into his office. "He was responsible for the whole of Abu Za'abal for a long time, and everyone talked about his cruelty. He had refused food and medicine to prisoners and many contracted diseases and were left to die." Walid was angry with Ahmad and wanted to know why he was refusing the Canadian officials' requests that he agree to meet with Canadian investigators. Ahmad thought carefully about what to say.

"This is your country, not theirs," he said. "I didn't want to antagonize you by accepting them here."

"That is not your business. It is ours to worry about. I'm going to raise this issue with my superiors," Walid said.

A couple of weeks passed without news, then Ahmad was transferred back to Istiqbal Tora prison. Looking back, he thinks it might have been after this transfer that he was questioned, but just for five minutes. "They took me in a room and told me to sit down. Then someone came up behind me and put his hand on my shoulder and said 'Don't look back.' Then he showed me two pictures, and asked if I knew the people in them. I said no."

"I know you don't," the man said.

The man asked if Ahmad recognized his voice, and Ahmad replied yes—he knew it was the same interrogator who had tortured him with the electric shock at the Mabahith Amn al-Dawla al-'Ulya, the State Security Investigations services facility in Nasr City. The interrogator left the room, and Ahmad was taken back to the common cell where he was being kept.

Samira saw Ahmad again just a few weeks later, in mid-February, for Eid al-Adha, the Muslim feast marking the culmination of the hajj. Because of the holiday, many families were visiting and they weren't as closely watched, so Ahmad was able to speak more freely with his mother. He didn't dare say anything about what was happening to him in Egypt, but he did tell her about his experience in Syria. He described the grave-like cell and the torture, and that he had been forced to sign a confession he couldn't read.

Samira says she wasn't surprised. "I know these people, and I had heard a lot about what they do. But you never think bad things will happen to your loved ones. In spite of everything, I always thanked God that Ahmad was alive and I could see him."

Three weeks later, on February 27, Bale and the other consular officials came again, this time with Ahmad's mother, sister, and sister's husband. Bale's notes from the visit indicate that Ahmad said for the first time that he would be willing to meet with a Canadian investigator, but Ahmad remembers it differently. He insists he still said no, not until he was home in Canada. He thinks that it was after this visit that he was taken downstairs to a waiting van and again made to lie, covered, in the back. For the third time, he was transferred to the State Security facility in Nasr City and locked into the same solitary confinement cell he had occupied previously.

This time, however, when the guards came for him, they undid his handcuffs, yanked his arms behind his back, and locked them in place. "I knew immediately this meant that I would be tortured." They led him out of the cell, down the hall, past the elevators, and into one of the interrogation rooms.

"Tell us about your will," one of the men in the room said.

Ahmad didn't know at first what the interrogator was talking about. When he asked him to explain, the torture started. The men slammed Ahmad on the back of the head with their fists, forcing him onto his knees, and pulled out a black rod. He felt the electricity shoot through him. Again, they aimed for his genitals and handcuffs. They asked him about the will again. Ahmad remembered he had prepared a will, back in 1999, before performing the hajj. He asked them if this is what they meant. "I was asking myself, 'How would they know about this? I didn't even remember this!'"

What Ahmad didn't know then was that the will he prepared before his pilgrimage had been among the items seized by RCMP agents when they searched his father's apartment in January 2002. The pilgrimage to Mecca is demanding and dangerous. Preparing for death, both spiritually and logistically, is expected. Every year, more than two million pilgrims brave the crowds and scorching heat, and every year there are deaths. The journey itself is often referred to as *jihad* or struggle. The year before Ahmad went to Mecca, more than one hundred pilgrims were trampled to death. For Muslims, to die this way is to die a martyr. Ahmad's will, like those of all Muslims undertaking the pilgrimage to Mecca, was written in anticipation of the possibility that he would die a martyr.

In his will, Ahmad asked his father and mother for forgiveness—again customary among Muslims who are near death or about to take a long trip. The idea is to make peace with one another and ensure all transgressions, large and small, are forgiven. It's likely that the RCMP, with so little knowledge of Islam, misinterpreted the meaning of the will, especially as it contained the words *jihad* and *martyr*, and asked for forgiveness. Faisal Kutty, a lawyer who in his practice draws up many wills for Muslims, says that this kind of misunderstanding "shows a lack of nuance or sophistication on the part of investigators and analysts." "Many hajjis—those who perform the hajj—in fact hope and pray that they die on their way to, during, or on their way back from hajj so that they may die as a *shaheed*, or martyr," Kutty says. "There is nothing insidious or abnormal about this practice or belief from an Islamic perspective. This is based on the belief that a person who dies while performing a good deed or carrying out his or her religious obligations, including performing the hajj, is considered a *shaheed*."[8]

It isn't publicly known if the RCMP, or CSIS, sent the will and other information from the searches to Ahmad's interrogators, either directly or through American authorities. But somehow, the will itself, or information about the will, had ended up in Egypt.

His interrogators also ordered Ahmad to consent to the Canadians' requests that he meet with a Canadian intelligence official in Egypt. "I just wanted the torture to stop, so I said yes."

A few days later, Ahmad was taken, handcuffed and blindfolded, into an interrogation room yet again. A man removed his blindfold, then sat behind a desk in front of Ahmad. He was in his late fifties, partially bald, with a moustache. "I can't be sure, but he looked a lot like Omar Suleiman. It was someone very high-ranking, anyway," says Ahmad. Ahmad had seen Suleiman, the head of Egyptian intelligence, on television. To Ahmad's right was a one-way window. "I've always wondered who was watching there. Was it [the] Canadians?"

The man offered Ahmad tea. "I didn't know what was going on. This was the first time I had seen an interrogator face to face in Egypt. And now he is offering me tea, as if he is trying to show someone he is treating me well." With or without the tea, Ahmad says, it would have been obvious to whoever was watching that Ahmad was in very bad condition; he'd been subjected to electric shock just a few days earlier. After the guards brought tea, the questioning started. Every so often the man in charge would order the guards to take Ahmad back to his cell. They'd come back for him a while later, and the questions would continue, probing areas that had already been gone over. "This interrogation was my life story again," says Ahmad. "It was a marathon interrogation. I would guess it went on for at least ten hours."

Ahmad says it was around this time that he fell on the knee he had injured in high school. "There is a step down from the cell into the hall. They were rushing me, yelling at me to move faster. I was blindfolded and I could not see, and I tripped over the step. I landed with all my weight on my knee. The pain was excruciating. My knee swelled up and I was limping, badly." The fall he experienced that day, along with the forced kneeling during torture and interrogations, would eventually turn what was once a minor injury into a crippling one.

The interrogations eventually ended, and, after about ten days at the Nasr City facility, Ahmad was returned to Istiqbal Tora prison, and then transferred to Abu Za'abal. The truck drove past the armed guards and through the fortress-like gates into the complex. This time, however, it stopped in front of the older Liman Abu Za'abal prison instead of continuing on to the newer maximum security complex where Ahmad had previously been kept. Ahmad had heard horror stories about this prison, a crumbling, decrepit building where prisoners were sent to "rot to death." He thought of the interrogation he'd just endured, and the one-way window, and wondered if the Egyptians had been asked to put him somewhere where he'd never be heard from again. "I knew [Liman Abu Za'abal] is a place where people just disappear, for years and years, with no family access." One of his fellow inmates at Istiqbal Tora prison had told him how ten of his friends had died in this building. "They'd just been left there, to die a slow death."

Inside, Ahmad could smell the decades of decay and suffering. He was locked in a cell that was about six feet wide and ten feet long. The only thing in it was a bucket, to use as a toilet.

He had arrived in the afternoon. By nightfall, Ahmad was out of his mind with worry. "Compared to the other prisons, the conditions were the worst. It was really hard. I didn't sleep, because I thought that was it for me. I really thought that this was big punishment and because I didn't know what was going on, I thought I was being put there to die."

The next morning Ahmad was let out of his cell and allowed to walk around in the hall with the other prisoners in his wing for a few minutes. He remembers meeting a man who was in his early forties. "He told me he'd been in this place for twenty-two years. I couldn't believe it."

It turned out Ahmad had just been put there for the night. Later that morning, he was moved back to his former cell in the newer maximum security prison, where he was kept for a few more days before being transferred back to Istiqbal Tora prison.

Tuesday, April 22, 2003
Far' Falastin, Damascus

IN APRIL 2003, Maher was published. His article appeared in that month's issue of *Wireless Systems Design* magazine.

"Modern communications systems employ bandwidth-efficient modulation techniques, such as quadrature amplitude modulated (QAM)," he wrote. "With QAM, the amplitude and phase of a sinusoidal signal are both varied to transmit digital information."[9]

Maher had submitted the article to the magazine some time before his detention. It was the first time he had been published and the magazine is an important publication in his field. It would have normally been reason to celebrate. But Maher didn't know he'd been published. He'd been in the grave for more than six months; more than two months had lapsed since the last consular visit in February. It was a Tuesday morning when he was taken out of his cell at Far' Falastin. His beard was shaved and he was told to wash his face and comb his hair well. He hoped this meant there would be another visit and news from his family. But this time, the guards took him outside to a waiting car. Maher asked where he was being taken, but, as always, they refused to say.

Maher, not having been in Damascus since he was a boy, couldn't tell where they were headed as they drove though the busy downtown streets. Eventually arriving at an office building, he was put in a room on the second floor and served tea. Maher used the opportunity to lobby his escorts to get the hot water fixed at Far' Falastin. They said they would try.

After about ten minutes, Khaled and Colonel Salloum entered the room. Khaled looked tired, and they both looked anxious. "You will be put in front of a judge and justice system. Are all your needs taken care of?" Salloum asked.

"I don't need anything," Maher replied.

"There are people from Canada to see you," Salloum said, the usual warning implicit in his tone.

"I won't tell them anything."

Maher was led to a nearby room, where a man introduced himself to Maher as the Canadian ambassador, Franco Pillarella. Another man from the embassy was there also. A third man identified himself as Sarkis Assadourian, an Armenian-Canadian Member of Parliament who spoke Arabic. Khaled took notes as Salloum watched Maher. A young Syrian official acted as interpreter. Then a woman entered the room and introduced herself as Maher's Member of Parliament, Marlene Catterall.

Salloum instructed Maher to speak in Arabic and to not speak about the security aspects of his case. He was to speak only about matters relating to his health, family, and prison conditions. Maher, of course, didn't dare speak about the prison conditions.

Catterall did most of the talking. She explained that she was there because of the hard work of his wife. She had been to his home and had spent time with Monia and his children. She handed Maher two letters from Monia and photos and drawings from the children. Maher looked at them, tears streaming down his face. Then he looked at Catterall.

"I want to go home to Canada."

"Yes, but we need to respect Syrian law," she said.

"But I am innocent and I know I will be released soon."

Salloum reminded him not to discuss his case. Maher dictated a letter for Monia, slipping into English. In front of the parliamentarians, Salloum had to tolerate it. Maher also asked that Monia send more money—he needed it to buy extra food and supplies from the guards at Far' Falastin. He would need money every six months, he said, though he couldn't imagine surviving another six months.

Only fifteen minutes had passed when Salloum stood up to signal that the meeting was over. Maher followed Salloum into another room, where he overheard two officials discussing how

Canadian media coverage was negatively portraying Syria. Hearing this, Maher became angry with himself, and the anger grew as he was driven back to Far' Falastin and locked in his cell. If his wife was speaking out at home, he should have spoken out also. "I was so angry at myself. Why hadn't I spoken up? Why didn't I tell them where I was being kept, and about the beating I endured at the beginning of my detention? I made a decision that the next time, no matter how afraid I was, I was going to tell the truth."

Catterall was upset, too. Her concern was that she and her colleague had not been fully briefed by Foreign Affairs before leaving Ottawa. Before the two parliamentarians had met with Maher, Pillarella had told them that the Syrians believed Maher had trained in Afghanistan and was linked to al-Qaeda. Pillarella did not say that the allegations were likely the product of torture. Catterall was shocked by the gravity of the case. She had thought that the allegations against Maher were to do with his military service and possible links to the Muslim Brotherhood. This was the first she'd heard about training in Afghanistan.[10]

The group had also met with Syrian deputy Foreign minister Walid Mouallem that morning. Catterall had hoped to be able to hand him a letter signed jointly by Solicitor General Wayne Easter and Minister Graham. But Easter refused to sign. So in the end, the letter she handed to Mouallem was from Graham. It read, "There is no Canadian government impediment to Mr. Arar's return to Canada."[11] This was a significant change from the wording originally proposed by Pardy, which was that Maher "has not contravened any Canadian laws and since arriving in Canada with his family many years ago has been a good citizen of this country."[12] Catterall later said she understood the wording had been changed to reflect a "security perspective."[13]

Mouallem told the parliamentarians that Syria had been surprised by Maher's arrival. Because of the international "war on terrorism," they'd had no choice but to detain and question him about his role in al-Qaeda, he said. They'd finished their investigation, he said, and soon, Maher would stand trial on charges of belonging to al-Qaeda and having trained in Afghanistan.

Later that day, Pillarella wrote to Ottawa that, had the parliamentarians "been more fully briefed in Ottawa, they would have reconsidered undertaking their mission to Damascus." The ambassador concluded his briefing by lauding the Syrians' "remarkable" cooperation, and noting how clear it was that they did "not wish this case to hinder, in any way, our bilateral relationship."[14]

SEVENTEEN

The American Resolve Effect

Sometime in April 2003
Far' Falastin, Damascus

ABDULLAH HAD BEEN LIVING UNDERGROUND for almost a year. He had been called up and questioned in early March about whether he had raised money in Canada for al-Qaeda. His answer was the same as it had always been: No, he had nothing to do with al-Qaeda.

Abdullah's physical condition was deteriorating. The eleven months spent in the dark had taken its toll. He was covered in huge welts from insect bites that had become infected. He'd lost a lot of weight. "You could see many, if not most, of my bones," he says. He remembers a guard looking him over one day and remarking that the prisoners in the graves weren't even worth feeding. In March, tuberculosis had started to spread in the detention centre, so the prisoners were allowed in the court-yard—one at a time, to prevent them from seeing each other. When it was Abdullah's turn, he grabbed his blankets to take them to air out, and struggled to get up the stairs. "I had already lost a lot of muscle. I remember having a hard time carrying my blankets," he says.

It had been more than four months since Abdullah had had contact with the outside world. The last visit from his family was when his cousin and uncle had been allowed to visit in late December. Abdullah believes that the visits were blocked whenever there was another round of interrogations: "Any time that a report came and there were a lot of interrogations, the visits would stop, and these visits were my only lifeline."

They were finally successful in April. Abdullah was elated to see his father sitting with his cousin in the prison manager's office when he entered. He hadn't seen his father since leaving Canada a year and a half earlier. "One of my wishes was to see my father. I wanted to know that he was okay. I wanted to tell him that I was fine, and to forgive me and pray for me. It is a Muslim tradition that we ask forgiveness of our loved ones when we are going away, or when we are close to death. I was not sure I was going to survive." But his father was clearly horrified when he saw his son's condition. "His eyes got red almost instantly and filled with tears," Abdullah recalls.

The prison manager and several officials sat in close around them, listening and watching. Abdullah's father is a proud man, used to being in control. Now he was unable to help his son and barely able to stop himself from crying. "I felt very proud of my father, how he managed his emotions and the way he talked. He was, even under the circumstances, the father I always knew, the father that I am always proud of. I felt sorry for him, I felt his pain that he tried to hide," says Abdullah.

Abdullah asked his cousin to push the Syrians to release him. His cousin told Abdullah that his family had been talking with Syrian officials but had been repeatedly told that his was an international problem. His family in Canada had been working on it also, but with no results. Abdullah didn't tell his father about the grave, or the torture: "I wanted to tell him that everything was fine and that I was okay and that I was being treated well. His well-being was more important to me than anything else, and I know that if he got to know what I went through, that might have killed him." Even so, Abdullah's father was very upset, and seemed almost relieved when the visit was over. "He had to leave. He couldn't take it. He couldn't take seeing me like this."

When Abdullah's mother came for the next visit, in June, she told him that he looked as thin as a fifteen-year-old boy. She brought him a Qur'an. It meant the world to Abdullah. He had managed to persuade the prison manager to give him one some time ago, but the print was small. "My eyes were getting really, really bad and I couldn't see it anymore," says Abdullah. The Qur'an his mother brought had larger print.

It wasn't just his eyesight that was failing. "My vision was getting exponentially worse, the same with my mental power, physical power, concentration, and memory. I remember that I started forgetting parts of the Qur'an that I had memorized if I did not review it every second or third day. Even songs that I used to know and enjoy, I could only remember … a word or two."

The family visits helped him survive. But survival sometimes meant forgetting, and the visits, Abdullah says, made it hard to not think of life outside and his family. When things got really bad, Abdullah says, he sometimes even wanted to be tortured to death, just so that he could be spared the anguish.

"Number seven," the man in a cell across from him, had arrived the day after Abdullah. They were by now the most senior inmates of the cells on that end of the corridor. He warned Abdullah not to reveal his hopelessness, as it would demoralize the other prisoners and hurt their chances of survival. "Even if I was feeling really bad, I had to sound okay, the same with him, number seven.… That was not easy to do. And some people, like number five, would know from my tone, no matter how much I tried to hide it, that I was feeling down or hopeless."

The year had been difficult for Abdullah's wife, Khuzaimah, too. His family had urged her to focus on her health and the well-being of the five children while they worked to help Abdullah in Syria and Canada. Khuzaimah was forced to move into a less expensive apartment, and daily life was very difficult on her own with five children. "I tried to keep sane and take care of our children and that was as much as I can handle. It was very stressful and I was really depressed. Simple tasks like doing groceries were challenging to me because I could not move around freely and leave the children by themselves."

Khuzaimah hadn't told the children what was happening. "I wanted to protect them from getting hurt, from being unhappy or confused.... So when they asked, when is Daddy coming home, initially, I'd said 'Soon.' But after a while, I'd say I didn't know."

Wednesday, April 30, 2003
RCMP headquarters, Ottawa

RCMP INVESTIGATORS WERE WORRIED. Inspector Rick Reynolds, now in charge of the National Security Investigations Branch at headquarters, had received the consular reports detailing the parliamentarians' visit to Syria and could see that political momentum was building around efforts to get Maher released. Reynolds' response was to draft a briefing note for Commissioner Zaccardelli. The briefing reported on the media coverage resulting from the MPs' trip to Syria and summed up the reasons the RCMP were interested in Maher. It noted that Maher had refused an interview with A-O Canada, which was false; that Maher had left for Tunisia "shortly" after refusing the interview, which also was false; that he had "volunteered" that he had been to a training camp in Afghanistan, which was false; and that he was a "highly connected individual associated with several criminal extremists," which was again untrue. Then he wrote, under the heading "Concern":

> The lobbyists are pressuring for quick intervention in an attempt to effect a return prior to ARAR being charged by the Syrians. The potential embarrassment exists should the Prime Minister become involved in a similar fashion to the incident following the Egyptian Embassy bombing in 1995 in Pakistan.[1]

He was referring to Prime Minister Chrétien's intervention on behalf of Ahmed Said Khadr while he was in Pakistani detention in 1996. Warnings like this would be made several times over the next few months, scaring many politicians from speaking out on

behalf of Maher, Ahmad, and Abdullah and others detained
abroad, a consequence that would later be dubbed the "Khadr
effect."[2]

The contents of the briefing reveal just how worried the
RCMP investigators must have been. Given, however, that they
still had no evidence linking Maher to terrorism, it's likely they
were less worried about politicians ending up embarrassed than
they were about the prospect of public accountability for their
role in what had happened to the three Canadian detainees.

2 P.M., Thursday, May 8, 2003
DFAIT headquarters, Ottawa

BY MAY 2003, Syria was finally acknowledging that it was
holding Abdullah. But officials there had waited until his military
service deferral had expired in March to reply to the Canadian
government's letter, sent on August 18 of the previous year. The
memo, dated April 26, 2003, noted Abdullah's Syrian citizenship
and stated that "Mr. Malki is also on the Syrian territories and he
has defaulted to join his military service. Hence the Syrian law
applies on him."[3]

Gar Pardy still knew very little about Abdullah's case, and how
he'd ended up in Syria, and still thought he'd arrived there
sometime in the summer of 2002. As for Ahmad, Pardy had come
to the conclusion by then that his case "seems to be a case of little
evidence to support the allegations of involvement in terrorist
activities but rather one of associating with others who may
have."[4]

In his role heading up consular affairs, Gar Pardy was
contending with many demands on his time in the spring of 2003.
There was the war in Iraq, of course, the SARS outbreak in
Toronto and China, and eleven Canadians who had been
detained abroad on security-related grounds. He was retiring in
three months and had decided there were two things he could
realistically strive to accomplish before leaving. He wanted
William Sampson released from custody in Saudi Arabia, where

he'd been detained for thirty-one months, and returned to Canada. He wanted Maher Arar home, too. But given the lack of cooperation of the Syrian and Egyptian governments when it came to Abdullah and Ahmad, he wasn't sure what he could do for these men in the short time he had left.

But things weren't going well in Maher's case either. Ever since CSIS officials had travelled to Syria in November, the Syrians had believed CSIS didn't want Maher back in Canada. Whether CSIS had meant to leave that impression or not, the damage was done, and proving difficult to undo, especially as CSIS itself was refusing to clarify the matter. Furthermore, the Syrians were understandably preoccupied with events in neighbouring Iraq—the Americans had invaded March 17. Consular access was becoming more difficult and, when the MPs had visited Maher in April, they'd been told he was going to be charged and tried, likely in a secret military court. Pardy knew this was bad news: Maher wouldn't get a fair trial in Syria. And, there had still been no formal response to the letter from Minister Graham that the parliamentarians had delivered. To make matters worse, U.S. ambassador Cellucci had been quoted in the media again on April 29 as saying that the United States had sent Maher to Syria because Canadian officials said they didn't want him back. That message didn't help Maher.

Late one Friday night in early April, Pardy had expressed his frustration in an email to Monia. "A major part of the problem here is that not everyone in the government of Canada agrees with what we are doing in support of Maher," he wrote. "The Syrians are well aware of that and that undoubtedly influences their willingness to be more cooperative."[5]

Gaetan Lavertu, Canada's deputy minister of Foreign Affairs, was travelling to Syria on May 19, and Pardy saw this as an opportunity to help Maher by sending along a letter to the Syrian Foreign minister, Farouk Shara'a. "There is a need for an unambiguous statement by the government of Canada," he wrote in a memo to Minister Graham, "preferably signed by the

Solicitor General and the Foreign Minister, to the effect that we have no evidence in Canada, or from foreign sources, that Mr. Arar is or was a member of al-Qaida, that we do not believe that such information exists and that Mr. Arar should be permitted to return to Canada."

So on Thursday afternoon, May 8, he met with representatives of CSIS, the RCMP, and DFAIT's intelligence division to pitch his idea. For it to work he needed the support of the RCMP and CSIS. Pardy provided everyone with an overview of Maher's case. He told them he wanted a letter demonstrating that Canada had one position on Maher Arar, signed by both the Foreign Affairs minister and the solicitor general. Of course, since the RCMP had supplied the information to the United States that had led to the decision to send Maher to Syria, they couldn't really agree with that wording. They *didn't* have any evidence linking Maher to al-Qaeda, though, so they could have agreed with that part. Instead, the RCMP officials said they needed to meet in-house before responding to Pardy's request.

The next morning, Pardy met with Monia. He told her about Lavertu's upcoming trip to Syria and that he might be taking an official government letter with him stating that Maher had no links to terrorism and should be returned to Canada. What Pardy didn't know was that on the same day, May 9, CSIS was doing what it could to stop the "one-voice" letter. A briefing note to Solicitor General Wayne Easter dated May 9 warned that if he were to sign such a letter, "the US Government may ... question Canada's motives and resolve, given that they had deported ARAR to Syria because of concerns about alleged terrorist connections."[6] This would later be dubbed the "American resolve effect." CSIS had also warned the solicitor general about the "Khadr effect," spelled out in the RCMP's briefing note to Zaccardelli just a few days earlier. In Deputy Director Hooper's mind, it would be "political jeopardy" for Easter to sign the letter.[7] The CSIS briefing "strongly advised" that the solicitor general refuse the request. The following Monday afternoon,

Pardy sat down with the agencies to try again. There was quite a crowd in attendance, he says.[8] He and Myra Pastyr-Lupul, DFAIT's case management officer for the Middle East, represented the consular affairs division, while Scott Heatherington was there from Foreign Affairs' intelligence division. Helen Banalescu attended on behalf of Solicitor General Wayne Easter's office. Glen Robinson had come from the Privy Council Office, and Rick Reynolds was there from RCMP headquarters, along with two other officers, and at least two CSIS representatives.

Again, Pardy summarized Maher's case. CSIS and the RCMP officials raised concerns about the letter's wording. By the end of the meeting, it was clear to Pardy that neither CSIS nor the RCMP were prepared to help. Officials from both agencies said they would not support any letter that stated that Canada had no evidence Maher is or was a member of al-Qaeda, even though they didn't.

In the end, Gaetan Lavertu didn't have a letter to take to Syria with him and didn't even raise Maher's case in his meeting with the Syrian Foreign minister. He would later say that it had been impossible, given that the meeting had been so focused on the war in neighbouring Iraq. When Pardy heard that, he felt even more frustrated. That the issue hadn't been raised sent the wrong message entirely. Never mind the failed attempt at the letter.

By early June, Pardy had given up on the idea of a joint letter. He amended his action memo for the minister, proposing that Graham send a letter to his Syrian counterpart, Foreign Minister Farouk Shara'a. Having no choice, Pardy used the exact wording that had been used in the letter MP Marlene Catterall delivered to Syrian deputy Foreign minister Walid Mouallem—language the Syrians had already ignored: "I assure you, that there is no Canadian government impediment to Mr. Arar's return to Canada."[9] In the meantime, he continued to push Minister Graham to agree to meet in person with Monia.

The minister agreed, and a meeting was arranged for Thursday, June 12. In addition to the minister, Robert Fry,

Graham's senior policy adviser, was there, as was Daniel Costello, Graham's executive assistant. Catterall was there too, and was particularly taken aback that Monia had not come alone. Aiming to demonstrate the growing support for her struggle, Monia had invited Riad Saloojee from the Canadian Council on American Islamic Relations, along with a representative from the Canadian Labour Congress, to accompany her.[10] Monia noted that Alex Neve from Amnesty International had very much wanted to attend but was overseas and wasn't able to change his plans on such short notice.

Minister Graham told Monia that his letter to Shara'a would say that there was no Canadian impediment to her husband's return to Canada. Monia told Graham that she wanted a clearer position. Riad Saloojee suggested the minister's letter say that the Canadian government has no evidence linking Arar with terrorist activities.

As the meeting ended, Monia handed a letter to the minister that asked for a coherent, official statement from Canada before Parliament recessed for the summer.

The minister listened. Over the next few days, his advisers drafted new text and asked Pardy to get CSIS, the RCMP, and the solicitor general to sign it. The new wording was unequivocal: "I assure you that there is no evidence he is involved in terrorist activity nor is there any Canadian Government impediment to Mr. Arar's return to Canada."[11] The next day, Monia received a couriered letter from Prime Minister Chrétien. It read: "I want to take this opportunity to reiterate the determination of the Canadian government to provide all possible consular assistance to Mr. Arar, as well as to yourself and other members of his family, and to press the Syrian government for his release and return to Canada as soon as possible. We will not relent."

Later in June, Monia shared the prime minister's letter and Gar Pardy's April 12 email with the media.[12] She wanted Canadians to know about the divisions impeding Maher's return.

The RCMP and CSIS, however, had moved even further into damage-control mode in their apparent mission to block efforts aimed at winning Maher's release. When they saw the revised wording proposed by Graham's office, CSIS headquarters sent an email to the CSIS liaison officer at DFAIT calling the attempt "nonsense," saying that CSIS had already told DFAIT it wouldn't support this statement and had warned DFAIT that "this could go down the same road as Ahmed Said KHADR; people run to his defense only to find out later he was one of the major players within the AL-QAIDA network."[13]

RCMP deputy commissioner Loeppky responded to the revised wording by saying that he had "major concerns with the misleading statement" that there was no evidence linking Maher to terrorism. He added that if Maher returned to Canada, the RCMP would continue to investigate him.[14]

The RCMP and CSIS effectively shut down any possibility of the joint letter being sent to Syria by proposing the following wording instead, wording that both Graham and Pardy recognized would make matters worse for Maher: "Mr. Arar is currently the subject of a National Security Investigation in Canada. Although there is not sufficient evidence at this time to warrant Criminal Code charges, he remains a subject of interest. There is no Canadian government impediment to Mr. Arar's return to Canada."[15]

By June 24, Jim Gould, the deputy director of the Foreign Intelligence Division, was worried that the dispute could poison the working relationship between DFAIT and CSIS in particular. He drafted a memo saying:

> CSIS has made it clear to the Department that they would prefer to have him [Arar] remain in Syria, rather than return to Canada. CSIS officials do not seem to understand that guilty or innocent, Maher Arar has the right to consular assistance from the Department and that in the circumstances in which he presently finds himself, the best outcome might be his return to Canada. Even though there is a risk that Arar

might later be found to have been involved in extremist activities of one sort or another, his right to consular assistance must be honoured.[16]

Now that CSIS and the RCMP had successfully blocked a more strongly worded letter from Minister Graham, Pardy and officials in Graham's office tried another route. Senator Pierre de Bané was to travel to Saudi Arabia in July to deliver a letter about William Sampson's case on behalf of the prime minister. Why not send him to Syria with a letter on Maher's case from the prime minister too?

Granted, the wording could not go beyond what the RCMP and CSIS would approve, but Pardy hoped that having the letter go from Prime Minister Chrétien to President al-Assad would carry weight. In the letter, dated July 11, 2003, the prime minister asked that Arar be released and returned to Canada and, no surprise, said: "I can assure you there is no Canadian government impediment to his return."

On July 22, Senator de Bané delivered the letter on behalf of the prime minister to Syrian deputy Foreign minister Mouallem.

EIGHTEEN

Smear Campaign

Sometime in June 2003
Far' Falastin, Damascus

MAHER SAYS he was at the "peak of his mental destruction" by June. He had been in the grave for eight months. His skin was turning yellow, and so he found the courage to ask one of the friendlier guards to arrange for him to see Khaled. He hadn't been upstairs since the parliamentarians had visited in April.

A few days later, he was taken upstairs. Maher pleaded with Khaled, saying he'd been in the grave for too long and that if they were going to keep him, they had to move him to a place fit for humans.

"Don't you know the news? The United States has attacked Iraq, so we are very busy. You will be lucky if we don't take you to court."

Maher replied that he wanted to appear in court.

"You and your wife are causing us a lot of headaches," Khaled complained. "You think you are in Canada? If we release you and you go back there, the Canadians will arrest you."

Nevertheless, the risk Maher had taken by asking to see Khaled paid off in a small way. In the two weeks after that meeting, he was allowed to take some air in the courtyard twice.

Friday, July 4, 2003
Ottawa

IT WASN'T JUST WHAT THE STORY SAID. It was the way the story was laid out, with the headline, and the photos. Under the headline "'Canada's al-Qaeda' still behind bars: Only five of seven alleged suspects known to public," the *Ottawa Citizen* placed photos of Maher with Monia and their daughter, Ahmed Said Khadr, Mohammed Jabarah, and Ahmed Ressam. Jabarah had been detained in Oman in early 2002 before being transferred to Canada, then handed over to the United States, without an extradition or other legal process, and accused of links to terrorism plots in east Asia. Ressam was the so-called "millennium bomber" caught crossing into the United States from Canada with a trunk-load of explosives in 1999. Granted, the first sentence of the *Ottawa Citizen* story said that the seven Canadian men with *alleged* links to terrorism were in detention, but it went on to say that "collectively, they are known as 'Canada's al-Qaeda,' although their suspected ties to terror in some cases expand beyond Osama bin Laden's group itself."[1] It was this kind of careless labelling that fed public doubt about Maher's innocence.

Three days later, Abdullah was named for the first time in the media. Sources had given Abdullah's name to at least one journalist in November 2002, but he had heeded Abdullah's family's requests to keep his name out of the news. This time, however, a *Globe and Mail* story named Abdullah, saying that he had been detained "under mysterious circumstances in his native Syria for nearly a year." According to the article, "some sources in Syria suggest that it was Mr. Almalki who mentioned Mr. Arar's name to interrogators," setting in motion the "chain of events" leading to Maher's detention.[2] The story also noted that, according to intelligence sources, Abdullah had passed through Indonesia and Malaysia months before his capture. Abdullah had been in Malaysia, of course, but had not been to Indonesia. The story went on to note that Abdullah's family was worried publicity "could cause serious consequences for him and his relatives," which was why DFAIT wasn't naming him.

Then, in the same week that the prime minister's letter was being delivered in Syria, the Canadian agencies launched a new strategy. Ahmad's "confession" wasn't just being used in the courts to justify search warrants and telephone taps anymore. It was about to be used in the media to sway public opinion against efforts to get any of the men released.

At the end of July, *The New Yorker* published a story by Pulitzer Prize–winning author Seymour Hersh about cooperation between Syrian and American intelligence agencies since 9/11. American intelligence and State Department officials told Hersh that "by early 2002 Syria had emerged as one of the C.I.A.'s most effective intelligence allies in the fight against Al Qaeda, providing an outpouring of information that came to an end only with the invasion of Iraq." Because of that, Hersh wrote, the head of the CIA, George Tenet, "had become one of Syria's champions in the interagency debate over how to deal with its government." Apparently, Tenet was up against officials in the Pentagon, who saw Syria as a problem, and had "prevented all kinds of action against Syria." The intelligence that had won Tenet's support included information that helped avert attacks on American targets, including "a suspected plot against an American target in Ottawa."[3]

Here in Canada, *The Globe and Mail*'s Colin Freeze and CanWest's Ottawa bureau chief, Robert Fife, chased the story about the Ottawa target. American and Canadian sources were all too happy to oblige, and turned to Fife.

Happy to oblige, but not on the record.

Fife's story, subtitled "Tipoff from Syria bears fruit," ran on the front pages of the *National Post*, *Ottawa Citizen*, and several other CanWest newspapers, and cited unnamed "American intelligence sources" confirming that Syrian authorities had provided the CIA with intelligence that helped avert an al-Qaeda conspiracy to attack the U.S. Embassy in Ottawa.[4] The "intelligence" bore striking resemblance to the "confession" Ahmad had been forced to make under torture in Syria. According to the headline, the terrorists' objective was to "at least kill Marines guarding [the] diplomatic site." Fife quoted "one high level source" as saying, "We were basically able to round up a network that was going to carry out the plot."

"Sources would not give a time frame for the attack nor say whether it involved a bomb," Fife wrote, but said that it was Syrian intelligence that had tipped off the CIA, which in turn tipped off Canadian authorities. Fife wrote that "one official would only tell CanWest News Service that Mr. Arar, a 36-year-old engineer, is a 'very bad guy'" who received training at an al-Qaeda base. Flynt Leverett, a former CIA analyst, also confirmed the existence of the Ottawa plot, describing the "intelligence" received from Syria: "We could break up networks. Bad guys got arrested. It was useful stuff."[5]

At the end of the story, Fife mentioned that Monia had denied allegations that Maher was linked to terrorism. But Fife didn't contact Amnesty International or any other human rights experts to inquire about Syria's human-rights record. Nor did he question the credibility of information from the Syrians or raise the possibility that the information was the fruits of torture.

Setting aside the credibility of Syrian intelligence, or the credibility of information from sources who refuse to go on record, it turns out that one of the sources who was willing to be named didn't have much credibility himself. Testifying under oath at the Arar Inquiry two years later, former CIA analyst Flynt Leverett, when asked if he had any direct knowledge of any specific plot to attack the U.S. Embassy, as he had told Fife, replied simply, "I don't know about specific plots, no."[6] His quotes were accurate, he maintained; it was just the way the story was written that was the problem.

Leverett was quoted in Seymour Hersh's story, too, which reported that the Syrians had helped the United States prevent an attack on an American target in Ottawa. In 2005, Hersh was in

Montreal to speak at a Canadian Association for Security and Intelligence Studies conference and commented on his story about the plot in a casual conversation with other journalists there. Asked about the plot to blow up the U.S. Embassy, he said, "I don't believe it anymore." He added that, at the time, even Ambassador Pillarella thought "it was a given that [Maher] was bad, and the case was good."[7]

In the Arar Report, Justice O'Connor concluded that, over time, government officials "intentionally leaked classified information" and "used the media to put a spin" on Maher's case and damage his reputation. Commenting on the leak in Fife's story in particular, he said that "the apparent purpose behind this leak is not attractive: to attempt to influence public opinion against Mr. Arar at a time when his release from imprisonment in Syria was being sought by the Government of Canada, including the Prime Minister."[8]

Fife still believes today that his sources believed what they were saying. "These were serious and senior and credible people who were in the loop," he says. "The only thing I would do differently now is I would have worked harder to provide a balance. I do feel bad, as a journalist, that I didn't work harder to provide that balance."[9]

Fife's story, of course, was just one of several in which Canadian government officials attempted to sway public opinion against the men and their advocates.[10] The leaks worked, for a while anyway, doing irreparable damage to the reputations of Maher, Ahmad, and Abdullah. In the long run, however, the leakors' attempts at damage control would backfire. In the meantime, Monia was forced once again to defend her husband's reputation. Her letter to the editor, titled "Where's the Evidence?" was published in the next day's *National Post*.[11] In it, she pointed out that for three and a half months, the Syrians had denied access to Maher, and asked if the leaks were to justify something that had happened to Maher: "Have the Syrians hurt my husband? Is this why my husband is being put on trial in the media now? Is my husband still alive?"

Maher's identity as a father and professional engineer was being stripped away, and any efforts to help him were being cast in a negative light now, too. It was during this week that the government told the media about the prime minister's letter to the Syrian president delivered by Senator de Bané on July 22. The prime minister had intervened to help a "terror suspect," the *National Post*'s front-page headline read.[12] Not a father, husband, or brilliant engineer.

James Bissett, who wrote the ill-informed commentary in November 2002 blasting parliamentarians for criticizing U.S. authorities for their treatment of Maher, decided it was time to speak up again. "If Canadians require further evidence why our allies in the war against terrorism no longer trust us, they need look no further than the Maher Arar case," he wrote in a commentary published in the *National Post*.[13] Despite allegations that he is a terrorist, Bissett wrote, "our government has gone to extraordinary lengths to demand Mr. Arar's release and his return to Canada." Bissett, it seems, had already concluded that Maher was guilty. Or didn't care if he wasn't.

It was in this week on July 30 that the *Ottawa Citizen* article by Robert Fife reported that Solicitor General Wayne Easter "would not discount the possibility ... that rogue elements in the RCMP passed on intelligence information to U.S. authorities leading to [Maher's] arrest and deportation."[14] Easter would later say that he'd never used the term *rogue elements* and that Fife had taken "a lot of journalistic liberty" in the story.[15] The RCMP had assured him, Easter said, that there hadn't been any official discussions with the United States approving Maher's deportation. His published remarks and Fife's story sparked a storm of controversy, helping to turn the media's questions back to what the RCMP, not Maher, had done wrong.

Back at the Integrated National Security Enforcement Team's operational room at the RCMP's "A" Division headquarters, someone had posted a sign on the bulletin board reading:

"Beware rogue elephants ... The Easter Bunny."[16] The sign stayed up for two weeks.

The RCMP had, of course, provided information that had led to the U.S. decision to send Maher to Syria. It had labelled him an Islamic extremist with suspected ties to al-Qaeda and had asked that he be put on a U.S. watch list. The request had gone, in writing, from the RCMP, making it "official." But the RCMP swung into action to "correct" the record anyway. Assistant Commissioner Proulx, the head of national security investigations at RCMP headquarters, urged the Americans to officially state that the RCMP had not asked that Maher be sent to Syria. Commissioner Zaccardelli met with U.S. ambassador Cellucci to ask the same thing.[17] Within twenty-four hours on July 31, the U.S. Embassy had released a statement saying that the decision to send Maher to Syria had been its own. The Americans also said that although they "consult and exchange information all the time, in the case of the detention of Maher Arar, the U.S. did not consult with any Canadian law enforcement organization."[18] This just wasn't true. There had been ample consultation.

The back-and-forth about who said and knew what prompted calls for answers. Amnesty International, the Canadian Council on American Islamic Relations, NDP leader Jack Layton, and former ambassador to Israel Norman Spector called for a parliamentary inquiry into what role the RCMP may have played in what happened to Maher.

NINETEEN

3' x 6' x 7'

11 A.M., Friday, August 7, 2003
Room 130S, Centre Block, Parliament Hill, Ottawa

IT HAD BEEN FOUR MONTHS since the parliamentarians' fifteen-minute visit with Maher in April, and since then, the Syrians had been ignoring requests for consular access. The RCMP and CSIS were thwarting efforts to get Maher home, and unnamed Canadian officials continued to use the media to label Maher a terrorist. The London-based Syrian Human Rights Committee (SHRC) had mentioned Maher in its annual report, prompting Monia to ask the SHRC for more information. The committee sent Monia a letter claiming it had received "confirmed reports from confidential and knowledgeable sources" that Maher had been a subject to torture and mistreatment: "The torture includes beating by sticks and shredded cables on the sole[s] of his feet and on his body, the use of electricity and being squashed in a car tier [sic] for long hours, etc.... SHRC was told also that Syrian and foreign investigators interrogated Mr. Maher Arar, and that he was in a very weak condition because of torture and deprivation from sleep. It is worth mentioning that the conditions of the Syrian prisons are appalling, and that detainees are exposed to malnutrition, diseases, and many other risks."[1]

It was time to step up the public campaign.

On August 7, Monia held a news conference along with Alex Neve of Amnesty International and former Ottawa mayor Marion Dewar. She had released SHRC's letter to the media, and now, she said, it was time for Canada to increase the pressure and recall Ambassador Pillarella for consultations. Neve described the SHRC as a credible organization whose report should be taken seriously, especially given the time that had lapsed since anyone had had access to Maher. "Canada needs to be allowed back in there immediately. It's been nine or ten months since the detention began. That's far too long for anyone to be held without charges or a trial." Monia voiced her worst fears. "I am left asking why there has been no access to my husband. Is he so badly hurt they want no one to see him? Is he still alive?"[2]

The Syrian ambassador to Canada, Ahmad Arnous, denied the allegations: "Mr. Maher Arar has been met by two Canadian Members of Parliament accompanied by the Canadian ambassador in Syria and they reassured us that Maher Arar is in good health and good shape."[3] DFAIT's spokesperson backed up Arnous, saying that MPs Assadourian and Catterall, and the Canadian ambassador, had seen no signs of torture when they saw Maher in April.[4] But, of course, the parliamentarians had not had private access to Maher. "Torture is insidious and often invisible," Neve later told Canadian Press reporter Alexander Panetta, adding that he was certain Maher hadn't been "allowed to take off his shoes and socks and put his feet on the table" for the parliamentarians.[5]

Within hours of the news conference, Minister Graham's office called Ambassador Pillarella. Because of the torture allegations and intense media interest, Pillarella was asked to immediately press again for consular access. On the same day, Syria's ambassador to Canada was called into DFAIT and told Canada wanted access to Maher.[6]

Four days later, Pillarella informed senior Foreign Affairs officials by email that the Syrians had arranged a meeting with General Khalil on August 14, and that the visit with Maher "should help us to rebut the recent charges of torture."[7] Pillarella says he wrote this because he had no visible proof that torture had occurred. Justice O'Connor, in his report, describes the ambassador's choice of words as "troubling," because "on its face, it reveals an interest in disproving the allegations of torture, hardly the attitude one would expect from the Canadian ambassador with respect to allegations of torture against a Canadian citizen."[8]

Thursday, August 14, 2003
Far' Falastin, Damascus

MAHER, MEANWHILE, was wracking his brain for answers. "Who is William Sampson? Is he a journalist? Is he someone from the embassy?"

The Syrians had hauled him up to the interrogation floor two days earlier to ask about Sampson. Maher had no idea who Sampson was. Back in his cell, he agonized. "Because they make the detainees doubt themselves, it comes to the point where you doubt yourself. You think, 'If they are asking me about him, it must mean I know him.' That's what you start believing," he says. "And because of the low threshold for [anything suspicious] after 9/11, you start wondering 'Did I meet this person once in the mosque? Did I meet this person once in the street?'"

The next time the guard came to get him again, Maher guessed he was going to have a visitor because he was allowed outside in the courtyard. It was the fourth time he'd seen the sun in ten months. He paced around the courtyard, preparing himself to speak out. "I decided I had nothing to lose. I would rather be tortured physically than remain in the grave one more day." After about ninety minutes, the guard escorted him to a nearby building, where Salloum was waiting for him. "Martel is here. Do like every time," he instructed. But Maher had already decided that this time would be different.

"When will I be released?" Maher asked.

"Your case is not easy because it has an international dimension," he replied.

The two men entered General Khalil's huge, luxurious office. Maher was ordered to sit in a chair about twenty-five feet from

Martel's. Khalil was sitting behind his desk. Salloum sat between Khalil and Martel, giving him a clear view of Maher. There was also an interpreter present.

Martel spoke first, explaining circumstances had made it difficult to visit earlier. "I understand that you are exhausted like all prisoners, but has anything happened to you recently?" he asked.

"I am asking Syria to release me or let me see a judge. I want to know which Syrian law I have broken," Maher responded.

"There are negative reports in the media about you, saying you are being beaten. Are you being beaten?"

Maher spoke as quickly as he could. "Not now, but in the beginning, yes. You have to understand, I have been living in a grave. My cell is very small. It is only three by six by seven feet, there is no light, no heat, no mattress, no reading, and I have no hot water even in winter. And I am sleeping on the floor."

"No, no, this is not true!" the interpreter interrupted.

Salloum glared at Maher. "Have you forgotten your Arabic?" he asked him in Arabic.

"Were you beaten recently?" Martel persisted.

Maher didn't respond. He felt frustrated. Didn't the man hear what he'd just said about the grave? "I thought to myself, 'I am already scared. Why does he want me to repeat it?'"

"Were you beaten? The newspapers say you are paralyzed," said Martel.

"I am not paralyzed," he responded excitedly. Was that supposed to make the beating any less significant? he wondered.

"I took office recently and I am going to help you," Khalil said, trying to calm Maher down. This was a lie, of course. Khalil had been at Far' Falastin for three and a half years.

Maher turned to him. "I am going crazy, do you understand that?" Then he turned to Martel. "I am mentally destroyed."

"Are all prisoners treated this way? I hope he is not being treated differently from other prisoners," Martel said to Khalil.

Khalil didn't answer but said, through the interpreter, that Maher's case would go to court within a week. Maher told

Martel he wanted to appoint his own lawyer, but Khalil refused, saying, "We have hundreds of lawyers." Maher then asked Martel to enlist the help of Monia and his father's cousin.

As the meeting ended, Maher shook hands with everyone, making a point of thanking Salloum, who was fuming.

"Tell him the media reports are not true," he ordered Maher.

"The press will know the truth when I get back," Maher said.

Maher had caught the Syrians by surprise. They had taken it for granted that he would stay submissive. Back in his cell, he sat terrified, waiting to be dragged upstairs and tortured. Salloum was angry. The guards were angry. Everything had changed. "Not knowing what they would do to me—it was hard. It was mental torture."

Nothing happened for five days. Then, on Tuesday, he was taken to see Khaled. "He made me sit on the floor and gave me a couple of sheets of paper," Maher recalls. "Khaled said, 'Write down your confession.' He was so angry, because of what I had done. And then when I was sitting down he kicked me on my shoulder. That was painful for four or five days. He threatened me, saying I deserved to be put in the tire." Maher told Khaled he didn't know what to write. Khaled dictated to him from a written report. "He said, 'Write down what I tell you. My name is Maher Arar. I live in Montreal.' I tried to correct him and he hit me again. He told me, 'Just write down what I tell you to write!'"

After Maher finished writing his "confession," Khaled forced him to sign it and place his thumbprint on it.

"No one has ever done what you did," Khaled said, referring to Maher's outburst.

What would happen next? Maher asked. Khaled told him he'd be handed over to the Canadian Embassy. "I felt some hope, but because they had always lied I didn't believe him," Maher says. Maher was left in his cell for about thirty minutes, then taken to the military investigations branch, Far' Tahkek Alaskare, in the same security compound. There, Maher waited in a room for nine hours before being escorted to a common cell. Forty-six prisoners were crowded into the twenty-by-fifteen-foot cell. "There was nothing on the ground, no blankets," Maher recalls. "Just people packed in. The guards could barely open the door because it was so full of people." The heat was stifling, so most of the prisoners had stripped down to their underwear. The prisoners were shocked to hear that he'd been in the grave for ten months and ten days.

The next morning, guards blindfolded Maher and took him into a room. When the blindfold was removed, Maher saw a car tire and a cable on the floor. Interrogators read through his "confession," then took his photograph. Blindfolding him again, the interrogators made him stand in a hallway facing the wall for two hours before taking him back to the cell. Thirty minutes later, the guards, armed with rifles, came to the cell and called his name, telling him to bring his things. They handed him his wallet, then took him upstairs to sign for all of his belongings. Then, led outside, he was put in the backseat of a station wagon, blind-folded, and ordered to put his head down.

"Where are you taking me?" Maher asked.

"To Sednaya prison."

Thursday, August 14, 2003
Ottawa

MONIA HAD BEEN AT A FRIEND'S HOME doing an interview with CBC television when she learned that the Syrians had agreed to let Martel see Maher. The call came from Myra Pastyr-Lupul at the consular division. Keep it quiet, she advised; don't tell the media. Monia rushed home to anxiously wait by the phone for news.

The next morning, Pastyr-Lupul phoned again to say the visit had taken place and that she wanted Monia to know before Minister Graham spoke with the media. A few minutes later, the media calls began. A *Globe and Mail* journalist said she'd just spoken with Gar Pardy. She said that a consular official had reported that Maher had confirmed he wasn't tortured and wanted Monia to be more discreet—he didn't want adverse media attention because it would only hurt his case. More calls came, this time from CBC's *The National* and from the *National Post*. These journalists said that, according to Minister Graham, consular officials had seen Maher privately and he'd confirmed he hadn't been tortured. And they all wanted to know if Monia was going to respect her husband's wishes to keep quiet.[9]

As much as she would have liked to believe Maher hadn't been tortured, Monia wouldn't until she could see him for herself. She soon learned what Graham had told the media: "I've just been speaking to my officials in Ottawa, who have been on the phone to Damascus this morning. Mr. Arar has been visited by our consular officials in jail. Our consular officials have assured us that he's in good physical condition. He personally, totally rejects all allegations of torture. He was interviewed independently by our consular officials and he has stated that his condition is better than it was before we started to intervene on his behalf."[10]

All those asked about this statement at the Arar Inquiry said they couldn't remember who briefed Minister Graham that day. He'd been on his way to a press scrum about the William Sampson case—Sampson had been released a few days earlier—when a call came in about the consular visit to Maher. Graham says he just repeated what he'd been told.

The implications were startling. Would Canadians stop caring when they read in the next day's papers that Maher hadn't been tortured? How could anyone be so sure he hadn't?

Then the lights went out and the media calls stopped. At 4:11 P.M., much of Ontario and the northeastern United States experienced the biggest blackout in North American history. Fifty million people, including the journalists chasing the story, were suddenly without electricity. The next day, few newspapers were published in Ontario, and in the coming days, most of the coverage of the minister's ill-advised statement was buried in the news about the blackout.

But the impact of the statement was to linger for years. Justice O'Connor would later say in his report of the Arar Inquiry that the minister's statement had been "inaccurate " and "unfortunate":

> While there might have been no immediate consequence, statements like the Minister's create perceptions in the public mind, particularly in newsworthy cases such as Mr. Arar's. The perception that Mr. Arar had not been tortured was wrong and, no doubt, the Minister's statements planted the seeds of that misperception in the minds of some. Tellingly, even during the early stages of the Inquiry, some government officials still believed that Mr. Arar had not been tortured. In all likelihood, those officials and probably some members of the public were influenced by the inaccurate message taken from the August 14 consular visit. It is ironic and disappointing that the consular visit of August 14, which was meant to help Mr. Arar, ended up being turned against him in this way.[11]

As it turned out, Martel's report on the visit had been misleading too. "He was able to express himself freely at times," Martel wrote, "and he indicated that prison conditions had been more difficult in the past than now."[12] Martel wrote that Maher "mentioned that he did not wish to have adverse media publicity as he felt this would only harm his case," something Maher says he didn't say. According to Martel's report, Maher's "long detention had destroyed him mentally," yet "he confirmed he had not been beaten nor tortured." Years later Martel would admit that Maher had told him the dimensions of his cell—and he had jotted them down in the notes he was taking during the meeting—but he didn't include that detail in the report he sent to the decision makers in Ottawa. At the Arar Inquiry, Martel testified that, "if he had a window or a grate, even if he was sleeping on the floor, I couldn't at the time conclude it was inhumane. It was small, yes, but that didn't mean it was inhumane. Hundreds of people are in that situation."[13]

Wednesday, August 20, 2003
Sednaya prison, Sednaya, Syria

THREE STOREYS HIGH and shaped liked the three-pronged
Mercedes-Benz logo, the German-designed Sednaya prison is
located in the town of Sednaya, in the mountains north of
Damascus.[14] While it was being built in 1987, the townspeople
were told it was to be a hospital. It turned out to be one of Syria's
most infamous detention centres instead. Each floor of each wing
contains twenty common cells, measuring about twenty by fifteen
feet. The total number of detainees is often double the intended
capacity of five thousand. The Syrian Human Rights Committee
says that its interrogation offices "are equipped with the most
modern and developed torture instruments."[15]

Maher had heard about Sednaya when in the Far' Tahkek
Alaskare at Far' Falastin. He'd been warned that detainees are
tortured when they arrive at Sednaya, so during the ride there he
tried to think of ways to avoid being tortured. When he arrived
at the prison, an official asked if he'd met bin Laden. He replied
that he had never met the man and had nothing to do with
al-Qaeda. Officials searched Maher's bag, taking most of his
belongings, though they let him keep some clothes in a bag. Then
they took him to a large room where he could see other detainees.
Maher later learned they'd just been beaten. Maher hoped that
by saying he'd met with General Khalil and the Canadian consul
just days before, he'd avoid torture. It seemed to work—he
wasn't subjected to the same initiation ritual as the others but
instead taken to a common cell.

Of the nine other prisoners in Maher's cell, most had university degrees. Maher later learned that the wing they were in was
dubbed the "al-Qaeda wing." Most of the detainees, however,
weren't even accused of being part of al-Qaeda.

The cell contained a toilet and a shower, but no running water.
Instead, guards refilled buckets. The prisoners kept themselves
and the cells clean to curb the spread of disease. Prisoners slept
on the floor with blankets. The electricity cut out several times a

day, partly because the prisoners, many of whom where engineers, had invented a way to heat water by tapping into the electrical system. They hooked wires up to a used sardine tin and dropped it into a bucket of water as a heating element. But if more than two or three prisoners did this at once in their various cells, they'd overload the system and the power went out.

The food was better than it had been at Far' Falastin, but it was still often rotten and inedible. Many prisoners used their own money to buy food. Once a month they could order basic staples, and twice a month they could order vegetables. Maher thinks he had lost about forty pounds since being detained. At Sednaya he started gaining his weight back. "I realize now that part of the reason I was sent there was to fatten me up before being released," he says. No one was allowed to pray. If caught, they were beaten. They weren't allowed to grow their beards, either.

But Maher found the conditions at Sednaya so much easier than at Far' Falastin. After Maher had been at Sednaya for about a week, the guards let the seventy-five or so prisoners of his wing walk around together in a common area. "This was paradise," Maher says. "To be able to walk and stretch and move."

Sometimes, he heard news from outside. A prisoner in another cell had somehow managed to get a radio and keep it hidden. One day he passed the news along to Maher that he'd heard a report that the Canadian prime minister had sent a letter to the Syrian president about Maher's case.

A few weeks after arriving at Sednaya, Maher was teaching English to his cellmates when they heard a commotion in the hallway.

"There is another Canadian! There is another Canadian!" someone said.

"I looked up, and saw a man, but I did not recognize him," Maher recalls. "His head was shaved, and he was very, very thin and pale. He was very weak. When I looked closer, I recognized him. It was Abdullah."

Monday, August 25, 2003
Far' Falastin, Damascus

ABDULLAH HAD MISSED MAHER AFTER HE WAS TRANSFERRED. "He was the only person around me who I had known before," he says. "No matter how much I got to know the others, I always trusted Maher the most." Most importantly, he says, he knew what Maher looked like. He'd been living in the dark for more than fifteen months and had never seen any of the prisoners he whispered with. "At least I knew Maher's face. When I spoke with other people I couldn't even imagine what they looked like. I knew what he looked like. He wasn't just a voice like the others."

A few days after Maher left, two of the interrogators, Abdallah and Haitham, told Abdullah that he would be going to a more comfortable place, where he'd see Maher. The next morning he was taken upstairs. This time, Haitham gave him a falafel sandwich for breakfast. "He was very nice and waited in the room until I finished eating, then sent me back downstairs." A few days later, Abdullah was called up again, this time to sign some papers. Haitham gave Abdullah a pen and paper. He had a handwritten report in his hands and dictated from it, ordering Abdullah to write down what he said. Abdullah was then told to sign and place his thumbprint on each page. Haitham told him that he would be transferred the next day—to where he didn't say—then taken to a court, which would order his release, because there was no evidence that he'd done anything wrong or illegal.

"How will I go to court without a lawyer?" Abdullah asked.

"You don't need one, because there is no evidence you did anything wrong," Haitham replied.

The next day, after having lived there for one year, three months, and twenty-five days, Abdullah was released from the grave. Like Maher, he was brought to Far' Tahkek Alaskare. "As soon as we arrived, the guards started insulting me," Abdullah remembers. "They swore at me in English. They must have learned these words from movies."

The guards left him to wait for hours in an interrogation room, then took his bag and ordered him to hand over his eye glasses. "I told them I needed them to see, but they said [glasses] were forbidden." Then they took him to a common cell. "The cell was very small, with more than twenty-five people crowded in … we each had a space about twenty centimetres wide when it came time to lie down and sleep. We all had to lie on our sides, and couldn't move." Ten days later, Abdullah was loaded onto a bus with other prisoners. One of them told Abdullah they were going to Sednaya.

When they arrived at the immense facility, the prisoners were lined up against a wall inside. An officer asked Abdullah what he'd been accused of.

"I was accused of being a member of al-Qaeda, but I have been cleared. I will be going to court before being released," Abdullah said.

"Oh, yes," the man replied sarcastically. "That's why they sent you here! What they really meant was that they just didn't know how to make you confess. Once we hook you up to electricity and do our work, you will confess."

The other prisoners tried to reassure Abdullah—it was just a threat. The prisoners were taken up to the second floor. "I was so frail I could hardly get up the stairs," Abdullah recalls. "One of the other prisoners who was more than sixty years old had to help me carry my bag up the stairs." Most of the prisoners were led away, but Abdullah and two others were left in a large hallway for about an hour. Several officers approached with their commander, Mouhanad. One ordered Abdullah to take what he needed from his bag, so Abdullah grabbed a plastic bag and some clothes. Before long, the initiation ritual began. More prison officials came in with hand-held manual hair clippers—the kind used in barber shops. But at Sednaya, these clippers, with their dull blades and sharp teeth, were instruments of torture. Mouhanad ordered the officers to shear the hair off the prisoners' heads and to be ruthless. They jammed the clippers' sharp prongs into the prisoners' scalp, then squeezed the clippers' handles together to trap the hair and yank it out. "This was very painful and we were left bald except for uneven patches of hair all over our heads," Abdullah says.

They started with the oldest, a fifty-nine-year-old man. "They started shouting at him and calling him names and then slapped him hard on the face, which threw him several feet away on the floor," Abdullah says. "They asked him to get up and then did it again. Then they made him lie on his stomach with his feet up and beat him on the soles of his feet with a wide, thick, long belt. I couldn't watch and had to turn away."

The second man was beaten much like the first before the officers turned their attention to Abdullah. They slapped his face and kicked him, then, ordering him to lie on his stomach with his feet up, beat the soles of his feet. Abdullah heard Mouhanad ask whether he was the Canadian. The guards answered yes. In that case, Mouhanad said, he would like to continue the beating himself. "This was different than what I had experienced before—the torture was short and intense and they didn't want information," Abdullah recalls.

After the beatings, Abdullah and the other two prisoners were ordered to keep their heads and eyes down and walk. They were led down narrow stairs to a set of metal doors that when opened, Abdullah says, revealed what looked "like an opening to an underground hole," opening onto a hallway lined with single cells.

"Do they have hotels like this in Canada?" Mouhanad mocked Abdullah.

The cell was dark and filthy. About six feet wide and nine feet deep, it had an open toilet stall, and the stench was terrible. The officers brought each prisoner a gallon of water, four blankets, and a pillow. "I was in a lot of pain, and very cold," Abdullah remembers, "so I just tried to clean an area on the floor, then folded three of the blankets in half to lie on, and covered myself with the fourth. The next day I started cleaning the washroom.

This took four days to do, as there was feces all over the floor and urine on the walls."

The cell had no running water, so each day a guard took the water bucket to refill. In the washroom was a second, damaged container, which Abdullah fixed by lining it with his plastic bag and then used to collect dirty water to flush the toilet with at the end of the day. After a few days, another prisoner, one who had been at Sednaya for one and a half years, talked a guard into passing along his undamaged container to Abdullah. Abdullah used this to save a little water each day to wash himself and his clothes.

The only light in Abdullah's cell filtered in from down the hall and through the bars at the top of the cell's solid door. "I agonized over my situation. What I would do if it got colder, what I would do when I ran out of the little soap I had, and what if I never got out of this cave. It was very, very quiet and I felt like I was behind the sun," he says. After a few days one of the guards showed some compassion, putting a light bulb in a socket close to Abdullah's cell. Abdullah spent ten days locked in the cell before being taken to see an official.

"Are you a member of al-Qaeda?" the official questioned Abdullah.

"No, I have said before, I am not. I do not share their beliefs. I do not believe in violence."

"Are you related to Adnan al-Malki?" the official asked. This was not an interrogation question. He was just curious.

Abdullah told him that Adnan al-Malki had been his father's cousin. (It turned out that the prisoners at Sednaya, especially the younger ones, knew more about Adnan al-Malki than Abdullah did, as they had learned about him in school.)

Guards took Abdullah to a door leading into the "al-Qaeda wing," then pushed him through. He was immediately surrounded by dozens of prisoners. Who was he? Where did he come from? What was he accused of? "They led me towards one of the cells, and I then I saw Maher. He led me into his cell and then they all took care of me. I must have looked very bad because they were all very concerned. They took my clothes to clean and heated water so I could wash."

A few days later, a guard took Abdullah to an office. He was surprised to see his mother and cousin there, waiting for him. Abdullah saw the shock on their faces when he walked in the room. "I was shaved and mostly bald except with patches of hair sticking out. I felt and must have looked terrible."

Abdullah's mother was furious to see what they'd done to his head—it was clear that he'd been humiliated.

Abdullah asked his mother why his father wasn't there.

"He cannot take it," she said. "He just cannot stand to see you in jail."

Looking back, Abdullah doesn't know why he took the risk and decided to speak openly. Maybe it was because the officials watching on were with the prison rather than with the Syrian Military Intelligence. Or maybe he just didn't care anymore. "I was beaten," he told his mother and cousin. "There was a report that came from Canada before I was detained in April 2002. That's why they took me. Also I know that a Canadian delegation was in Syria on November 24," he said, recalling the cover of the report he had seen during an interrogation round.

The prison officials seemed unconcerned with Abdullah's statement. They simply said they had nothing to do with any beatings.

TWENTY

"You Are Safe Now"

Saturday, September 20, 2003
Abu Za'abal prison, northeast of Cairo

"MOM, I THINK IT IS TIME to go public and get my story out," Ahmad whispered.

His mother was visiting him at Abu Za'abal, and the Egyptian officials watching over the visit had left the room for a moment. Samira agreed. It was time to speak out. She was returning to Canada soon; she would talk to the family and they would go to the media.

After spending more than four months at the Istiqbal Tora prison, Ahmad had been transferred back to Abu Za'abal, in August. He was locked into the same cell as before, for nineteen hours a day. But this time, between ten in the morning and three in the afternoon each day, guards would open his and the other prisoners' doors so that there were free to mix and spend time in the courtyard. It made a huge difference to have that small bit of freedom, he says. He didn't have to squeeze his wet clothes through the hole in the door for other prisoners to hang out to dry—he could hang out his own laundry now. He had bought a small radio from one of the guards, too, and, when the signal was good, could listen to Radio Canada International and the BBC news.

Ahmad was having a lot of difficulty walking because of his fall in the Nasr City facility. His knee was painful and swollen. It wasn't just his knee, though. "I was suffering a lot.... It had been too long and my body was in bad shape," Ahmad remembers. "I had constant diarrhea. My skin was awful. Now I had severe bronchitis too and was spitting up green phlegm. My feet were swollen and dark. My back was in constant pain."[1]

Back at Abu Za'abal prison, he had another visit with consular officials on September 24. He hadn't seen anyone from the embassy for seven months, and he was furious when they finally came. A man named Roger Chen was there instead of Stuart Bale. Anna Papas, who visited previously, was there also, as was Mira Wassef. As always, both prison and SSI officials were watching over the visit.

Ahmad asked the Canadian officials why it had been so long since they'd visited. They were following policy, they replied— they were to visit four times per year. There had been staff changes, too. And besides, Ahmad was getting family visits. This infuriated Ahmad. He'd heard about the William Sampson case on the radio. Why did the government seem to care more about that case than his? "I felt that my government did this to me, and now they were doing nothing to help me. It is like they wanted to leave me to rot," Ahmad says.

Like Bale had before, Chen asked if Ahmad would agree to meet with a Canadian security official. Remembering the torture he'd faced at Mabahith Amn al-Dawla al-'Ulya, the State Security Investigations services facility in Nasr City, Ahmad said he would agree. Then he told them about his knee. "I fell six months ago, and now I can hardly walk." He had asked prison officials for medical attention but they ignored his requests.

Ahmad explained to the consular officials that he'd been transferred several times among Abu Za'abal, Istiqbal Tora, and the Mabahith Amn al-Dawla al-'Ulya facility. They asked why, and Ahmad, in front of the Egyptian officials, said he didn't know. He couldn't tell them that each time he was sent to Nasr City, it was for more interrogation and torture, and that much of the information being used in those sessions could only have come from Canada. At one point in the meeting, Ahmad noticed that the Egyptian officials were distracted and so took a chance, hurriedly whispering in Arabic to Mira Wassef, "When I am transferred to Nasr City, it is for interrogation." He hoped she'd figure out the rest.

"I wanted them to know I was being interrogated and tortured when those transfers happened," Ahmad says. "I did not dare to say torture, but she should have known from what I did say."

Ahmad can't remember for sure, but thinks it was soon after this consular visit that he was transferred to the Giza province branch of the State Security Investigations Service. His release order had been confirmed for the third time, so he was being transferred to be rearrested. The Giza branch is located in a residential area about an hour's drive from Abu Za'abal. Ahmad would later learn that his aunt lived only two blocks away. He was kept, along with the other prisoners, in a crowded holding area. Ahmad remembers hearing the screams of someone being tortured when he first arrived. After a few days, the holding area was so overcrowded that Ahmad and several others were transferred to a paramilitary camp on the outskirts of Cairo. They had more room there, Ahmad says, with far fewer prisoners in each holding area. He was kept there for about two weeks before being transferred back to Abu Za'abal.

11:00 A.M., Thursday, September 25, 2003
Room 269, West Block, Parliament Hill, Ottawa

IT WAS STANDING ROOM ONLY in the parliamentary committee room. Media, Members of Parliament, and their aides crowded in, and Monia was there with her supporters, too. RCMP assistant commissioner Richard Proulx had had the misfortune of being chosen to represent the RCMP at a Commons Foreign Affairs Committee hearing. The committee wanted to know what the RCMP's role was in Maher's case.

Asked several times whether the RCMP had provided the United States with information leading to the decision to send

Maher to Syria, Proulx was evasive. "The RCMP does not, as a matter of practice or procedure, reveal details regarding operational police matters in order to protect the integrity of on-going investigations and to respect the privacy of individuals involved," he said.[2] The irony of this statement, coming so soon after a flurry of leaks to the media, wasn't lost on the committee members.

When a frustrated Tory MP, Bill Casey, pointed out that several operational details had been provided in published media reports, Proulx said that yes, "there were some comments in the media that the RCMP was involved in the decision made by the Americans. I'm saying here today before you that I want to make it clear that the RCMP was not involved in the decision made by the U.S. authorities to arrest or to deport Mr. Arar."

Proulx was visibly uncomfortable with the questions. He shifted in his seat and cleared his throat repeatedly. He became more uncomfortable when Liberal MP John Harvard asked why the RCMP wouldn't help get Maher freed.

"Mr. Proulx, you look a little uncomfortable in your chair. Imagine what Mr. Arar must feel stuck in a hell hole in Damascus," Harvard said. "When you take this 'no comment' position behind an operational barrier, some people would assume you have information that is bad about him.... Does the RCMP feel no obligation whatsoever to clear Mr. Arar?"

"First of all, I'm not feeling uncomfortable in my chair.... I fail to see what I could do with the Syrian authorities. I am a police officer and I don't know the reason why Mr. Arar is detained in Syria so how can I help?... What I am trying to say, Mr. Chair, is that we are not dealing with the Syrian authorities. This is really a case for the Department of Foreign Affairs to deal with," Proulx replied.

When it was Monia's turn to speak, she didn't appear uncomfortable at all. The room fell completely silent.

"Today it's exactly one year since I saw my husband for the last time," she began. Her six-year-old daughter, she continued, had started school. "[My] son hasn't seen his father for one year; he was only 7 months when he saw his father for the last time. Now he's a baby of 19 months, he walks, he runs, he's even started talking, but he doesn't know his father," she said.

Monia said she wanted the prime minister to state clearly that Maher must not face trial in Syria but be returned to Canada immediately: "If the Syrian President and the Syrian authorities continue to ignore the Canadian government, then Syria must know Canada will suspend its ongoing efforts to accelerate trade and investment in Syria." She called on the committee to urge the American government to take responsibility for sending a Canadian citizen to a country that it acknowledges abuses human rights. "The United States must be asked to intervene on my husband's behalf," she demanded.

Monia also called for an inquiry into the contradictory statements made by the solicitor general and the RCMP. She and her children had the right to know if the security agency had any role in Maher's detention, she said. "Canadians have a right to know if our own security agencies are choosing to use the courts in authoritarian regimes instead of our own justice system. If they didn't find anything on Maher Arar, they should say publicly today to the Syrians that Canada doesn't have any evidence to link Mr. Maher Arar to terrorist activities."

Liberal MP Irwin Cotler outlined a plan for the committee: Canada should ask the United States to intervene; demand Maher be returned before an unfair trial; work through the United Nations and urge allies such as France to back appeals to Syria; and, if these steps fail, apply economic and trade sanctions against Syria.

On the same day the committee met in Ottawa, Minister Graham met with Syrian Foreign minister Farouk Shara'a at the U.N. General Assembly in New York. Graham told Shara'a he wanted Maher back and raised the possibility that bilateral relations, and Canadian investment in Syria, could be jeopardized if he wasn't released. Shara'a said he'd do his best to ensure a positive outcome, but a Syrian intelligence official at the meeting commented that the media attention wasn't helpful.[3]

A few days later, on October 1, Graham raised Maher's case with Amr Moussa, the secretary-general of the Arab League. He urged Moussa to help push for Maher's release, saying that consular cases in the Middle East were giving Canadians a poor perception of the Arab world. Moussa promised to urge Syria's Foreign minister to settle the case.[4]

Sunday, September 28, 2003
Sednaya prison, Sednaya, Syria

WHEN THE GUARD FIRST CALLED OUT HIS NAME, Maher didn't rush. Usually, guards called once, then returned fifteen minutes later. But it was Mouhanad, the senior guard, and he expected Maher's immediate attention. When Maher approached him, Mouhanad slapped him, hard, across the face. As Maher leaned forward, covering his face, Mouhanad hit him on the back of the head. Dizzy, Maher almost fell to the ground.

He was taken to a room where two officials ordered him to shave. Then they left him to wait. Eventually, the guards came back and accompanied Maher downstairs. Maher realized he was being transferred again. But when he asked where he was being sent, the men just swore at him and told him to shut up. "Don't ask questions or you'll be in trouble," they warned.

Put blindfolded in a car, Maher was taken to what he guessed was Far' Tahkek Alaskare, the military investigations branch, then directed onto a bus. After only a two-minute drive, he was led off the bus and into a building, where his blindfold was removed. He was back at Far' Falastin, in the prison manager's office.

"What brought you back here?" the manager asked.

"I don't know," Maher responded. "No one would tell me anything."

Maher was put in an interrogation room, then later transferred to a room across the hall. It was mid-afternoon by now. Maher paced. He could hear prisoners in nearby rooms being tortured and screaming, and felt very afraid. It was evening when the guards took him outside, where Khaled was waiting for him.

"How did you find your vacation?" he asked, mocking.

Maher didn't answer.

Khaled led Maher into another building and up to the third floor. There, Salloum walked up to him, shook his hand, and took him into a luxurious office, where a colonel sat behind a desk watching the Al Jazeera station on television. He turned to Maher, smiling. "If you go back to Canada, what will you say about us?"

"I will keep silent."

"We did not beat you."

No, Maher said. Salloum and others *had* beaten him.

"But only in the first week," Salloum said.

"Oh, probably because you refused to confess," the other colonel interjected.

Salloum and Khaled took him back outside. They were angry. "Why don't you love your country of origin?"

"I love this country, but my affairs and family are in Canada," Maher responded.

Maher spent the night in the room he'd waited in earlier. What was happening? he wondered. Why was he back here? Again he was being forced to hear the constant screams of others being tortured, and felt devastated. Aside from guards bringing him food, Maher saw no one for a week.

It was a Saturday morning when Khaled finally came and asked Maher where his belongings were. Still at Sednaya, Maher told him. That night, Khaled asked him to list his possessions. "We have decided to send you back to Sednaya," he said, then paused. "No, I am lying to you. You are going to Canada today or tomorrow."

Maher didn't believe him. The next morning, Khaled returned with Salloum, who was still very angry. He barked at Maher to wash his face.

Handcuffed, Maher was put in a car and taken to the Supreme State Security Court. At the courthouse, Maher waited, still chained, for almost two hours. The guards told him he would be seeing the prosecutor. When Maher asked for a lawyer, he was told he didn't need one. "Don't think you are safe in Canada, so don't say bad things there," one of the guards warned.

They took him up to the second floor. The colonel from Far' Falastin come out of a room, then Maher was shown in. Maher thinks one of the two men in the room was the prosecutor. "What is going on? I need a lawyer," Maher said.

"You don't need a lawyer."

The prosecutor read from Maher's "confession," while the other man took notes. Maher told him he was beaten and did not go to Afghanistan. The prosecutor told Maher to sign and stamp his fingerprint on a document, which he did, though he wasn't permitted to see what had been written.

"We are letting you go," said the prosecutor.

"What do you mean, am I being released?"

"Yes."

Maher didn't believe him. But arriving back at Far' Falastin, Maher caught sight of Martel in another car and wondered if it was indeed true. Was he really being released?

Inside, Khaled brought Maher his bags, computer, and cellphone. "We've never had a case like yours," he said. "I have had nightmares. It caused us a lot of trouble. We don't normally have visits and media coverage to deal with. I just want you to disappear from here."

Maher was taken to General Khalil's office. Martel was there with another man from the embassy, who introduced himself as Tracy Reynolds, the *chargé d'affaires*.

Khalil spoke to Maher in Arabic. "The president was calling me every week and wanted me to take care of you. Not only you, but all prisoners. How is the Syrian community in Canada? Is it big?"

"No, it is small," Maher replied. "But there's an excellent Syrian pastry shop in Montreal."

"I'll come and visit you one day," Khalil said. Then he pointed his finger at Maher. "I want you to say good things about this country. Are you friends with George [Salloum] now?"

"I have nothing against George," Maher said.

Martel asked if Maher could leave Syria that day, and Khalil assured him he would issue a statement so that there was no issue at the airport. The men all stood and shook hands. Salloum, waiting for them in the hall, was still angry. He escorted them outside, where he shook hands with each of them. Then Martel and Maher climbed into the waiting embassy car and drove off, winding their way through the grounds of the security compound, out through the gates, and into the busy Damascus streets.

12:30 P.M., Monday, October 6, 2003
Dorval International Airport, Montreal

WHEN A-O CANADA TEAM MEMBERS heard through the media about Maher's release, they decided to deactivate the customs lookout issued in his name. Apparently, "they felt a secondary examination would not be useful under the circumstances."[5]

Maher's Air France flight touched down at Montreal's Dorval International Airport in the early afternoon of Monday, October 6. He'd gone from the Far' Falastin to the embassy with Martel, then to Martel's house to shower before going to the airport to catch a flight home the same night. He was accompanied on the journey home by Leo Martel, who asked many questions about what had happened. Maher was still in shock and didn't know yet who to trust, so kept his answers brief. After some negotiation, Minister Graham's office had arranged for a van large enough to carry Monia, her children, and her mother to the

airport to meet him. The group of people who'd worked closely
with Monia through the year were there too, including Alex Neve
of Amnesty International and Riad Saloojee of the Council on
American Islamic Relations.[6] On the way there, Monia worried
about how much Maher, and she, had changed since they last saw
each other. Myra Pastyr-Lupul, from DFAIT's consular division,
sat in the passenger seat and seemed preoccupied with other
matters, though she turned to Monia several times to remind her
that Maher had said he didn't want media attention.

At the airport, they joined Maher's sister and mother in the Air
France executive lounge to wait for Maher's arrival as more than
two hundred journalists and camera operators jostled for space
outside the lounge entrance. When the call came to say Maher
had landed, Monia was escorted to the secure arrivals area to
meet him on her own. The man who walked through the door
was very pale and thin, and wearing a black sweater much too
big for him. His beard and hair were uncharacteristically untidy.
And he was visibly scared.

"You are safe now," Monia whispered in his ear.

Taking his hand, she led him through a back corridor and up
to the lounge, passing a hallway packed with the media on their
way. Maher was shocked—he hadn't been told how much media
interest there was in his case.

In the lounge, the family reunion was tearful, an overwhelming
mix of nervous laughter and crying. "I was still in shock and
disoriented," Maher recalls. "Until I de-boarded the plane, I
didn't know what was coming next. I wasn't told about the
media interest. I didn't trust anything people told me then. It was
like someone coming out of the grave.... You have to learn again
and adapt again. Those first moments were not easy."

After some discussion, Maher decided he'd say a few words to
the media. Just as he and Monia were about to walk out to face
the cameras, MP Sarkis Assadourian stopped Maher to fasten a
red maple leaf pin onto his sweater. The two walked past the
hundred or so assembled journalists, cameras flashing, to sit side

by side at a table in front of a mass of microphones and cameras. Clutching Monia's hand beneath the table, Maher said in a voice that was barely audible, "I'm very glad to get back home. I'm so excited to see my family again. My kids grew up in the past year. I want to thank my fellow Canadians who helped to get me back."

To the journalists, Maher appeared "pale," "sickly," "visibly exhausted," "nervous," and "subdued," his "face gaunt" and his "skin grey."[7]

Monia was anything but subdued. "This has been a terrible tragedy for our family," she said. "I wish to thank all Canadians who helped us during this nightmare so that there would be justice for my husband." Then, wagging her finger back and forth, she continued, "This is just [the] beginning of justice." Asked what she meant, she explained, "It's only the beginning. We are going to take some time to get together and to spend it with the children. And I think after that time, we are going to answer all the questions, not all the questions of you, but all the questions of Canadians. They must know the truth."[8] The couple stood up and slowly made their way back to the lounge, leaving Saloojee and Neve to answer the media's questions so that they could dodge the cameras and retreat to the privacy of Maher's mother's home.

"The full narrative of what happened is yet to be uncovered," Saloojee told journalists. "We've called before, and we will be calling more strenuously now, since he's now home and he's safe, for a full public inquiry to find out exactly what transpired and the nature of our government's involvement in sending a Canadian citizen to a foreign country where he has languished for one year and faced severe torture." Neve emphasized the need for an inquiry so that Maher could clear his name. "Clearly this shadow hangs over Mr. Arar and his family. What kind of information did Canadian authorities possess? Who did they share it with? He should be given the chance to clear his name or be cleared."

Just after noon, Wednesday, October 7, 2003
Room 269 West Block, Parliament Buildings, Ottawa

BACK IN OTTAWA, on the day of Maher's return, journalists had surrounded Solicitor General Wayne Easter as he stepped out of his caucus meeting. Would there be an inquiry into the case? "No, I will not agree to an inquiry," he said.[9]

The next day, he and RCMP deputy commissioner Loeppky faced the wrath of the Commons Foreign Affairs Committee. That the committee was dominated by Liberals didn't help either of them. The two didn't say much, but what they did say, they said over and over again, regardless of the question. Easter's mantra was that "the RCMP was not involved in the decision by American authorities to arrest and deport Mr. Arar"; that American authorities "acted independently and in accordance with their domestic laws"; and that "the RCMP did not at any time suggest to the United States authorities that Mr. Arar should be deported to Syria."[10]

Committee member after committee member pointed out that if the Americans had based their decision on information from Canada, then the decision wasn't really the point. They wanted to know if the information *behind* the American decision had come from Canada. Loeppky said he couldn't say, because to do so would be to confirm that the RCMP had been investigating Mr. Arar, and to do that would be to disrespect his rights. "We need to respect the rights of an individual to be presumed innocent," he said. "If we were to start talking publicly about anyone in our communities who is a suspect, that would really be an infringement of their rights and it would be inappropriate."

The cold answers from Loeppky and Easter angered Liberal MP John Harvard. "Aren't you as mad as a wet hen over the behaviour of the Americans?" he asked, incredulous. "They took a Canadian citizen, Wayne, and they sent him to a Syrian gulag.... He hasn't been proven guilty of anything. He was stuck in that Syrian gulag for one year. As a human being, Wayne

Easter, does that not depress you? Can you look me in the eye and say the system works?"

Prime Minister Chrétien, meanwhile, was also fending off calls for an inquiry. "Every time that we have a problem in government, we cannot have an inquiry on everything," he told reporters as he left a cabinet meeting. "It's no inquiry unless you have something to tell me I don't know."[11]

But the stonewalling by the prime minister, Easter, Loeppky, and other officials only served to fuel the call for a public inquiry, echoed in hundreds of newspaper editorials, columns, and letters to the editor over the course of the week.

Maher, needing time to recover and reconnect, spent the next several days at a friend's home, away from the reporters who had surrounded his home. He needed time with his family. He needed to get to know his son. He needed time to digest what had happened since he'd been detained, what had happened while he and his wife were apart. He needed to sit down with his supporters, including Alex Neve and Riad Saloojee, and provide them with an accurate account of what had happened.

While Maher sequestered himself with his family, much of the Canadian public and media were very clearly on his side, so Canadian officials tried to undermine Maher's credibility. They beat back calls for a public inquiry by selectively leaking information, much of it classified, and much of it untrue and the product of torture. Without evidence to back the allegations against Maher, Ahmad, or Abdullah in a court of law, the men would be tried in the media. The contrast between what the officials would say on the record and anonymously was stark.

On October 9, just three days after Maher returned home, the *Toronto Star* reported that "an official closely involved in the case [speaking] on condition that he not be quoted by name," said that Maher had been watched because "he had been to Afghanistan several times."[12] The source recounted a conversation to journalist Graham Fraser between a Canadian and an

American official while Maher was in U.S. detention. The account is remarkably similar to Sergeant Rick Flewelling's recollection of a phone conversation he had with an FBI official on October 5, 2002.[13] According to the unnamed official, the American asked if Canada would detain Maher if he returned; the Canadians had responded that they could not, as they didn't "have anything [with which] to lay charges against him." The Charter of Rights wouldn't allow it, the Canadian apparently said. The American official was apparently frustrated by the answer. The effect, of course, was to cast more suspicion on Maher and to make the RCMP look like it had staunchly defended his charter rights.

Two more stories ran the next day. This time an anonymous official contacted *The Globe and Mail*'s Jeff Sallot. The goal this time was to leave the impression that Maher hadn't been tortured. "Arar was not tortured, officials say; Engineer held in 'very bad' conditions, suffered psychological stress," the headline read.[14] Maher had "complained he was roughed up in Jordan and held in appalling physical conditions in a Syrian prison, but not physically tortured," said unnamed Canadian government sources. He "suffered enormous psychological stress and anguish during his 12 months in Syrian custody," and was "slapped around," but wasn't physically tortured, the officials maintained. Sallot would later personally and publicly apologize to Maher for writing the story: "I was trying hard to get a fresh angle on the story in advance of Maher's upcoming news conference and I wasn't skeptical enough about my source's information. I also didn't think about the impact this story would have on Maher. I have no excuse for being so careless. I am sorry for what I did."[15]

Sallot thinks the source believed what he said, and it could have been any number of officials. Martel had debriefed DFAIT on October 7 about what Maher had told him after his release and during the journey back to Canada. According to Martel, Maher had said he was "beaten" during the first two weeks in

Syrian detention but that he was not subjected to electric shock or stuffed into a tire. This information was shared within DFAIT and then with CSIS; someone there circulated a memo by email noting that Maher had claimed he hadn't been physically abused, except for being slapped a few times early on. The memo noted that Maher's conditions of detention had seriously affected his physical and mental health. The memo's author concluded that Maher "was not subjected to the physical abuse that is commonly associated with torture."[16]

In his report on the Arar Inquiry, Justice O'Connor concluded that the memo was "consistent with the reaction of several Canadian officials on Mr. Arar's return to Canada: they attempted to downplay the seriousness of the ordeal he had endured in Syria ... if Canadian officials were in any way involved in what happened to Mr. Arar, it would be better from their standpoint if he had not been seriously mistreated."[17]

The Ottawa Sun ran a story that day, too, in which an unnamed source claimed Maher had become a "person of interest" because "he had associates with alleged links to terrorist groups." The story went on to say that those "associates are now believed to be held in detention."[18]

But the leaks didn't have any impact on the calls for a full public inquiry being voiced by members of all political parties, several prominent Canadians, and, as before, in editorials in most national, regional, and local newspapers across the country.

Then unnamed "senior government officials" told Craig Oliver at CTV News that the Syrians had released Maher because he'd given them information about al-Qaeda and the Muslim Brotherhood. According to these government sources, "Arar also provided information to the Syrians about four other Canadians: Arwad al-Bushi, Abdullah al Malki, both Syrians being held in a Syrian jail; Ahmed Abu al Maati, an Egyptian Canadian in custody in Egypt; and Mohamed Harkat. Born in Algeria, [Harkat has] been held under an anti-terrorism security certificate at the Ottawa Detention Centre."[19] Oliver later explained he felt this was a credible story because these sources were senior in two separate departments.[20]

Curiously, whoever leaked the information appears to have tagged on Harkat and al-Bushi's names. Ahmad and Abdullah were named in information the Syrians had provided to Canadian officials about Maher; neither Harkat or al-Bushi were.[21] (Al-Bushi had been detained for past membership in the Muslim Brotherhood—his case was not related to national security investigations in Canada, and he has been released.) Maher had heard about al-Bushi while he was at Sednaya, but had never heard of Harkat until after he was released and read his name in media reports.

As Justice O'Connor later concluded, "this leak was timed to implicate Mr. Arar in a terrorist scheme just after his return to Canada. Obviously, being called a terrorist in the national media will have a severe impact on someone's reputation."[22] He also concluded that the leaks were "potentially very dangerous, not only for the Arar family, but also for the individuals allegedly named by Mr. Arar and still in detention abroad in countries known to practice torture."[23] The RCMP knew about the leak before it was reported. Sergeant Rick Reynolds wrote about the story in a briefing note to Commissioner Zaccardelli, warning about "a potential CTV news report tonight, 23rd of October, 2003, quoting unnamed government sources as saying Maher Arar is part of an al-Qaeda cell in Canada and was only released from Syrian custody because he agreed to tell about other members of his cell." The briefing note suggests that, in the event of media inquiries, "the standard line be issued that the RCMP can neither confirm nor deny these allegations."[24] So, while it has never been proven that the leak came from the RCMP, it is certain that both Reynolds or Zaccardelli could have intervened to stop it but didn't. Their concern at the time, according to Deputy Commissioner Loeppky, was to ensure media was coordinated out of headquarters.[25]

Several years later, once the Arar Inquiry's report had exonerated Maher, CTV's Craig Oliver made a point of apologizing to him, in person, for running the story. He also told Maher about a story he'd been offered and turned down. A source had told Oliver they had a photograph of Maher in a training camp in Afghanistan. "[The source] wanted me to use the information without showing me the photograph. That was a very solid source. I wonder now if this person was assured it actually existed. The photograph didn't exist, of course. This experience has made me more skeptical.... I knew these people very well."[26]

Maher, Ahmad, and Abdullah weren't the only subjects of leaks by unnamed officials in the fall of 2003. On October 15, Ahmad's brother, Amr, was mentioned in a *Washington Times* article. Journalist Bill Gertz doesn't name his sources, who claim that an FBI informant said that he'd seen FBI suspect Adnan El Shukrijumah in Hamilton, Ontario, sometime in 2002, and that three other "al-Qaeda terrorists" were seen there also.[27] The informant claimed Amr El Maati was there too, and that El Shukrijumah had posed as a student at McMaster University, which has a five-megawatt research reactor. "According to the officials," Gertz wrote, "the al Qaeda members were sent to North America and assigned with making the bomb from materials acquired there, rather than trying to smuggle conventional explosives and radioactive material into the United States.... The terrorists were to buy or steal radioactive material with help from people who had access to research reactors or radioactive medical waste." According to Gertz's sources, El Shukrijumah became an FBI suspect after being identified by captured al-Qaeda leader Khalid Sheikh Mohammed.[28]

The report was picked up by several Canadian newspapers the following day. Officials at McMaster countered that they had no evidence of any threat to their nuclear facility, or that El Shukrijumah had ever been a student there. Spokespersons for CSIS and the RCMP said they'd already investigated the allegations and found no evidence of a threat. "We've worked very closely with McMaster security to determine there has not been a threat or a breach of security to the university or its grounds," the RCMP's Michele Paradis told *The Hamilton Spectator*.[29] CSIS spokesperson Nicole Currier noted that CSIS had investigated the claim back in March when the information first came to its attention and found no evidence of a Canadian connection.

Former CSIS analyst David Harris helped to hype the threat, telling journalists that the "cold, chilling reality is that we in the West have been a target of Islamic extremists since well before Sept. 11 and that continues to this day.... There are people of intelligence and maturity who spend their days plotting and scheming ways to destroy as many Western lives as possible." As for why Hamilton would be targeted, he asks, "Who's to say it isn't happening all over the place?" Just to be sure his point was made, he added that "the truth is that fabulously-damaging weapons can be put together using conventional explosives and radioactive material that is readily available in hospitals, some dental facilities and a great many university research centres."[30]

Paul L. Williams, an academic and consultant to the FBI, later wrote about the apparent threat in his book, *Dunces of Doomsday*, claiming that "at McMaster University, where the al-Qaeda agents may have registered under fictitious names, Shukrijumah and friends wasted no time in gaining access to the nuclear reactor and stealing more than 180 pounds of nuclear material for the creation of radiological bombs."[31] For that, he's being sued by McMaster for $2 million for damages. The university claims there is no nuclear material missing and no evidence that any of the men Williams names, including Amr, were ever anywhere near the university. "Mr. Williams' allegations about McMaster [are] on a par with UFO reports and JFK conspiracy theories.... The notion that because there are people on faculty from Egypt that McMaster is then a haven for terrorism is not only logically offensive, it smacks of racism," the university's lawyer, Peter Downard, says.[32] Williams' publisher retracted publicity statements about the book that repeated Williams's claims that 180 pounds of nuclear material had been stolen and that the university has been infiltrated by terrorists and is a risk to the public. The statements "were without basis in fact" says the publisher.[33]

TWENTY-ONE

"It Is in Allah's Hands"

Morning, Wednesday, October 22, 2003
Sednaya prison, Sednaya, Syria

ABDULLAH DIDN'T KNOW WHAT TO THINK when the guards called his name and told him to get ready for court. He and another prisoner were taken outside to a waiting military car. Both were handcuffed, then driven to a building in Damascus.

Abdullah was led to an office where a man in civilian clothing was seated behind a desk, dictating something to another man. They didn't introduce themselves. The man behind the desk consulted a report, then asked Abdullah how he knew Ibrahym Adam and Ahmad El Maati. Abdullah told him that Ibrahym was a friend. He didn't know Ahmad as well; Ibrahym had introduced them. The man asked Abdullah about his volunteer work in Pakistan and Afghanistan and about his export business. Why had Abdullah been questioned by Canadian intelligence in Canada?

"I don't know why I was questioned," Abdullah said.

"You are just a casualty of the West's war. The West used to support the mujahideen, and now they just need someone to blame," the man replied.

Abdullah can't remember if he pointed out that he'd never been with the mujahideen. Did Abdullah want to change anything in the handwritten report he had signed at the interrogations branch? the man asked. "I was too afraid to say anything [else] so I just said, 'No.'" The man asked whether Abdullah agreed with the reports. Abdullah said he hadn't read the reports.

The man told his colleague to write down that Abdullah agreed with everything in the reports. Abdullah was then asked to sign and fingerprint this new report.

"Can you please add that I never belonged to a political or a religious organization?" Abdullah asked.

It was added to the report, and Abdullah signed and finger-printed it as he was instructed.

"I am going to report that you are accused of activities and knowing people that are a threat to Syria," the man told Abdullah. "I will look at the laws very carefully and ensure you are treated fairly."

Later that day, Abdullah returned to Sednaya, where other prisoners, based on his description, told him he had been at the State Supreme Security Court and that the man he had seen was a prosecutor. Abdullah wished he could get a message to his family about appointing a lawyer.

10:30 A.M., Tuesday, November 4, 2003
National Press Theatre, Ottawa

IT HAD BEEN ONE MONTH since Maher's release and he was now ready to tell his story. He'd gained some weight back. He was sleeping more, despite the continued nightmares. He'd negotiated a friendship with his youngest child, who was still wondering who this mysterious man was who'd suddenly wandered into his mother's life. He'd described to Monia what had happened to him and she'd recounted some of what the family had been through in his absence. He'd started reading the media coverage about his case. He'd been fully debriefed by Amnesty International. He'd met with doctors and lawyers. He'd met with Abdullah's family to consult with them about talking publicly about Abdullah's case. He'd met with Minister Graham, to whom he had emphasized that given what he'd told them about Abdullah's torture, it was very important for the Canadian government to immediately step up pressure for Abdullah's release.

Maher was angry about the untrue statements the anonymous government sources were leaking to the press and he wanted them to stop. When he was ready, he wanted to tell Canadians, and the world, who he really was, and demand a public inquiry. Broadcasters all over North America were competing to carry Maher's first public interview. But Maher wanted to be fair so chose to speak to all the journalists at once in the National Press Theatre across from Parliament Hill. The media had been growing impatient.

By the time Maher and Monia arrived at the National Press Theatre, just before 10:30 A.M., it was packed. As Maher, Monia, Alex Neve, and lawyer Lorne Waldman stepped onto the platform and took their seats, the room went quiet. And it stayed that way for more than an hour. Maher, reading from a prepared statement, was confident and poised, occasionally pausing momentarily to regain his composure. Journalists sat perfectly still, on the edge of their seats, listening attentively to every word Maher had to say:

> I am here today to tell the people of Canada what has happened to me. There have been many allegations made about me in the media, all of them by people who refuse to be named or come forward. So before I tell you who I am and what happened to me, I will tell you who I am not. I am not a terrorist. I am not a member of al-Qaeda and I do not know anyone who belongs to this group. All I know about al-Qaeda is what I have seen in the media. I have never been to Afghanistan. I have never been anywhere near Afghanistan, and I do not have any desire to ever go to Afghanistan.
>
> Now, let me tell you who I am.
>
> I am a Syrian-born Canadian. I moved here with my parents when I was 17 years old. I went to university and studied hard, and eventually obtained a master's degree in telecommunications. I met my wife, Monia, at McGill University. We fell in love and eventually married in 1994. I knew then that she was special, but I had no idea how special she would turn out to be. If it were not for her, I

believe I would still be in prison. We had our first child, a daughter ... in February 1997. She is six years old now. In December 1997, we moved to Ottawa from Montreal. I took a job with a high-tech firm, called The MathWorks, in Boston in 1999, and my job involved a lot of travel within the U.S. Then in 2001, I decided to come back to Ottawa to start my own consulting company. We had our second child ... in February 2002. He is 20 months old now.

So this is who I am. I am a father and a husband. I am a telecommunications engineer and entrepreneur. I have never had trouble with the police, and have always been a good citizen. So I still cannot believe what has happened to me, and how my life and career have been destroyed.[1]

Maher said he'd seen Abdullah at Sednaya prison in September, and that he'd barely recognized him, he was so thin and pale and weak. Abdullah had been in the grave for much longer than he had, Maher emphasized. Fearing for the safety of Abdullah and other detainees still at Far' Falastin, Maher didn't reveal that he and Abdullah had been able to communicate through the walls there. "He told me he had been severely tortured with the tire, and the cable," Maher continued. "He was tortured much worse than me." He went on to say that he had no idea why the Syrians were holding Abdullah. "What I can say for sure is that no human deserves to be treated the way he was, and I hope that Canada does all they can to help him."

Maher's statement took an hour—ten times longer than the six minutes usually allowed for opening remarks at a press conference. CTV Newsnet and CBC Newsworld carried it live. And the next day, several newspapers ran full-page excerpts of the statement. The *Ottawa Citizen* published it in full on its first and second pages.

Jacques Bourbeau from Global National News says Maher was remarkable: "It was the silence ... you could almost hear people holding their breath as he spoke. I came back with the tape and said, 'I shouldn't say a word with this. Anything I'd have to say would be superfluous, Canadians need to hear what he said.' So we ran cuts of his statement. It was a dramatic and heart-wrenching story. I think that's when Canadians made their judgment of the man, and he was very, very articulate and very strong. Even if there were still people who thought there was something fishy about him, you couldn't help but feel some sympathy for what he went through."[2]

Within hours of Maher's press conference, the Commons Committee on Foreign Affairs called for a full public inquiry. That night and the next day, columnists and editorials across the country followed suit. "No one who watched Maher Arar of Ottawa speak live on television yesterday morning could fail to be shaken by his harrowing story," *The Globe and Mail*'s November 5 editorial read.[3] "Mr. Arar's case stands for nothing less than the presumption of innocence, and whether that presumption is to be a casualty of the worldwide war on terrorism," it continued. "The federal cabinet has the power to call an inquiry, and should do so. No Canadian should be dehumanized in this fashion without the country asking why."

By the morning of November 6, Maher's case was on the agenda at the White House. Michael Kergin, Canada's ambassador to the United States, was summoned for a meeting at the National Security Council with Frances Townsend, the U.S. national director for combating terrorism and deputy national security advisor. Maher's case, Kergin was told, had been discussed in a meeting at the White House that morning. Senior officials in the Bush administration were angry about Chrétien's recent remarks that the United States had unilaterally made the decision to send Maher to Syria. The decision, according to Townsend, had been a joint one.[4]

In the House of Commons that day, NDP MP Alexa McDonough asked members to stand in honour of Monia and the work she'd done, saying she had "inspired Canadians with her unrelenting efforts to raise awareness of what happens when the rights of citizens are trampled in the name of so-called national security."[5]

Late morning, Friday, November 7, 2003
Ottawa

MAHER'S MEDIA COORDINATOR was tipped off about the next leak before it was published. A caller warned that Canadian officials had given a journalist a file about Maher. The caller wouldn't say which journalist or even which media outlet but warned it was possible that the journalist in question would not be seeking Maher's perspective. This was, of course, troubling. After several calls and a lot of probing, she learned it was the *Ottawa Citizen*'s Juliet O'Neill.

It's unclear whether O'Neill had been digging for information from a source she'd worked with in the past, or if it was the officials who called her. O'Neill had never interviewed Maher or Monia, and unlike many other Ottawa and parliamentary reporters who'd been covering Maher's story for more than a year, she'd written only two stories on his case: one on the day Maher was released, the other the day before he told his story at the National Press Theatre. She didn't appear to have the detailed chronology and biographical information that had been distributed to journalists around the time of the first leaks. What she did seem to have, courtesy of Canadian officials, was a dossier about Maher containing his "confession" and a lot of the same inaccurate and misleading information that had been shared with the Americans.

It would have been difficult for any journalist to turn down the story. Maher's case had been front-page news for weeks. Moreover, the past leaks, like those to CanWest's Robert Fife, had been just verbal. This was the first time a file containing official government documents was handed to a journalist. The important question, then, was the angle O'Neill would take, and how much context she'd provide.

By now many observers believed the leaks were being orchestrated to fend off calls for a public inquiry by undermining Maher's credibility. Just a week earlier, Minister Graham had condemned the CTV coverage linking Maher to al-Qaeda, calling it "unsubstantiated allegations" and "speculative statements" unfair to the person and the process.[6] Two days earlier, O'Neill's colleague Susan Riley had written that one of the reasons an inquiry was needed was to answer questions about the leaks. "Why have federal officials been leaking damaging snippets on Arar to the media?" she asked. "There have been unsourced claims that he spent time in Afghanistan, that he gave the Syrians names of terrorists—completely unsupported, yet terribly damaging."[7]

Veteran *Globe and Mail* journalist Hugh Winsor also wrote about the leaks in his front-page November 5 column: "The more information that comes out over the handling of the Arar case, often through leaks from anonymous 'government sources,' the more this resembles the David Kelly case in Britain," he wrote. "Prime Minister Tony Blair's spin doctors arranged to leak Mr. Kelly's name to divert attention from Mr. Blair. In Canada, anonymous officials are feeding the media what might be seen as incriminating information about Mr. Arar's interrogation in an attempt to take the heat out of demands for a public inquiry."[8]

(Winsor was referring to a British weapons expert and former UN arms inspector at the centre of a scandal unfolding in the United Kingdom. David Kelly allegedly took his own life after a government leak identified him as the source of a BBC news report about Iraq. The report said that British intelligence had "sexed up" its dossier about Iraq's so-called "weapons of mass destruction" in an effort to justify Britain's support for U.S. plans to invade Iraq.[9])

"The media is equally complicit for printing or broadcasting this unverified spin," Winsor wrote.

When O'Neill was reached by phone, Maher's media coordinator urged her to recognize that the leaked file was part of a bigger strategy to discredit Maher's reputation and stave off an inquiry.[10] She remembers urging O'Neill to be careful reporting on information that was likely the product of torture and encouraging O'Neill to speak with Alex Neve at Amnesty International, or any other credible torture expert, about the unreliability of such information, given Syria's dismal human rights record. But O'Neill's questions focused on the information in the dossier that made Maher look like he had something to hide.

O'Neill's story ran in several CanWest papers and on the front page of Saturday's *Ottawa Citizen* with the headline "Canada's dossier on Maher Arar: The existence of a group of Ottawa men with alleged ties to al-Qaeda is at the root of why the government opposes an inquiry into the case."[11] Justice O'Connor would later say that the article "contained an unprecedented amount of classified information" and a detailed description of the inside of "A" Division's Integrated National Security Enforcement Team's offices, which offered clues as to the source of the leak, as only INSET and A-O Canada members had pass cards for those offices.[12] The RCMP, O'Neill wrote, "had caught Mr. Arar in their sights while investigating the activities of members of an alleged al-Qaeda logistical support group in Ottawa." Investigators "were suspicious when they saw Mr. Arar and their main target, Abdullah Almalki, talking outside in the pouring rain away from eavesdroppers." According to O'Neill, "one of the leaked documents" describes "in minute details" what Maher "allegedly told Syrian military intelligence officials during the first few weeks of his incarceration." She went on to describe the so-called confession in detail.

Some of the badly needed context was there. O'Neill did note that Maher had told the public that he had confessed under torture to things that weren't true. She also quoted Maher's media coordinator's response to some of the allegations outlined in the classified documents. But given that her story detailed Maher's apparent "confession," it was disappointing that she didn't provide more context on the unreliability of such information. Nor did she acknowledge the strategy behind the leak, which by this time was obvious to many. Looking back now, O'Neill says that what happened to Maher was horrible, but she has no regrets about the story. "I stand by what I wrote. I was explaining what went on. I was reporting on what officials were saying," she says. She says the necessary context was provided when the *Ottawa Citizen* devoted its two front pages to Maher's statement a few days earlier. "My assignment was 'Let's go back to the beginning and see what they have on him,' so that's what I did."[13]

Material had been leaked, O'Neill wrote, "in defense of their [A-O Canada's] investigation." Justice O'Connor points out in his report that the implication is that leaking classified information "is justified if it suits the interests of the investigators," noting that this reasoning means that "since the public does not have access to classified information, leakors can pick and choose what is released to suit their purposes."[14] He also points out that, during the Arar Inquiry, the government claimed national security confidentiality over a lot of the same kind of information in order to keep it out of the public domain. And on several occasions at the inquiry, Maher's legal team and intervening human rights and civil liberties groups pointed out that the government was picking and choosing embarrassing information to keep secret.

One of the more prescient parts of O'Neill's story came from an unnamed "security source" who told her that an inquiry could "open a can of worms involving Syrian, American and Canadian investigations into alleged terror plots in Ottawa and alleged shipments of electronic and computer equipment to al-Qaeda terrorists in Pakistan and Afghanistan." This would present a "dilemma" about what to do about the other suspects in overseas detention, the source said. "If Mr. Arar has caused such an uproar, others may do likewise."[15]

That, it seems, was the true motivation behind the leak. The leakor may have wanted Canadians to believe that a public inquiry would compromise an investigation into dangerous men, but in reality, the most dangerous thing about a public inquiry was the potential for opening another "can of worms" entirely: exposing the full extent of systematic Canadian complicity in the torture of not one but three Canadian citizens.

ABDULLAH'S FAMILY decided to speak out after they heard what Maher had to say. The youngest of Abdullah's brothers, Youssef, a medical student, travelled to Ottawa to speak on behalf of the family. He told the media that for eighteen months the family had chosen the route of diplomacy in Canada and Syria but were now ready to speak out. "The quiet diplomacy that we've been trying to do with Foreign Affairs, it seems that it's so quiet nobody hears it," Youssef said.[16] He emphasized that Abdullah had no ties to terrorism.[17] Speaking with CBC Radio's Curt Petrovich, he said he hoped that Minister Graham would do more and demand his brother's release. Petrovich reported that the minister had asked the Syrian ambassador for Abdullah's release the day after Maher's news conference.[18]

On the same day that O'Neill's story ran on *The Ottawa Citizen*'s front page, the first interview with Abdullah's wife, Khuzaimah, ran on page A5.[19] She told journalist Kate Jaimet that she'd decided to return home from Malaysia to help fight for Abdullah's release. Jaimet noted that although the RCMP were keeping quiet about Abdullah's case, media reports suggested that he was suspected of being part of a terrorist cell planning to bomb the U.S. Embassy in Ottawa. Khuzaimah countered that the allegations were lies. "They raided the house, and that was 22 months ago.... If they have anything against him, they should charge him," she said.

On November 7, the day before the O'Neill story ran, Abdullah's brothers went with lawyer Michael Edelson to meet with Inspector Warren Coons and staff sergeants Callahan and Corcoran from A-O Canada. They asked for a letter from the RCMP confirming that Abdullah did not have a criminal record, that there were no warrants for his arrest in Canada, and that there was no legal impediment to his return to Canada. Back in June, Edelson also asked for confirmation that Abdullah didn't have a criminal record, but so far, the RCMP hadn't complied.[20] This time, he and Abdullah's family stressed the urgency of the case and asked for a response by November 11. They didn't hear back until November 28, when Coons told Edelson that the letter was tied up in government bureaucracy and the RCMP's legal counsel office. Edelson followed up in writing, asking how such a simple request could "devolve into a vortex of procrastination of truly mind boggling proportions." He warned that there would be "very significant consequences ... if anything should happen to Mr. Almalki while [the RCMP] have been paralyzed in their analysis of these simple requests."[21]

In the meantime, the family had written to the prime minister and to Minister Graham, asking them to personally intervene by directly contacting the Syrian president, Syrian Foreign minister, and Syrian ambassador to Canada to demand Abdullah's immediate release. Prime Minister Chrétien responded by letter on November 25, saying that "the Government of Canada takes Abdullah's plight very seriously" and that Minister Graham and his officials were "energetically pursuing this matter with Syrian authorities," including the Syrian ambassador to Canada.[22]

David Pratt, the Member of Parliament for Abdullah's riding of Nepean-Carleton, also wrote to Minister Graham, asking for a briefing on DFAIT's efforts on Abdullah's case. Abdullah's brother Youssef later learned from someone at the consular division that the new Canadian ambassador to Syria, Brian Davis, was to meet with Syrian deputy Foreign minister Walid Mouallem on November 30 to discuss the torture allegations and consular access. The official also told Youssef that Senator Pierre de Bané was travelling in the region in December and planned to raise Abdullah's case in a meeting with the Syrian president.

But the most powerful letter to the prime minister would be written by Abdullah's oldest son, who was eight at the time. The

December 18 letter, addressed to Paul Martin and written just a week after he was sworn in as prime minister, read:

> Dear Prime Minister,
>
> *Please Bring Our Dad Home*
>
> I am happy that you have become our new prime minister. My father's name is Abdullah Almalki. I would like to ask you to bring my father back home to us. We have not seen him for 1 1/2 years. We miss him so much. He has not called or written to us and we have been waiting to hear from him for so long now. My mother told us that he is in a prison in Syria, and that he cannot phone or write to anyone. They put him there even though he has not done anything wrong. This is not fair. My little brother always says that he hopes our father is still alive. We hope you will bring him back and make all of us happy again.[23]

Sometime in November 2003
Sednaya prison, Sednaya, Syria

ABDULLAH REMEMBERS that it was some time in November that he was tortured for smiling.

He was still locked into the "al-Qaeda" wing at Sednaya prison. The wing contained ten cells, each with its own toilet and bathing area. The wing had no running water, so twice each day, early in the morning and again at noon, the prisoners took empty water containers to the door of the wing to be filled by the guards.

One day, when Abdullah was taking the containers out, he saw the guard who had put the light bulb outside his old cell. The guard smiled at him and congratulated him for having been moved. "When were you moved?" he asked.

"Some time ago," Abdullah said, smiling back at him. He hadn't noticed but the man who'd been in charge of his initiation, Mouhanad, was standing a few feet behind the guard and had seen Abdullah smiling.

"Bring him to me!" he yelled to the guard.

The guard took Abdullah over to Mouhanad, who immediately starting slapping him hard on the face. "When I raised my hands to cover my face, Mouhanad shouted at me to put my arms down and started kicking me. I refused, and said I wanted to see his commander."

For that, Abdullah was severely punished. "Mouhanad dragged me into a room, and told me to get on my knees. Several soldiers surrounded me and started kicking and punching me all over my body. I felt as if my eyes would come out."

A few minutes later, some officials came back with the commander. "I think Mouhanad told him I hit him," says Abdullah. The commander grabbed and pulled on Abdullah's ears, then slapped his face and called him names. He ordered the guards to bring the tire, the bar, and the cable. Abdullah was ordered to lie on his back with his legs bent so his knees were up. They shoved the tire over his knees and rammed the bar behind his knees, then turned the bar 180 degrees so that his body was upside down and completely restrained. Then it was the *falaka* again. This time they used a belt to whip the soles of his feet.

"I hope you will not do this again!" the commander barked. Abdullah was dragged back to his wing. The other prisoners there carried him to his cell and helped clean him up. "Some were crying because they could not help me," Abdullah says. "I had cuts and bruises all over my body, and my feet were punctured all over and bleeding. I think the belt must have had nails sticking out."

Wednesday, November 12, 2003
Constituency office of Foreign Affairs Minister Bill Graham, Toronto

AHMAD'S PARENTS HAD GIVEN UP on quiet diplomacy, too. Ahmad's mother, Samira, had spoken with a lawyer in Egypt before returning to Canada in late September. "He said very few words. He said, 'Go to Canada and publish your son's story. The public there, the opinion of the public can force the government to release him.'" Samira arrived back in Canada in time to see Maher make his brief statement at Dorval airport the night of his return. "I saw him on the TV. I was happy for him and for his wife and it gave me hope for Ahmad," she says.

For two years, Ahmad's family had heeded the advice of the consular officials at Foreign Affairs to stay quiet about Ahmad's case and let quiet diplomacy do its work. Now they'd seen how the publicity had helped in Maher's case. They too were angry about the leaks. Ahmad was right—it was time to speak out. Both Samira and Badr, Ahmad's father, spoke with journalists in October and again after Maher had told his story in November. On November 12, Badr spoke to media outside Minister Graham's Toronto constituency office. "I'm asking the Canadian government and Mr. Graham to do the same thing they did for Mr. Arar," he told the assembled journalists.[24]

Late morning, Eid-al-Fitr, November 2003
Abu Za'abal prison, northeast of Cairo

AHMAD WAS BACK AT ABU ZA'ABAL after having been sent to Nasr City again in October. There, one of the Egyptian officers had said something Ahmad would never forget. "We know it was Canada that did this to you, Ahmad. This is happening with a lot of American cases, too. Some people are being forced to be informants, and they are implicating other people. If you go back to Canada, get a good lawyer and fight back."

Ahmad's mother, Samira, had travelled back to Cairo in early November. She wanted to be back in time to visit Ahmad for the Eid-al-Fitr feast marking the end of the Ramadan fast. She had good news. They'd gone public, as he had wanted, and she'd smuggled the newspaper articles back to Cairo to show to her family. "I folded them up very small in my pocket," she says. She was worried she might be searched when she arrived in Cairo. She didn't dare take them with her to the prison, but she would tell Ahmad about them. Maher's release was good news, too, and she wanted to share that with Ahmad. But she had bad news also. She'd waited a year to tell him, and it was time.

Samira baked special Eid pastries stuffed with pistachios and dates and Ahmad's favourite chicken and rice dishes. There was so much food that her taxi driver had to help her carry it through the gate at Abu Za'abal.

Because this was a holiday visit, it took place in the large outdoor cage-like structure, where Ahmad had seen other prisoners being beaten on his first day at Abu Za'abal. Other prisoners were with their families and sat on the cement floor. But Ahmad's mother was having trouble with her hip, so he insisted that a guard bring her a chair. They had twenty minutes. Samira started with the good news, telling Ahmad that she and his father had spoken with journalists and there had been media coverage of his case in Canada. She told him about Maher's release, and they talked about how it might signal good news for his case.

The twenty minutes had almost passed, and Samira knew she had to tell Ahmad the bad news. Rola's family had waited a year to tell her, and now she had waited a year to tell Ahmad. It was time.

"I have news about Rola," she said.

Ahmad hadn't heard from Rola or her family since he'd been detained. He'd asked after her but understood that it was difficult for her to help given that she and her family were in Syria. And he worried about her—that she would be under a lot of pressure, and may have been questioned. Most of all, he dreamed of the day he would be released and they would be together.

"Rola's father and mother came to speak with me in Cairo. They came to say that they could not have picked a better husband for their daughter, but things are too dangerous for them, and they have had to void the marriage," Samira told Ahmad. "They are afraid of the intelligence. The intelligence called Rola to go to the prison many times by herself."

There was a long silence. Finally, Ahmad spoke.

"It is in Allah's hands."

TWENTY-TWO

"We Are Not a Police State"

Wednesday, November 19, 2003
Washington, D.C.

THE NEXT LEAK came from an unnamed American official and was timed to run on the same day Solicitor General Wayne Easter met with U.S. attorney general John Ashcroft in Washington. The *Washington Post* story revealed that a senior U.S. Justice Department official, Deputy Attorney General Larry D. Thompson, had signed Maher's removal order. Further, when Maher had been detained at John F. Kennedy Airport, he was carrying "the names of a large number of known al Qaeda operatives, affiliates or associates' in his wallet or pockets."[1] That story was picked up in the Canadian news that night and the next day, along with Easter's comments about his meeting. Easter admitted for the first time that Canada had shared information about Maher with the United States. But he did it in a way that left an impression that there had been international interest in Maher. "I think I can say that our discussions indicate that this information didn't just come from Canada alone. The information comes from a number of agencies," he told reporters.[2] Of course, Easter didn't specify whether Ashcroft was referring to information from Syria that was likely the product of torture, such as Ahmad's false confession that he'd seen Maher in Afghanistan. Easter also said that Ashcroft had assured him that the United States had not broken any laws and "were operating under their mandate in the interests of their laws and their national security policy."[3]

The next day, the *Washington Post* ran another story quoting a U.S. Justice Department official as saying that before shipping Maher off to Syria, the CIA had received assurances from Syria that Maher wouldn't be tortured. Journalist Dana Priest wrote that the official wouldn't say why they thought the assurances were credible, noting that just two weeks earlier President Bush had given a speech on the Middle East that had singled out Syria for criticism, saying the regime has left its people "a legacy of torture, oppression, misery and ruin."[4] The U.S. Department of Homeland Security's inspector general would reveal much later that, in fact, the Immigration and Naturalization Service (INS) didn't think the purported assurances were credible at all. "The INS concluded that Arar was entitled to protection from torture and that returning him to Syria would more likely than not result in his torture," he said. "The assurances upon which INS based Arar's removal were ambiguous regarding the source or authority purporting to bind the Syrian government."[5]

If the leakors in Canada and the United States hoped to quell calls for a public inquiry, they must have been disappointed, because the leaks were having the opposite effect. Throughout November and December, several organizations and public figures joined in the call for a public inquiry, including prominent Liberals such as Secretary of State Stephen Owen and Natural Resources Minister Herb Dhaliwal. Conservative MP Bill Casey wrote an open letter to Prime Minister Paul Martin calling for an inquiry. Several newspapers' editorials also made the pitch. Martin, in the weeks leading up to him being sworn in as prime minister, told reporters he wanted to see all the facts before making a decision but that he wouldn't close the door on the possibility of an inquiry.[6] Once Martin was prime minister, his newly appointed Justice minister, Irwin Cotler, repeated his call for an inquiry.

Monday, December 1, 2003
Office of Foreign Affairs Minister Bill Graham, Ottawa

"I WAS MISTAKEN."

It was the first time, after a full year of saying consistently, "your guys knew what we were doing all along," that U.S. secretary of state Colin Powell told Minister Graham that this wasn't the case.[7] Powell had telephoned Minister Graham to say that the United States had made the decision to send Maher to Syria on its own. But, he said, the decision had been based on information from various sources, mainly CSIS and the RCMP. Maher wouldn't have been on the United States' radar screen had it not been for the Canadians, he pointed out, but the Canadians had not been consulted before the deportation.

The news that both CSIS and the RCMP had provided the information was more evidence of the need for a full public inquiry, Maher's supporters suggested, but Graham maintained just the opposite. Interviewed on CTV's *Question Period*, Graham said, "We're not going to get (U.S. attorney general John) Ashcroft to come up to Canada and appear in a Canadian inquiry."[8] Not much later, Prime Minister Martin said he'd been briefed on the file and had seen no evidence of Canadian wrongdoing. He used national security confidentiality as a reason an inquiry might be a bad idea. Speaking during a year-end interview on CBC television, Martin said, "I want to know what happened on the Canadian side and I want to know what happened on the American side. I'm going to do this in a way that is, in fact, going to make sure that we do have the facts, but it is not going to imperil national security because there are things in there that perhaps should stay ... closed."[9]

12:15 A.M., sometime in December 2003
Abu Za'abal prison, northeast of Cairo

IT WAS JUST AFTER MIDNIGHT and Ahmad was doing what he did every night at that time—trying to tune in to Radio Canada

International's Arabic-language broadcast. It must have been a
clear night, because he was able to get a strong signal. He lay
back and listened, then sat upright. "I was astonished. It was an
interview with Maher Arar, in Arabic, talking about his detention
and release. Just hearing about his case, and knowing that he was
on national radio, I felt that this was a good sign for me. I was
very hopeful that I would have the same media interest and I
would be released soon," he says.

Not too long afterward, Ahmad's mother came to see him
again. She had good news, too, she said. She'd seen the Prophet
Mohammad in a dream—something which, for Muslims, signi-
fies a true experience. "I was in the Medina mosque. It was empty
and peaceful. I saw the Prophet Mohammad there, and standing
behind him was his wife, Khadija. I asked for Ahmad's release.
He put his hand on my shoulder and told me that Ahmad would
be okay." Samira understood this to mean that Ahmad would be
released.

A few days later, the Canadian consular officials visited
Ahmad. They had a letter of retainer with them from a lawyer in
Canada, Paul Copeland. They explained to Ahmad and the
Egyptian officials monitoring the visit that Ahmad's father
needed him to sign the letter so Copeland could represent Ahmad
in Canada. "The security officials grabbed the letter and got very
angry. They left the room and came back later, saying no, I
couldn't sign it."

The embassy had helped pressure the Egyptians into agreeing
to have Ahmad's knee examined at the hospital. An MRI was
scheduled for later in December. Ahmad thought this might be an
opportunity to sign the letter for Copeland, so he worked to get
a message out to his mother. He did this using a system well
known among the over eighteen thousand political prisoners and
their families in Egypt. Each time a detainee is transferred in a
prison truck, he or she can carry short messages, usually just
one or two sentences long and a phone number, to the outside
world on small, folded pieces of paper. When the truck stops at a

busy intersection, the prisoner tosses the messages through the window grates. "In the streets, people watch for those trucks containing prisoners in white, the political prisoners. They are like heroes in Egypt," Ahmad explains. "Women, especially, help by coming up and taking the message. They are thinking of their brothers or sons. Every family in Egypt knows somebody who is detained for political reasons." Ahmad's message to his mother included her phone number, the date of his appointment at the hospital, and a request for her to bring the lawyer's letter.

Sure enough, the message reached Samira by phone. She took a copy of the letter to the hospital on the appointed day, where she waited for five hours, but Ahmad never appeared. Back at the prison, on the morning of the appointment, Ahmad had been told to get ready to go, but then the guard never came back for him. In the end, Ahmad would have to wait until after he was released to sign the retainer letter. Later, Ahmad and his mother wondered whether Samira's phone had been wiretapped and if that was why the trip to the hospital had been cancelled.

Tuesday, December 30, 2003
Ottawa

THAT THE CALLS FOR A PUBLIC INQUIRY were still growing appears to have frightened intelligence agencies on both sides of the border. Clearly desperate, unnamed officials in Canada and the United States chose to use CanWest's Robert Fife again to take another swipe at Maher's reputation. The story ran on the front pages of the *National Post*, the *Ottawa Citizen*, and several other CanWest newspapers. "Canadian and U.S. intelligence officials are '100% sure'" that Maher "trained at the same al-Qaeda camp in Afghanistan as Ahmed Ressam, the former Montrealer convicted of planning a terrorist attack,"[10] the story began. This was the first time officials had identified the Khalden camp, Fife wrote. "High level sources in Canada and the United States who have had access to an extensive secret intelligence file on Mr. Arar say the 33-year-old Ottawa software engineer travelled to Pakistan in the early 1990s and then entered Afghanistan to train at the Khaldun camp," he wrote.

But the innuendo reached new heights when Fife quoted a "senior Canadian intelligence source, speaking on background," as saying, "this guy is not a virgin," and "there is more than meets the eye here." Fife added that, according to the source, "U.S. agencies have an extensive dossier" on Maher and "if the Americans were ever to declassify the stuff, there would be some hair standing on end."

Fife noted that Ressam had trained at Khalden and that "other graduates of the camp bombed the World Trade Center in 1993 and were part of the suicide team that drove truck bombs to U.S. embassies in East Africa in 1998, killing 224 people."

Maher issued a statement the next day, reiterating that he'd never been to Afghanistan. "I have nothing to hide and I want a public inquiry," he said. "If they [Canadian law enforcement and security agencies] have nothing to hide, they should want one too."[11]

Just before midnight, Monday, January 12, 2004
Cairo

AHMAD'S MOTHER, SAMIRA, was startled when the phone rang just before midnight. It was the state security officer from the State Security Investigations Service's Giza branch.

"You must bring us your son's passports. We want both the Canadian and Egyptian passports."

"Why?" Samira asked.

"We need information from his passports. You must bring them now."

"But it is almost midnight, and I am alone. I have nobody to bring me." Samira was frightened. She didn't want to go anywhere near the SSI branch, especially in the middle of the night.

"I don't care. Find a way and bring them now. We will give them back when we are done. Just bring them now."

Samira called the kind taxi driver who'd been shuttling her back and forth to the prison visits. He agreed to deliver the passports for her. After he picked them up, she began to pace and fret about the phone call. "The first thought that came to my mind was that they were sending Ahmad to Guantánamo. I was so worried." When the driver returned some time later, he told her that the officers had refused to return the passports to him. "Then I was sure," Samira says. "I was sure they were sending him to Guantánamo."

Even though it was two in the morning now, she called the Giza branch to ask why the passports hadn't been returned.

"You can visit [your son] tomorrow at the state security branch in Giza, and bring him clothes," an officer told her. Then the officer asked for her exact address. "I didn't know why he asked that. I thought 'Are they coming here?'"

Samira sat up all night, worrying. How would the family help Ahmad if he was sent to Guantánamo? In the morning, she went to the Giza branch with clothes and food for Ahmad.

"You cannot see him," was all the officials would say.

"I couldn't be alone, I was so worried. So I went to my daughter's home." It was there that her son-in-law suggested another possibility: "Maybe he is being sent to Guantánamo. But maybe he is being released. You should go home and stay there just in case."

Back at her apartment, the phone rang. It was the state security officer. "We will release Ahmad if you tell us where Amr is," he said.

"I don't know where Amr is," Samira replied. "What can I do? I don't know where he is."

"He was polite," Samira recalls, "but I didn't believe he would ever release Ahmad."

The next morning, Wednesday, Samira was up early. She says she felt unusually calm, and set about cleaning the apartment.

Her daughter called to say she wanted to bring Samira's grand-children over to spend the day with her—her grandson would make hamburgers.

The children arrived, and Samira's thirteen-year-old grandson made hamburgers, as promised, making extra. "These are for Uncle Ahmad," he said. "Just in case." Then they settled in to watch videos.

At about five-thirty in the evening, the grandchildren left to go home. Five minutes later there was a knock at the door. "I thought they had forgotten something," Samira says. "I opened the door, and Ahmad was standing there. And the children—they pushed him through the door."

Samira fainted. Ahmad caught her just before she fell to the floor.

A FEW DAYS EARLIER, Ahmad had been handcuffed, blindfolded, and transferred from Abu Za'abal to the State Security Investigations Service's Giza branch, where he was interrogated. "They reviewed everything, and asked me a lot of questions about my brother, Amr. When I told them I did not know where Amr is, one of the men grabbed me by the beard and ripped part of it out."

But after a few hours, they handed him his passports, his remaining canteen money, and a piece of paper with his mother's address written on it and told him he had to report to them every four or five days. They would want to know where he had been, whom he had talked to, and who had called him. Then they sent him out the door. It was 5 P.M., January 14, and it had been two years, two months, two days, and two hours since he was first detained in Syria.

Ahmad looked terrible. He was dressed head to toe in white, as are all political prisoners in Egypt. But his clothes weren't clean, and his beard was long and straggly. His chin was bleeding from where his beard had been ripped out. He climbed in a cab, but the driver had gone only a few yards when he turned around and got a good look at Ahmad. "I'm sorry. I cannot take you. I have to go," he said. Ahmad understood. The driver was scared. He got out and hailed another cab. That driver was more courageous, he says.

After a lot of stops along the way to ask for directions, the driver found his mother's apartment complex on the outskirts of Cairo. They drove into the parking lot. "It was after sunset, around 5:30, and was getting dark. I was paying the driver, and then I saw three kids standing in front of the entrance of the building. I didn't recognize them. It had been too long. [But] the youngest one had recognized me.... They ran to me, and I opened the door, and they were hugging me and laughing and screaming 'Uncle Ahmad, Uncle Ahmad!'"

The children pulled Ahmad out of the taxi and into the building, the youngest, seven years old, giggling and running circles around him. They knocked on the door to Samira's apartment. When it opened, they pushed him through toward his mother.

Wednesday, January 21, 2004
Ottawa

PRIME MINISTER MARTIN was still brushing off calls for a public inquiry by pointing to investigations underway by the Commission for Public Complaints Against the RCMP and by the Security Intelligence Review Committee. He said he planned to "get to the bottom" of what happened but hinted that a public inquiry risked jeopardizing national security confidentiality.[12]

But everything changed on the day the RCMP raided the home of *Ottawa Citizen* reporter Juliet O'Neill. The goal of the raid, said the RCMP, was to identify her source—to find out who had provided her with the classified information she wrote about in her November 8, 2003, article. For five hours, as journalists gathered outside, ten RCMP officers rifled through O'Neill's personal belongings, a violation she described as feeling like "slow-motion robbery."[13] Another RCMP team cordoned off and searched the *Ottawa Citizen* City Hall bureau.

Maher's attorney, Lorne Waldman, spoke to *Ottawa Citizen* journalist Kate Jaimet about what was unfolding. "I simply cannot believe that the commissioner of the RCMP cannot find out who leaked this information by calling the three or four people who have access to the file into his office and asking them," he said. "There's got to be a more effective way of getting to the bottom of the leaks, rather than using the extreme measures of the Security of Information Act, which is going to ensure that nothing will ever be made public."[14]

O'Neill later described her experience in an *Ottawa Citizen* story.[15] She was still in bed that Wednesday morning when the doorbell rang. When she peeked out the window, she saw unmarked police cars in her driveway and men standing on the doorstep. She got up and showered, hoping they'd go away, but the doorbell continued to ring. She went downstairs to the door, and Staff Sergeant Legresley held his identification up to the window. She opened the door, and Legresley walked in with two other officers. An officer read out the search warrant and told her she could call a lawyer if she wanted. She did, and within minutes a crowd of journalists was gathered outside her house. For the next five hours, ten RCMP officers rummaged through her home. Eventually they'd tell her that they were there to identify the source of the leak she'd reported on in her November 8, 2003, story on Maher Arar. She later learned that a simultaneous search was being conducted at the *Ottawa Citizen*'s offices. The RCMP made a copy of her laptop's hard drive but let her keep the computer. Before leaving, they made a videotape to show they hadn't ransacked the house.

O'Neill's experience was very different from the experiences of those targeted by the RCMP's Projects O and A-O Canada two years earlier. Ahmad's father, Badr, says the RCMP certainly hadn't told him he had the right to call a lawyer. And they'd walked away with not just his computer and some of his belongings but also with the trucking logs, papers, and other belongings of his son, who had still been in incommunicado detention in Syria. Abdullah says he doesn't know if the RCMP videotaped his parents' home after they ransacked it. If they did, he says, he'd sure like to see the tape. As for the search at his brother's and employee's homes, the RCMP certainly hadn't let them keep their computers either, Abdullah says.

That difference wasn't lost on O'Neill. Unlike Muslim Canadians who've talked about "the knock on the door from the RCMP," as a journalist, she experienced something she realized "would be more difficult to endure without a lawyer, without knowing my rights, and being confident of media attention."[16]

O'Neill had been under surveillance for more than a month before the searches. An RCMP team from Moncton had been brought in to investigate. By December 5, it had sifted through 1.8 million email messages sent to and from RCMP employees over a three-month period, searching for any messages sent to or from any of O'Neill's three email addresses. And it found a message, sent at 6:30 P.M. on November 7, 2003, from O'Neill's *Ottawa Citizen* email address to an RCMP officer attached to A-O Canada, with the words *Arar question* in the subject line.[17]

The search had been authorized under the Security of Information Act, part of the omnibus anti-terrorism bill C-36—legislation passed after 9/11. Public Safety Minister Anne McLellan had told a Quebec newspaper that her department was investigating the leaks.[18] The prime minister seems to have had some advance knowledge of the investigation. But both denied knowing any operational details of the investigation, such as how and where searches would be conducted. Either way, if this was Prime Minister Paul Martin's way of showing he was "going to get to the bottom" of what happened to Maher while avoiding a public inquiry, it wasn't very effective.

The need to get to the bottom of what happened was increasingly evident as the day unfolded. That night, the CBS's *60*

Minutes II aired its episode on Maher's case, revealing that, according to two unnamed American sources, Canadian intelligence agencies had approved Maher's removal to Syria. The program announced that Maher would be launching his law suit against U.S. attorney general John Ashcroft the next day.

By the next morning, anyone who hadn't already been calling for a full public inquiry was, and pretty much every journalist and media outlet in the country had made it their mission to win one. According to CanWest president Gordon Fisher, the search of O'Neill's home "smacks of a police-state mentality," and the tactics were like "one might equate with the former Soviet Union."[19] Surrounded by outraged journalists at a news conference at the World Economic Summit in Davos, Switzerland, the prime minister tried to demonstrate he was on the same side as the media. O'Neill "clearly" isn't a criminal, he said. Then he denied that Canada is a police state. "Very clearly, we are not a police state and we have no intention of being a police state."[20] He opened the door to an inquiry, too, saying, "We want to get all of the facts. There are many options to get them, certainly an inquiry is one of them."[21]

By Saturday, Richard Mahoney, the Liberal candidate for Ottawa Centre and close confidant of the prime minister, added his voice to the call for an inquiry. And Shirley Heafey, former chair of the RCMP's public complaints commission, spoke out to ensure the public understood that she wasn't conducting a review of the RCMP's role in the case—at this stage, the RCMP was still investigating itself. Only after that process finished would she be able to take the next step. Even if she did launch her own investigation, Heafey said, she didn't have the powers she needed. The legislation that had put the RCMP back into national security work didn't give her increased powers to oversee that work. "The most effective option to ensure that there is proper civilian oversight is to give this Commission the same powers over the RCMP that SIRC has over CSIS," she added.[22]

Early morning, Wednesday, January 28, 2004
Ottawa

MAHER AND MONIA decided to up the pressure by holding their first news conference since Maher had told his story in November. Together with their attorney Lorne Waldman and Alex Neve from Amnesty International, they would call on the public to pressure the prime minister to call a public inquiry. The Speech from the Throne would take place the following Monday, kicking off Paul Martin's first week in the House of Commons as prime minister. Maher and Monia wanted him to call an inquiry before the week was through. They planned to launch a website aimed at channelling public support and release proposed terms of reference for the inquiry. With a federal election looming, it would make sense for Martin to get this matter out of the way by giving in.

The news conference was to start at 1 P.M. But by early morning it was clear the campaign wouldn't be necessary. Public Safety Minister Anne McLellan held her own news conference at 10:30 A.M. to announce that the federal government was appointing Dennis O'Connor, associate chief justice at the Ontario Court of Appeal, to head up a public inquiry into Maher's case.

TWENTY-THREE

The Fourth Canadian into Far' Falastin

1:30 P.M., Thursday, December 11, 2003
Al-Ya'aruyba border crossing, Syrian-Iraqi border

THIRTY-SIX DAYS after Maher Arar told the world he'd been tortured in Syrian detention, the Syrian Military Intelligence detained another Canadian citizen. Muayyed Nureddin would be the fourth Muslim Canadian who, after being investigated by Canadian agents, was detained at Far' Falastin, tortured and interrogated with information from Canada, and locked into an underground cell.[1]

Muayyed had just spent two and a half months reunited with his family in his hometown of Kirkuk, north of Baghdad in Iraq. It was his third visit to his family since defecting from Saddam Hussein's Popular Army and fleeing Iraq in 1991. It was difficult to leave his family again, but his Canadian income had become essential to their survival. He was booked to fly out of Damascus at 2:13 in the morning on Saturday, December 13. So on Thursday morning, Muayyed, his mother, three brothers, and two sisters piled into the 1995 Mercury Grand Marquis sedan he'd shipped for them from Canada. His family wanted to drive with him to the Syrian border to say goodbye. Muayyed and his younger brother, Arsalan, would travel together by bus from the border to Damascus.[2] Muayyed had started a business exporting cars for resale in Iraq and wanted to show his brother how to pick up cars in Damascus. Arsalan would then return home to Iraq, and Muayyed would catch his flight to Canada.

The family pulled up to the Iraqi-Syrian border at about 1:30 in the afternoon. Muayyed and Arsalan went into the busy Syrian immigration office to present their passports. Another brother, Efa, waited at the back of the crowded office to see them off before driving back to Kirkuk with his family.[3] A Syrian official entered Muayyed's name into a computer, then asked him to wait. Another official took his passport into a backroom. Ten minutes later he returned and asked Muayyed his name and the names of his parents. Then he asked Muayyed to follow him into the backroom.

He'd be out in a minute, Muayyed told Arsalan as he followed the official. The official ordered him to sit in a chair beside an iron bed. Muayyed did as he was told, still certain he'd be on his way soon.

"You are wanted," the official said to Muayyed, and ordered another man to handcuff him to the bed.[4]

Muayyed's heart was pounding. Having grown up under Saddam Hussein's Ba'ath Party, he knew very well what these officials in the Syrian Ba'ath Party were capable of. "I was in shock, very terrified. If the Mukhabarat says you are wanted, that means you are in big trouble. I said to myself, 'I am finished. That is it.'"

BORN IN 1967, Muayyed is the oldest of seven children—five brothers and two sisters. They all grew up in Kirkuk, a city he says is "floating on oil." The centre of northern Iraq's petroleum industry, the oilfields outside Kirkuk contain almost half of the country's total reserves. As members of the Turkoman ethnic minority, however, like the Kurdish families in Kirkuk, Muayyed's family never saw any of that wealth, which went instead to Saddam Hussein, his family and friends, and officials in his Ba'ath Party. Muayyed's father earned very little as a clerk in the army, and the family of nine shared an army-subsidized, tiny two-bedroom home.

Muayyed dreamt of becoming a doctor, and did well in high school, but had to settle for geology in university. Like all Iraqi university students, Muayyed was forced to train with the Popular Army in the summertime. Muayyed had trained once already, at fifteen, and had hated it. Facing expulsion from university if he didn't report, he served in the summer of 1986 before completing his second year of university. His interest in geology had grown, and he was doing well.

Tragedy struck the following spring when Muayyed's uncle, Mohammad, a close friend, was killed. Mohammad had recently defected from the army and Muayyed's family believes it was because of that that he was denied the medical attention he needed to survive. The family was told that Mohammad had been struck by a car while trying to avoid detection by a passing military convoy. The senseless death hit Muayyed hard. He remembers going with his father to collect Mohammad's body from the hospital morgue. The man working there was a close friend of his father's and showed them the bodies of eight people who'd been tortured to death by officials of the Ba'ath Party. They were just skin and bones. One had had all his teeth pulled out and had black scars on his stomach. This scene, and his uncle's death, served as a poignant reminder to Muayyed of how precarious his future was if he remained in Iraq.

While Muayyed was still in mourning, Ba'ath Party officials posted the schedules for that summer's Popular Army training rotation. Muayyed didn't see until six days into the first rotation that he'd been listed in the first group. The student department at the Ministry of Defence ordered him to make up for it by reporting to the second rotation in June. But before June arrived, the second rotation was cancelled, and Muayyed was automatically expelled from university for having "failed" to report. He sunk into a deep depression, knowing that he'd have no choice now but to sign up in the regular army for good as soon as his student identification expired the following year. "Everywhere there was a checkpoint where you have to show your status," Muayyed says. "If you were a student, you were a student. If you were not a student, they took you to jail right away. In addition to the checkpoints, they had raids in the streets. You could wake up tomorrow, and the whole avenue is surrounded by security, going from house to house to search for people."

By the next year, checkpoints weren't the only problem. In the summer of 1988, Saddam Hussein ordered his henchmen to wait ten days and then execute anyone who was supposed to report and hadn't. Muayyed's father told him he had to surrender. If he ran away, his family would be punished. "He said, 'Do you want them to come to take your sisters?'" Muayyed knew his father was right. They'd come and take his sisters, they might be assaulted, and their lives would be over. His father took him by the hand and walked with him to the police station. For Muayyed, joining Saddam Hussein's army meant becoming a slave. "This is not about serving your country. This is not about doing good things. This is about serving the people in the power," he says.

For the next two years, Muayyed was miserable. Life in the army was a gruelling regimen of physical and infantry training, hard labour, and sleep-deprived night watch rotations. Once a month, he had a few days off to go home to visit his family. The pay barely covered food and trips home. Even if Muayyed had money, as a Turkoman, he had no right to own land. "I had no future, no money, no secure job, and no respect," he says.

Muayyed dreamt of following thousands of others who'd fled over the northern border into Turkey. When Iraq invaded Kuwait in August 1990, Muayyed tried to escape Iraq for the first time. By then, so many others were running that there was little chance of recrimination against his family. He and a friend waded across a river into Turkey, only to be turned back by Turkish troops who ordered them to swim back or be shot.

A year later, Muayyed tried again and succeeded. But life in Turkey wasn't what he'd expected. The country was overrun with refugees desperate for work, and he'd arrived with just five dollars in his pocket. He remembers sharing four eggs among six people for dinner on one of his first nights there. Muayyed eventually travelled to Istanbul where for two years he struggled to make ends meet. He found work but was rarely paid. He was desperate. "In the Iraqi military, we were slaves. In Turkey, as workers, we were slaves again," he says. He thought of the family he'd left behind and of the risk he'd taken to get to Turkey. "Is this the life I risked execution for?" he wondered. "Is this the life so many others have been executed for trying to get?"

Muayyed's luck changed when he was accepted and registered as a United Nations sponsored refugee. After a year's wait, he learned he'd be going to Canada, a country he knew nothing about. He arrived in snow-covered Ottawa on January 20, 1994. He remembers his two nights in a motel, shocked to have a room with a double bed and a washroom all to himself, and free breakfast in the morning. One week later he caught a bus to Toronto and reunited with other Iraqis he'd met in Turkey who had come to Canada. Muayyed was overjoyed. "I was in a safe place and had rights. I could go to school, establish a business, earn an income to support my family, and travel," he says. Muayyed phoned his family from Toronto. "Don't worry about me now," he told them. "I am in Canada now and I am happy."

Muayyed spent a year in English-language classes before enrolling in Centennial College in 1996, where he studied to be a computer programmer and analyst. Rather than taking out a loan to pay for school, Muayyed worked part time to pay the costs.

Muayyed didn't see his family again until late 1999. Going to Kirkuk would have meant risking execution, so his grandmother, mother, father, and sisters drove to stay with him in the city of Dahuk, in Kurdish-controlled Iraq, where Muayyed had rented a house. It was a tearful reunion, and Muayyed remembers being shocked at how much older everyone looked from the last time he had seen them. His youngest sister was now eighteen and wearing the hijab. His brothers came with their families, and Muayyed met their wives and his nephews and nieces for the first time. He visited them again in 2002, this time in Erbil, in northern Iraq, which was also under Kurdish control.

Having the right to travel also meant having the right to fulfil his Muslim duty to perform the hajj. Muayyed fulfilled his lifelong dream to make the pilgrimage in January 2003.

MUAYYED HAD NEVER HEARD of the Canadian Security Intelligence Service, or CSIS, before an agent came to see him sometime in late 1997 or early 1998. The agent who knocked on the door of Muayyed's Toronto basement apartment introduced himself only as Michel. Muayyed invited him in, and offered him tea, but the agent declined. Had he been to Afghanistan? No, Muayyed said, he hadn't. Did he know anyone in al-Jihad? No, he didn't. (The Egyptian al-Jihad's original aim was to overthrow the Egyptian regime and create an Islamic state. The organization merged with al-Qaeda in 2001.) The conversation was short and polite, and Muayyed, who'd grown up in a city of many check-points, didn't think much of it. "I thought this was because I am from Iraq. I thought, 'It's okay because I am in their country. I am praying. I am Muslim. I am a foreigner. It's okay.'"

CSIS came knocking again a few months later. This time two agents, a man and a woman, arrived a couple minutes after Muayyed had left for classes. His roommate told them that Muayyed had just left for school. The agents peered over his shoulder and commented on how clean the kitchen was. Yes, he said. Muayyed keeps a very clean kitchen.

Muayyed was surprised to hear about the visit. He remembered seeing the agents his roommate described when he'd left the apartment building—they'd walked past him while he was pulling out of the driveway and had looked right at him. He wondered why, if they wanted to speak with him, they hadn't just stopped him then. But Muayyed wasn't worried. He figured the agents would come again and he'd find out what they wanted then.

After graduating from Centennial College, Muayyed found work as a principal in the Salaheddin Islamic Centre's private elementary school. Located in the Toronto suburb of Scarborough, the centre is a place of worship for almost three thousand Muslims. Its school had over 150 students when Muayyed started there. Its former principal, Mahmoud Jaballah, an Egyptian-born Canadian, had been detained by the RCMP in 1999 and again in August 2001 on a national security certificate and accused of links to al-Jihad. Muayyed knew Mahmoud but not well. Mahmoud had come to Canada in 1996. At the time, because Mahmoud was a newcomer, Muayyed had offered him a ride when he needed one. But they never became friends, and Muayyed never knew much about the allegations against him.[5] CSIS had taken a great interest in the Islamic Centre, likely because Ahmed Said Khadr and his family had once attended. Not one to engage in politics or watch the news, Muayyed didn't realize the extent of the agency's interest in his workplace.

Muayyed stayed on at the school for two and a half years, before starting a business fixing up and exporting used cars to Iraq. The plan was to ship the cars to Jordan or Syria, where one of his brothers could receive them and take them into Iraq for resale. He hoped the business would help generate more financial support for his family. And, once the Americans had occupied Iraq, Muayyed had excitedly begun preparing to go to Kirkuk for the first time since he'd left in 1991. In anticipation of his trip, he shipped three cars to Jordan, planning to drive with his brother from Iraq to pick them up.

1:30 P.M., Tuesday, September 16, 2003
Pearson International Airport, Toronto

MUAYYED'S FRIEND YILMAZ drove him to the airport.[6] His KLM flight to Amsterdam was to leave at 4:35 P.M. From there he would continue on to Stuttgart, Germany, where his brother Efa lived. His brother had purchased a car in Germany for them to drive into Iraq, then sell. Muayyed was carrying a lot of money— about US$10,500 and 4000 euros—and had arrived early so he'd have time to declare it at customs. Most of the money wasn't his but from friends for their families in Iraq. At the time, securely wiring money to family in Iraq was next to impossible, so Yilmaz had asked him to deliver $5000 to his mother to buy land. Two other friends each asked him to take $3000 to their families.

When Muayyed checked in at the KLM counter, the ticket agent left for a moment to speak with a supervisor. She returned, checked him in, and Muayyed went through security, then lined up to declare the money. Two men approached him, the taller one showing Muayyed his badge and saying they were Canadian security agents. They asked Muayyed to follow them over to a row of seats in the waiting area.

"Don't worry," they told him, "you won't miss your flight."

But the questions took about forty-five minutes. How many times had he been to Iraq? He told them he'd been back in 1999 and then again in 2002. How much money was he carrying? How much did he carry before? Muayyed told them what he had with him this time, who it was for, and that he'd carried about $3500 in 1999, and $4500 in 2002.

The next questions were about people he knew. Did he know Hassan Farhat? Yes, Muayyed told them, like him, Farhat is a Turkoman, and his children had attended the elementary school at the Salaheddin Islamic Centre when he was principal. He told them that Farhat had taken his children out of the school in 2001 before returning to Erbil. Did he know Subghat Allah Rasul? Yes, Rasul is a Canadian from Iraq who led prayers at the Salaheddin Islamic Centre's mosque during Ramadan; they had been neighbours for a while. Did he know Ali Hindy? Hindy is the imam at the Salaheddin Islamic Centre, Muayyed replied, and had been his boss when he was the school's principal. Was he involved in the accounting department at the school? No, Muayyed said.

Muayyed could see that, by this time, the other passengers had boarded the flight. The more polite of the two agents took him by the hand, rushing, to the gate. Muayyed walked into the passenger bridge to find eight customs agents and a sniffer dog. "Give us your bag and your jacket please," a customs agent said.

Three or four agents stood with him and the sniffer dog, while the others searched his belongings. He could see agents leafing through his address book and other papers he was carrying, frantically copying everything down into their notebooks. Another agent asked Muayyed to sign a declaration for his money. One of the agents' cellphones rang. After conferring with whomever was on the other end, the agent turned to his colleagues and said, "Okay, he can board."

Muayyed had been more anxious about missing his flight than about being questioned. He attributed the incident to his destination—he was, after all, returning to Iraq—and the two and a half years he'd worked at the Islamic centre. He'd never had any reason to think that he, or the people they asked about, were suspected of links to terrorism. Muayyed would be travelling through Syria en route to Iraq, and his return flight was out of Damascus. But he wasn't worried about travelling through the Middle East. He hadn't heard about Maher Arar, who at the time was still in Syrian detention. He'd met Ahmad El Maati a couple of times in passing following Friday prayers, but didn't know him as a friend and had no idea he'd been detained. He didn't know Abdullah Almalki either. "Even if I had heard about their cases I would have gone to Syria," Muayyed says, "because I have nothing to hide and I wanted to see my family."

Muayyed arrived in Amsterdam early the next morning and caught his connecting flight to Stuttgart. He and Efa drove to Italy, catching the ferry to Greece. Their plan was to drive through Turkey and Syria and into Iraq—at the time it cost about US$1200 to cross the Turkish-Iraqi border, compared with US$300 to cross from Syria. They made good time, reaching the Turkish-Syrian border the morning of Saturday, September 27. When they presented their passports at the border control, Turkish officials asked them to pull aside and park. They were ushered into the immigration office and told to wait.

Turkish officials counted the money Muayyed was carrying, then asked if he worked at a Muslim centre. Muayyed, surprised by the question, answered yes but said he'd left his job there in June. Did he belong to any organizations? No, he replied. Muayyed and his brother were then told to sit and wait. When Muayyed went to use the washroom, one of the officials ran after him, yelling at him not to close the door. Muayyed was already seated, but opened the door as he was told. This is ridiculous, he thought.

Muayyed and his brother were ordered back into the car; an official drove it to a small jailhouse just metres away. The brothers watched for the next two hours as the car was thoroughly searched. "They took the doors apart, and even looked in the ceiling," Muayyed says. They found nothing.

The man who'd chased Muayyed to the washroom apologized. "I am sorry. We did this because we had orders from higher up."

Their photographs were taken before they were driven back to the immigration office. The officials asked the brothers to sign some papers noting they'd been searched. A few minutes later, one of the officials stepped aside to take a call. Muayyed heard him say to whomever he was speaking with on the phone, "Why are you exaggerating? He has nothing." He turned to Muayyed and his brother, signalling that they were free to go.

"Turkey had nothing to do with you. Only Canada," he said.

Muayyed and Efa continued through Syria, arriving in Kirkuk two days later, on September 29. Muayyed's worries about the questioning in Turkey quickly faded when he saw his grand-mother, parents, sisters, and brothers. He had missed them terribly and was proud to see that the money he sent had enabled them to buy land and build a new home. It was much larger than the tiny two-bedroom house they'd all shared when he was growing up. He could see now how important his income was to them. Kirkuk's infrastructure had seriously deteriorated since he'd left in 1991. The city was in the middle of a war zone, and earning any kind of income was next to impossible. The roads were crumbling and the electricity worked only for about four hours a day. Cooking fuel was scarce and pricey.

On November 17, Muayyed and Arsalan drove to Jordan to pick up the cars Muayyed had sent from Canada. At the

Jordanian border, an officer took their passports, leaving them waiting for half an hour before calling Muayyed into the office to ask why he was going into Jordan and where he'd be staying. Then he let the brothers continue on their way.

The cars from Canada hadn't been processed by Jordanian customs and wouldn't be before the Eid-al-Fitr, less than a week away, so Muayyed and Arsalan decided to go back to Iraq for the holiday and return for the cars later. On their way out of Jordan they were stopped again. This time a Jordanian official asked if Muayyed had been ordered to report to security officials in Jordan. No, he hadn't, Muayyed replied. Muayyed got the sense that the official didn't believe him, but he waved them on their way anyway. Five days later, Arsalan returned to Jordan by himself to pick up the cars, hiring drivers to bring them back. Arsalan knew where to go on his own now, and Muayyed wanted to spend as much time with his family as possible before leaving for Canada again. Those last days with his family would be more precious than he realized: In a few days' time, on December 11, Muayyed would be in the hands of Syrian Military Intelligence.

5 P.M., Thursday, December 11, 2003
Al-Ya'arubya border crossing, Syrian-Iraqi border

AFTER HANDCUFFING Muayyed to the bed and telling him he was "wanted," the Syrian officials searched his clothing and shoes.

"Maybe he has a bomb in his shoe," one of the officials said, laughing. "Which building are you going to bomb in Syria?"

"I am only trying to go back to Canada," Muayyed said, daring to hope it might help.

They asked if he had luggage. It was with his brother outside, Muayyed explained. He sat, still handcuffed to the bed, while an official searched his luggage and the others made phone calls about him. "He wasn't detained when he came through Syria the first time because the report came in on the fourteenth of November," he heard one of them say into the phone. Muayyed says that's when he realized that his being held must have something to do with the questions in Canada and Turkey.

One hour turned into two, and two into three. Finally, the handcuffs were unlocked from the bed and locked onto the wrist of an official, who led Muayyed out into the public area of the immigration office. Muayyed's younger brother, Arsalan, was still standing there, waiting.

"Where are you taking my brother?" he asked.

"He is not going to see the sun again," the senior official answered. "Get out of here!"

Arsalan grabbed Muayyed's hands and they embraced. "Go to Damascus and wait for me," Muayyed told him. "If I'm not there in two days, go back home and call my friends in Canada. Tell them what's happened."

"Promise me you'll take care of the family," Muayyed said as he was being led away.

"Remember Allah," Arsalan called after him.

The Syrian officials loaded Muayyed into a pickup truck and drove him to another building. There, in a second-floor office, an official counted his money. Then he was driven to a detention centre in the town of Kamishli, about a twenty-minute drive west of the Iraqi border.

The greeting was harsh.

"Face the wall! Don't look at us!" an official yelled as Muayyed was led into the detention centre. He was locked into a three-by-six-foot underground cell until the next evening, when he and the seven other detainees were handcuffed to each other and loaded onto a minibus. He overhead one of the detainees saying they were going to Damascus. Muayyed recalls two of the detainees whispering about the place they were going to as being crowded, and about torture.

Muayyed's brothers hadn't told their mother that he'd been detained. After waiting more than two hours, they'd known the situation was serious. Arsalan told Efa he'd better take the family back to Kirkuk: It would take four hours, and driving in Iraq after sunset was dangerous. Arsalan would wait, just in case he could somehow help Muayyed. Efa had hidden his fear, gone back to the car, and told his mother that Muayyed and Arsalan were on their way to Damascus. "She wouldn't have left the border if they told her," Muayyed says.

Arsalan did as Muayyed had instructed and waited in Damascus for two days. Then he went to a police station to ask after Muayyed. The police officers said they didn't know anything. When Arsalan insisted, they warned him to leave or he'd be detained, too. Reluctantly, Arsalan set out for Kirkuk, dreading the prospect of having to tell his mother that Muayyed hadn't showed up. "My mother has a heart condition. They told me later my mom fainted and was hospitalized for two or three days when she heard the news," Muayyed says.

THE MINIBUS WOUND ITS WAY through the Syrian Military Intelligence compound in Damascus and stopped outside Far' Falastin sometime after midnight on Friday, December 12. The prison manager wasn't there, so Muayyed and two other prisoners were ushered through his office and locked in an interrogation room for the night. But first, the guard took their belts, watches, and shoelaces. Muayyed looked up at the iron hooks on the walls of the interrogation room. He guessed they were used to suspend prisoners for torture.

He and the others waited, anxiously, for the morning. Eventually, a guard appeared and took them to the prison manager's office. The manager assigned the other two prisoners to a cell.

"What's your nationality?" the manager asked Muayyed.

"I'm Canadian," Muayyed replied.

"I know you're Canadian. I need your nationality."

"I'm Iraqi," he answered, then added, "I have a flight today."

The manager just shook his head.

Muayyed could see past the manager into a small room with hundreds of belts hanging from hooks on the wall. "That's when I realized how many people were kept there."

The manager put Muayyed's belongings into an envelope and ordered a guard to take him to cell number eight, a common cell.

Muayyed remembers seeing the picture of former Syrian president Hafez al-Assad and the verse from the Qu'ran on the wall on the way downstairs.

"In the cell, I was scared. Many of the prisoners stood up and came to me, [asking,] Where are you from? What's the news from Iraq? What's happening? What did you do? What are you accused of?" Muayyed recalls. One of the prisoners tried to hush the others, explaining to Muayyed that they'd not had news from the outside in a long time. Muayyed later learned that this man, whom the prisoners called the *chaoush*—Egyptian for sergeant— had been there for a year and a half. When Muayyed arrived, thirty prisoners were crammed into the fifteen-by-twenty-foot cell. Within a few days, ten more were added.

Because of the tight space, the prisoners had resorted to vertical storage—the cell's cement walls were crowded with bags hanging from hooks filled with their shoes and other items they were allowed to keep, as well as bags filled with yet to be eaten food rations. The door was solid, and the small window at the top of the wall opened onto a cement basin outside. The prisoners couldn't see out but could at least tell whether it was day or night. The fluorescent lights mounted on the cement ceiling were always on.

In the back corner of the cell was a bathroom with a pit toilet, its six-foot-high ceiling covered in cockroaches. "The ceiling was 90 percent black. Not a spot of white showed. They were on top of each other. If someone sits more than two minutes, the cockroaches start walking on [you]." There were roaches and other insects in the cell itself, too, but not as many.

The prisoners ate in groups of five, with each group sharing from one dish. There was only enough space for three or four groups to sit down at once, so they took turns.

The men slept like sardines, on their sides, straight, because there wasn't enough room to bend their knees. The cell was barely wide enough for two rows of prisoners to sleep head to toe. Two blankets were shared among every three or four prisoners. The five most senior prisoners slept during the day and kept watch through the night. It was rare for detainees to hurt, instead of help, each other, but this was a policy dictated by the guards.

A guard came to call for Muayyed at 10:30 P.M. the night after he arrived. He heard the guard call his first name through the door. The *chaoush*, who had a list of everyone's full names, read out Muayyed's given name and surname to confirm this was the "Muayyed" wanted. Yes, the guard said, he is the one. Muayyed later learned that the guards never revealed prisoners' full names in the hallway, so that prisoners wouldn't know if their relatives or friends were in other cells.

Muayyed was led to an interrogation room. He tried to explain that he'd planned to fly home from Damascus and that they had his airline ticket, but the interrogator just starting yelling questions at him: Tell me your life story. What do you do in Canada? What is the Salaheddin Islamic Centre? What did you do there? Who is the imam? How much money did you take to Iraq? Do you belong to any organizations? Do you belong to Ansar al-Islam? What did you do in Iraq? Why did you come to Syria?

Muayyed had heard most of the questions before—in Canada, and again in Turkey—but he hadn't heard the question about Ansar al-Islam before and knew nothing about the group. He didn't know that, at the time, American agencies believed Ansar al-Islam, a militant Islamic group fighting for control of northern Iraq, had been a link between Saddam Hussein and al-Qaeda.[7] Muayyed told the interrogator he wasn't a member of Ansar al-Islam or any other religious or political organization. But when he told him he'd worked at the Salaheddin Islamic Centre, the interrogator insisted he was lying and had worked at the al-Uhm Islamic Centre in Toronto. Muayyed said he didn't know about this centre.

"You are a liar, and you have ten minutes to think of better answers!" the interrogator barked.

"This is my story and this is the truth. I have nothing to hide," Muayyed insisted.

"We have a report on you. We know exactly how much money you had when you left Canada, and we have your passport number and your name."

Muayyed later learned the interrogator was Haitham, the same man who'd tortured and questioned Ahmad, Abdullah, and Maher. Haitham left, returning a few minutes later.

"Do you have anything new to say?" he asked.

Muayyed said no, he had told the truth. Haitham ordered Muayyed to strip to his underwear and stand facing the wall, then asked another man to douse him with cold water. The ceiling fan was turned to high speed, and the interrogators left the room. He stood there, shivering, until the interrogators returned and asked Muayyed again if he had anything new to say. When Muayyed said no, Haitham ordered him to lie on his stomach on the floor, then poured more cold water on his back before leaving the room. Again they came back and asked if he had any new answers. When he answered no, Haitham asked the other man to get a cable, then ordered Muayyed to crawl into the corner and bend his knees so his feet were in the air. Haitham took the cable and whipped the soles of Muayyed's feet. The pain, Muayyed says, feels like hot water is being pouring on a bad burn. "It's like fire on your skin. I was screaming and begging him to stop, but he just kept beating, beating, beating." After fifteen minutes or so, Haitham told Muayyed to get up and jog on the spot. The jogging brought some relief. Haitham told him to get water in the washroom if he was thirsty. The pain came back as Muayyed walked. "I think the purpose of telling me to jog and to go to the washroom is to make me feel the pain again.... When I saw myself [in the mirror] I asked, 'Is this me?'" He was dripping with sweat, and his face, stomach, and underwear were filthy from being on the floor.

Back in the interrogation room, it started again, with Haitham asking the questions while the other man whipped Muayyed:

Who did you give your money to? Did you give your money to an organization? Was it Ansar al-Islam? Muayyed told them the money was for his family and the families of his friends. But his answers just made the interrogators angrier.

"I was screaming, 'If you want to kill me, kill me, but don't torture me like this!' I tried to kiss Haitham's shoes, but he pulled his feet back."

Muayyed was losing consciousness. The whipping stopped and Haitham ordered Muayyed to stand and jog on the spot, then sent him to the washroom again.

"Oh, you can still walk," Haitham said as Muayyed came back into the room. "Get back on the floor again!"

The cable came out. Muayyed remembers that his feet were bright white—almost glowing, as if fluorescent, he says.

The interrogation continued until about 1:30 in the morning. Haitham warned him not to talk to the other prisoners. He'd be calling for Muayyed again at 6 A.M. that morning. He pointed his index finger at the hooks and the chair. "Think about what you are going to say. It is going to be worse tomorrow. We're going to hang you from those hooks all day, and then we're going to use the chair. We're not in a rush, you will be here at least a year."

Back in the cell, barely able to walk on his swollen feet, and drenched in sweat, Muayyed took his place between the other sleeping prisoners. He lay awake, terrified by any sound, thinking that the interrogators were sending for him again. "There were two things that wouldn't let me sleep. The pain, and the fear." The next morning one of the detainees asked what they'd done to him; he'd seen Muayyed's swollen feet. Muayyed just said he was fine and kept quiet. He couldn't walk, or touch his feet, for four days.

Each day the guard came for three or four prisoners, but Muayyed's name wasn't called again until December 21. This time the men only threatened to torture him, barking out questions about two of the people he'd been asked about at the airport in Toronto—Farhat and Rasul. Muayyed repeated what he'd told the Canadians.

THINGS SUDDENLY CHANGED two days later, on December 23. At around 7 P.M., Muayyed was called up to see the prison manager. The manager saw him shaking with fear.

"Calm down, calm down. Nobody will touch you again," he said, offering Muayyed tea.

"I knew then that something must have happened. Something from Canada," Muayyed says.

The manager asked for his parents' names and how much money he had. Then he asked if Muayyed had been beaten. When he answered yes, the manager told him he was now safe and not to worry. Just then they heard screaming from an interrogation room down the hall. "This manager is trying to give the picture, 'We don't torture,' and then the yelling came. He put his head down and covered his face."

When Muayyed was taken back to his cell, a cellmate was lying on his back on the floor, groaning in agony. The others were gathered around him trying to help. This, it turned out, was the man Muayyed had heard screaming.

"They used the chair on him," one of his cellmates explained.

At about 10 P.M. Muayyed was called up to an interrogation room and ordered to take a seat, with his back to the door. A man he later learned was Colonel George Salloum came into the room. He was wearing a suit and tie, and his shoes were polished.

"*Merhaba*." Salloum spoke Iraqi. Welcome. He noticed Muayyed's feet were bare and ordered a guard to take him down to his cell for his shoes. Back in the interrogation room, Salloum asked if "anything bad" had happened.

"Yes, the interrogator tortured me," Muayyed replied.

"Sometimes mistakes can happen," Salloum said.

Haitham entered the room, and Salloum ordered him to shake Muayyed's hand. Haitham didn't apologize, but his actions betrayed his regret, Muayyed says. "He told me, 'I didn't call you the next day because I felt I trusted your story. I had a feeling you are honest. I was just doing my job. I had no choice. We received a report about you, and we had to verify it." He didn't say where the report had come from.

Salloum's tone was friendly, but he had more questions, again about the money Muayyed had been carrying and the men he'd been asked about before. He was rushing, and as he wrote the answers, he handed them one page at a time to a guard, ordering him to take each page to be typed.

The next day one of Muayyed's cellmates, an Iraqi prisoner who'd been detained for about six weeks, cracked. The guard delivering the food told the prisoners he didn't have as many pita loaves as usual: "We didn't receive enough to feed everybody. There are 400 prisoners, and we only have enough for 350. So today you will only get two each, not three."

The Iraqi prisoner demanded to see the prison manager. The guard ran into the cell, shouting, "You want to see the director? Come with me!"

Muayyed recalls that the prisoner was so scared that he ran into the washroom and started cutting himself with an empty can, trying to commit suicide. The *chaoush* and other prisoners managed to open the door. The guards dragged the bloodied and terrified man out of the cell. About a half hour after Muayyed was back in the cell the guards opened the door and tossed the Iraqi man in. He was unconscious.

A few minutes later, the guard transferred Muayyed to what the prison manager referred to as the "best cell," a thirteen-by-sixteen foot cell shared by just eight prisoners. The prisoners there told Muayyed that the minimum stay at Far' Falastin was one year.

BACK IN CANADA, Muayyed's friends were trying to help. Muayyed's brother, Arsalan, had called Yilmaz in Toronto after returning to Kirkuk. Yilmaz told him that CSIS had questioned him about Muayyed. Two agents had come to his home a week or two after Muayyed left in September. They'd implied that Muayyed was in trouble and said they wanted to help him. Did

Yilmaz know the route Muayyed would take to travel to Iraq? Yilmaz said he thought Muayyed would cross from Turkey. The agents asked Yilmaz about Farhat and Rasul, alleging that Farhat and two of Rasul's sons were linked to Ansar al-Islam. Yilmaz told them that if this was true, the men were misguided. Muayyed isn't politically active, he said, and if they wanted to know more about him, they should speak with him directly. The agents said they wanted to but had missed him. But then they asked whether any of the money Muayyed was carrying to Iraq belonged to Yilmaz— demonstrating that they hadn't missed Muayyed at all, as this was information Muayyed had told them at the airport. Yilmaz confirmed that Muayyed was taking money to his mother for him.

Yilmaz wasn't the only person CSIS visited after Muayyed left Canada. Muayyed learned much later that CSIS agents also questioned two other friends he'd carried money for.

Yilmaz hadn't thought much of the questions until Muayyed's brother called from Iraq to say that Muayyed had been detained. Yilmaz talked to Ali Hindy, the imam at the Salaheddin Islamic Centre. Another of Muayyed's friends called the consular division at DFAIT on December 18. He eventually spoke with Myra Pastyr-Lupul in the consular division, who advised Muayyed's friends not to speak to the media. On December 21, DFAIT sent a diplomatic note to the Syrian Ministry of Foreign Affairs, asking if Syria had Muayyed in detention. By January 2, Syria had still not officially confirmed that it was holding Muayyed, so Muayyed's friends decided it was time to talk to the media. It had worked for Maher Arar, and it might help Muayyed.

Yilmaz told the Toronto Star's Michelle Shephard about Muayyed's detention and the CSIS questioning. Coming on the heels of the publicity around Maher's case, Muayyed's story was big news. For Maher and his supporters, it was evidence of a pattern of complicity in overseas detentions. This wasn't a coincidence, or a series of mishaps. Now four Canadians, all of interest to Canadian investigators, had ended up in Syrian detention. Worst of all, no one could claim ignorance about what would happen to someone in Syrian detention if Canada sent information—it was clear that this man had been detained after Maher had told everyone his story.

Thursday, January 8, 2004
Far' Falastin, Damascus

BACK AT FAR' FALASTIN, Muayyed had been invited for tea with the prison manager almost every day since being moved from cell number eight. Two days earlier, the manager had asked him whom he should contact in case of an emergency.

"The Canadian embassy, please."

"Where are you going to go when you are released? Why don't you stay in Syria a while, then go back to Iraq?"

Just don't go back to Canada and do what Maher Arar is doing, he must have been thinking.

Now, on January 8, Muayyed was instructed to sign and place his thumbprint on several statements. One he had been asked to write the day before about his family and his life. Another was a declaration that he had been treated nicely and not tortured. Another contained the answers he'd provided about Rasul, Farhat, and Hindy on December 23, but he wasn't permitted to read it, so it's unclear whether his answers had been embellished.

Five days later, on January 13, Muayyed was called out of his cell. This time, he wasn't just served tea. He was given his passport, his expired airline ticket, and other belongings and told he was being released. George Salloum and Haitham took him to see a senior official, who told him to say he'd been treated nicely. Then he was taken to see another senior official. When asked, he said he hadn't been tortured. "I think this was a final test," Muayyed says. The official asked if he needed anything.

"An airline ticket, please."

The official told Muayyed not to worry and ordered a guard to bring him a cup of Turkish coffee. A few minutes later, Muayyed was taken into General Hassan Khalil's office. A man stood and introduced himself as Leo Martel, the Canadian consul. Khalil asked Muayyed if he'd been tortured. Again, Muayyed replied that he hadn't been.

"Syria is your second country now. If you want to come back, you can come anytime, and we are your brothers," Khalil told Muayyed.

Muayyed was released and allowed to leave with Martel. A Syrian official drove them to the nearby Sheraton Hotel in Omayad Square. There, Martel took Muayyed for lunch, with a woman named Maha joining them from the embassy. Martel and Maha asked Muayyed to tell them everything that had happened. They emailed the report to Ottawa that same day.[8] Muayyed remembers Martel telling him that a Canadian security agent had called the embassy from Canada that morning to say he'd be released. Muayyed assumed he meant CSIS, and wondered if CSIS had arranged for his detention, too.

Martel took him to an American medical clinic, where a doctor gave him a prescription for scabies. Then Martel took him back to the Sheraton Hotel for the night. Muayyed learned later that he'd be billed for that. The next morning, Muayyed was taken to the embassy, where he was asked further questions about his ordeal. The Canadians asked Muayyed to sign a note promising to repay the Canadian government the cost of the hotel, a jacket they'd bought for him to wear, and his airline ticket—the ticket was in first class. The total cost was a whopping $3069. Muayyed paid it back in less than a month but wishes that money could have gone to his family instead.

When Martel told him he'd fly with him to Canada, and their flight would leave at 2:15 A.M., Muayyed suggested Martel simply accompany him to the airport—he could get home on his own. "Martel told me, 'I advise you that when your government offers you any service, you should take it.' I didn't feel I had any choice but to show I was grateful." Martel introduced him to Brian Davis, the Canadian ambassador to Syria, then took him to a guesthouse to await his flight.

At the airport, Muayyed had another scare. "When I gave them my passport, I saw a red bar across the computer screen. It said '*Matlobe, Matlobe, Matlobe*,' which is 'wanted' in Arabic. I was scared, but I knew if they took me, the consul would witness it." The immigration official asked Muayyed and Martel to follow him into a security office, where he handed Muayyed's passport to a uniformed security official, who told them to wait. After a forty-minute delay, during which Muayyed believes the security official checked in with the Syrian Military Intelligence on his status, they were allowed to board the flight. Muayyed says he was feeling conflicted and confused as they left Syria. "I was very happy to be out of that cell, but I was also very confused about why this happened and who was behind it. I worried I wouldn't be able to travel again. How would I see my family?"

Muayyed's friends and lawyer, who'd heard from someone at Foreign Affairs that he was on his way home, along with a horde of journalists and television cameras, were waiting in the arrivals area at Pearson International Airport in Toronto. One of those reporters, the *National Post*'s Stewart Bell, spoke to an unnamed source about Muayyed's case. "Intelligence officials are concerned he may have served as a courier of money and information for an organization, sources said," his story, published the day after Muayyed's arrival home, read.[9] "But no evidence has been made public that would support the allegation." It's not known whether the statements Muayyed had been unable to read but forced to sign had made their way back to Canada.

It was only after Muayyed returned to Canada that he learned about the detentions of Maher Arar, Ahmad El Maati, and Abdullah Almalki. Just a few weeks after Muayyed returned to Canada, another former principal of the Salaheddin Islamic Centre, Helmy Elsherief, was detained for three weeks in Egypt on his way from the hajj in Saudi Arabia. The Egyptian government told Elsherief that a foreign government had requested his detention. CSIS had visited Elsherief after 9/11, and he was likely under investigation because, like Abdullah Almalki, he'd worked with Human Concern International in Afghanistan in the 1990s.

Aly Hindy, the imam at the Salaheddin mosque whom Muayyed had been asked about, had been detained and questioned in Egypt, too. Hindy had been on his way to hajj in January 2004 when he was arrested at the airport in Cairo, blindfolded, handcuffed, thrown into a van, and taken to a detention centre, where he was interrogated for thirty-four hours. He says he was asked about the Salaheddin Islamic Centre and people involved in it who had been accused of terrorist links. He was told CSIS didn't want him released. His interrogators threatened to make him disappear or to send him to Guantánamo. Hindy says he was released only because of family connections.

Muayyed didn't learn until after his release that Farhat and two of Rasul's sons had been publicly accused by the Patriotic Union of Kurdistan (PUK) of involvement in Ansar al-Islam. He doesn't know whether there's any basis to the allegations.

8:30 A.M., Thursday, February 12, 2004
Home of Muayyed Nureddin, Toronto

MUAYYED WOKE UP when he heard someone knocking on his door at around 8:30 in the morning. He ignored the knocking until he heard it again about twenty minutes later. He got out of bed and opened the door. The two men standing there introduced themselves as Ian Ferguson and Mike from CSIS.

"We want to speak with you," Ferguson said.

"I would like to have my lawyer here first," Muayyed answered.

"Why do you need a lawyer?" Mike asked. "They are so expensive. Listen, we didn't do this to you, and you are a good man, and we just want to clear your name."

It was snowing outside, so Muayyed invited the agents in and offered them tea. Then he called his lawyer, Barb Jackman, and his friend Yilmaz, leaving messages for them both. The agents settled in for the conversation they wanted to have without a lawyer present. How many times had he been to Iraq? they asked. Muayyed handed them his passport. "I felt like they were being honest," he says. Ian continued to ask questions while Mike copied down the dates of the passport stamps. What was the purpose of his last visit? To see his family, and to expand his used-car export business, he said. His mother had phoned him after Saddam fell, asking him to come to Kirkuk. Many other Iraqis returned home then, he explained. How much money did he take? Muayyed told the agents what he'd told the agents at the airport, the Turkish officials, and the Syrians. Did he see anyone from Toronto in Iraq, such as Farhat? No, Muayyed said.

The questioning continued for about twenty minutes before the phone rang. It was Yilmaz calling to say that he'd tracked down Muayyed's lawyer—she would be phoning in a moment. In the meantime, he said, she wants him to stop the meeting. Jackman called a couple of minutes later and spoke to one of the agents. If they wanted to meet with her client, she said, they'd have to do it with her in her office. The agents scheduled a meeting for the next morning. As they were leaving, Muayyed asked them for their cards. Mike said he didn't have one, but Ian reluctantly handed his over.

They met again the next day in his lawyer's office. This time both agents had cards. The other agent's name was Mike Boehm. A no-nonsense lawyer used to dealing with CSIS, Jackman pulled out a recorder and put it on her desk. Ferguson pulled out one too. "Like we told Muayyed yesterday, this is a voluntary interview," Ferguson said. Muayyed told Jackman later that he'd told them he wanted a lawyer but that they had made him feel as if he had no choice but to speak with them right then. This time they wanted to know if Muayyed had met with anyone on his way to Jordan, and when he had planned his latest trip to Iraq. Barb asked whether they had concerns about Muayyed. Ferguson said no, Muayyed was clear now; they just wanted to know if Muayyed was being used by a third party without his knowledge.

Muayyed told them that was impossible. These people were his friends, and the money had gone to their families.

Within two weeks of his return, Muayyed had met with Alex Neve at Amnesty International Canada, and told him his story. Amnesty International's international office wrote to the Canadian prime minister, urging him to consider adding a second phase to the Arar Inquiry to examine Muayyed's case. "Amnesty International is also concerned about the possibility that CSIS may have played a role in this case," wrote Amnesty's international secretary general, Irene Khan. "The similarity of the questioning Mr. Nureddin faced in Canada and in Syria points in that direction, as does the fact that Canadian consular officials reportedly learned of Mr. Nureddin's release from CSIS sources."[10]

10 A.M., Wednesday, February 25, 2004
Religious Society of Friends (Quakers), Friends House, Toronto

ALEX NEVE sat next to Muayyed when he told his story publicly for the first time, on February 25.

"It has become clear that there is a pattern of people who held my job at the Islamic school being viewed with suspicion by the authorities," Muayyed told the media.[11] "Helmy Elsherief was the principal at one time. He was held in the Egyptian jail for close to one month this year. Mahmoud Jaballah was the principal at one time. He has been held in a Canadian jail for more than two years. I was principal at one time and I have been tortured in Syria. I did know these men. I know nothing about them doing anything illegal." Muayyed asked why he had been targeted, called for a public inquiry to examine his case, and listed the questions he wanted answered.

"I want to know why I was detained in Syria. I want to know if CSIS or any other Canadian security agency was responsible for my detention and torture in Syria. I do not want this to happen to others ever again. It is wrong."

The day after Muayyed's statement, the *Toronto Star*'s Tom Walkom summed up the questions on many people's minds in a front-page column. "To put it bluntly," he wrote, "there is growing suspicion that these kinds of things are happening on purpose—that CSIS and the RCMP have adopted their own version of what the U.S. calls 'extraordinary rendition' and are making quiet deals with foreign dictatorships to interrogate Canadians abroad using methods that would be illegal at home."[12]

TWENTY-FOUR

Release and Return

Sometime in January 2004
Sednaya prison, Sednaya, Syria

IT HAD BEEN A LONG TIME since Abdullah had had any contact with the outside world, so he was overjoyed when both his parents visited him in January. He hadn't seen his father since his visit at Far' Falastin. "I didn't learn until later how not being able to help his own son had destroyed him. He couldn't face me until he could do something. He was able to face me now because there was some kind of process, and he felt like he had some sort of control again, like he was able to do something." Abdullah's parents had returned to Syria with a letter from the RCMP. Signed on December 11, 2003, by RCMP assistant commissioner Ghyslaine Clément, the letter confirmed that Abdullah had no criminal record and was not the subject of any arrest warrants in Canada. His parents delivered it to the headquarters of the Syrian Military Intelligence. There was going to be a hearing in February, his parents told him, and they were hopeful he'd be released. They'd appointed a lawyer who they believed could speed up what would normally be a very long process.

By now, however, Abdullah didn't believe he'd ever be released—even talking about it was a waste of valuable visit time. "[It] was frustrating for me ... I wanted to talk about something that would be useful. I wanted more information about the family, my wife, my kids, and what was happening with them. But [my father] kept talking about lawyers, and the letter from the RCMP."

The visit didn't last long. When Abdullah returned to his cell, he told his fellow inmates about the lawyer. They recognized the name and said he was well known. "I was a little comforted by that, but others warned that in [the State Supreme Security] court a lawyer can't do much, if anything. But at the same time there was the hope that something is moving, not forgotten," Abdullah says.

In early February, the guards told Abdullah that he was going to court. "I was very afraid. I do not know why, maybe because I was going to be taken from Sednaya, the place that I felt the least terrible in, a place where I was surrounded by [prisoners] who cared a lot about each other. But also there was hope, hope to help others," Abdullah says. Detainees were sometimes able to see family in court, and Abdullah had been asked to request tuberculosis medication for a detainee who was near death because of the lack of medication at Sednaya.

Abdullah, shackled and chained at the wrists and ankles, was put in a military truck with three other prisoners and driven to the State Supreme Security Court. They waited in a cell for hours before a clerk asked Abdullah to sign for his lawyer. Once he did, his father and the lawyer came to the cell. His father was visibly shaken when he saw his son in chains. Abdullah asked him to help get TB medication. "The guard overheard me calling him 'Dad' and made him leave." The guard had assumed Abdullah's father was just a lawyer. Two hours later, a clerk came to say the hearings were postponed because the judge hadn't shown up. The prisoners were taken back out to the truck. "As we drove off, I saw my father standing out by the street," Abdullah says. "I will never forget his face. He looked devastated."

Back at Sednaya, Abdullah learned that George Salloum had come looking for him. He came again on February 25, with Haitham and a new report. It was about a Canadian family Abdullah knew. "I couldn't believe how detailed the information was. They had everyone's names, including the children's and the in-laws." The men wanted to know if any of them had been to

Afghanistan. Abdullah said he didn't know. Salloum, unhappy with his answers, threatened Abdullah with more torture. At the end of the interrogation, Salloum asked Abdullah if he thought there were innocent prisoners at Sednaya.

"There are many innocent people here," Abdullah answered.

"Who?"

"Me, for example."

"Your case is special." Salloum said.

Four days later, Abdullah was taken back to the court. This time, the judge showed up. Abdullah was escorted into the courtroom and asked to stand before the judge. The judge looked him over. "Did you attend the mosque in Ottawa? Did you attend lectures there?" he asked.

"Yes," Abdullah replied.

"Do you know Ibrahym Adam?"

"Yes. He has never been charged with anything in Canada."

"Did you work with Human Concern International in Pakistan?"

"Yes. I worked on their UNDP-funded projects," Abdullah said, referring to the United Nations Development Programme he had been involved with. "But I left and went back to Canada."

Abdullah's lawyer entered the room and asked if he could stand next to Abdullah so he could hear the conversation. But the judge ordered him to the back of the room. "Does anyone else have anything to add?" he asked. A man in a military uniform spoke from his chair.

"Do you still share al-Qaeda's views?"

"No. I have never shared al-Qaeda's views," Abdullah answered. "People who know me know I do not follow the Wahhabi teachings, and I do not believe in violence."

There were no more questions. Abdullah was taken out of the courtroom and locked into a cell. His lawyer came a few minutes later. Abdullah's family was arranging to pay his bail and then he'd be released, the lawyer explained. He'd have to appear in court again on April 25. "I didn't believe him," Abdullah recalls.

"I just worried that they would lose the money." He didn't know then that the bail amounted to only about 5000 lira, or Can$125.

The next day Abdullah was transferred to Far' Falastin. But detainees at Sednaya had warned him that only the branch that had originally detained him could release him, so he wasn't surprised. "I knew I would end up back at Far' Falastin, and I didn't know for how long. I'd heard stories that this step could take months or even years." This time he was locked him in one of the common cells directly below the interrogation floor. "We could hear the prisoners being tortured and screaming. It was very clear and loud, as if they were in the next room. Occasionally, people would be taken from our cell for torture. It was awful ... we would all hear them being tortured and then see them when they were brought back to the cell. We had rubbing alcohol to help clean the wounds."

Ten days later, Abdullah was taken back upstairs and told he'd have to remain in the country for a year. Then, after one year, ten months, and seven days of detention, he was released.

"The first thing I did was phone Khuzaimah. I told her I had to stay in Syria and she said they'd come if I had to stay. I talked to all my kids; some did not say a word. I remember the youngest saying, 'Baba, Baba,' which was all he knew of his father—a picture and the word *baba*.'"

1 A.M., Sunday, March 7, 2004
Cairo International Airport, Cairo

AHMAD AND HIS MOTHER knew through the media that embassy officials had escorted Maher Arar and Muayyed Nureddin home from Syria. They'd pleaded with officials at the Canadian Embassy in Egypt to do the same for them. But they refused, saying they would write a letter for Ahmad to carry and would accompany them to the airport, but they would not escort them home. "I was very frightened I would be prevented from leaving the country, or worse, arrested again or kidnapped. I begged them, but they just said no, no, no," Ahmad says.

It was 1 A.M., March 7, when the embassy van picked them up to take them to the airport. Once there, they checked their bags, got their boarding passes, then went to the immigration area. An Egyptian staff person from the embassy, Ayman, took Ahmad and his mother's passports over to the immigration office. Several minutes passed with no sign of Ayman. An airline representative came to see what was happening—their flight was boarding, she said. Ahmad assured her they'd be along soon. But Ayman didn't emerge for another half hour.

"They'll let you go," Ayman said to Ahmad's mother. "But Ahmad cannot go."

Ahmad's heart sunk. Samira stood up, angry. "I am not leaving without my son," she said.

The airline representative came over again to say she couldn't hold the flight any longer. She needed their tickets, she said, so their bags could be taken off the plane.

Ahmad's departure wasn't a problem with the State Security Investigations Services, Ayman later told Ahmad. It was a problem with General Intelligence—they were the ones blocking his departure. It isn't clear whether CSIS or any other Canadian agency had anything to do with the problems Ahmad experienced that day, but Ahmad says that Ayman spent several days trying to sort it out, while he and his mother waited back at Samira's apartment.

After rebooking their flight, Ahmad and his mother asked the Canadian Embassy again if, given what had happened, an official could accompany them home. "Why was I different from Maher Arar? Why was I different from Muayyed Nureddin? They kept refusing. They just said they it wasn't their policy," Ahmad says. He was furious and said, "I told them I have nothing personal against you. If anything happens to me or my mother while we are travelling, I will hold you personally responsible. If my mother sees her son being detained in front of her, you will be responsible. She is not in good shape health-wise. Remember, my case is being watched very carefully in the media."

They went to the airport again on Monday, March 29, this time making it through immigration. As they waited to board the airplane for their flight to Frankfurt, Ahmad telephoned his father in Canada. "We are in line now," he said, "and we are coming soon. If anything happens to us, tell the media." Ahmad's father promised he'd be waiting for them, with the media, at the airport in Toronto.

"All the way home I was looking over my shoulder. The whole time," Ahmad says. Samira remembers sitting guard outside the men's washroom at the airport in Frankfurt, waiting for Ahmad, "in case someone came and took him." But nothing happened, and soon they were on board Air Canada flight 586 to Toronto. "On the flight I felt I could breathe easily. I was heading back home. Let Canadian security people do whatever they like. At least I will be at home and can speak out." The RCMP, Ahmad learned later, considered questioning him at the airport when he arrived in Toronto. But, after speaking with Ahmad's lawyer, Paul Copeland, they changed their mind.

They arrived at Pearson International Airport at three in the afternoon on March 30. Ahmad thought back to November 11, 2001, the day when he and his mother had been questioned at that same airport. At the immigration counter, they were, of course, pulled aside for a secondary inspection. "The guy asked what my story was. I said I had been detained for over two years in Syria and Egypt and now I was home." A second official came over and spoke in a low tone to the first: "His lawyer is outside. He gave me his card."

The two officials talked for a while. They seemed to be arguing about what to do, Ahmad says. Then he overheard one saying, "Well, he's a Canadian, I have to let him in."

When Ahmad and his mother finally walked through the door into the arrivals area, his father ran over, photojournalists close on his heels, snapping photos. Journalists asked Ahmad what had happened. Ahmad's lawyer advised him to wait before speaking publicly. "You don't need to talk about it now," he said. "Take some time first."

"I just want to say thank you," Ahmad said. Then he turned to the media. "I'm very happy actually to be back home, and I'd like to thank the Canadian people who have supported me in this dilemma," he said, beaming. He said he was grateful to the Egyptian authorities, too, for giving him the chance to come home and tell the truth.[1]

TWENTY-FIVE

"Abundance of Caution"

Afternoon, Wednesday, May 26, 2004
Washington, D.C.

"GOOD AFTERNOON. Today, Director Mueller and Deputy
Attorney General Comey and I want to announce developments
in the war on terror. First, credible intelligence from multiple
sources indicates that al-Qaeda plans to attempt an attack on the
United States in the next few months. This disturbing intelligence
indicates al-Qaeda's specific intention to hit the United States
hard."[1] This was how U.S. attorney general John Ashcroft
opened the news conference about the latest threat. He went on
to ask local law enforcement and the public to help track down
seven terror suspects, including two Canadians, Amr El Maati
and Abderraouf Jdey. Mueller described Ahmad's brother, Amr,
as "an al-Qaeda member and a licensed pilot, [who] is believed
to have discussed hijacking a plane in Canada and flying it into a
building in the United States.... They all are sought in connection
with the possible terrorist threats in the United States, they all
pose a clear and present danger to America, they all should be
considered armed and dangerous."

This was the first time anyone but Ahmad's Syrian interrogators had suggested Amr had discussed any kind of attack or
hijacking an airplane. The December 2002 episode of Fox's
America's Most Wanted had first alleged Amr had a pilot's
licence. As Ahmad wasn't able to read the "confessions" he was
forced to sign in Syria and Egypt, he doesn't know whether his
interrogators had added that allegation to the list.

FBI director Robert Mueller spoke again. "Unfortunately, we currently do not know what form the threat may take," he said. "And that is why it is so important that we locate the seven individuals shown to my right," he added, pointing to mug shots of the six men and one woman listed. "Though we do not have any reason at this time to believe that they are working in concert, we will not take any chances."[2]

Asked whether there was any reason to think that an attack was being planned from Canada, Ashcroft clarified that he did not have specific information about any plan or its origin. Asked why, given that authorities had been looking for these suspects for a long time, they were reissuing alerts for them now, Ashcroft replied, "Well, we believe that the public, like all of us, needs a reminder." Neither Ashcroft nor Mueller could answer why, in light of the news conference, the threat level wasn't being raised in the United States. When asked whether he thought Americans might be sceptical about the announcement, he replied, "I just don't think my job is to worry about what skeptics say."[3]

And there were many skeptics. *The New York Times* reported that Democrats backing presidential hopeful John Kerry, including the influential police and firefighter unions, thought the announcement was suspicious and timed to divert attention from Bush's plummeting poll numbers and bad news in Iraq. Intelligence officials told the *Times* that "they were uncertain that the link between the fresh intelligence and the likelihood of another attack was as apparent as Ashcroft made it out to be." The day before the press conference, the *Times* reported, officials in the Department of Homeland Security had said "they had no new intelligence pointing to the threat of an attack."[4]

Even Reid Morden, the former director of CSIS, greeted the news with some skepticism. It is important to be vigilant, he said, but like many in the United States, he wondered if the news conference timing was less about security and more about political strategy in an election year.[5] Skepticism aside, the announcement was big news in Canada. The RCMP said publicly that it had known of both men for some time. Both Prime Minister Paul Martin and Public Safety Minister Anne McLellan addressed the warning, saying they did not believe there was an immediate threat to Canada. Nor did they believe either of the Canadian men were in Canada.

That night's television news and the next day's newspapers carried Amr's photograph, including the front page of the *Ottawa Citizen* and in several other CanWest papers. Reporter Sheldon Alberts said that Mueller had "disclosed new information that Mr. El-Maati, a trained pilot, was suspected of planning a Sept. 11-style attack against the U.S." Amr's brother, Ahmad, Alberts wrote, "confessed in writing to plotting to drive a truck bomb into the Parliament buildings, though he has now recanted."[6] Alberts didn't mention that Ahmad had been held in detention in Syria and Egypt for more than two years, and likely tortured. Much of the coverage linked Amr to Abdullah and Maher as well. The *National Post* story, whose headline read "Arar linked to wanted Canadian," noted that Amr's brother, Ahmad, had given Syrian authorities the names of "alleged accomplices" Maher and Abdullah.[7] This story, at least, did say that Ahmad and Maher had been tortured, and that the allegations against Maher had not been substantiated.

The media calls to Ahmad's father's home were unrelenting. Badr El Maati repeatedly denied that his son was in any way involved in terrorism and pointed out that Amr's eyesight was so poor it was unlikely he could fly a plane, let alone get a pilot's licence. (Colin Freeze of *The Globe and Mail* later reported that he could find no official record of Amr having a pilot's licence.)[8] Some reporters came knocking on the doors of Badr's neighbours, too. One neighbour told *Toronto Sun* reporter Kevin Connor that he wasn't sure if the person he'd seen in the apartment hallway some time ago had been Amr, but his "appearance was radical and he had a fanatical certain way of being," and that this was "an indication of that kind of (terrorist) involvement."[9] The neighbour, a former brigadier general in the Egyptian army, said he'd felt uncomfortable when the family tried to befriend him. The landlord, on the other hand, said Badr was a model tenant. Connor also interviewed pundit David Harris, who warned that CSIS would "have a special interest in the father (Badr El-Maati) because he would have a special knowledge of the son. They would want a conversation with him to develop leads." CSIS, the RCMP, and immigration officials wouldn't comment on Amr's case.[10]

They didn't need to. Ashcroft had taken care of that. Besides, it would have been unwise for Canadian officials to leak information now, given that the Arar Inquiry's public hearings were to start the following week and RCMP deputy commissioner Garry Loeppky, CSIS director Ward Elcock, and CSIS deputy director Jack Hooper would be among the first people in the witness box.

4 P.M., Saturday, May 29, 2004
Home of Badr El Maati, Toronto

DAVID HARRIS WAS RIGHT. The knock on the door came at about four o'clock in the afternoon on Saturday, May 29, just three days after Ashcroft and Mueller's news conference. Badr opened the door to find two men in suits.

"Are you the father of Amr El Maati?" one asked.

"Yes, I am."

"May we speak with you?"

"They were already at the door, and I didn't want my neighbours to see. I felt I had no choice but to ask them in," Badr says. The men gave Badr their cards. They were William Jones and Justin Wallace from CSIS. Had he heard the news about Amr? they asked. Badr said yes. Had he heard from him lately? No, Badr replied, he hadn't heard from Amr in many years.

"We are concerned about his safety," one of the agents said. "He is a Canadian, and we wouldn't want him to fall into American hands and end up in Guantánamo or somewhere else, or be killed."

Badr told Jones and Wallace what he'd told the media. "What's in the news is old news from 2001. It's just hype to keep everyone on their toes. They [security agencies] have cried wolf several times before."

The agents told Badr to tell Amr, if he heard from him, to report to the nearest consulate office and come back to Canada. Then they asked how Ahmad was doing, and whether he was still suffering from his detention. Badr was angry. "He is trying to recover from his ordeal," he said, "and maybe trying to marry after CSIS ruined his marriage and his life." They hadn't done that, the agents said.

"You were following him with several cars at a time for twenty-four hours, and I saw that myself. Wasting taxpayers' money on hired cars and overtime paid when you could have sat with him and his lawyer like they asked. You declined. Someone has to answer for his ruined life," Badr exclaimed.

Badr says the agents didn't answer. Instead, they asked if Ahmad prayed. Badr was incredulous. "Don't you pray in your church?

"Then they asked if Ahmad has a grudge. I told them that anyone who'd been through what he'd been through would want someone to be held responsible. They said they wanted to talk with him and I told them to call his lawyer. Then they left."

Thursday, March 18, 2004
Canadian Embassy, Damascus

EIGHT DAYS AFTER BEING RELEASED, Abdullah went to the Canadian Embassy to get his passport renewed. After he asked to meet with an official, a man came to the security window and introduced himself as Leo Martel. He seemed surprised to see Abdullah, and started talking to him through the window. Abdullah interrupted him, saying he would like to speak to him face to face. Martel seemed reluctant but led Abdullah to an office. Martel asked why Abdullah needed a passport if he wasn't supposed to leave the country. "I told him I wanted to be ready to leave the minute I could. He said I could apply after I was allowed to leave. It seemed he didn't want to help," Abdullah says. But Abdullah insisted on filling out an application.

Martel remarked that he was surprised Abdullah had been released. He then mentioned that MP Dan McTeague would be in Damascus on March 22 and wanted to meet with Abdullah. A parliamentary secretary to Minister Graham, McTeague had recently been assigned to help with cases of Canadians in trouble abroad. Martel suggested that he and Abdullah meet for lunch before meeting with McTeague. It was during that lunch, four days later, that Martel told Abdullah about Senator Pierre de Bané's December 2003 meeting with the Syrian president. President al-Assad had apparently been frustrated by de Bané's entreaties on behalf of Abdullah. According to Martel, the president had told de Bané something like this: "First you tell us to detain people. Then you criticize us for detaining them and ask us to release them. Then, when we release them, we get criticized for mistreating them." De Bané later testified at the Arar Inquiry, and, just as he was about to describe his conversation with President al-Assad, the commission counsel cut him off, saying that, "unfortunately," the Canadian government had claimed national security confidentiality over the content of the meeting. De Bané seemed surprised.[11]

After lunch Abdullah and Martel went to meet with McTeague, who remembers the meeting well. "Abdullah showed me his teeth had been smashed somewhere in the back, then he showed me his foot, and scars on his wrists, it was obvious that emotionally and physically he was a mess. I have no doubt he'd been badly tortured."[12] McTeague told Abdullah to give him three weeks to try to help get him back to Canada. If Abdullah wasn't out of Syria by then, McTeague would come back and refuse to leave without him. "As far as I'm concerned, you're innocent," he told Abdullah. "I believed it then and I believe it now," McTeague says. "If he weren't, he would have been detained by the guys with yellow stripes on their pant legs [RCMP] when he came home, which is what I told him."[13]

JUST A FEW DAYS BEFORE Abdullah was to appear in court, he got a call from an interrogator saying that George Salloum wanted him to report to Far' Falastin. The Syrian authorities still had his computer and said they wanted to give it back to him. Abdullah didn't want to go anywhere near Far' Falastin but knew he had no choice. "I thought I'd better go there and cooperate rather than getting dragged there—either way if they want me they'll get me, I'd better show cooperation," he says. He packed a bag in case he was detained. He prepared in other ways too, by recording everything he knew about Canadian involvement in his case on paper. He left his notes in a safe place and returned, as instructed, to Far' Falastin, on April 14. There, he was questioned briefly but told Salloum was busy and he should report again. He returned on April 22. This time he was put him in a room with an interrogation team: Haitham, Khaled, and Abu Elnour. The men showed Abdullah photographs of ten or so people, asking if he recognized anyone. He didn't. The photographs had been faxed; Abdullah saw that the date on the fax was March 29, 2004. Abdullah was then questioned about people whose names he didn't recognize— except for one, who was a friend in Canada. Abdullah noticed the people in the pictures were very young. The interrogators were getting angry and yelled at him: "They are from the prayer group. How can you not know them when you are their spiritual leader?"

"How can I be their leader? They are all very young. I've been living downstairs [at Far Falastin] for more than two years. They would have been kids. These reports don't make sense. When are they going to stop?"

"The Canadians are not happy that you are released, and they want you back in jail," Haitham said.

After a while, Abdullah was taken to Salloum's office. "Why haven't you been visiting?" Salloum asked, mocking him. "We are like family now."

Salloum gave Abdullah his computer and let him leave. As soon as he could, Abdullah called his family to tell them what had happened. They in turn told McTeague. Three days later, Abdullah went to court, as scheduled. But his hearing was postponed to June 6. On June 6, he was told it was postponed again, this time until July 25.

WHEN IT HAD BECOME CLEAR that Abdullah wouldn't easily be able to leave Syria, he and Khuzaimah decided she and the children would join him in Damascus. "He needed us, I could tell from his phone calls that he needed us. Also, I was afraid, anything could happen. I wanted to see him as soon as I could."

Getting there from Malaysia wouldn't be easy. The Canadian Embassy there seemed to be stalling her attempts to get a passport for her youngest child. After numerous delays, she and the children were finally able to leave on June 19.

Abdullah booked a taxi to go to the airport to pick them up. "I was desperate to see them. I wanted to hold and touch my kids," he says. The oldest would be ten now, and the youngest, two and a half. Abdullah hadn't seen him since he was an infant.

When Abdullah arrived, he waited in the arrivals area, watching nervously through the doors to the customs area and baggage carousel for a glimpse of his family. Then he saw them. He saw a little boy running around his mother's skirts—that must be my youngest son, he thought. They moved in and out of sight. At one point Abdullah had a fright when he saw a man walk over to speak with Khuzaimah—it would turn out he was just offering to help.

A half hour later, his family came through the doors.

"I walked alongside them, on the other side of the rail, but they did not notice me. At the end of the rail, I stood in front of them, but still they looked at me, but as if I was a stranger. I greeted them and wanted to hug them all. That is when my wife told the kids, 'This is Papa.'" They hadn't recognized their father.

"He looked very different—so much thinner," Khuzaimah says. "His face was covered in red spots, and his hair was very short. But we were so happy and it was so overwhelming to see him. Even thinking about it today I cry."

The kids smiled, and were a little shy at first, but the oldest quickly adjusted to the way Abdullah looked and embraced him. The youngest didn't know who Abdullah was, and was a bit frightened of him. They piled into the car and made their way back to Abdullah's parents' home. The youngest of the girls sat on Abdullah's lap during the drive. "We had our first meal together in years. For a few hours, I forgot almost everything I went through, I felt I had it all," Abdullah remembers.

On July 25, Abdullah returned to court. He was relieved to see that Brian Davis, the Canadian ambassador to Syria, was there. The judge reviewed the prosecutor's charge that Abdullah was linked to al-Qaeda and involved in illegal activity that would endanger Syria. Abdullah was acquitted of all the charges, the judge said. But there was a catch. He was to be handed over to the military police to complete his military service. "It was like the end of me. I was in no shape to do any military service. I didn't know what to do. Were they going to arrest me right there?" Then a strange thing happened. Another court official ordered the military police not to arrest him, telling Abdullah to resolve the issue of his military service. "I'll give you two days to manage your affairs," the official said.

Ambassador Davis drove Abdullah back to his family. "Please contact the Syrian minister of Foreign Affairs," he urged Davis. "You have to explain that the only reason I am in default for my military service is because I was detained." The ambassador promised to speak with people in Ottawa.

Khuzaimah knew Abdullah was in no shape, physically or psychologically, to endure military service. "He couldn't even walk properly, how was he going to run? He walked with a huge limp on his left foot. I didn't see him resting peacefully, he had a lot of physical pain, he had a lot of nightmares, he talked in his sleep, and almost every night the pillow and sheet covers were wet from his sweat. I used to put a dry towel on them. While sleeping he made strange sounds and used to get up in his sleep and look at the door or point to it. It was very painful to see him like that," she says.

The next day, McTeague's executive assistant, Glenn Bradbury, spoke with Abdullah's brother, saying Abdullah should try to seek refuge at the Canadian Embassy or the ambassador's residence in Damascus and stay there until the issue of his military service was resolved. Abdullah arrived at the Canadian Embassy on July 27. Because he didn't trust Martel, he called his brother in Martel's presence to confirm what McTeague had said. His brother said yes, this is what McTeague had told him. Abdullah repeated what his brother was saying out loud, then told his brother to call back later to check on him. Hanging up the phone, Abdullah turned to Martel. "As you heard, I'm staying here."

"Not in my lifetime," Abdullah remembers Martel saying. "You are a dual national, and we have to consider the local laws of this country."

"I'm Canadian, and I am staying on Canadian soil," Abdullah insisted.

"McTeague doesn't have the authority to do this, only the minister can do this," Martel countered. "You will have to leave the embassy before it closes at 4:30 P.M. today."

"If Martel expelled him it was in bad judgment, as this Canadian citizen's life was in jeopardy," says Bradbury. "If an embassy can't afford protection to its own citizen, that's morally wrong and not in keeping with what Canadians expect."[14]

Abdullah sat in the embassy's reception area, waiting for his brother to call him back. But when the receptionist told him he had a call, it turned out to be CBC Radio's Curt Petrovich.

Abdullah's brother had called Petrovich to alert him to what was happening.

Listening to his recording of the interview years later, Petrovich says Abdullah wouldn't let him report on much, warning he'd be detained if he talked about what happened in detention: "They [Abdullah and his brother] wanted him to sound thankful and not insulting to Syria."[15] Abdullah told Petrovich he was in no shape to go into the military.

Petrovich said Abdullah expressed his gratitude to the Canadian ambassador for having been at the court hearing but was "surprised and confused" by Martel's actions. Petrovich asked if Abdullah thought there were officials who didn't want him to return to Canada. "The government has faced some embarrassment at the Arar Inquiry and you might say something there that might be embarrassing," Petrovich told him. "I agree, I agree a thousand per cent," was Abdullah's response. But had the Canadian officials been helping him? Petrovich asked. Abdullah said he hadn't expected to be told he couldn't stay at the embassy: "You tell me. The consul, Leo Martel, said, 'No way, you can't stay here,' and I say to him 'But it's Canadian soil.'" Abdullah warned Petrovich not to report on this. "If this talk [about Canadian officials not wanting him home] goes out, I bet you won't hear or see me again.... You wouldn't understand what two hours in there would be like. I can be back where people will never hear my voice again."[16]

Petrovich tracked down then–Foreign Affairs Minister Pierre Pettigrew that same day. He'd replaced Bill Graham just seven days earlier but was, according to Petrovich, nonetheless, "obviously well briefed by the embassy and was being told what their position was," though he would only say, "Well, there's nothing we can do about it."[17]

Petrovich filed his report with what he could say later that day for CBC national radio news. "I would expect that the prime minister calls his equal here and asks him to solve this problem and get me immediately back into Canada. That is what I expect. Enough is enough," he quoted Abdullah as saying.[18]

Abdullah was on the phone with his brother, Youssef, when the receptionist told him he had to leave. "It's 4:30," she said. "We're locking up."

Abdullah was too frightened to return to where he was staying—the two days he'd been given to report for military service had passed and he fully expected to be arrested. After getting a message to his wife that he wouldn't be back that night, he wandered downtown to old Damascus, then made his way to a relative's home for the night. In the morning he went to a friend for advice. What he said surprised Abdullah: "If the judge really wanted you to do military service, they would have detained you then and there. It seems to me that the judge has signalled that you should leave."

Abdullah was skeptical but went to the immigration office. To his surprise, officials there gave him an exit visa. Abdullah rushed to a travel agency and asked for a ticket on the first flight to Europe. The soonest flight was leaving Beirut for Vienna just after midnight, the agent told him. There was just enough time. He bought the ticket, got a friend to drive him to the Lebanese border, only fifteen minutes away from Damascus. He cleared Syrian customs and immigration, obtained an entry visa to Lebanon, crossed without delays, and continued the rest of the two-hour trip to Beirut. Abdullah caught his flight, emailing Khuzaimah as soon as he arrived in Vienna. He was out, he told her, and he wanted them to leave Syria as soon as possible. He didn't tell her where he was, in case his email was being monitored. "I was very worried that my family could be used to get me back to Syria. I just wanted them out," he says.

Khuzaimah says she "worked like a robot" to get the children organized. Friends of the family helped. She had a return ticket for Malaysia, but there were no flights available with six open seats for her and the children. The first available flight with enough seats was three days later, on Saturday, July 31, on

Austrian Airlines, Damascus to Vienna. She would have to stay in Vienna for two nights before catching a connecting flight to Montreal. Not only did she have no idea that Abdullah was in Vienna, she didn't even know when she'd see him next. She worried about being stopped at the airport, but all went well. When the plane landed in Vienna, she was anxious to email Abdullah to say they were safe and to make sure he was, too. "I saw some computers at the airport and I wanted to email Abdullah, but it was so hard," she says. "I had five kids with me, they were so restless after the flight, it was a new environment, new country, new language. So, I decided to calm them down first. I went to the closest hotel, which was opposite the airport, and got my kids settled down. Then I went to ... the hotel lobby and emailed Abdullah, telling him that we were in Vienna."

Still in Vienna, Abdullah was dumbfounded when he read Khuzaimah's email. He emailed her back, asking for the hotel's phone number. Receiving her answer, he called to say he was in Vienna, too. By now it was late at night and the kids were sleeping, so Abdullah and Khuzaimah agreed that they would come to his hotel in morning.

The next day, for the first time in more than two years, the family was together in what they felt was a safe place. Abdullah booked himself on the flight to Montreal. Then they played tourist. "It was like a whole-family honeymoon—a one-day vacation that was long overdue," Abdullah remembers. "It was a total surprise. It was a gift from God that showed me again that He was looking after us. Had we planned it, it would not have been as good."

Monday, December 20, 2004
National Press Theatre, Ottawa

CANADIANS WOULD HAVE TO WAIT for more than a year for public hearings on factual evidence to start at the Arar Inquiry. In the spring of 2004 there had been five days of hearings on background information on CSIS, the RCMP, and DFAIT. But then everything went behind closed doors. Public hearings on factual evidence—about what actually happened—were supposed to start that July, beginning with testimony by Monia and others in Maher's family. But with just a week to go, the inquiry announced a change of plans. The government wanted to keep so much of the factual evidence secret that holding public hearings was impractical. Instead, Justice O'Connor decided, the inquiry would start with in-camera, or secret hearings, first. He'd release summaries of the factual evidence heard in camera in time to inform the public hearings.

But when it came time to release the first summary—a summary of evidence about CSIS's role in what had happened to Maher—the government and the Arar Inquiry reached an impasse. After a long period of negotiation, Justice O'Connor ruled on what he believed the public had a right to know, information he determined that, if public, posed no threat to national security. The government responded by blacking out much of the summary, and parts of Justice O'Connor's ruling about the summary, and initiated proceedings in the Federal Court to try to use the Canada Evidence Act, as amended by the Anti-terrorism Act, to enforce the secrecy it wanted.

In frustration, the Inquiry's counsel called a news conference and distributed the heavily censored summary of CSIS evidence and the ruling to reporters. Waving the blacked-out pages in front of him, the inquiry's lead counsel, Paul Cavalluzzo, was visibly furious. "This government called a public inquiry and not a private investigation," he said repeatedly. He pointed out that some of the material the government had blacked out was already public, including published newspaper articles. He couldn't be more specific with examples, he said, because to do so he'd be risking fourteen years in jail. He was "very surprised and disappointed with the government's position on what the public is entitled to know," he told reporters. "There is a great deal of information out there, most of which is unsubstantiated, which is damaging to Mr. Arar." Justice O'Connor's ruling, Cavalluzzo said, had attempted "to balance that out by showing a truer status of the picture of Mr. Arar." Moreover, he said, a lot of the information blacked out related to CSIS's role during the crucial period that Maher had been in U.S. detention. Even if the inquiry won the battle in court, Cavalluzzo said, the government could, using anti-terrorism laws, issue a security certificate to keep the information secret. Asked whether the actions of the government were being directed at a senior level, Cavalluzzo responded, "I get the feeling that it goes pretty high up."[19]

Maher, who had just been named *Time* magazine's Canadian Newsmaker of the Year, told reporters he was shocked at the secrecy and wondered what the government was trying to hide. He called on Prime Minister Paul Martin and Public Safety Minister Anne McLellan to back down. "There must be a balance between the national security and the public's right to know, but what we're seeing here is undermining both," he said.[20] Speaking to *Sun News* reporter Kathleen Harris, McLellan dismissed the charges by Maher and the inquiry. "They're entitled to their opinion," she said. "They are not in charge of the national security of this country."[21]

The government's litigation threatened to stop the entire process. "The prospect of litigation at that point in the Inquiry was very troubling. It seemed evident that litigating the government's NSC [National Security Confidentiality] claims on a piecemeal basis, ruling by ruling, was a course that would at best lead to enormous delays and could actually bring the Inquiry to a complete and final halt," Justice O'Connor wrote in his report.[22] The only way forward was to abandon efforts to release summaries of the in camera evidence. Once the summaries were abandoned, the government withdrew its threat of litigation. The consequence was that public hearings could deal only with information the government did not make secrecy claims over. It didn't have to win the argument. It didn't matter whether Justice O'Connor agreed. It merely had to assert a claim. *We want that information secret, so nobody can talk about it, or read about it, or ask questions about it, whether the judge agrees with us or not.*

As if to add insult to injury, lawyers representing the government, the RCMP, and Inspector Michel Cabana, the former head of A-O Canada, in particular, then argued that because of the secrecy, it was unfair to expect anyone from the RCMP to testify in public. The secrecy claims would prevent them from providing complete evidence, they could be unfairly prejudiced, and the public could be misled. Not surprisingly, Justice O'Connor rejected their arguments.[23]

The secrecy did make it very difficult for Maher to testify. Maher's counsel, and intervening organizations, suggested that Justice O'Connor appoint a fact-finder to interview not just Maher but also Ahmad, Abdullah, and Muayyed about their experiences. Justice O'Connor agreed but limited the fact-finder's mandate to examining Maher's experience in Syria and Jordan, not the actions of Canadian officials. The fact-finder, Dr. Stephen Toope, an expert on torture and professor of law at McGill University, interviewed all four men and concluded that what they'd told him about their treatment was credible, and that they had all been tortured.[24]

Public hearings finally began in the spring of 2005. The process was plagued by what organizations with intervenor status described as "the government's seemingly and at times evidently random claims of National Security Confidentiality over documentary evidence and testimony."[25] Information in documents released at the inquiry was often redacted, or censored, in ways very different from that in the same documents obtained through requests under the Access to Information Act. One of the more striking examples was differently censored versions of Leo Martel's consular report about his first visit to Maher. The version released through the inquiry said, "When asked if [Maher] wished the Embassy to provide him with anything he might need he answered that his needs were all taken care of by his Syrian hosts."[26] The rest of the sentence was blacked out. The version released through access requests revealed that the government had blacked out "his answer was dictated to him in Arabic by the Syrians."[27] Clearly, this secrecy was about downplaying the gravity of Maher's situation, not safeguarding national security. Over the course of the public hearings, several documents were released again and again, with each new version revealing a new word, sentence, or paragraph.

Many of the government's secrecy claims related to information about the other cases. Ahmad, Abdullah, and Muayyed had initially been denied standing. Now it seemed that every time anyone had a question about their cases, government lawyers asserted NSC claims to stop witnesses from answering. Marlys Edwardh, counsel for Maher Arar, asked Jim Gould of DFAIT's intelligence branch whether his agency had ever passed on information to foreign intelligence agencies. Government counsel objected:

> I'm sorry, sir, I have no idea what the answer would be, so I'm having some difficulty here. If it deals with other individuals, I have some difficulty, and out of an abundance of caution I have to say that if we are dealing with whether or not ISI or ISD facilitated the transfer of policing information to other police or security authorities in respect of other individuals, I would first argue that it is not relevant, and out of an abundance of caution I would have to take the position that we claim national security with respect to any answer relating to that.[28]

The "abundance of caution" approach to claims of secrecy dominated the government's approach throughout the inquiry, leaving intervening organizations with the impression much of the secrecy was "more about avoiding accountability than about safeguarding national security." They agreed that there were sometimes "very legitimate reasons for making these claims" but said that the "frequency and enormity of the claims made, and the redacting, re-redacting and re-re-redacting of documents that ... plagued this process," was "alarming."[29]

It wouldn't be until much later that the public learned the full extent and implications of what Justice O'Connor called the government's "overclaiming" of national security confidentiality over crucial evidence. In his report, Justice O'Connor pointed to two examples of information over which the government claimed National Security Confidentiality until the public hearings were finished. These examples happen to be the two most explosive and damning pieces of public evidence the inquiry uncovered. The first was that the RCMP had, in its requests to the United States to post border lookouts, labelled Maher and Monia as "Islamic Extremist individuals suspected of being linked to the Al Qaeda terrorist movement."[30]

The second was evidence that the RCMP had sent questions to Syrian interrogators to ask Abdullah. "Given the Syrian record for torturing detainees being interrogated, these events are very troubling," Justice O'Connor wrote.[31] "The Government only withdrew its position that this information was subject to a claim of NSC after the hearings were completed." The point, says Justice O'Connor, is that these issues should have been addressed in the public hearings. Justice O'Connor concludes "it would have been preferable if all the information now being made public [in the report] had been disclosed prior to the public hearings. To the extent that this did not happen, the public hearings process suffered."[32]

It wasn't just the public hearings process that suffered in the end. That the RCMP sent questions for Abdullah was the smoking gun—the evidence of torture by proxy—that Maher's team, intervening organizations, the media, and the public had been looking for. If that information had come out during the public hearings, it would have no doubt generated a lot of public interest in, and support for, the need to either open up the process to examine the other men's cases or call another public inquiry.

Instead, this damning information would be all but ignored in the media coverage surrounding the report's release, overshadowed by the exoneration of Maher Arar.

Thursday, September 1, 2005
Tunney's Pasture Government Complex, Ottawa

AT THE INQUIRY'S PUBLIC HEARINGS, RCMP witnesses repeatedly referred to Ahmad and Abdullah as "main targets" of their investigations. When it became clear that their reputations were at stake, Justice O'Connor granted them a form of "limited party standing"—their lawyers were limited to addressing only the evidence that directly related to reputational interests, to help minimize any damage. As their frustration about having been excluded from the process grew, Ahmad and Abdullah decided to go public with their full stories and grant their first interviews since returning home to Canada. *The Globe and Mail*'s Jeff Sallot interviewed them both, and their in-depth stories ran in late August. Then both men filed detailed chronologies, brief biographies, and other background documents as public exhibits at the inquiry.

As the hearings were drawing to a close, Sallot decided he wanted to know more about the mysterious map that seemed so central to allegations made against Ahmad, Abdullah, and Maher. During his interview with Ahmad, he'd learned about how Ahmad had been stopped at the U.S. border on August 16, 2001, and questioned about the map. Ahmad showed him the letter from his employer saying that the map could have belonged to another driver. Ahmad described how CSIS had questioned him about the map on September 11, 2001. Sallot remembered how, in October 2001, the map had somehow found its way into the news, hyped as evidence that al-Qaeda was plotting attacks on Canadian nuclear facilities. In the interview, Ahmad described how scared he'd been when he'd seen the news and explained how his lawyer had tried to reach CSIS to clear things up, but his calls had not been returned. Then he described how, one month later, in Syrian detention and under torture, he'd been forced to "confess" that it was his brother, Amr, who'd sent him the map and instructed him to attack an Ottawa target. He described how his Egyptian interrogators had shown him the map on a television screen. Sallot remembered the July 2003 media reports that Syrian intelligence had helped thwart an Ottawa attack, and leaks to the *National Post* about the alleged plot.

Sallot called Ahmad's lawyer and asked her to send him a copy of the letter-sized map. It was a crudely drawn outline of the buildings and streets that make up an Ottawa government complex, just west of downtown, called Tunney's Pasture. Each building on the map, including the Health Canada virus labs and the Atomic Energy of Canada office, were numbered from one to twenty-three. Other areas were marked with four-digit numbers.

Sallot decided to investigate. He got into his car and drove to Tunney's Pasture. "The first thing I noticed was that the numbers on the map corresponded to the numbers in the parking lots. Then I noticed that some of the buildings weren't there anymore."[33] In particular, the two buildings on the map that had caused so much concern, the Atomic Energy of Canada building and the virus labs, seemed to be missing entirely. He decided to go into building number eight to ask where they were.

"I haven't seen one of those in a long time," a friendly commissionaire said.[34] "That's an old map. Those buildings are gone."

The buildings, it turns out, had moved long before Ahmad was even asked about the map in 2001.

"[The commissionaire] had a stack of more recent maps of Tunney's Pasture to help visitors to the complex. She happily handed out a copy, noting the lab and the nuclear building are now parking lots," Sallot wrote in his story a few days later. He got "the same friendly co-operation and copies of newer maps from commissionaires at the next four buildings as well."[35]

"This was just the sort of map they hand out to the FedEx people so they can find their way around the complex," Sallot says.[36]

Sallot called CSIS and the RCMP, but CSIS wouldn't comment, and an RCMP spokesperson just said it would be inappropriate to comment. "I realized that nobody in the government or the security agencies had bothered to check out the map, or if they did—and this is even worse—they realized there was nothing to the map, but it was a good story to have out there."[37]

The Globe and Mail waited until the following Tuesday to run the story, wanting to be able to devote most of its front page to it. The paper ran an almost full-sized photo of the map itself, under the headline "It was hyped as a TERRORIST map: It was cited by Egyptian TORTURERS; It is a VISITOR'S GUIDE to Ottawa." A couple of days later, Sallot got a call from an anonymous caller who he says was "obviously connected to either the RCMP or CSIS or the Canadian Security Intelligence Establishment." The caller was upset with the story. "This person was trying to put me in my place. He said, 'But when you were out there did you even notice there's a minaret on a mosque just down the street?' And I said, 'Yeah, so? If you look on the other corner there's a Baptist church. What does that mean?' ... He just wanted to give me the gears. You know, 'You think you're such a hot shot reporter but we have to worry about what's going on in that mosque.' Whoever this person was seemed to think there was something very sinister about that mosque and that it was very close to government installations."[38]

You see this often in the secret world of spies, and in some journalists too, Sallot says. "They have little pieces and they think of it as a puzzle, and they think all the pieces fit in a certain way. But they never get out to see if the pieces fit in another way. I am sure there have been all kinds of efforts to get warrants for wiretaps and so on, to get information they could probably had just had if they just sent someone out to take a look at the situation." The problem, he says, is that very often these people think the only kind of information that is valuable is what's collected by clandestine means, "but often when you compare it to what's on the ground, there's nothing sinister about it at all."[39]

For Ahmad and his family, the story brought an enormous wave of relief. "It was like a huge weight lifted from my shoulders," Ahmad says. "I had been asking myself about that map every day in Syria, and Egypt. Now I finally knew what it was."

Noon, Monday, September 18, 2006
Government Conference Centre, Ottawa

THE ARAR INQUIRY RELEASED ITS REPORT almost a full year after the public hearings ended in the late fall of 2005. Media, intervenors, and the parties had a couple of hours to read the report in a lock-up before it was made publicly available. Maher and his lawyers read the report in one room, and Ahmad, Abdullah, Muayyed, and the organizations with intervenor status read it in another. For Maher, the report was vindication. Justice O'Connor had granted his first wish:

> Mr. Arar has asked that I "clear his name." His concern, understandably, is that the publicity surrounding his case has raised suspicions that he has been involved in illegal activities. Unfortunately, Mr. Arar has been the subject of a good deal of publicity, some of which has inaccurately portrayed his status in Canadian investigations and his possible connections to terrorist activities. The result has been that Mr. Arar, already the victim of inhumane and degrading treatment in Syria, has been subjected to further suffering owing to the release of information that has unfairly damaged his reputation here in Canada.
>
> I have heard evidence concerning all of the information gathered by Canadian investigators in relation to Mr. Arar. This includes information obtained in Canada, as well as any information received from American, Syrian or other foreign authorities. I am able to say categorically that there is no evidence to indicate that Mr. Arar has committed any offence or that his activities constitute a threat to the security of Canada.[40]

Justice O'Connor had also determined that American authorities "very likely" based their decision to send Maher to Syria on erroneous information they received from Canada, including information that described Maher, and his wife, Monia, as Islamic extremists with suspected ties to al-Qaeda. "There was clearly no basis or justification for this description," he said. "Moreover, it was highly inflammatory and, in the post–9/11 environment in the United States, had the potential to prove enormously prejudicial to them."[41]

For Abdullah, Ahmad, and Muayyed, the report was a mix of good and bad news. The good news was that Justice O'Connor had clearly fought, and won, a struggle over NSC claims and the limits of his mandate to release at least some important information about their cases. Importantly, he also identified what he called "a pattern of investigative practices" at work in all the cases "that point to systemic problems that go beyond Mr. Arar's case—problems that should be addressed by the relevant agencies through policies or guidelines."[42] Those practices included sharing information with foreign agencies that they could use to detain Canadians; sharing information about detained Canadians that could be used in interrogations; pushing forward with investigations into detained Canadians, "sometimes in conflict with or to the prejudice of diplomatic efforts to have those Canadians released to Canada;" relying on information that may be the product of torture; and being "dismissive" or careless about allegations of torture.[43] In addition, he said, Canadian agencies informed American agencies any time a person suspected of links to terrorism travelled outside the country. Justice O'Connor says that given American practice at the time, it is likely that the American agencies in turn notified the country of destination.

Justice O'Connor also recommended their cases be investigated, something the intervening organizations, and Maher's team, had pressed for. It had been raised by the United Nations Committee on Human Rights, too, which, after examining Canada's compliance with the International Covenant on Civil and Political Rights, noted concern about allegations that Canada "may have cooperated with agencies known to resort to torture with the aim of extracting information from individuals detained in foreign countries." The committee called on Canada "to ensure that a public and independent inquiry review all cases of Canadians citizens who are suspected terrorists or suspected to be in possession of information in relation to terrorism, and who have been detained in countries where it is feared that they have undergone or may undergo torture and ill treatment. Such inquiry should determine whether Canadian officials have directly or indirectly facilitated or tolerated their arrest and imprisonment."[44]

Ahmad, Abdullah, and Muayyed were disappointed that Justice O'Connor didn't recommend there be a second phase to his inquiry and that he didn't believe a public inquiry would be the best forum. He did say that he'd heard enough evidence about the cases to conclude they should be reviewed "through an independent and credible process that is able to address the integrated nature of the underlying investigations." Whatever the process, he said, "it should be one that is able to investigate the matters fully and, in the end, inspire public confidence in the outcome."[45]

"The Lucky Ones"

Spring 2008
Canada

EVERY TIME Ahmad El Maati hears the sound of rushing water, he's reminded of the underground cell in Cairo. Sometimes the sound triggers flashbacks that force him to relive his experience there—the buzz of the electric shock torture, the sound of prisoners screaming, his own torture and the fear, humiliation, and hopelessness he felt. His nightmares often wake him.

Unlike many survivors of modern-day "stealth" torture, Ahmad has visible scars.[1] They're from the cigarette burns administered to his shin in Syria. But the scars are the least of his problems. Ahmad has endured seven surgical procedures since his release. Most have been to help him walk properly again. Before his detention, his knee injury from wrestling in high school was an annoyance that stopped him from running long distances. Now he can barely walk more than a city block without resting. The injury was exacerbated by the crippling fall in Nasr City, the forced kneeling during the long torture sessions, and the trauma of the beatings themselves. And then there's his back—he's had surgery to decompress a herniated disk that shot pain down his right leg. His doctors say that was likely brought on by the cold, confined cell in Syria and positional torture in Egypt. Lately he's noticed that his entire left leg goes numb if he stands for more than five minutes, so doctors are sending him for a new round of tests. Unable to exercise, Ahmad is battling his weight, and that, of course, is causing a litany of other complications.

But it's the emotional scars that torment him the most. Ahmad has difficulty remembering what happened to him at what time—a common coping mechanism among torture survivors. He has been diagnosed by Dr. Donald Payne, a psychiatrist specializing in treating victims of torture, as suffering from post-traumatic stress disorder. The symptoms include "difficulty sleeping, with bad dreams of his experiences; frequent intrusive memories of his experiences, marked upset with reminders of his experiences in detention, excessive anxiety and depression, excessive irritability and poor concentration."[2] Ahmad worries that his mother bears the brunt of his irritability. "I have lost my patience. This just kills me. My mother is suffering from that because she's the one who lives with me." More than anything, he says, he wishes he could return to his life on the road as a truck driver. But even if his physical condition improved enough, the inability to concentrate and memory problems make retraining almost impossible.[3]

Now, Ahmad rarely leaves the apartment he shares with his mother. When he does, it's usually to see lawyers or doctors. Sometimes journalists too. And they all want him to remember what he has both consciously and subconsciously tried to forget. He has stopped going to places where people know him. He can tell they're all scared that, just by associating with him, they'll incriminate themselves. It's not just that people are afraid of him. Now he's afraid of others, too. "I'm now very suspicious of people," he says. Convinced that his phones are tapped and that he's still being followed, he feels he has no privacy. He has tried making new friends, but that hasn't been easy either. There's the trust issue, and then there's CSIS. Not long ago Ahmad suggested to a friendly neighbour that they go to the mosque together. Their friendship grew until CSIS came knocking on the man's door. "They tried to scare him off, and it frightened him," Ahmad says.

It has been six and a half years since Ahmad left for his wedding in Syria. The future he'd imagined for himself back then—a simple life with Rola, children, and steady work—bears no resemblance to the shattered existence he struggles through today. Four and a half years after his release, he wonders if he'll ever be able to marry or find work again. Physical and psychological issues aside, being labelled a terrorist doesn't do much for one's eligibility for either employment or marriage.

Like Ahmad, Abdullah has visible scars. The nail on one of his big toes is deformed from the *falaka*—the beating on his feet. He has scars on his right ankle from where the flesh tore away and on his right wrist from being suspended. And, like Ahmad, it's not the visible scars he worries about. It took years to diagnose the source of some his most debilitating pain. Now he's in physiotherapy for soft-tissue injuries. After four years of working to regain his strength and stamina, he was thrilled to be able to play basketball with his kids for about five minutes. His wife, Khuzaimah, is constantly reminding the children about their father's physical limitations. "What they hear from my wife is, 'Your father can't do this because he has a fragile body. He needs a place to rest comfortably.' I have a fragile body. This is the reality," Abdullah says.

Unlike Ahmad, Abdullah remembers what happened when and is a confident public speaker. He thinks that talking about what he endured helps him cope. He has assembled an hour-and-a-half-long PowerPoint presentation documenting his experience, which he takes to church halls, schools, and conferences. But while he is describing being stuffed into a tire or suspended and whipped, his face is often expressionless. He shows very little emotion and has had to work hard to remember to use the words *I* or *me* instead of talking about his experience in the third person. Dr. George Fraser of the Ottawa Trauma and Anxiety Clinic says Abdullah is suffering from major depression and post-traumatic stress disorder. Abdullah's "coping strategy of blocking out emotional feelings and emotions ... in order to cope with his isolation" has made reconnecting with his family and friends difficult, Fraser adds. "Such a survival tactic is not one we usually deal with, and we do not have a diagnostic category to indicate its significance ... or do justice to the degree of impairment this has had in [Abdullah's] post-prison life."[4]

Like Ahmad, Abdullah finds it hard to trust people, especially officials with government and police, and says he feels socially isolated. "Some people have made it clear they don't want to associate with me. They know me, I did them favours in the past, but now they don't want to know me ... and people who know me walk by as if they don't know me. But not everyone is afraid. Others who I never thought would be supportive are."

He worries most about the impact on his wife and children. "I am learning how to be a father again, because for two years I wasn't a father. I'm not patient enough with the kids, but it's better now than before." He credits his wife, Khuzaimah, for her strength. "I don't know how she managed, but she walked a fine line and managed to keep the whole family together." Since he was released, Abdullah and Khuzaimah have had their sixth child, another boy, who is very close to Abdullah. It has been hardest to bond, Abdullah says, with his second-youngest son, who spent all but the first weeks of his first two and a half years without his father. "For all the kids, I missed two years, which, for each of them was important in different ways to learn something from me. The youngest ones, for bonding. The older ones, for exploring."

Abdullah remembers how much of what he calls his "real education" came from watching his father and uncle run their businesses. "My kids do not have this. Now they're learning what? They're learning about torture. They're learning about a father who is broken." His twelve-year-old daughter recently spoke alongside Abdullah at an event organized to raise awareness about Canada's involvement in torture. "When I found out what happened to him, I felt anger, frustration, and could not believe the inhumanity of the people who did all this to him," she said. "I had nightmares and have trouble understanding why this happened to him."[5]

Like Ahmad, Abdullah has flashbacks and nightmares. His are triggered by things like the sight of a car tire, the size and layout of stalls in some public washrooms, the sound of screaming on the television, and some insects. He has trouble reading and concentrating, and sometimes forgets how to say words. "I can remember the word but can't say it. There are certain words that just do not come anymore."

Abdullah wonders how he'll ever work again. "Engineering and business are part of me. I loved my company because I was able to combine both. Now not being able to do either, part of me is gone, and I constantly feel its absence." He can't sit in front of a computer for more than an hour without experiencing intense back pain. Even standing for a half hour hurts. And his concentration is impaired. "Combine that with being smeared. Why would anyone hire me? If I want to start a business, how could I? Is there someone who can tell me how I could start a business again? I would not do business with me, and I would excuse anyone who would not want to do business with me. If they buy products from me, they could lose their money or their reputation or get accused of links to terrorism."

Muayyed frequently dreams he's back in Far' Falastin, in a panic about how to get out. He has flashbacks, too. "The bright white colour of my feet's soles always comes to my eyes, and the sound of the cable on my soles. When I remember that, I get tense inside, a tightness in my chest, and I clench my fists. Whenever I have time to think, it comes to me. And I think too much. Especially when I am alone." And Muayyed is alone a lot. Unlike the others, he has no family in Canada and cannot risk going to Iraq to see his relatives until his name is cleared. His mother is seriously ill, and Muayyed is devastated that he can't be with her.

Missing his family has been made worse by the isolation Muayyed has felt since his release. People who once were friends now avoid him. Some pretend they never knew him. Life got even lonelier after an incident in January 2006. At the time, Muayyed was working in a shoe warehouse that supplied Toronto shoe stores. He got a call from Rima Masri, who explained that her husband, Sami Kahil, was in trouble and had given her Muayyed's number, because "he knows media and lawyers." Muayyed gave Masri his lawyer's phone number and that of the *Toronto Star*'s Michelle Shephard, who had interviewed Muayyed just a few days earlier.

He later learned that Kahil and his family had been on their way to Mexico for a vacation when their Air Transat flight was suddenly flanked by U.S. fighter jets because Kahil's name had appeared on a no-fly list. Masri had called Muayyed while Kahil was in detention—he had been detained overnight in Mexico before being escorted back to Canada by the RCMP. When Shephard asked Masri how she got her number, Masri told her she got it from Muayyed. Shephard wondered if Kahil's link to Muayyed was the reason he was listed. She tried to reach Muayyed but couldn't: His lawyer said he wasn't doing interviews. She decided to write about the connection anyway. "There's also the potential that Kahil's name has been connected by security services to another Canadian, who was once under investigation and detained abroad in 2004," she wrote. "An associate of Kahil's at the Mississauga shoe store knows Iraqi-Canadian Muayyed Nureddin, who now imports shoes to China, according to Masri."[6]

The implication was that just being "an associate" of Muayyed Nureddin could land you on a no-fly list, or worse.

"I thought the connection was important to mention because I knew from past cases, and Arar's story in particular, that just knowing someone who the security agencies were investigating could make you a target or person of interest," Shephard says.[7] "But there's a good lesson in this story now in hindsight. We have to always be very careful when mentioning someone's name in connection with a security case because once it's out there, there's a stigma that's hard to shake."

Kahil was eventually cleared by a letter from the U.S. Department of Homeland Security.[8] Muayyed wishes he never gave Shephard's number to Masri that day. He'd just been trying to help, but after Shephard's story was published, even more people were afraid to associate with him. Today, he's looking for work again but never knows what to say to potential employers. "I don't know whether to tell the employer about my case or not. And I don't want to be in a situation after I am hired where they say, 'Why didn't you tell us?'"

American authorities insist on keeping Maher's name on a terrorist watch list. This, despite the fact that Public Safety Minister Stockwell Day, having viewed the Americans' file on Maher, says there is nothing there to justify Maher's name remaining on the list. There is some hope that Maher might get some answers once President George W. Bush finally leaves the White House. As this book went to print, Democratic members of Congress were pushing for an independent examination into Maher's case.

In Canada, Maher's exoneration at the Arar Inquiry led to an official government apology and financial compensation for the role Canadian agencies played in his ordeal. But, he says, no amount of money can compensate for what he's lost. He's rebuilding his life piece by piece, and is back in school, trying to finish his Ph.D. It's a struggle, because, like the others, his ability to concentrate has been so diminished. And Maher copes with a whole other level of stress—the stress of being recognized every-where he goes. Despite having been exonerated, he still sees suspi-cion in the eyes of some people. As Justice O'Connor wrote in his report, "labels, even unfair and inaccurate ones, have a tendency to stick."[9] No doubt, the Americans' reluctance to clear Maher's name doesn't help. Speaking to a room full of journalists at the 2007 Global Investigative Journalism Conference in Toronto, Maher talked about how tough it is to shed the stigma of being labelled a terrorist. "In our society, to be labelled with this 't-word' is worse, unfortunately, than a serial killer," he said.[10]

Like Maher, Ahmad, Abdullah, and Muayyed have all been labelled as terror suspects in the media. Unless they can clear their names, it will be impossible to rebuild their lives in any meaningful way. For all of them, it's about justice. It's about their reputations, their careers, and being able to travel freely. For Ahmad, it's also about being able to fulfill his dream of marrying and having a family. Muayyed hopes to marry, too, but for now, his priority is being able to see his family again. For Abdullah, it's about his children being able to grow up without the stigma of having a father who's been branded a terrorist. And then there's Ahmad's brother, Amr. A *New York Times* reporter did find documents addressed to Amr in a safe house in Kabul in 2001. But, as *Times* reporter David Rohde wrote at the time, "It was not clear whether Mr. Abouelmaati was a member of the group or whether his identity was stolen, a tactic Al Qaeda members have used in the past."[11] Amr's family wants to know why, a year after the documents were found in Kabul, the FBI issued an alert in his name. Did the FBI rely on the "confession" in which Ahmad, under torture in Syria, falsely implicated his brother? Was the alert issued in November 2002 simply to help cast suspicion on Maher? Almost six years later, nothing has yet been produced publicly to substantiate the allegations made against Amr in the media. Neither Canada nor the United States appear to have issued warrants for his arrest.

At the Arar Inquiry, Justice O'Connor found that in Maher's case, Canadian officials "intentionally released selected classified information" to the media.[12] "Several of the leaks," he wrote, "were inaccurate, unsupported by the information available from the investigations, and grossly unfair to Mr. Arar." He found that the leaks had "deleterious effects on Mr. Arar's reputation, psychological state and ability to find employment."[13] Ahmad, Abdullah, and Muayyed were named and labelled by these officials, too, sometimes in the very same documents. And, as in Maher's case, no evidence has been produced that would demonstrate that they are in any way linked to terrorism or any other illegal activity.

Ironically, not one of the officials who broke the law by leaking classified information about these men to the media has been publicly identified, let alone charged and prosecuted.

Carleton University journalism professor and former *Globe and Mail* reporter Jeff Sallot says that there are lessons for the media in these cases. The implication of getting the story wrong, he says, "causes real pain to real people.... There's a real soul searching that still needs to go on about how we [the media] were badly abused in the Arar case, and, I think in the Almalki case and in the El Maati cases as well," he says. "The big lesson is to always question your sources—not just because they may have an agenda, but because they may have imperfect knowledge. I think a lot of the people who were saying this stuff believed it." What's frightening, Sallot says, is "they believed it because under torture he said that, and that this was somehow evidence of guilt." Sallot says there's too strong a temptation to "draw too many conclusions from scant evidence, evidence that nobody's willing to stand behind. They say, 'We've got the transcript of the confession.' Well, do you have the audiotape? Was he screaming? You have to be so skeptical, particularly when people are not prepared to go on the record—it indicates that they're not so sure themselves."[14]

Sallot says that, for example, he knew to be cautious about drawing conclusions about allegations that people had been in Afghanistan because he'd been there himself. "I had been to Afghanistan, and I knew that a lot of people had been to Afghanistan for all kinds of reasons. I was there for journalistic reasons, others were there because it was an adventure.... Are we going to question every CIA officer who was in Afghanistan or Pakistan at that time about their loyalty because they may have known bin Laden?"[15]

The trouble with leaks, Alex Neve, secretary general of Amnesty International Canada, says, is that they circumvent the international legal system and international standards for fair trials. Instead of having allegations presented in a court of law, where the accused can know the source of the allegations, defend themselves in a meaningful and fair way, and have an impartial judge or jury rule on their guilt or innocence, "leaks mean an individual is accused, charged, and convicted through whispers and innuendo on the front page of newspapers."[16]

And, while no evidence has been produced that would substantiate the allegations against Ahmad, Abdullah, and Muayyed, there is a lot evidence on the public record that the agencies involved in their cases breached Canada's obligations under international human rights law. The full extent to which CSIS may have countenanced torture in these cases is, unfortunately, still shrouded in secrecy. But it is known that CSIS received information obtained under torture in Maher's case, failed to analyze it for reliability, and even assumed that the information demonstrated he hadn't been tortured. The Arar Inquiry also determined, among other things, that the RCMP sent questions for Abdullah to his Syrian interrogators and used Ahmad's torture "confession" in legal proceedings in Canada. It is likely that, like Maher, these men were labelled "Islamic extremists" in information ultimately shared with Syria and Egypt, and that this information was shared with the full knowledge that it would lead to their initial and prolonged detention, and to the risk of interrogation and torture.

Canada was one of the first countries to ratify the United Nations Convention Against Torture and Other Cruel, Inhuman or Degrading Treatment or Punishment. Canada has also acceded to the International Covenant on Civil and Political Rights.[17] As such, Canada's political leadership, agencies, and officials have an obligation to uphold the absolute prohibition of the use of torture and ill treatment by refraining from directly or indirectly causing human rights violations and torture, and by taking steps to prevent those violations from happening in the first place. Amnesty International's Alex Neve says that it is clear that in these cases, Canada breached both of those obligations. "By sharing information with security agencies in Syria and possibly also Egypt, knowing that there was a real likelihood that this could lead to interrogations involving torture, Canada breached its obligations not to cause abuses," he says. "And, by failing to prioritize consular assistance over security cooperation, Canada breached its positive obligation to do everything possible to *prevent* torture."[18]

And national security is no excuse. As Peter Burns, dean emeritus at the University of British Columbia's law school, testified at the Arar Inquiry, "as long as the person rendering the information knew, or should have known, or was wilfully blind to the fact that [the information] would be utilized for that purpose," this would be a breach of Canada's obligations under the Convention Against Torture. Under article two of the convention, Burns says, "necessity is not a defence." Further, he says, the Convention against Torture prohibits "the use of torture-obtained admissions in legal proceedings except against the torturer."[19]

There are three critical reasons why the ban on torture is absolute, says Neve. First, the notion that torture works is "completely fallacious and unfounded," he says. "We know from these cases and thousands of cases around the world that people will say anything, finger anyone, confess to any plot, simply to bring torture to an end, and while there may occasionally be grains of truth among those confessions, there is also a lot of misinformation and false confessions." That, he says, is why security experts themselves say that relying on information from torture is bad practice, because "it leads to all sorts of false leads, and it distracts police from doing the sort of solid, more time-consuming, and difficult policing work that will actually give rise to good leads."[20]

Second, Neve says, the notion that the use of torture can be confined to serious terrorism cases is misguided: "Once you allow torture in the case of the individual who is supposedly the mastermind of the next mass terrorist attack, well, surely that means you can use it against someone who knows where that person is hiding, against their sister, against people who go to their mosque and so on. That is the reality of torture. It doesn't shrink and get confined. It expands and it claims ever more victims."[21]

Finally, Neve says, the most vital reason that the ban on torture is absolute is that it is simply wrong: "Torture is a human rights violation that shatters the very notion of human integrity that is at the very heart of why we have human rights in the first place. Suggesting that allowing torture will bring us a greater sense of security is completely wrongheaded. Instead, torture is an abuse that simply creates more victims, leads to greater resentment and disenfranchisement, lays the groundwork for more violence, more acts of terrorism, further repression, and on and on it goes."[22]

Ahmad, Abdullah, and Muayyed want answers. So do many Canadians. Beyond what we already know, what role did CSIS, the RCMP, and other Canadian agencies play in these men's detention and torture? Who provided the information that led to their detentions, interrogations, and torture? What did Canadian agencies do with the fruits of that torture? Who is going to be held accountable? How can we ensure that what happened to these men doesn't happen to anyone else? And, most importantly, for Ahmad, Abdullah, and Muayyed, how can they clear their names?

They may get some answers from an internal inquiry led by retired Supreme Court Justice Frank Iacobucci. Created in December 2006, the Iacobucci Inquiry was mandated to examine whether the men's detention or "mistreatment" (the government refrains from using the term *torture*) "resulted, directly or indirectly, from actions of Canadian officials, particularly in relation to the sharing of information with foreign countries and, if so, whether those actions were deficient in the circumstances." The inquiry was also tasked with determining whether there were "deficiencies" in the provision of consular services. "While public hearings are possible, it is likely the Inquiry will be carried out largely in private," the government warned, because the inquiry is expected "to deal with sensitive national security matters."[23]

The government's terms of reference meant this inquiry would become one of Canada's best-kept secrets and would exclude the very people at the heart of the process: Ahmad, Abdullah, and Muayyed. By the time final submissions were made in the summer of 2008, there had been just two days of public hearings, on standards of conduct, in January 2008. The men, their lawyers, and the human rights and civil liberties organizations with intervenor status weren't permitted to see any documents presented as evidence to the inquiry. Nor were they able to cross-examine a single Canadian official, or given access to transcripts of what any of these officials said. Toward the end of the process, lawyers for the men and the intervenors were allowed to see a "draft factual narrative," outlining evidence heard about what officials were doing when. But Ahmad, Abdullah, and Muayyed weren't allowed to see the narrative. And, because their lawyers' final submissions dealt with information in the secret narrative, the men weren't even allowed to read those.

Representatives of Amnesty International, Human Rights Watch, the International Civil Liberties Monitoring Group, and the Canadian Council on American Islamic Relations were among the intervening organizations at the inquiry and drafted an op-ed about their frustrations with the process: "Secrecy takes a terrible toll. It undermines public confidence. It makes it more difficult to monitor human rights protection. But perhaps most critically, it slowly destroys the psyche of individuals whose reputations and well-being are directly implicated by the proceedings but who are excluded from participating in any fair or meaningful manner."[24]

Without any opportunity to participate in a meaningful way in the inquiry, the men's role was reduced to having to prove, again, that they were tortured. The government had already accepted the findings of the Arar Inquiry's fact-finder, Dr. Stephen Toope, that Maher was tortured, but would not accept Toope's findings that the others were also tortured. So the men have had to endure interviews by the commissioner and commission counsel and a new round of independent psychiatric and psychological assessments to once again prove they were tortured.

Alex Neve at Amnesty International interviewed and assessed the men very soon after they returned to Canada, long before the Iacobucci Inquiry was a possibility, and determined they were tortured. He says that given Amnesty International's interviews, Toope's findings, and the human rights records of Syria and Egypt, "the government's starting point should have been to acknowledge that the likelihood of torture in these cases was substantiated, unless something were to arise that cast doubt on that. Instead, it seems its starting point was that the men's allegations of torture aren't founded and they must disprove the government's doubt."[25]

And then there's the impact of that doubt on the men themselves. The trouble with doubting torture, according to torture expert Dr. Donald Payne, is not just that it re-traumatizes victims; it also makes it difficult for them to move on. "It is just one more obstruction in the long process of not being able to heal," he says. "The doubt [in these cases] re-traumatizes and gives a sense of despair that this is arbitrary doubt," and a sense that the government "is focused on not wanting to believe." Payne says that, given the record for torture in Syria and Egypt, ironically, "it must be much harder for a political detainee in Syria or Egypt to prove that they *weren't* tortured."[26]

As they awaited the outcome of the Iacobucci Inquiry, Ahmad, Abdullah, and Muayyed were understandably worried that the government might use the inquiry to label them as terrorists all over again. Their concerns are well founded. The government has a history of doubting allegations of torture and believing tortured confessions about links to terrorism. Justice O'Connor notes that that's what happened at the Arar Inquiry:

> At the beginning of the Inquiry, it was obvious to me that many within government believed that Mr. Arar had not been tortured and that he had voluntarily admitted links to terrorist activity to the Syrians. They were of the view that

the truth would come out during the Inquiry. Well, the truth did come out. When Professor Toope's report was made public over a year later, the government did not challenge the findings in the report and, indeed, through counsel, the government indicated that Mr. Arar had given "a credible"account that he was tortured. The disturbing part of all of this is that it took a public inquiry to set the record straight.[27]

At the time this book went to print, the men and the public were still waiting to learn whether Iacobucci's inquiry would set the record straight in these cases.

One person who says he never doubted that Maher Arar, or any of these men, were tortured, is Gar Pardy, the now-retired director general of Consular Affairs. He retired before Muayyed was detained, so can't comment on his case. But he's frank in his assessment of Ahmad, Abdullah, and Maher, whose cases he came to know well in his last years of service: "These men are totally innocent, and until somebody in the Canadian government is prepared to write a bill of particulars and bring them into court, there's nothing that will change that, and no one is going to do that because the evidence isn't there in anything I know or anything I've seen."[28]

The Hon. Dan McTeague, a Privy Council member and the former parliamentary secretary to then–Foreign Affairs minister Bill Graham, was assigned in late 2003 to help Canadians in trouble abroad and worked on Abdullah and Muayyed's cases. He sometimes sparred with Pardy over consular issues, especially when it came to the case of William Sampson (who'd been detained and sentenced to death in Saudi Arabia but later released) but is quick to agree with him on this issue. He believes the men are all innocent. "I never saw anything that would disprove their innocence," he says. "If they weren't innocent, they would have been detained and charged in Canada. Instead, they've all been out for four years, free."[29]

Pardy is not as generous when it comes to assessing the actions of the RCMP. "We had very inexperienced and, up to a point, inept people dealing with a subject matter that they knew nothing about and ... absolutely no supervision of these people at a level that should have been taking place," he says. Pardy finds some solace in the fact that Giuliano Zaccardelli, the commissioner of the RCMP who oversaw the force's actions in all of these cases, was forced to resign after giving conflicting testimony on Maher's case before a parliamentary committee.[30]

But how about the heads of CSIS, such as Jack Hooper, or the heads of the intelligence agencies within Foreign Affairs? No other Canadian official involved in these cases has been held to account in any formal way. Many have since been promoted. Former RCMP commissioner Zaccardelli has done well, having recently been appointed a senior position in Interpol (the International Criminal Police Organization) to help Africa fight crime. That he was "expected to provide abroad the leadership that was so conspicuously missing at home" was "a surprising choice," in the words of *Toronto Star* columnist James Travers.[31]

And what of accountability for those who set the national security agenda for Canada after 9/11? Prime Minister Chrétien, deputy prime ministers John Manley and Anne McLellan, and Solicitor General Wayne Easter come to mind. Neither the Arar Inquiry nor the Iacobucci Inquiry has adequately scrutinized the actions of Canada's political leadership in these cases. Instead, both inquiries were set up to focus in at the level of political officials. "It's the political leaders who set the tone and the framework, and they are the ones who have the responsibility and the power to intervene to ensure that actions of officials best ensure the protection of human rights," says Alex Neve.[32]

Pardy agrees. "I believe that most RCMP and CSIS guys aren't evil people. To the extent that they do wrong, it probably has more to do with the environment that is created for them. What amazes me is that there isn't anyone above the level of director general who gets held to account. All the ministers and the prime ministers— ultimately they're the ones who are responsible. These are the people who set up the conditions for this to happen," he says.[33]

And the Conservative government has allowed those conditions to remain in place. Justice O'Connor had a second and very important component in his mandate—to recommend how to improve oversight of the RCMP. For more than two years, the Arar Inquiry's counsel examined international and domestic review models, and heard from experts and advisers on what would work best for Canada. Justice O'Connor released his findings in a second report, in November 2006, recommending an integrated approach to reviewing not just the RCMP but five other federal agencies involved in national security activities, such as the Border Services Agency and the intelligence bureaus within Foreign Affairs.[34]

Nearly two years later, the Conservative government has yet to implement any of the recommendations from Justice O'Connor's report on oversight and review. In a letter to intervening organizations on April 10, 2008, Public Safety Minister Stockwell Day wrote: "I can assure you that this government is working diligently to determine the best model for a review mechanism of Canada's national security activities."[35] Diligently, maybe, but also slowly. Reg Whitaker, an adjunct political science professor at the University of Victoria who served as an expert adviser to the Arar Inquiry's examination of oversight and review mechanisms, says enacting those reforms is crucial "unfinished business."[36] Neve agrees. "The broader institutional changes haven't been put in place. Without them, how can we ensure that injustices like these don't occur again and, if they do, that the people in cases that emerge today have somewhere to turn?"[37]

CSIS and the RCMP are working hard to discourage any added scrutiny of their work. Ben Soavé, who once served as the RCMP's liaison officer to the Middle East and was head of the RCMP's Toronto Integrated National Security Enforcement Team in November 2001, told *The Globe and Mail*'s Colin Freeze that he considers the scrutiny brought on by federal inquiries "judicial terrorism." Jack Hooper, the former deputy director of CSIS, calls it "legal jihad." Paul Cavalluzzo, who served as lead counsel at the Arar Inquiry, says that the comments by Soavé and Hooper are "unbelievably disrespectful" and that it was those agencies' actions that brought on the inquiries.[38]

And while the RCMP and CSIS continue their national security work without improved oversight and review, many other cases have emerged. One of the first involved an aeronautical engineer from Algeria. On September 12, 2001, six days after making a refugee claim in Canada, Benamar Benatta was illegally transferred over the border and handed over to U.S. officials, seemingly suspected of terrorist links simply because he knew about airplanes and was from Algeria. He spent the next five years in U.S. detention, despite having been cleared of any links to terrorist activities by the FBI within two months of his initial detention. In 2006, he was finally released, returned to Canada, and granted refugee status. He had to launch a lawsuit against the Canadian government to get answers.[39]

In the spring of 2008, Abousafian Abdelrazik, another Canadian citizen, spoke with *The Globe and Mail*'s Paul Koring from the Canadian Embassy in Khartoum. Abdelrazik told Koring that he was harassed by CSIS in Canada before travelling to his native Sudan to visit his ailing mother, where he was soon detained by Sudanese officials, in September 2003. The Canadian government has not challenged an assertion in one of its own documents that Abdelrazik was detained "at our request." He spent the next two years in Sudanese prisons, where he says he was repeatedly tortured and, at one point, interrogated by two CSIS agents. Sudanese prisons, like those in Egypt and Syria, are notorious for abuse and torture. Abdelrazik's name had appeared on an international watch list for suspected links to al-Qaeda— he says he has no idea why and has never had anything to do with terrorism. In June, Abdelrazik was still at the Canadian Embassy in Khartoum, where diplomats granted him refuge after his case was made public, although they were refusing to issue him a new passport or help him get back to Canada.[40]

Internationally, it's been the work of a handful of determined activists and investigative journalists that has exposed the breadth of the U.S.-led "extraordinary rendition" program and forced the Bush administration to acknowledge the program's existence.[41] But it's still unclear how many hundreds of people deemed terror suspects have been disappeared into the torture chambers in Jordan, Syria, Egypt, and other countries. As author Stephen Grey recently wrote, "much remains a deep secret." Most of the victims are in custody and can't speak out. "We know the fate of just a small fraction of the thousands of prisoners captured by U.S. forces around the world since 9/11."[42]

Ahmad, Abdullah, Maher, and Muayyed often think of the fellow prisoners they left behind—not just those detained because of the so-called war on terror, but the political prisoners jailed for advocating for democracy in their countries. And that work is even more dangerous because of how regimes like Syria and Egypt have been used in the "war on terror." Haitham al-Maleh, a prominent human rights activist and lawyer living in Damascus (and barred from leaving the country) says that conditions in Syria have seriously declined in the last few years. "It's like it was in the eighties again," he says. Al-Maleh says they had to relocate Far' Falastin because it wasn't big enough to hold detainees. Sometime in the summer of 2007, he says, it was moved to a larger facility outside Damascus.[43]

Walid Saffour, president of the London-based Syrian Human Rights Committee, points to the hypocrisy of extraordinary rendition. "These governments say, 'We adhere to human rights,' but they deport people to dictatorial regimes who do not hesitate to torture people to death or to the brink of death." This, he says, has made people in Syria lose faith in the value of struggling to improve human rights conditions in their countries. "Now people in Syria say, 'Look, what you are doing is nonsense. All the world are against you.... It makes our work harder."[44]

Canada has yet to issue a statement that clearly and unequivocally condemns the CIA's rendition program or any use of torture in the "war on terror." Perhaps it's because, like many other governments after 9/11, ours has been implicated in aiding and abetting the program.

Ahmad El Maati says that despite everything that's happened, he still thinks that he, Abdullah, Maher, and Muayyed are the lucky ones. "Since 9/11, so many others have just disappeared, or are still in secret prisons, with no right to ask questions. At least we have the right to ask questions about why this happened. At least we might get answers," he says. "It's immensely important to feel that you can at least try to regain your dignity and try to have justice from anyone who caused you harm. Not to be able to do that, that is torture itself."

NOTES

To tell their stories, I have relied on first-hand interviews conducted with the men and their families that began in the fall of 2003 with Maher Arar; then in the summer of 2005 with Ahmad El Maati, his mother, Samira al-Shallash, his father, Badr El Maati, Abdullah Almalki and his wife, Khuzaimah. I've also relied on their public statements and interviews with their counsel. I have used their accounts to reconstruct narrative by American, Canadian, German, Syrian, Egyptian, and Jordanian officials. I have not provided a note for the date of every interview with these men and their families.

Author's Note
1 "Hold an inquiry into the Arar case," *Globe and Mail* (Toronto), editorial, November 5, 2003, A20.

One: The Man with the Map
1 Ann Armstrong, manager, Recruiting and Training, Highland Transport, letter in author's files, August 27, 2001.
2 For more on this period in Afghanistan's history, see Eric Margolis, *War at the Top of the World: The Struggle for Afghanistan, Kashmir and Tibet* (New York: Routledge, 2000).
3 CSIS later alleged in court documents that HCI was connected to al-Qaeda, and those allegations were repeated in the media, seriously harming the charity's reputation. In 2006, HCI filed a complaint with the Security Intelligence Review Committee (SIRC), the organization mandated to oversee CSIS. SIRC found that the allegations were "unsubstantiated," and recommended that CSIS formally retract the statement and apologize. CSIS continues to refuse to do so. See Security Intelligence Review Committee, *SIRC Annual Report 2005–2006: An Operational Review of the Canadian Security Intelligence Service* (Ottawa: Public Works and Government Services Canada, 2007), 29–30. Available at www.csars.gc.ca; and Jim Bronskill, "Watchdog calls for apology

from CSIS over unsubstantiated statement about charity," Canadian Press, November 5, 2007.

4   For more on the Khadr family, see Michelle Shephard, *Guantanamo's Child: The Untold Story of Omar Khadr* (Mississauga, ON: Wiley and Sons, 2008).

5   This man has asked that his name not be used. Ibrahym Adam is a pseudonym.

Two: "Your Name Is 'Number Five' Now"

1   Peter Cheney, "Kuwaiti found with papers on sensitive Ottawa sights," *Globe and Mail*, October 13, 2001, A1.

2   Patrick J. McDonnell and William C. Rempel, "U.S. strikes back: The investigation," *Los Angeles Times*, October 12, 2001, A1.

3   Melanie Brooks, "Terrorists eye nuclear plants, expert says: 'Ample evidence': Kuwaiti man had sensitive documents on N-plant, virus lab," *National Post*, October 15, 2001, A8.

4   The list, naming 370 people, was obtained by United Press International (UPI) after it was posted on October 3 on Finland's Rahoitustarkastus (Financial Supervision Authority) website. The FBI told UPI that the only list that had been circulated internationally was a continually updated watch list of people authorities were investigating regarding their possible connections to the 9/11 hijackers. Diplomatic sources said that the list had been initially circulated to them from the U.S. Justice Department. Within twenty-four hours, the list had been removed from the website, but the media had it, and were knocking on the doors of many of those listed. It is likely that Canada had provided the Canadian names to the Americans.

5   Seymour M. Hersh, "The Syrian bet: Did the Bush administration burn a useful source on al-Qaeda?" *New Yorker*, July 28, 2003, www.newyorker.com/archive/2003/07/28/030728fa_fact?currentPage=1 (accessed March 1, 2008).

6   This is an excerpt from Chapter 16, verse 118, of the Qur'an: "Al-Nahl" (The Bee).

Three: The Ressam Effect

1   Address by John Manley to the Trilateral Commission 2005 North American Regional Meeting, Montreal, November 4–6, 2005.

2   For a comprehensive account of the Ressam case, see Hal Bernton, Mike Carter, David Heath, and James Neff, "The terrorist within: The story behind one man's holy war against America," *Seattle Times*, June 23-July 7, 2002. France's terrorism magistrate Louis

Bruguière had discovered Montreal phone numbers in the electronic organizer belonging to Christophe Caze. In March 1996, Caze was killed in a shootout with police after they discovered that he and a group he led had planted a car bomb near the site of an upcoming Group of Seven industrialized nations meeting in Lille, France. The group was linked to the GIA, Groupement Islamique Armé, an Algerian terrorist group in France. See Bruguière testimony, *United States v. Ahmed Ressam*, No. CR 99-666-JCC (W.D. D.C.).

3 Stuart Bell, "CSIS watched Ressam for years before arrest: Spy agency gives details," *National Post*, April 7, 2001, A2.

4 Hal Bernton, Mike Carter, David Heath, and James Neff, "Chapter 7: Joining Jihad," in "The terrorist within: The story behind one man's holy war against America," *Seattle Times*, June 23–July 7, 2002, http://seattletimes.nwsource.com/news/nation-world/terroristwithin/ (accessed March 1, 2008).

5 Trial testimony of Ahmed Ressam, *United States v. Mokhtar Haouari*, No. S4 00 Cr. 15 (S.D. N.Y.), July 3, 2001, transcript pp. 536-69; July 5, 2001, transcript p. 624.

6 Ressam eventually told all about his plot: how he eluded Canadian investigators and the training he received in Afghanistan. See Ahmed Ressam testimony, *United States v. Mokhtar Haouari*, July 3 and 5, 2001.

7 Ibid., July 3, 2001, transcript pp. 559–60.

8 Ibid.

9 Bruguière testimony, *United States v. Ahmed Ressam*, April 2, 2001, transcript pp. 17–18.

10 Hal Bernton, Mike Carter, David Heath, and James Neff, "Chapter 10: The mission," in "The terrorist within: The story behind one man's holy war against America," *Seattle Times*, June 23–July 7, 2002, http://seattletimes.nwsource.com/news/nation-world/terroristwithin/.

11 Andrew Duffy, "RCMP missed clues on map: Airports circled, Ressam trial told," *Ottawa Citizen*, March 24, 2001, A13.

12 Hal Bernton, Mike Carter, David Heath, and James Neff, "Chapter 16: The reckoning," in "The terrorist within: The story behind one man's holy war against America," *Seattle Times*, June 23–July 7, 2002, http://seattletimes.nwsource.com/news/nation-world/terroristwithin/.

13 Curiously, the RCMP's deputy commissioner, Garry Loeppky, would later characterize the Ressam operation as a success, saying "that was an operation that required close collaboration between ourselves, CSIS, a variety of United States agencies and the international

community and was an example, I think, where that integrated approach, that close collaboration, resulted in the prevention of what could have been a significant activity at the Los Angeles airport." See Loeppky testimony at the Commission of Inquiry into the Actions of Canadian Officials in Relation to Maher Arar (hereafter "Arar Inquiry"), June 30, 2004, transcript p. 756. Note that transcripts of testimony at the Arar Inquiry are available at www.ararcommission.ca.

14 For a stunning and fulsome account of intelligence failures in the lead-up to 9/11, see Lawrence Wright, *The Looming Tower: Al-Qaeda and the Road to 9/11* (New York: Vintage Books, 2006), especially "Revelations," Chap. 20.

15 In fact, the myth persisted for years. Newt Gingrich, former Republican Speaker in the U.S. House of Representatives told Fox News on April 19, 2005, that "far more of the 9/11 terrorists came across from Canada than from Mexico." In fact, none came from either Canada or Mexico. Gingrich later apologized for the error. On December 19, 2005, Republican Senator Conrad Burns told a news conference that "we've got to remember that the people who first hit us in 9/11 entered this country through Canada." See Sheldon Alberts, "U.S. senator revives 9/11 myth about Canada: Embassy demands he retract claim terrorists came from here; U.S. TV host calls us 'retarded,'" *Ottawa Citizen*, December 20, 2005, A1; and Doug Struck, "Canada fights myth it was 9/11 conduit: Charge often repeated by U.S. officials," *Washington Post*, April 9, 2005, A20.

16 Testimony of John Manley at the Arar Inquiry, May 31, 2005, transcript p. 4349.

17 "Attack on America: Interview with John Manley," interview with Charles Adler, *Global Sunday*, Global TV, September 16, 2001.

18 Jeff Sallot, "The aftermath: The strategic response," *Globe and Mail*, September 14, 2001, A3.

19 Kent Roach, *September 11: Consequences for Canada* (Montreal: McGill-Queen's University Press, 2003), 148.

20 David Frum, "Canada was purposefully cut from 2001 speech, Frum says," *Globe and Mail*, January 8, 2003, A8.

21 Manley had to stop in on U.S. senator Hillary Clinton, too, to set the record straight: Earlier in the week, Clinton told a reporter from *La Presse* that "some of the 19 terrorists crossed the border several times to come into Canada." See Michelle MacAfee, "Manley discusses border issues with Clinton," Canadian Press Newswire, October 24, 2001.

22 Government of Canada, "Government of Canada introduced Anti-terrorism Act," news release, Canada NewsWire, October 15, 2001.

23 Justice Minister Anne McLellan, evidence provided to the Standing Committee on Justice and Human Rights, meeting no. 49, November 20, 2001.

24 Roach, *September 11*, 23.

25 Ibid., 21, 23.

26 Criminal Code, R.S.C. 1985, c. C-46, s. 83.01 (1) (b) (i) (A).

27 Roach, *September 11*, 27. The Superior Court of Ontario ruled in 2006 that the contentious religious and political "motive" provision of the definition was unconstitutional, but a parliamentary subcommittee tasked with reviewing the Anti-terrorism Act disagreed, and the controversial definition, as laid out in the ATA in 2001, remains in effect today. See *R. v. Khawaja*, [2006] O.J. No. 4245 and Government of Canada, "Government's Response to the Seventh Report of the House of Commons Standing Committee on Public Safety and National Security-Rights, Limits, Security: A Comprehensive Review of the Anti-Terrorism Act and Related Issues," July 18, 2007, www.justice.gc.ca/en/anti_terr/rep_res/cc_hc/index.html (accessed March 14, 2008).

28 Kent Roach, professor, University of Toronto, quoted in "Legal experts urge senators to change anti-terror bill: Bill C-36 still goes too far, they say," *Toronto Star*, December 6, 2001, O8.

29 Jim Bronskill, Janice Tibbetts, and Norm Ovenden, "Police get new powers to fight terrorism: 'Peace and security' of Canadians at stake, federal minister says," *Vancouver Sun*, October 16, 2001, A1.

30 Ibid.

31 Testimony of Justice Minister Anne McLellan before the Special Senate Committee on Bill C-36, Proceedings of the Special Senate Committee on Bill C-36 (formerly the Subject Matter of Bill C-36), Issue 7—Evidence (Afternoon Sitting), December 4, 2001.

32 Ibid.

33 Shirley Heafey, phone interview with author, April 13, 2008.

34 Jack Aubry and Rick Mofina, "Terror bill's powers 'exorbitant': Spy agency watchdog says government would gain power to break privacy laws," *Ottawa Citizen*, October 23, 2001, A1.

35 Tim Harper, "'Big brother' looms with terrorism bill: Watchdog," *Toronto Star*, October 24, 2001.

36 Roach, *September 11*, 37.

37 Reporters without Borders, "The Anti-Terrorism Law Threatens Press Freedom," December 19, 2001, www.rsf.org/article.php3?id_article=322 (accessed March 25, 2008).

38 Canada Evidence Act, R.S.C. 1985, c. C-5, s. 38.13, as amended by the ATA.

39 See, for example, Chapter 25, on how the Government of Canada used these provisions to attempt to block sections of the Arar Inquiry's report from being released. Some of the information the government attempted to conceal was related to Canadian agencies' knowledge about and use of information likely obtained under torture.

40 Manley testimony at the Arar Inquiry, May 31, 2005, transcript pp. 4338–39.

41 Ibid., p. 4354.

42 Coalition for Secure and Trade-Efficient Borders, "Rethinking our borders: A plan for action," December 3, 2001, www.cme-mec.ca/pdf/planforaction.pdf (accessed March 25, 2008).

43 Manley testimony at the Arar Inquiry, May 31, 2005, transcript p. 4353.

44 CEO of Canadian Pacific, Robert J. Ritchie, as quoted in Roach, *September 11*, 135.

45 The laws were eventually amended with the passage of the Public Safety Act in May 2003.

46 By this time (on September 12, 2001), a young Algerian asylum seeker named Benamar Benatta had been, without benefit of legal counsel or any formal hearing, handed over to the United States by Canadian officials. The officials alleged that as a Muslim with aeronautical experience Benatta may have been connected to the events of 9/11. Benatta spent almost five years in detention in the United States under conditions the United Nations concluded were tantamount to torture, even though the FBI cleared him of any allegations in November 2001. See Andrew Duffy, "Five lost years: How Benamar Benatta 'disappeared' after 9/11; The Canadian government sent him to the U.S. where he was accused of being behind the 9/11 bombings; 'The way they accused me, I thought my life was over,'" *Ottawa Citizen*, January 26, 2008, B1.

47 Proceedings of the Standing Senate Committee on National Security and Defense, no. 11 (February 24, 2003): 16.

48 Arar Inquiry, Report of the Events Relating to Maher Arar, Factual Background, vol. 1, p. 14. Note that the Arar Inquiry report is available at www.ararcommission.ca.

49 Testimony of Jack Hooper at the Arar Inquiry, August 25, 2005, transcript pp. 10740 and 10746.

50 Arar Report, Factual Background, vol. 1, p. 15.

51 Ibid., pp. 15–16.

52 Ibid., p. 20.

53 Ibid., p. 117, note 15; Hooper would also later tell a Senate committee that the Crown said there was "not sufficient evidence to proceed with charges." See Proceedings of the Standing Senate Committee on National Security and Defence, no. 2 (May 26, 2006): 18.

54 Proceedings of the Standing Senate Committee on National Security and Defence, no. 2 (May 26, 2006): 18.

55 Ibid.

56 Ibid.

Four: Squeezed Out of Canada

1 Krista Foss, "Hate incidents up in large cities, police forces say," *Globe and Mail*, October 15, 2001, A6.

2 John MacFarlane, "Medical resident tells of assault," *Gazette* (Montreal), September 18, 2001, B6.

3 Karina Roman and Alison Korn, "'People are scared, they don't come': Attack on Ottawa teenager keeps many Muslims home," *Ottawa Citizen*, September 19, 2001, A4.

4 Arar Report, Factual Background, vol. 1, p. 51.

5 "Personal notes of Michel Cabana," Arar Inquiry, Exhibit P-166, p. 2.

6 Testimony of Michel Cabana at the Arar Inquiry, June 29, 2005, transcript pp. 7758–60.

7 Ibid., p. 7762.

8 The Office of the Privacy Commissioner of Canada examined a sample of Project Shock's 2002 records and found that many of the tips the project received "appeared innocuous in nature, and in some cases seemed to amount to little more than public hysteria during a time of crisis." See "Audit Report of the Privacy Commissioner of Canada: Examination of RCMP Exempt Data Banks; A Special Report to Parliament," February 13, 2008, www.privcom.gc.ca/media/nr-c/2008/nr-c_b-di_080213_e.asp.

9 Cabana testimony, June 29, 2005, transcript p. 7766.

10 Ibid., p. 7785.

11 Ibid., p. 7784.

12 Arar Report, Analysis and Recommendations, p. 71.

13 Arar Report, Factual Background, vol. 1, p. 22.

14 Ibid., pp. 35–36.

15 Ibid., p. 51.

16 Ibid., p. 62.

17 Riad Saloojee, email interview with author, June 10, 2008.

Five: "Tell Us About the Map"

1 Walsh ITO (Information to Obtain), Arar Inquiry, Exhibit P-179, p. 77.

2 Ahmad's family eventually had further proof he was on the flight: He used his credit card to buy perfume for Rola from the in-flight shopping service, so his bill would have shown that.

3 David Rohde, "A nation challenged: Kabul; In 2 abandoned Kabul houses, some hints of Al Qaeda presence," *New York Times*, November 17, 2001.

4 U.S. Department of State, "Syria: Country reports on human rights practices-2001," March 4, 2002, www.state.gov/g/drl/rls/hrrpt/ 2001/nea/8298.htm# (accessed January 6, 2008).

5 Amnesty International, *Amnesty International Report 2002*, index number POL 10/001/2002, p. 237.

6 The entrance gate to the security compound housing the Far' Falastin can be located on "Google Earth" at the following coordinates: 33 30 30.96 N; 36 16 27.76 E.

7 Michelle Shephard, "Untangling tale of tortured Canadian: *The Star* retraces Arar's steps in Syria," *Toronto Star*, May 1, 2004.

8 As described by former detainees to Abdullah Almalki.

9 Walid Saffour, director, Syrian Human Rights Committee, telephone interview with author, April 16, 2008.

10 Arar Report, Factual Background, vol. 1, p. 252.

11 Zammar was questioned by German intelligence agencies after 9/11 and accused of supporting terrorism. The Germans did not have enough evidence to charge him. Zammar travelled to Morocco, where he was detained and questioned in early December 2001, then flown on a CIA plane to Syria. (The German authorities had supplied his travel information to the CIA.) The CIA says it sent questions for Zammar to his Syrian interrogators. He was held at Far' Falastin in one of the grave-like cells for almost three years, until around October 2004, when he was transferred to the Sednaya detention centre. In February 2007 he was tried and sentenced to twelve years in prison for belonging to the Muslim Brotherhood (which he denies) and three other offences related to posing a domestic threat to Syria. See Amnesty International, "Europe: Victims of Rendition and Secret Detention Still Seeking Justice," index number EUR 01/012/2008, June 24, 2008, www.amnesty.org/ en/library/info/EUR01/012/2008/en (accessed July 1, 2008).

Six: Seven Searches

1   It's not clear whether CSIS or the RCMP had assumed that Ahmad had Syrian citizenship and had mistakenly informed the Americans, or the Syrians, that Ahmad was Syrian before or during his initial detention.

2   Testimony of Franco Pillarella at the Arar Inquiry, June 14, 2005, transcript p. 6694.

3   Memo to Officer in Charge, Project O Canada from RCMP liaison officer Steve Covey in Rome, January 2, 2002, Arar Inquiry, Exhibit P-171.

4   Gar Pardy, interview with author, Ottawa, March 31, 2008.

5   Ibid.

6   Arar Report, Factual Background, vol. 1, p. 64.

7   Ibid., p. 104.

8   Ibid., p. 105.

9   Arar Report, Analysis and Recommendations, p. 72.

10 Ibid.

11 See Arar Inquiry transcript of cross-examination of Inspector Cabana by counsel for Ahmad El Maati and Abdullah Almalki, and the corresponding National Security Confidentiality claims filed by government counsel Simon Fothergill, August 9, 2005.

12 By the summer of 2002, there was some dispute within the RCMP's "A" Division about whether the threat still existed, given that Ahmad and Abdullah were both in detention and Maher was in Tunisia. RCMP headquarters had concluded that the threat was no longer imminent. One analyst listened to A-O Canada, based in Ottawa, argue with O Canada, based in Toronto, about whether the threat was to Ottawa or Toronto, and walked away "sceptical" about the threat. By the time Flewelling had been brought in to monitor A-O Canada and reinstate policies that existed before 9/11, he felt the threat was no longer imminent and therefore did not justify any deviation from policy. Arar Report, Factual Background, vol. 2, p. 510.

13 Walsh ITO, Arar Inquiry, Exhibit P-179, p. 1. At the time this book went to print, significant portions of the ITO remained censored and efforts to seek its full disclosure remained before the Federal Court.

14 Ibid., Appendix D, p. 97.

15 Arar Report, Disclosure of information authorized by the Federal Court of Canada in accordance with Sections 38.04 and 38.06 of the Canada Evidence Act, Analysis and Recommendations, p. 99. Note that Inspector Cabana testified that if Project A-O Canada was going to use information that might have been obtained under

torture to justify a search warrant, A-O Canada would analyze it and corroborate it, "so if there was an issue of torture, we would make sure that the judicials are aware of the existence of that possibility." See Arar Inquiry transcripts, August 9, 2005, pp. 9380–81.

16 Walsh ITO, Appendix D, pp. 45 and 90.

17 Ibid., p. 90.

18 Youssef Almalki, "An Interview with Youssef Almalki," interview with Carole MacNeil, *CBC News: Sunday*, CBC, November 7, 2003.

19 Ibid.

20 Walsh ITO, Appendix D, pp. 86–87.

21 Arar Report, Factual Background, vol. 1, p. 73.

22 Maureen Murray, "Watchdog to probe arrests by Mounties: Agency concerned about RCMP use of anti-terror powers," *Toronto Star*, January 31, 2002, A2.

23 Youssef Almalki, "An Interview with Youssef Almalki," interview with Carole MacNeil, *CBC News: Sunday*, CBC, November 7, 2003.

24 Siri Agrell, "RCMP 'violation' leaves Muslim family terrified: No charges laid after six-hour search under anti-terror law," *Ottawa Citizen*, January 27, 2002, A11.

25 Shirley Heafey, phone interview with author, April 13, 2008.

26 If Canadian agencies were behind this questioning, they put Abdullah at risk of indefinite detention and ill-treatment in Malaysia. Human rights groups have long criticized Malaysia's Internal Security Act (ISA), enacted in 1960, which allows for indefinite detention. In 2006, Amnesty International reported that "in the context of the 'war on terror,' hundreds of individuals alleged to be Islamist militants have been arrested on suspicion of links to terrorist networks. At least seventy of them remain detained under the ISA, many of whom have been detained since 2001." See Amnesty International, "Another Guántanamo in Malaysia? Indefinite detention and risk of torture," March 22, 2006, www.amnesty.org/en/news-and-updates/feature-stories (accessed March 13, 2007).

27 White House Office of Management and Budget, "President Bush releases $1.7 billion in emergency funds to provide for the security and humanitarian needs related to the attack on America," news release, October 23, 2001. U.S. military aid to Pakistan climbed from $9.1 million in the three years preceding 9/11 to $4.7 billion in the three years after 9/11. See Sarah Fort, "Billions in Aid, With No Accountability: Pakistan Receives the Most Post-9/11 U.S. Military Funding, Yet Has Failed to Ferret Out Al Qaeda, Taliban Leaders,"

May 31, 2007, Center for Public Integrity, www.publicintegrity.org/Content.aspx?src=search&context=article&id=877 (accessed March 26, 2008).

28 Colin Freeze, "Torture, radios and why the U.S. won't let go," *Globe and Mail*, March 17, 2007, A8.

29 Arar Report, Factual Background, vol. 1, pp. 77–78.

30 Ibid., p. 78.

31 Hussein was later given a settlement by the government after he lost his business due to the mistaken allegations. See Jake Rupert, "Government pays off victim of terror smear: Ottawa man was arrested, his business ruined," *Ottawa Citizen*, October 2, 2003, A1.

Seven: Damascus to Cairo

1 Jane Mayer, "Outsourcing torture: The secret history of America's 'extraordinary rendition' program," *New Yorker*, February 14, 2005, www.newyorker.com/archive/2005/02/14/050214fa_fact6.

2 Adrian Levy and Cathy Scott-Clark, "'One huge jail,'" *Guardian* (London), March 19, 2005, 16.

3 Amnesty International, "Amnesty International's Briefing to the Human Rights Committee on the Arab Republic of Egypt," May 2002, www.amnesty.org/en/library/asset/MDE12/019/2002/en/7eLGVtyhDBkJ (accessed March 29, 2008).

4 Ibid.

5 U.S. Department of State, "Egypt: Country Reports on Human Rights Practices-2002," March 31, 2003, www.state.gov/g/drl/rls/hrrpt/2002/18274.htm (accessed March 29, 2008).

6 Ibid.

7 Arar Report, Analysis and Recommendations, p. 533.

8 Arar Report, Factual Background, vol. 1, p. 105.

9 Ibid., p. 19.

10 Ibid.

11 Ibid., p. 85.

12 Ibid., vol. 1, p. 89.

13 Ibid., vol. 1, p. 88.

14 Testimony of Garry Loeppky at the Arar Inquiry, July 27, 2005, transcript pp. 8424–26.

15 Arar Report, Factual Background, vol. 1, p. 92.

16 Arar Report, Analysis and Recommendations, p. 122.

17 Ibid., vol. 2, p. 562.

18 Ibid., vol. 1, p. 143, note 609.

Eight: The Prevention Side of the Mandate

1   Among the documents seized from Abdullah's office during the
    January 22, 2002, RCMP searches was a 1996 fax to Ibrahym
    Adam. At the time, Ibrahym operated a business in a New York
    warehouse, and Abdullah contracted Ibrahym to process a shipment
    for him. The fax seized by the RCMP directed Ibrahym to remove
    labels and repackage a shipment for him. The RCMP appears to
    have have told the FBI that the fax demonstrated Abdullah was
    concealing the contents of the shipment. The other documents
    relating to the shipment, however, demonstrate that all was above
    board. A quick search of the internet shows dozens of companies
    that offer import/export businesses, the same processing service
    Ibrahym provided Abdullah, for example www.apwl.net/; www.
    truckingdistribution.com/warehousing.html; and www.trancy
    america.com/html/services_fs_waredist.htm. Abdullah later
    provided the documents relating to that shipment to journalist
    Andrew Duffy. See "Almalki linked to U.S. terror trial: Papers taken
    by RCMP during raid on Ottawa man's home surface as court
    exhibit," *Ottawa Citizen*, March 14, 2007, p. A1. Note that the
    Ottawa Citizen later issued the following apology about the
    misleading headline attached to this story: "The *Citizen* article was
    never intended to suggest that Mr. Almalki is a terrorist or is linked
    to any terrorism trials. The *Citizen* regrets any confusion caused by
    the headline, and apologizes to Mr. Almalki for any distress the
    Citizen may have caused him."

2   Douglas Little, "Excerpts from 'Cold War and Covert Action: The
    U.S. and Syria, 1945–1958,'" *Middle East Journal*, Winter 1990, as
    reprinted in Coalition to Oppose the Arms Trade, *Press for
    Conversion*, May 2003, 51: 12.

3   Yehezkel Hameiri, *Prisoners of Hate: The Story of Israelis in Syrian
    Jails* (Jerusalem: Keter Books, 1969), 43–45, quotes on 44.

4   Little, "Excerpts from 'Cold War and Covert Action,'" 12.

5   Ibid.

6   Andrew Rathmell, *Secret War in the Middle East: The Covert
    Struggle for Syria, 1949–1961.* (London: I.B. Tauris, 1995), 97–98.

7   Mohammad Amir Al-Shallash had been the deputy chief of staff
    under al-Shishakli.

8   Hadith 19, *An Nawawwis Forty Hadith*, by the Islamic scholar
    Yahia bin Sharaful-Deen An-Nawawi. Muslims believe that the
    Hadiths are the sayings of the Prophet Mohamed.

9   Stephen Grey, *Ghost Plane: The True Story of the CIA Torture
    Program* (New York: St. Martin's Press, 2006), 4.

10 Arar Report, Factual Background, vol. 1, p. 102.

11 Ibid., pp. 100–101.

12 Ibid., p. 102. Cabana also testified at the Arar Inquiry that at the time he left Project A-O Canada, in February 2003, the team had no plans to charge Maher.

13 Ibid., p. 102.

14 Ibid., p. 107.

15 Security Intelligence Review Committee, *SIRC Annual Report 2005–2006: An Operational Review of the Canadian Security Intelligence Service* (Ottawa: Public Works and Government Services Canada: 2007), 13.

16 Ibid. In conducting its investigation, SIRC didn't get everything it asked for from CSIS. SIRC requested records of secure telephone conversations between CSIS headquarters and the CSIS security liaison officer in the region; that person would have been in direct contact with the Syrians and the CIA. CSIS said there no written records of these conversations. SIRC warns CSIS's actions were fully compliant with its policy framework, which, it argues, needs to be changed to reflect relations with countries with poor human rights records. SIRC also recommended that CSIS keep written records of telephone conversations with its security liaison officers. See *SIRC Annual Report 2005–2006*, p. 14.

17 Proceedings of the Standing Senate Committee on National Security and Defence, no. 2 (May 26, 2006): 18.

18 Personal notes of Rick Flewelling, Arar Inquiry, Exhibit P-211, pp. 21–22.

19 Arar Report, Factual Background, vol. 1, p. 108. At the Arar Inquiry, CSIS officials rejected the RCMP's assertion that CSIS had given the RCMP the impression that the agency was able to secure Abdullah's release.

Nine: Extreme Treatment

1 The Mabahith Amn al-Dawla al-'Ulya (State Security Investigations Services) facility in Nasr City can be located on Google Earth at the following coordinates: 30 04 02 08 N; 01 17 50.23 E. Although technically the Nasr City facility is a "branch," it is one of the biggest, if not the biggest, and appears to serve as the central hub for interrogation by the State Security Investigation (SSI) Services.

2 Testimony of Michel Cabana at the Arar Inquiry, June 29, 2005, transcript pp. 7866–67.

3 Ibid., pp. 7868–69; personal notes of Michel Cabana, Arar Inquiry, Exhibit P-166, p. 40.

4　Arar Report, Factual Background, vol. 1, p. 106.

5　Personal notes of Sergeant Rick Flewelling, Arar Inquiry, Exhibit P-211, p. 24; personal notes of Inspector Michel Cabana, Arar Inquiry, Exhibit P-166, p. 39.

6　Arar Report, Addendum, Factual Background, vol. 1, p. 103.

7　Arar Report, Factual Background, vol. 1, p. 245.

8　Diplomatic note from Syrian Ministry of Foreign Affairs to Canadian Embassy in Syria, July 2, 2002, Arar Inquiry, Exhibit P-256.

9　Ibid., DFAIT case note, 01-DMCUS-725675, July 17, 2002.

10　Gar Pardy, interview with author, Ottawa, March 31, 2008.

Ten: "I Was Tortured"

1　The State Security Investigations (SSI) Services facility in Lazoughli Square in Cairo can be located on Google Earth using the coordinates: 30 02 21.93 N; 31 14 23.34 E.

2　The Istiqbal Tora prison is just one of the facilities in the Tora Prison Disrict. It can be located on Google Earth at the following coordinates: 29 56 56.58 N; 31 16 57.14 E.

3　Arar Report, Factual Background, vol. 1, p. 107.

4　Testimony of Michel Cabana at the Arar Inquiry, June 29, 2005, transcript p. 2916; Exhibit P-83, tab 1, p. 182.

5　Arar Report, Addendum, Addendum, Analysis and Recommendations, pp. 127-127a. The Canadian government took the Arar Inquiry to court to keep this information secret, and lost.

6　Ibid.

7　Ibid.

8　Arar Report, Factual Background, vol. 1, p. 107. See also note 702 on page 146.

9　Ibid., vol. 1, p. 109.

10　Ibid., vol. 1, p. 146, n. 713.

11　Testimony of Michel Cabana at the Arar Inquiry, June 29, 2005, transcript p. 7872.

12　Arar Report, Factual Background, vol. 1, p. 109.

13　Ibid.

14　Ibid., pp. 108–110.

15　Ibid., p. 107.

16　Ibid., p. 109.

17　The location of Ahmad's cell (as well as the whole of the Abu Za'abal prison compound) can be viewed using Google Earth at the following coordinates: 30 16 4.12″ N, 31 21 26.43″ E.

Eleven: Tunis to New York

1 Arar Report, Factual Background, vol. 1, p. 152.
2 Ibid.
3 Arar Report, Analysis and Recommendations, p. 150.
4 Maher Arar, statement at a news conference, National Press Theatre, Ottawa, November 4, 2003, Ottawa, www.maherarar.ca/cms/ images/uploads/Maher_statement_nov04.pdf.

Twelve: New York to Damascus

1 Arar Report, Factual Background, vol. 1, p. 184.
2 Ibid., p. 157.
3 Ibid., p. 160.
4 The Arar Inquiry accepted Flewelling's testimony on this issue. See Arar Report, Analysis and Recommendations, p. 152.
5 Estanislao Oziewicz, "Ottawa man feared being sent to Syria, U.S. lawyer says," Globe and Mail, October 15, 2002, A5.
6 "Statement of Complaint and Demand for Jury Trial," Maher Arar vs. Ashcroft, United States District Court, Eastern District of New York, January 22, 2004, 14, http://www.maherarar.ca/cms/images/ uploads/Arar_Complaint_FINAL.pdf (accessed April 10, 2008).
7 Arar Report, Factual Background, vol. 1, p. 171.
8 Arar Inquiry, Exhibit P-20, "Decision of the Regional Director of the Immigration and Naturalization Service," October 7, 2002.
9 Ibid.
10 Ibid.
11 Testimony by Nancy Collins at the Arar Inquiry, May 19, 2005, pp. 3095–96.
12 Arar Report, Factual Background, vol. 1, p. 203.
13 Ibid., p. 177.
14 Ibid., p. 180.
15 Arar Report, Addendum, Factual Background, vol. 1, p. 245.
16 Presidential Aviation website, www.presidential-aviation.com/ fleet.html (accessed April 11, 2008).
17 Stephen Grey, Ghost Plane: The True Story of the CIA Torture Program (New York: St. Martin's Press, 2006), 69.
18 Ibid., 69.
19 Ibid., 71.
20 Ibid., 70.

Thirteen: "Tell Us You Went to Afghanistan"

1 Peter Cheney, "Canadian's deportation causes furor," Globe and Mail, October 12, 2002, A1.

2   "Ontario: United States deports suspected terrorist to Syria,"
    National Post, October 12, 2002, A9.
3   Anthony DePalma, "Threats and Responses: Detainee; Canadian
    immigrant arrested at J.F.K. is deported to Syria," *New York Times*,
    October 12, 2002.
4   Gar Pardy, interview with author, Ottawa, March 31, 2008.
5   Arar Report, Factual Background, vol. 1, p. 232.
6   Ibid., p. 233.
7   Gar Pardy, email intervview with the author, May 5, 2008.
8   "The alarming case of Maher Arar," editorial, *Globe and Mail*,
    October 19, 2002, A24.
9   Testimony of Gar Pardy at the Arar Inquiry, May 24, 2005,
    transcript pp. 3390–91.
10 Arar Report, Factual Background, vol. 1, p. 95.
11 Allan Thompson, "Lost Canadian in Syria: Damascus tells envoy
    deportee was in Jordan," *Toronto Star*, October 22, 2002, A21;
    Allan Thompson, "Deported Canadian surfaces in Syria," *Hamilton
    Spectator*, October 22, 2002, D4.
12 Testimony of Franco Pillarella at the Arar Inquiry, June 14, 2005,
    transcript p. 6779.
13 Gar Pardy, interview with author, Ottawa, March 31, 2008.
14 Ibid.
15 Memo from Franco Pillarella to DFAIT Ottawa, October 22, 2002,
    Arar Inquiry, Exhibit P-137, p. 1.
16 Ibid.
17 Arar Report, Factual Background, vol. 1, p. 257.
18 "Ambassador Pillarella: Newly redacted documents," Arar Inquiry,
    Exhibit P-134, tab. 3, p. 2.
19 See, for example, Allan Thompson and Tonda MacCharles, "PM
    speaks out on U.S. deportation: Ottawa turning to Syria for help
    finding Canadian," *Toronto Star*, October 18, 2002, A6: "U.S.
    authorities initially accused Arar of being linked to the Al Qaeda
    terror network, but foreign affairs department spokesperson
    Reynald Doiron said Canada has seen no evidence of any such
    connection."
20 Bob Harvey, "Don't forget Ottawa man deported to Syria by U.S.,
    McDonough says," *Ottawa Citizen*, October 21, 2002, A5.
21 Mike Trickey, "RCMP 'betrayed' man sent to Syria: Canadian's wife
    links deportation by U.S. to earlier Mountie probe," *Ottawa
    Citizen*, October 23, 2002, A3.
22 Ibid.

23 Email from Ambassador Pillarella to DFAIT Consular Affairs Bureau and DFAIT's Foreign Intelligence Division, November 3, 2002, Arar Inquiry, Exhibit P-138, p. 1. See also Arar Report, Factual Background, vol. 1, p. 275.

24 Email from Ambassador Pillarella to DFAIT Consular Affairs Bureau and DFAIT's Foreign Intelligence Division, November 3, 2002, Arar Inquiry, Exhibit P-138, p. 1. See also Arar Report, Factual Background, vol. 1, p. 275.

25 Testimony of Franco Pillarella at the Arar Inquiry, June 14, 2005, transcript pp. 6849–50. In testimony before the Arar Inquiry, the ambassador said it was important to point out that he had not asked for the information—it was offered by the general in response to the ambassador's apparent assertion that Maher should be returned to Canada. Justice O'Connor concluded that the ambassador's actions in receiving the report were not unreasonable or improper. However, he does recommend that "in these types of situations that Canadian officials exercise caution, to avoid taking any action that appears to condone or encourage human rights abuses." See Arar Report, Analysis and Recommendations, p. 196.

26 Arar Report, Analysis and Recommendations, p. 196.

27 Ibid.

28 Testimony of Franco Pillarella at the Arar Inquiry, June 14, 2005, pp. 6798–99. Justice O'Connor would later agree with this reasoning. See Arar Report, Analysis and Recommendations, p. 195.

29 Arar Report, Factual Background, vol. 1, p. 277.

30 Testimony of Michel Cabana at the Arar Inquiry, June 29, 2005, p. 8034.

31 It was not considered within the mandate of the Arar Inquiry to rule on how Pillarella's conversation may have affected Abdullah Almalki or Ahmad El Maati.

32 "Redacted personal notes of Richard Roy," Arar Inquiry, Exhibit P-206, p. 23.

33 Arar Report, Factual Background, vol. 1, p. 309. The government redacted part of a sentence in the Arar Report that showed that Cabana also said at this meeting that he wanted "more detailed information from the Syrians ... relative to their interview" of El Maati and Almalki. This is part of what was revealed in the Arar Inquiry's addendum to the report after the government lost its fight to keep it secret. Arar Report, Addendum, Factual Background, vol. 1, p. 309.

34 Arar Report, Factual Background, vol. 1, p. 309.

35 Ibid., p. 311.

Fourteen: "Your Guys Knew"

1 Arar Report, Factual Background, vol. 1, p. 284.
2 Patti Edgar, "Canadian held in Syria is no terrorist: Colleagues," *Montreal Gazette*, November 2, 2002, A14.
3 Testimony of Bill Graham at the Arar Inquiry, May 30, 2005, transcript pp. 4148–49.
4 Arar Report, Factual Background, vol. 1, p. 298.
5 Testimony of Bill Graham at the Arar Inquiry, May 30, 2005, pp. 4109–10.
6 Ibid., pp. 4149–50.
7 Arar Report, Factual Background, vol. 1, p. 298.
8 See alert on the FBI's website at www.fbi.gov/terrorinfo/elmaati.htm.
9 David Guy, "FBI seeks Canadian terror suspect: Authorities vague on reasons for year-long delay in seeking shadowy Kuwaiti immigrant," *Ottawa Citizen*, November 13, 2002, A4; [unauthored] "FBI won't explain sudden interest in terrorism suspect," *Edmonton Journal*, November 13, 2002, A6.
10 Michael Higgins, "FBI seeks terror suspect with Toronto ID," *National Post*, November 14, 2002, A10.
11 Stephen Thorne, "Officials say missing Canadian citizen is al-Qaida held by Syrians," Canadian Press Newswire, November 14, 2002.
12 Stephen Thorne, telephone interview with author, June 10, 2008.
13 Mike Trickey, "FBI told RCMP Ottawa man had terror link: Embarrassed officials admit U.S. sent evidence about Maher Arar," *Ottawa Citizen*, November 18, 2002, A1. The article prompted the RCMP's superintendent, Wayne Pilgrim, to draft a briefing note for Commissioner Zaccardelli about "recent press reporting [that] has indicated RCMP involvement in the deportation and subsequent detention of Maher Arar." The memo is heavily censored, but the Arar Inquiry would later reveal that in it, Proulx warned the commissioner that, given the RCMP's exchange of information with the Americans before Ahmad's departure from Canada, the RCMP can be seen as complicit in Ahmad's detention. Proulx later said that what he meant by this was that the media might see the RCMP as complicit. See Arar Report, Factual Background, vol. 1, pp. 64 and 301; "Briefing note to the Commissioner" from Wayne Pilgrim, November 21, 2002, Arar Inquiry, Exhibit P-83.
14 Mike Trickey, "FBI told RCMP Ottawa man had terror link: Embarrassed officials admit U.S. sent evidence about Maher Arar," *Ottawa Citizen*, November 18, 2002, A1.

15 This and subsequent quotations from the House of Commons question period are found in 37th Parliament, 2nd Session, Edited Hansard, number 026, November 18, 2002.

16 "Foreign Affairs distances itself from Maher Arar," CTV, *CTV News*, November 18, 2002.

17 "No shortage of questions about Canadian being held in Syria," CBC, *The National*, November 18, 2002.

18 37th Parliament, 2nd Session, Edited Hansard, number 027, November 19, 2002.

19 Ibid.

20 James Bissett, "Our timid anti-terrorism: The Maher Arar affair shows that Canada still doesn't take the danger seriously, says James Bissett," guest column, *Ottawa Citizen*, November 20, 2002, A17.

21 Allan Thompson, "Terrorism link in dispute," *Toronto Star*, November 20, 2002, A27.

22 "Chronology of events," contained in email message from Myra Pastyr-Lupul to Badr El Maati, October 28, 2003, Arar Inquiry, Exhibit P-257.

23 Email from Myra Pastyr-Lupul to Reynald Doiron, November 19, 2008, Arar Inquiry, Exhibit P-104. Pastyr-Lupul clarified this on Pardy's behalf.

24 Jacques Bourbeau, interview with author, Ottawa, May 9, 2008.

25 Ibid.

Fifteen: "Dark Days"

1 Arar Report, Factual Background, vol. 1, pp. 499–500, 509.

2 Testimony of Michel Cabana at the Arar Inquiry, June 29, 2005, transcript pp. 7868–69; personal notes of Michel Cabana, Arar Inquiry, Exhibit P-166, p. 40.

3 Arar Report, Factual Background, vol. 1, p. 498.

4 Arar Report, Analysis and Recommendations, pp. 30, 140, and 157.

5 Ibid., p. 110.

6 Ibid., p. 111.

7 Ibid.

8 Michelle Shephard, *Guantanamo's Child: The Untold Story of Omar Khadr* (Mississauga: John Wiley and Sons Canada, 2008), 115.

9 Arar Report, Factual Background, vol. 1, p. 315.

10 This statement was blacked out in the Arar Inquiry's public report. The Government of Canada sought to keep it secret but lost its fight in court, so it appears in the addendum to the Arar Report, released in 2007.

11 Arar Report, Analysis and Recommendations, pp. 214–16.

12 Arar Report, Factual Background, vol. 1, p. 315.

13 In the ITO for the search warrants conducted on January 22, 2002, Walsh draws on his experience with drug traffickers to describe someone's use of a public internet space as "suspicious" (Walsh ITO, Arar Inquiry, Exhibit P-179).

14 Walsh ITO, Arar Inquiry, Exhibit P-179.

15 Gar Pardy interview with the author, April 8, 2008.

16 Arar Report, Factual Background, vol. 1, p. 319.

17 Alex Neve, email interview with author, June 9, 2008.

18 This was contained in a DFAIT memo written after the meeting, but several years later, in testimony before the Arar Inquiry, that official said he had expected Maher to be released before Christmas. Arar Report, Factual Background, vol. 1, p. 317.

19 Lee Greenberg, "'Canadians are losing their freedom': Wife of Ottawa man deported by U.S. to Syria tells public the nightmare she's experiencing should worry everyone," *Ottawa Citizen*, December 17, 2002, A3.

20 Ibid.

21 Emanuella Grinberg, "Alliance MP sorry his aide belittled Arar vigil invitation: Cummins' assistant replied 'get a life' to boss's e-mail," *Ottawa Citizen*, December 18, 2002, D8.

22 Arar Report, Factual Background, vol. 1, p. 343.

23 Ibid.

24 Arar Report, Analysis and Recommendations, p. 211.

25 Arar Report, Factual Background, vol. 1, p. 344.

26 At the request of Gar Pardy, a diplomatic note about Abdullah was sent to the Syrians on August 14, 2002. It was followed up on again two weeks later, but there was no reply.

27 Arar Report, Factual Background, vol. 1, p. 343.

28 Arar Report, Analysis and Recommendations, pp. 211–12. Note that government witnesses at the Arar Inquiry almost always used the word mistreatment rather than torture.

29 Ibid.

30 Arar Report, Factual Background, vol. 1, p. 344.

31 Ibid.

32 In the Arar Inquiry's report, Justice O'Connor pointed out that by this time, the threat the RCMP had been investigating—a plot to blow up the Parliament buildings—was over a year old. In addition, both of the main targets of the investigation had been in detention for months. So the threat was not "imminent." See Arar Report, Analysis and Recommendations, p. 13.

33 Arar Report, Factual Background, vol. 1, p. 344.

34 Ibid.

35 Ibid., p. 340.

36 Ibid., p. 341.

37 Arar Report, Analysis and Recommendations, p. 212.

38 Gar Pardy, interview with author, Ottawa, April 8, 2008.

Sixteen: One-Way Window

1 Gar Pardy, interview with author, Ottawa, April 8, 2008.

2 Ibid.

3 Arar Report, Analysis and Recommendations, pp. 214–15.

4 Ibid., pp. 204–05. Graham would later testify that he did not remember why the phone call had been postponed.

5 Arar Report, Factual Background, vol. 1, p. 332.

6 Ibid., p. 335.

7 Hijazi was sentenced to death but had his sentence commuted to twenty years of imprisonment with hard labour. See Amnesty International, "Jordan: 'Your confessions are ready for you to sign'; Detention and torture of political suspects," July 24, 2006, www.amnesty.org/en/library/info/MDE16/005/2006.

8 Faisal Kutty, email interview with author, July 7, 2008.

9 Maher Arar, "A modified constant modulus algorithm enters the scene," Wireless Systems Design, April 2003: 35.

10 Testimony by Marlene Catterall, Arar Inquiry, May 31, 2005, transcript pp. 4547–4548.

11 Arar Report, Factual Background, vol. 1, p. 351.

12 Ibid.

13 Ibid., p. 354.

14 Ibid., p. 354.

Seventeen: The American Resolve Effect

1 Briefing note to RCMP commissioner Zaccardelli from Sergeant Reynolds, April 30, 2003, Arar Inquiry, Exhibit P-79. See also testimony of Wayne Easter at the Arar Inquiry, June 3, 2005, transcript pp. 5204–06 and Arar Report, Factual Background, vol. 1, pp. 364–65.

2. Ibid.

3 Department of Foreign Affairs and International Trade, Case note 02-DMCUS-851152, April 26, 2003.

4 "Action memorandum for the Minister of Foreign Affairs," from Gar Pardy, April 7, 2003, Arar Inquiry, Exhibit P-238.

5 Email message from Gar Pardy to Monia Mazigh, April 12, 2003, Arar Report, Factual Background, vol. 1, p. 360.
6 Arar Report, Factual Background, vol. 1, p. 364.
7 Ibid., p. 365.
8 Testimony of Gar Pardy at the Arar Inquiry, May 25, 2005, transcript p. 3696.
9 Arar Report, Factual Background, vol. 1, p. 369.
10 The author was at this meeting as well.
11 Arar Report, Factual Background, vol. 1, p. 374.
12 Jeff Sallot, "PM vows help for Canadian held in Syria," *Globe and Mail*, June 26, 2003, A4.
13 Arar Report, Factual Background, vol. 1, p. 375.
14 Ibid., pp. 377–78.
15 Ibid., p. 375.
16 Ibid., p. 379.

Eighteen: Smear Campaign

1 Sheldon Alberts, "'Canada's al-Qaeda' still behind bars: Only five of seven alleged suspects known to public," *Ottawa Citizen*, July 4, 2003, A5.
2 Alan Freeman and Colin Freeze, "Second Canadian held in Syrian prison," *Globe and Mail*, July 7, 2003, A6.
3 Seymour Hersh, "The Syrian bet: Did the Bush administration burn a useful source on Al Qaeda?" *New Yorker*, July 28, 2003, www. newyorker.com/archive/2003/07/28/030728fa_fact?currentPage=1 (accessed May 1, 2008).
4 Bob Fife, "Al-Qaeda Ottawa plot foiled: U.S.; Tipoff from Syria bears fruit; 'Bad guys got arrested'; Sources say terrorist objective was to at least kill Marines guarding diplomatic site," July 25, 2003, A1.
5 Ibid.
6 Testimony of Flynt Leverett at the Arar Inquiry, November 10, 2005, transcript pp. 12430. Leverett, called to testify in support of Pillarella and Martel, testified that it was reasonable that Pillarella had not assumed that Maher had been tortured despite being held incommunicado by the Syrian Military Intelligence.
7 James Gordon, "Gadfly journalist's memory can be hazy, but opinions are firm: Pulitzer Prize–winner Seymour Hersh admits he was wrong about a plot to bomb the U.S. Embassy in Ottawa, but he has other interesting theories," *Ottawa Citizen*, October 21, 2005, A7.
8 Arar Report, Analysis and Recommendations, pp. 257, 258.

9 Robert Fife, telephone interview with author, June 12, 2008.

10 In the Arar Report, Justice O'Connor found that Fife's story was just one in a series in which "government officials took it upon themselves to leak information to the media, much of which was unfair to Mr. Arar and damaging to his reputation." He wrote:

> over a period of time, Government of Canada officials intentionally released selected classified information about Mr. Arar or his case to the media…. Typically, the leaked information was attributed to an unnamed government official, an official closely involved in the case, or some similar source…. Several of the leaks were inaccurate, unsupported by the information available from the investigations, and grossly unfair to Mr. Arar…. Quite predictably, the leaks had a devastating effect on Mr. Arar's reputation and on him personally. The impact on an individual's reputation of being called a terrorist in the national media is severe. As I have stated elsewhere, labels, even unfair and inaccurate ones, have a tendency to stick. Professor Toope, the fact-finder I appointed to report on the circumstances of Mr. Arar's detention in Syria, has indicated that the leaks have had severe psychological and emotional impacts on Mr. Arar. Moreover, Mr. Arar, an educated, hard-working engineer, has had great difficulty finding employment. It seems likely that the smear of his reputation by the leakors has taken its toll.

See Arar Report, Analysis and Recommendations, p. 46.

11 Monia Mazigh, "Where's the evidence?" Letter to the editor, *National Post*, July 26, 2003, A17.

12 Robert Fife, "PM asks Syria to free terror suspect: Ottawa man was intercepted while en route to Canada," *National Post*, July 29, 2003, A1.

13 James Bissett, "Why our allies don't trust us," *National Post*, July 31, 2003, A14.

14 Robert Fife, "Chrétien wants to know who gave up Ottawa man to CIA, Syria: Rogue elements in RCMP not out of the question, solicitor general admits," *Ottawa Citizen*, July 30, 2003, A1.

15 Testimony of Wayne Easter at the Arar Inquiry, June 3, 2005, transcript pp. 5244–48.

16 Appendix B of an affidavit in support of application for a search warrant, Corporal Daniel Quirion, paragraph 13, Arar Inquiry, Exhibit P-187.

17 Testimony of Wayne Easter at the Arar Inquiry, June 3, 2005, transcript pp. 5252–53.

18 Robert Fife, "U.S. denies RCMP aided in Arar's deportation," *National Post*, August 1, 2003, A3.

Nineteen: 3' x 6' x 7'

1 Letter to Monia Mazigh from Saleem el-Hasan, Syrian Human Rights Committee, July 29, 2003. It is curious that the description more accurately describes how Abdullah was treated. This would be an easy mistake to make on the part of the source—both were known as Canadians, and neither were ever referred to by name at Far' Falastin.
2 Author's notes from news conference, August 7, 2003.
3 Anne Dawson, with files from Erin Conway-Smith, "Canadian tortured in Syrian jail: Rights group; Canada vows to investigate allegations Ottawa man was beaten, shocked," *Ottawa Citizen*, August 7, 2003, A1.
4 Ibid.
5 Alexander Panetta, "Wife of man held in Syria asks Chrétien to play diplomatic hardball," Canadian Press Newswire, August 7, 2003.
6 Arar Report, Factual Background, vol. 1, p. 385.
7 Arar Report, Analysis and Recommendations, p. 236.
8 Ibid.
9 These journalists spoke with the author as well as Monia.
10 Arar Report, Factual Background, vol. 1, p. 393.
11 Arar Report, Analysis and Recommendations, p. 240.
12 Email from the Canadian Embassy in Damascus to DFAIT in Ottawa, August 14, 2003, Arar Inquiry, Exhibit P-134, tab 25.
13 Testimony of Leo Martel at the Arar Inquiry, August 30, 2005, transcript p. 11150 (translation in the transcript from the French).
14 Sednaya prison can be seen on Google Earth at these coordinates: 33 39 54.11N; 36 19 45.71 E.
15 Syrian Human Rights Committee, *Sednaya Prison: The Continual Human Tragedy; When Will the Chronic Series of Detention in Syrian Come to an End?* June 1, 2004, www.shrc.org/data/aspx/d9/1749.aspx (accessed May 1, 2008).

Twenty: "You Are Safe Now"

1 After his release in January 2004, Ahmad was diagnosed during a medical examination as having had severe bronchitis for four to five months.
2 This and subsequent quotations taken from this meeting are found in Evidence, Standing Committee on Foreign Affairs and International Trade, 37th Parliament, 2nd Session, September 25,

2003. Proulx's testimony is a translation in the Evidence from the French. http://cmte.parl.gc.ca/cmte/CommitteePublication.aspx? SourceId=61410&Lang=1&PARLSES=372&JNT=0&COM=3272 (accessed May 1, 2008).

3 Arar Report, Factual Background, vol. 1, p. 407; Kathleen Harris, "Feds get nowhere with Syria: Access to Canuck trial unsure," *Toronto Sun*, September 26, 2003, 39.

4 Arar Report, Factual Background, vol. 1, p. 407.

5 Ibid., vol. 2, p. 503.

6 The author was present. The government initially resisted Monia's request that the vehicle be large enough to hold her children, her mother, and her supporters. Monia wanted her supporters there to help field questions from reporters. She wanted Maher to see his family as soon as possible and knew the media attention would be intense.

7 Jeff Sallot, "Arar thanks Canadians, Ottawa rules out inquiry," *Globe and Mail*, October 7, 2003, A1; Juliet O'Neill, "Maher Arar released: 'I am very glad to be back home,'" *Ottawa Citizen*, October 7, 2003, A5; Miro Cernetig and Graham Fraser, "Arar arrives home as new questions fly; Canadian citizen spent a year in Syrian prison Solicitor-General dismisses demands for public inquiry," *Toronto Star*, October 7, 2003, A1.

8 This and subsequent quotations from press conference taken from author's notes.

9 Cernetig and Fraser, "Arar arrives home as new questions fly."

10 This and subsequent quotations taken from this meeting are found in Evidence, Standing Committee on Foreign Affairs and International Trade, 37th Parliament, 2nd Session, October 7, 2003, time range 12:05–12:40.http://cmte.parl.gc.ca/cmte/Committee Publication.aspx?SourceId=64032&Lang=1&PARLSES=372&JNT =0&COM=3272 (accessed April 1, 2008).

11 Sandra Cordon, "Demands continue for independent inquiry into Arar jailing in Syria," Canadian Press Newswire, October 8, 2003.

12 Graham Fraser, "U.S. urged Canada to hold Arar: Canada refused to make arrest; Americans sent him to Syria; Arar watched because of Afghanistan trips," *Toronto Star*, October 9, 2003, A1.

13 See Chapter 12; see also Arar Report, Factual Background, vol. 1, pp. 168–69.

14 Jeff Sallot, "Arar was not tortured, officials say: Engineer held in 'very bad' conditions, suffered psychological stress," *Globe and Mail*, October 10, 2003, A1.

15 Jeff Sallot, email interview with author, June 12, 2008.

16 Arar Report, Factual Background, vol. 2, p. 473.

17 Arar Report, Analysis and Recommendations, p. 258.

18 Kathleen Harris and Stephanie Rubec, "Arar pals allegedly linked to terror," *Ottawa Sun,* October 10, 2003.

19 "The case of Maher Arar takes more twists and turns," CTV, *CTV News*, October 23, 2003.

20 Craig Oliver, phone interview with author, June 11, 2008.

21 Arar Report, Factual Background, vol. 2, pp. 492–93.

22 Ibid., p. 487.

23 Arar Report, Analysis and Recommendations, p. 258.

24 Briefing note to the commissioner, October 23, 2003, Arar Inquiry, Exhibit P-84, p. 96.

25 Testimony of Garry Loeppky at the Arar Inquiry, July 27, 2005, transcript pp. 8646–47.

26 Craig Oliver, phone interview with author, June 11, 2008.

27 Bill Gertz, "Al Qaeda pursued a 'dirty bomb,'" Washington Times, October 16, 2003, www.washtimes.com/news/2003/oct/16/20031016-110337-4698r/.

28 Khalid Sheikh Mohammed was captured in Pakistan in March 2003 and held by the CIA in undisclosed locations for two years. He was reportedly subjected to simulated drowning, or "waterboarding," before confessing. See Jane Mayer, "The black sites: A rare look inside the C.I.A.'s secret interrogation program," *New Yorker*, August 13, 2007.

29 Joan Walters, "Al-Qaeda story sparks Mac alert: RCMP dismisses nuclear 'bomb' scare," *Hamilton Spectator*, October 18, 2003, A1. See also Adrian Humphreys and Michael Friscolanti, "McMaster dismisses terror threat: No evidence al-Qaeda suspect had access to university's reactor," *Ottawa Citizen*, October 18, 2003, A5, and *National Post*, October 18, 2003, A6.

30 Joan Walters, "Al-Qaeda story sparks Mac alert: RCMP dismisses nuclear 'bomb' scare," *Hamilton Spectator*, October 18, 2003, A1.

31 Adrian Humphreys, "McMaster's atomic PR fight: An Ontario university is suing a U.S. author who alleges the school has lax nuclear security," *National Post*, April 21, 2007, A7.

32 Ibid.

33 Ibid.

Twenty-One: "It Is in Allah's Hands"

1 Statement by Maher Arar, November 4, 2003, Ottawa.

2 Jacques Bourbeau, interview with author, Ottawa, May 9, 2008.

3   "Hold an Inquiry into the Arar case," editorial, *Globe and Mail*, November 5, 2003, A24.

4   Arar Report, Factual Background, vol. 2, pp. 482–83.

5   37th Parliament, 2nd Session, Edited Hansard, number 151, November 5, 2003.

6   Dennis Bueckert, "Graham furious at leaks linking Canadian Maher Arar with al-Qaida," Canadian Press Newswire, October 30, 2003.

7   Susan Riley, "Maher Arar's story demands a sequel," *Ottawa Citizen*, November 5, 2003, A18.

8   Hugh Winsor, "What Canada owes Mr. Arar," *Globe and Mail*, November 5, 2003, A1.

9   See John Cassidy, "A scientist's death, a reporter's credibility, and the unravelling of Tony Blair's case for war," *New Yorker*, December 8, 2004, hwww.newyorker.com/archive/2003/12/08/031208fa_fact2?currentPage=1.

10 This conversation was between the author and O'Neill on November 7, 2003.

11 Juliet O'Neill, "Canada's dossier on Maher Arar: The existence of a group of Ottawa men with alleged ties to al-Qaeda is at the root of why the government opposes an inquiry into the case. Juliet O'Neill reports," *Ottawa Citizen*, November 8, 2003, A1.

12 Arar Report, Factual Background, vol. 2, pp. 487–88.

13 Juliet O'Neill, phone interview with the author, July 17, 2008.

14 Arar Report, Analysis and Recommendations, p. 260.

15 Juliet O'Neill, "Canada's dossier on Maher Arar."

16 "Prisoner's brother begs for his release," *Winnipeg Free Press*, November 6, 2003, A15.

17 Kate Jaimet, "Prisoner's family shocked by Arar's revelations," CanWest News Service, November 4, 2003.

18 Curt Petrovich, "A family appeal for another Canadian in a Syrian prison. The family of a Syrian born Canadian is demanding Ottawa do something to win his release. Abdullah Almalki has been held without charge," CBC Radio, *World Report*, November 5, 2003.

19 Kate Jaimet, "Second Canadian in Syrian jail has no terror links, wife says: Khuzaimah Kalifah plans to return to Canada to fight for Almalki's release," *Ottawa Citizen*, November 8, 2003, A5.

20 Letter from Michael Edelson to Corporal Randy Walsh of A-O Canada, June 30, 2003.

21 Letter from Michael Edelson to Inspector Warren Coons, November 28, 2003.

22 Letter to Khuzaimah Almalki from Prime Minister Jean Chrétien, November 25, 2003.

23 Letter from Abdullah's son to Prime Minister Paul Martin, December 19, 2003.
24 "Man demands Ottawa help son tortured in Syria before being jailed in Egypt," Canadian Press Newswire, 13 November 2003.

Twenty-Two: "We Are Not a Police State"

1 Dana Priest, "Top justice aide approved sending suspect to Syria," *Washington Post*, November 19, 2003, A28.
2 Sheldon Alberts, "U.S. broke no laws deporting Arar: Ashcroft: Meets with Easter," *National Post*, November 20, 2003, A2.
3 Ibid.
4 Dana Priest, "Man was deported after Syrian assurances," *Washington Post*, November 20, 2003, A24.
5 Statement of Richard L. Skinner, Inspector General, U.S. Department of Homeland Security before a Joint Hearing of the Subcommittee on the Constitution, Civil Rights and Civil Liberties Committee on the Judiciary and the Subcommittee on International Organizations, Human Rights and Oversight Committee on Foreign Affairs, U.S. House of Representatives, June 5, 2008, 6, www.dhs.gov/xoig/assets/testimony/OIGtm_RLS_060508a.pdf (accessed May 1, 2008).
6 Anne Dawson, "Martin opens door to Arar inquiry," CanWest News Service, November 25, 2003.
7 Arar Report, Factual Background, vol. 2, p. 484.
8 "Graham rules out inquiry into Maher Arar case," Canadian Press Newswire, December 22, 2003.
9 As quoted in Anne Dawson, "No sign of wrongdoing in Arar case, Martin says: Some facts may be kept secret for security reasons," *National Post*, December 24, 2003, A4.
10 Robert Fife, "Officials link Arar to Qaeda camp: Family says claim is part of smear campaign by anonymous officials, demands inquiry," *National Post*, December 30, 2003, A1.
11 Maher Arar, statement to the media, December 31, 2003.
12 Peter Mansbridge, "Year-end interview with Prime Minister Paul Martin," CBC, *The National*, December 23, 2003.
13 Juliet O'Neill, "'It felt like slow-motion robbery,'" *Ottawa Citizen*, January 23, 2004, A1.
14 Kate Jaimet, "Arar lawyer calls raid an attempt to intimidate the media," CanWest News Service, January 21, 2004.
15 O'Neill, "'It felt like slow-motion robbery.'"
16 Ibid.

17 Appendix B of an affidavit in support of application for a search warrant, Corporal Daniel Quirion, paragraph 20, Arar Inquiry, Exhibit P-187.

18 Bruce Garvey, "RCMP raids on reporter's home, office spark wave of protest," CanWest News Service, January 21, 2004.

19 Jim Bronskill and Sue Bailey, "RCMP searches journalist's home and office for leaked Arar material," Canadian Press Newswire, January 22, 2004.

20 Mark Kennedy, Mike Blanchfield, and Anne Dawson, "O'Neill 'clearly' no criminal: PM: 'We are not a police state,' Martin insists; Charges now unlikely," *Ottawa Citizen*, January 23, 2004, A1.

21 Robert Fife, "PM denies accusations feds okayed deportation," *Montreal Gazette*, January 23, 2004, A12.

22 Commission for Public Complaints Against the RCMP, Media advisory, January 26, 2004.

Twenty-Three: The Fourth Canadian into Far' Falastin

1 Author has recreated Muayyed Nureddin's story based on interviews conducted in person and by phone in the spring and summer of 2008, his public statements, and notes taken in interviews with his lawyer.

2 "Arsalan" is a pseudonym.

3 "Efa" is a pseudonym.

4 Author has recreated the dialogue based on Muayyed Nureddin's description. The conversation took place in Arabic.

5 Mahmoud Jaballah, an Egyptian citizen and father of six, says he was repeatedly detained and tortured in Egypt before seeking asylum in Canada in 1996. He was detained in 1999 after CSIS accused him of having links to al-Qaeda, released nine months later for lack of evidence, and detained again in August 2001. He is one of five men accused of links to terrorism and being held on security certificates, federally issued certificates allowing non-Canadians to be held in custody pending deportation. Courts have blocked his deportation to Egypt because of the risk of torture. Mahmoud was detained for six years before being released subject to strict bail conditions, including almost total house arrest. In March 2007, the Supreme Court of Canada ruled that the security certificate regime was unconstitutional and gave the government one year to find a solution. In 2008, the government set up a regime allowing "special advocates" to see the secret information that CSIS says is behind the allegations against these men.

6   Muayyed's friend has requested his name not be published. "Yilmaz" is a pseudonym.

7   Founded in September 2001, Ansar al-Islam fi Kurdistan (Supporters of Islam in Kurdistan) is among the many Sunni Islamist groups fighting for control of the Kurdish-controlled regions of Northern Iraq. Their main rival is the Patriotic Union of Kurdistan (PUK). After 9/11, the Bush administration said it believed that Ansar al-Islam was Saddam Hussein's link to al-Qaeda. See Human Rights Watch, "Background on the crisis in Iraq: Ansar al-Islam in Iraqi Kurdistan," www.hrw.org/backgrounder/mena/ansarbk020503.htm (accessed July 8, 2008).

8   "ZJGR0112: Syria: (NUREDDIN) MUAYYED," email from the Canadian embassy in Syria to Graeme McIntyre, January 14, 2004, Arar Inquiry, Exhibit P-245.

9   Stewart Bell, "Canadian home after month in Syrian prison: Former Islamic school principal arrested on Iraq trip," *National Post*, January 16, 2004, A2.

10 Letter from Irene Khan to Prime Minister Paul Martin, February 17, 2004. In author's files.

11 Statement by Muayyed Nureddin at a news conference, Toronto, February 25, 2004.

12 Thomas Walkom, "New torture claim shows Arar's case isn't unique," *Toronto Star*, February 26, 2004, A1.

Twenty-Four: Release and Return

1   Michelle Shephard, "Man's detention ordeal over; Returns to Toronto after being held 2 years in Syria, Egypt may provide a vital link in upcoming inquiry into Arar case," *Toronto Star*, March 30, 2004, A10.

Twenty-Five: "Abundance of Caution"

1   CNN, "Transcript: Ashcroft, Mueller news conference," May 26, 2004, www.cnn.com/2004/US/05/26/terror.threat.transcript/ (accessed June 7, 2008).

2   Ibid.

3   Ibid.

4   Richard W. Stevenson and Eric Lichtblau, "As Ashcroft warns of Qaeda plan to attack U.S., some question the threat and its timing," *New York Times*, May 27, 2004.

5   Ravi Baichwal, "Reassuring Canadians there is no immediate terror threat here," interview by Lloyd Robertson, CTV, *CTV News*, May 26, 2004.

6 Sheldon Alberts, with files from Sean Gordon and Susan Riley, "Two Canadians on FBI list of terrorists plotting attacks," *Ottawa Citizen*, May 27, 2004, A1.

7 Michael Friscolante, "Arar linked to wanted Canadian," *National Post*, May 27, 2004, A4.

8 Colin Freeze, "Search continues for elusive terrorism suspect," *Globe and Mail*, May 28, 2004.

9 Kevin Connor, "Suspect's dad lives in Toronto: Cops likely to quiz father about alleged al-Qaida plotter," *Toronto Sun*, May 28, 2004, 59.

10 Ibid.

11 Testimony of Senator Pierre de Bané at the Arar Inquiry, June 1, 2005, transcript pp. 4660–62. (Translation in transcript from the French.)

12 Dan McTeague, interview with author (by phone), July 10, 2008.

13 Ibid.

14 Glenn Bradbury, interview with author (by phone), July 10, 2008.

15 Curt Petrovich, phone interview with author, June 27, 2008.

16 Ibid.

17 Ibid.

18 Abdullah Almalki, interview with Curt Petrovich, "Ottawa man facing Syrian military stint begs PM for help," CBC Radio, www.cbc.ca/canada/story/2004/07/27/almalki_syria040727.html (accessed June 9, 2008).

19 Canada Newswire transcript of the news conference held at the National Press Theatre, Ottawa, December 20, 2004.

20 Sean Gordon, "Censors black out CSIS report on Arar: Government turning public inquiry into private probe, chief counsel says," *Ottawa Citizen*, December 21, 2004, A1.

21 Kathleen Harris, "Blacked-out Inquiry report a black mark; Arar 'shocked' by fed censorship of public probe into his jailing," *Ottawa Sun*, December 21, 2004, 7.

22 Arar Report, Analysis and Recommendations, p. 302. See also p. 296.

23 Arar Report, Factual Background, vol. 2, appendices, "Ruling on RCMP Testimony," p. 773.

24 Toope Report in Arar Report, Factual Background, vol. 2, Appendix 7, pp. 789–819.

25 "Joint Intervenors' Submission to the Commission of Inquiry into the Actions of Canadian Officials in Relation to Maher Arar," September 10, 2005, filed on behalf of Amnesty International Canada, the Association for the Prevention of Torture and the World

Organization against Torture (OMCT), the British Columbia Civil Liberties Association, Canadian Arab Federation, Canadian Islamic Congress, Canadian Labour Congress, Council of Canadians, Council on American Islamic Relations (Canada), International Civil Liberties Monitoring Group, International Coalition Against Torture, Law Union of Ontario, Minority Advocacy Rights Council, Muslim Canadian Congress, Muslim Community Council of Ottawa-Gatineau, National Council on Canada-Arab Relations, Polaris Institute, Redress Trust, p. 2.

26 Consular report emailed from the Canadian Embassy in Syria to DFAIT, Ottawa, October 23, 2002, Arar Inquiry, Exhibit P-42, tab 131.

27 Re-redacted version of the consular report emailed from the Canadian embassy in Syria to DFAIT Ottawa, October 23, 2002, Arar Inquiry, Exhibit P-134, tab 3.

28 Testimony of Mr. James Gould at the Arar Inquiry, August 24, 2005, transcript pp. 10398–99.

29 "Joint Intervenors' Submission to the Commission of Inquiry into the Actions of Canadian Officials in Relation to Maher Arar," September 10, 2005, www.bccla.org/othercontent/jointintervenor-submission.pdf.

30 Arar Report, Factual Background, vol. 1, p. 62.

31 Arar Report, Analysis and Recommendations, p. 303.

32 Ibid.

33 Jeff Sallot, interview with author, Ottawa, April 19, 2008.

34 Jeff Sallot, "It was hyped as a TERRORIST map: It was cited by Egyptian TORTURERS; It is a VISITOR'S GUIDE to Ottawa," *Globe and Mail*, September 6, 2005, A1–A5.

35 Ibid., A5.

36 Jeff Sallot interview with author, Ottawa, April 19, 2008.

37 Ibid.

38 Ibid.

39 Ibid.

40 Arar Report, Analysis and Recommendations, p. 59.

41 Ibid., p. 115.

42 Ibid., pp. 274–75.

43 Ibid., pp. 275–76.

44 "Consideration of Reports Submitted by States Parties under Article 40 of the Covenant: Concluding Observations of the Human Rights Committee, Canada, CCPR/CO/85/CAN," para.16, p. 4, www.unhchr.ch/tbs/doc.nsf/0/7616e3478238be01c12570ae00397f5d/$FILE/G0641362.pdf (accessed June 1, 2008).

45 Arar Report, Analysis and Recommendations, p. 278.

Afterword: "The Lucky Ones"

1 Darius Rejali uses the term *stealth torture* to describe "painful physical torture that leaves few marks" and writes about how the demand for this kind of torture is increasing. See Darius Rejali, *Torture and Democracy* (New Jersey: Princeton University Press, 2007), 406.

2 Letter from Dr. Donald E. Payne, M.D., F.R.C.P. (C), psychiatry, to Dr. James H. Choi, October 27, 2005, p. 1. In author's files.

3 For a comprehensive overview of physical and psychological impacts of torture, see *The Manual on Effective Investigation and Documentation of Torture and Other Cruel, Inhuman or Degrading Treatment or Punishment* (known as the Istanbul Protocol), www.unhchr.ch/pdf/8istprot.pdf. This United Nations document provides international guidelines for documentation of torture and its consequences.

4 Letter from Dr. George A. Fraser, M.D., F.R.C.P.C, medical director, Ottawa Trauma and Anxiety Clinic, to Ms. Jasminka Kalajdzic, counsel to Abdullah Almalki, "Re. Abdullah Almalki," December 21, 2005, p. 1. In author's files.

5 Speech by Abdullah's daughter (name withheld on request), as part of the May 1–8, 2008, "Caravan against Torture," All Saints Anglican Church, Ottawa, May 7, 2008.

6 Michelle Shephard, "Mississauga man detained: Father's name on U.S. no-fly list; Fighter jets follow Air Transat flight," *Toronto Star*, January 7, 2006, A1.

7 Michelle Shephard, phone and email interviews with the author, June 26, 2008.

8 Karen Howlett, "U.S. clears Canadian for takeoff: No-fly list corrected, but anguish lingers," *Globe and Mail*, September 27, 2006, A9. The RCMP later interviewed Kahil and asked him whether he'd travelled to Panama. Kahil demonstrated this would have been impossible. Soon after, he received the letter saying his name had been removed from the list. Neither the RCMP or U.S. officials ever gave any explanation as to why he had been put on the no-fly list in the first place, or whether the RCMP had supplied faulty information to the United States.

9 Arar Report, Analysis and Recommendations, p. 47.

10 Author's notes from the conference.

11 David Rohde, "A nation challenged: Kabul; In 2 abandoned Kabul houses, some hints of Al Qaeda presence," *New York Times*, November 17, 2001.

12 Arar Report, Analysis and Recommendations, pp. 46–47.

13 Ibid., p. 262.

14 Jeff Sallot, Interview with the author, Ottawa, April 19, 2008.

15 Ibid.

16 Alex Neve, phone interview with the author, July 8, 2008.

17 See "Convention against Torture and Other Cruel, Inhuman or Degrading Treatment or Punishment," www.unhchr.ch/html/menu3 / b/h_cat39.htm, and the International Covenant on Civil and Political Rights, www.unhchr.ch/html/menu3/b/a_ccpr.htm (accessed June 1, 2008).

18 Alex Neve, phone interview with the author, July 7, 2008.

19 Testimony of Peter Burns at the Arar Inquiry, June 8, 2005, transcript p. 5934.

20 Alex Neve, phone interview with the author, July 7, 2008.

21 Ibid.

22 Ibid.

23 "About the Inquiry," Internal Inquiry into the Actions of Canadian Officials in Relation to Abdullah Almalki, Ahmad Abou-Elmaati and Muayyed Nureddin, www.iacobucciinquiry.ca/en/home.htm (accessed July 1, 2008).

24 Warren Allmand, Nehal Bhuta, Alex Neve, and Sameer Zuberi, op-ed drafted in July 2008 for publication.

25 Alex Neve, phone interview with the author, July 7, 2008.

26 Dr. Donald E. Payne, M.D., F.R.C.P. (C), psychiatry, phone interview with the author, July 5, 2008.

27 Arar Report, Analysis and Recommendations, p. 61.

28 Gar Pardy, interview with author, Ottawa, March 31, 2008.

29 Dan McTeague, phone interview with the author, July 10, 2008.

30 Gar Pardy, interview with author, Ottawa, March 31, 2008.

31 James Travers, "Zaccardelli rides into African sunset," *Toronto Star*, May 22, 2008, AA08.

32 Alex Neve, phone interview with the author, July 7, 2008.

33 Gar Pardy, interview with the author, Ottawa, July 10, 2008.

34 A New Review Mechanism for the RCMP's National Security Activities (Ottawa: Public Works and Government Services Canada, 2006), www.ararcommission.ca.

35 Letter from Public Safety Minister Stockwell Day to Alex Neve, Amnesty International, April 10, 2008. In author's files.

36 Andrew Thompson, "Government slow to implement findings of Arar Inquiry: Expert; Adviser says probe focused too much on ethics, not enough on effectiveness," *Ottawa Citizen*, May 31, 2008, A7.

37 Alex Neve, phone interview with the author, July 7, 2008.

38 Colin Freeze, "Surveillance: Balancing national security and civil liberties; State agents say inquests causing 'judicial terrorism,'" *Globe and Mail*, June 9, 2007, A4.

39 See the Bennata Coalition for a Public Review, http://benamarbenatta.com, and Andrew Duffy, "Five lost years: How Benamar Benatta 'disappeared' after 9/11," *Ottawa Citizen*, January 26, 2008, B1.

40 Paul Koring, "Diplomats knew of his torture, Canadian says; CSIS agents were sent to Sudan to interrogate Abdelrazik while officials ignored abuse at prison, documents suggest," *Globe and Mail*, June 24, 2008, A13.

41 See Stephen Grey, *Ghost Plane: The True Story of the CIA Torture Program* (New York: St. Martin's Press, 2006).

42 Stephen Grey, "The agonizing truth about CIA renditions," Salon.com, November 5, 2007, www.salon.com/opinion/feature/2007/11/05/rendition/index.html (accessed July 1, 2008).

43 Haitham al-Maleh, phone interview with the author, July 6, 2008.

44 Walid Saffour, phone interview with the author, April 14, 2008.

CAST OF CHARACTERS

Ibrahym Adam Author's pseudonym for a Montreal businessman who knows Abdullah Almalki, Ahmed El Maati, and Maher Arar. Questioned by CSIS after 9/11. Home and business searched January 2002. Has never been charged with a crime.

Bashar al-Assad Became Syrian president in June 2000 after the death of his father, former president Hafez al-Assad.

Abdullah Almalki Canadian detained at the Damascus airport on May 3, 2002. Imprisoned in "grave" at Far' Falastin for 482 days. Transferred to Sednaya prison in August 2003. Released March 10, 2004, after more than twenty-two months in detention. Has never been charged with a crime.

Youssef Almalki Abdullah Almalki's youngest brother. Questioned by RCMP on January 22, 2002. Spoke to media on behalf of family.

Samira al-Shallash Mother of Ahmad and Amr El Maati. Travelled with Ahmad on his way to Syria before he was detained. Visited him several times while he was in Egyptian detention. Currently lives with Ahmad in Toronto.

Maher Arar Canadian detained in New York in September 26, 2002. Rendered by the CIA to Jordan, then Syria. Kept in "grave" at Far' Falastin for ten months and ten days, then moved to Sednaya prison August 2003. Released October 5, 2003, after 361 days in Syrian detention. Exonerated by the Arar Inquiry.

John Ashcroft U.S. attorney general. His deputy signed Arar's removal order. Ultimately responsible for Arar's extraordinary rendition to Syria. Held May 2004 news conference accusing Amr El Maati as a terrorist threat.

Sarkis Assadourian One of two Canadian Members of Parliament who travelled to Syria to see Arar in April 2003. Was at Dorval airport when Arar arrived home.

Stuart Bale Consul in Canadian Embassy in Egypt. Visited El Maati several times in Egyptian detention.

Randy Buffam RCMP corporal who arrived at Arar's home on January 22, 2002, and requested an interview with Arar.

George W. Bush U.S. president who declared the "war on terror" and oversaw U.S. anti-terrorism initiatives, including the extraordinary rendition program.

Michel Cabana Led the RCMP's Project A-O Canada from October 5, 2001, to February 4, 2003. Promoted from inspector to superintendent when he left the project. Now assistant criminal operations officer for the province of Quebec.

Patrick Callaghan Staff sergeant seconded to Project A-O Canada from the Ottawa Police Service. Worked closely with the FBI. Part of the team who flew to Washington in May 2002 to give presentation about A-O Canada targets.

Marlene Catterall Arar's Member of Parliament. Travelled with MP Sarkis Assadourian to Syria to see Arar in April 2003. Was at Dorval airport when Arar arrived home.

Paul Cavalluzzo Lead commission counsel at the Arar Inquiry.

Paul Cellucci U.S. ambassador to Canada from April 2001 to March 2005. His public statements fuelled speculation that Canadian authorities approved Arar's removal to Syria.

Hon. Jean Chrétien Prime minister who oversaw implementation of Canadian national security initiatives after 9/11. In power while El Maati, Almalki, and Arar were detained and tortured (Nureddin was detained on Chrétien's last day as prime minister).

Garry Clement Criminal operations officer at the RCMP's "A" Division in Ottawa. Assigned Inspector Cabana to lead Project A-O Canada, declaring it an "open book" investigation. Actively sought access to El Maati in Syrian detention. Now chief of police in Cobourg, Ontario.

Warren Coons Officer in charge of the RCMP's Project A-O Canada beginning February 2003, continuing through the period that El Maati, Almalki, and Arar were in detention.

Kevin Corcoran Seconded to Project A-O Canada from the Ontario Provincial Police. Worked closely with the FBI. Part of the team who flew to Washington in May 2002 to give presentation about A-O Canada targets.

Steve Covey RCMP liaison officer for the Middle East while El Maati and Almalki were detained in Syria, and while El Maati was transferred to Egypt. Met with General Khalil on July 4, 2002. Replaced by Dennis Fiorido in July 2002.

Antoine Couture Officer in charge of "A" Division's Criminal Operations unit. Received daily situation reports from A-O Canada.

Brian Davis Replaced Franco Pillarella as Canadian ambassador to Syria beginning in the summer of 2003. Attended Almalki's trial in Syria.

Hon. Stockwell Day Public Safety minister in the Conservative government. Called the "internal" Iacobucci Inquiry in December 2006, setting terms of reference. Yet to implement Arar Inquiry recommendations on oversight for national security agencies.

Hon. Wayne Easter Solicitor general from October 2002 to December 2003. Refused to sign on to a "one voice" letter to the Syrians about Arar.

Marlys Edwardh Co-counsel to Maher Arar at the Arar Inquiry.

Ward Elcock CSIS director from 1994 to May 2004, while El Maati, Almalki, Arar, and Nureddin were detained and tortured overseas. Now a senior adviser to the Privy Council Office.

Ahmad El Maati Canadian detained at the Damascus airport on November 12, 2001. Imprisoned in "grave" at Far' Falastin for seventy-four days. Rendered to Egypt on January 25, 2002. Released on January 11, 2004, after two years, two months, and two days in detention. Has never been charged with a crime. Whereabouts unknown.

Amr El Maati Ahmad El Maati's brother. Left for Pakistan in 1996, where he worked for the Health and Education Project, a charity run by Ahmed Said Khadr, then the Canadian government–funded Canadian Relief Foundation in Afghanistan. Implicated in Ahmad's false confession under torture in Syria in November 2001. Documents allegedly belonging to Amr were found in an apparent al-Qaeda safe house in Kabul. Neither Canada nor the United States appear to have issued a warrant for his arrest.

Badr El Maati Father to Ahmad and Amr El Maati.

Staff Sergeant Dennis Fiorido RCMP liaison officer for the Middle East from around July 10, 2002. Drafted cover letter for the questions for Almalki later delivered to Syrian interrogators.

Rick Flewelling Senior officer in the National Security Investigations Branch at RCMP headquarters. Played supervisory role to Project A-O Canada beginning in mid-June 2002. Spoke with the FBI in the lead-up to Arar's removal to Syria. Promoted from corporal to sergeant in April 2005.

Jim Gould Deputy director of DFAIT's Foreign Intelligence Division. Present for discussions about sending questions for Almalki to Syrian interrogators.

Hon. Bill Graham Minister of Foreign Affairs from January 2002 to July 2004, while El Maati, Almalki, Arar, and Nureddin were in detention.

Suleiman Haddad One of two Syrian deputy Foreign ministers who told Canadian ambassador Pillarella that CSIS said it did not want Arar back in Canada.

Hon. Stephen Harper As prime minister, issued a formal apology and compensation package to Arar. Oversaw appointment of retired Supreme Court Justice Frank Iacobucci to the Iacobucci Inquiry, and the formulation of the terms of reference.

Shirley Heafey Two-term chairperson of the Commission for Public Complaints for the RCMP from 1997 to October 2005. Began speaking out in 2002 to say the commission lacked sufficient powers to provide effective oversight of the RCMP's national security work.

Scott Heatherington Director of DFAIT's Security and Intelligence Bureau. Present for discussions about sending questions for Almalki to Syrian interrogators. Says he believed questions were never sent.

Jack Hooper Director general of CSIS Toronto regional office from 2000 to June 2002, then CSIS deputy director until retiring in April 2007. Provided information to the RCMP that led to the creation of Projects A and A-O Canada. Approved November 2002 CSIS visit to Syria.

Justice Frank Iacobucci Appointed as commissioner to the "Internal Inquiry" examining the role of Canadian officials in the cases of El Maati, Almalki, and Nureddin.

Barbara Jackman Counsel to El Maati and Nureddin.

Khuzaimah (surname withheld on request) Abdullah Almalki's wife. Stayed in Malaysia to care for their five children until returning to Ottawa in late 2003 to help fight for her husband's release.

Ahmed Said Khadr Egyptian Canadian who worked as the regional director of Human Concern International in Pakistan in the 1990s. Accused of financing terrorist attacks. Friend of bin Laden family. Target of Project O Canada in Toronto. Killed by Pakistani forces in October 2003.

General Hassan Khalil Head of the Syrian Military Intelligence until February 2005. Retired but still has considerable influence in Syria.

Dan Livermore Director general of DFAIT's Foreign Intelligence Division. Present for discussions about sending questions for Almalki to Syrian interrogators. Says he believed questions were never sent.

Garry James Loeppky Deputy commissioner operations, RCMP, throughout the period that El Maati, Almalki, Arar, and Nureddin were detained and tortured. Would not support helpful language about Arar in a proposed letter to the Syrians from Minister Graham. Honoured in March 2003 by the Governor General as an officer of the Order of Merit of Police Officers.

Hon. John Manley Chairman, ad-hoc cabinet committee on Public Security and Anti-terrorism, set up to oversee Canada's response to 9/11. Served as counterpart to Tom Ridge, the U.S. advisor on Homeland Security. Deputy prime minister from January 2002 to December 2003.

Leo Martel Consul at the Canadian Embassy in Damascus from September 2002 to summer 2005. Visited Arar while he was in Syrian detention. Would not let Almalki take refuge in embassy. Now retired.

Hon. Paul Martin Prime minister from December 12, 2003, to February 2006. Oversaw the appointment of Justice O'Connor to head up the Arar Inquiry.

Monia Mazigh Led the campaign for the release of her husband, Maher Arar, from Syrian detention.

Alexa McDonough Former leader of the New Democratic Party, Foreign Affairs critic, and one of the first politicians to speak out on Arar's case.

Hon. Anne McLellan Justice minister and attorney general until January 2002. Pushed anti-terrorism legislation through into law. Deputy prime minister and Public Safety minister from December 2003 to February 2006. Resisted calls for inquiry into Arar's case until February 2004.

Hon. Dan McTeague Parliamentary secretary to Foreign Affairs Minister Graham, appointed in late 2003 to help with cases of Canadians in trouble abroad. Visited Almalki in Damascus after his release. Also worked on Nureddin's case.

Scott Mills Ontario Provincial Police officer seconded to Toronto's Project O Canada in September 2001. Led investigation into Ahmad El Maati's case. Likely one of the officers who questioned him at the airport on November 11, 2001.

Walid Mouallem One of two Syrian deputy Foreign ministers. Told Canadian ambassador Pillarella that CSIS said it did not want Arar back in Canada.

Alex Neve Secretary general of Amnesty International Canada. Played a pivotal role in the cases of El Maati, Almalki, Arar, and Nureddin.

Muayyed Nureddin Canadian Iraqi detained at the Iraqi-Syrian border on December 11, 2003. Taken to Far' Falastin until being released on January 13, 2004, after thirty-four days in detention. Has never been charged with any crime.

Justice Dennis O'Connor Associate chief justice of Ontario, appointed commissioner at the Arar Inquiry.

Juliet O'Neill *Ottawa Citizen* reporter whose home was raided by the RCMP on January 21, 2004.

Henry Garfield "Gar" Pardy Director general of DFAIT's consular division from 1995 until August 2003. Worked on El Maati, Almalki, and Arar cases. Retired.

Myra Pastyr-Lupul Case manager for the Middle East region in the consular division at DFAIT headquarters. Worked on the cases of El Maati, Almalki, Arar, and Nureddin.

Wayne Pilgrim Officer in charge of the RCMP's National Security Investigations Branch. In July 2002, briefed Commissioner Zaccardelli about indications El Maati had been exposed to "extreme treatment" in Egyptian detention. Approved of questions for Almalki's interrogators but says he didn't know they were sent.

Franco Pillarella Canada's ambassador to Syria from November 2000 to August 2003 while El Maati, Almalki, and Arar were detained there. Oversaw delivery of questions for Almalki to Syrian interrogators. Now working at Foreign Affairs in Ottawa.

Colin Powell U.S. secretary of state. Told Foreign Affairs Minister Bill Graham in November 2002 that Canada had approved Arar's removal to Syria.

Richard Proulx Assistant RCMP commissioner singled out in the Arar Report for failing to provide clear direction to RCMP officers regarding how to share information. Told a parliamentary committee in 2003 that the RCMP was not "dealing with the Syrian authorities." Honoured in 2004 by the Governor General as an officer of the Order of Merit for Police Officers.

Ahmed Ressam Algerian refugee claimant. Dubbed the "millennium bomber," Ressam was arrested at the U.S. border in December 1999 before he could carry out a plot to attack the Los Angeles International Airport. Convicted in 2005 on nine counts. Now serving a twenty-two-year sentence in a U.S. prison.

Rick Reynolds RCMP inspector in charge of the National Security Intelligence Branch at headquarters in 2003. Briefed Zaccardelli on concerns about efforts to help Arar after parliamentarians' visit to him in April 2003.

Jeff Sallot Senior political correspondent at *The Globe and Mail* who discovered the origins of the map that El Maati was questioned about in Canada, Syria, and Egypt.

Riad Saloojee Executive director of the Canadian Council on American Islamic Relations from 2001 to 2006. One of the first people to speak out publicly on Arar's case. Played a pivotal role in the campaign for his release.

Jonathan Solomon Policy adviser in DFAIT's Foreign Intelligence Division. One of the few officials who is on the record as objecting to sending questions to Syrian interrogators for Almalki.

Colonel George Salloum Head of the counter-terrorism interrogation team at Far' Falastin. Oversaw and participated in the interrogation and torture of El Maati, Almalki, Arar, and Nureddin. His team of interrogators included Haitham, Khaled, Abdallah, and Abu Elnour.

Erika Sheridan One of the RCMP officers involved in the searches on January 22, 2002. Asked Abdullah Almalki's cousin if she thought Abdullah would be travelling to Syria.

Larry D. Thompson U.S. deputy attorney general. Signed Arar's removal order.

Lorne Waldman Co-counsel to Arar before and during the Arar Inquiry.

Corporal Randy Walsh Assigned on October 5, 2001, as lead investigator of Project A-O Canada. Signed affidavits, containing information that was likely the product of torture, for search warrants executed on January 22, 2002.

Adrian White One of two CSIS agents who questioned El Maati about the map on September 11, 2001.

Giuliano Zaccardelli Commissioner of the RCMP from September 2000 until resigning in December 2006. Commanded the RCMP throughout the period that El Maati, Almalki, Arar, and Nureddin were detained, tortured, and interrogated overseas. Recently appointed to senior position in Interpol in Africa.

ACKNOWLEDGMENTS

First to Ahmad, Abdullah, Muayyed, and your families (especially Samira, Badr, Sana, and Khuzaimah) for inviting me into your homes, opening your lives to even more scrutiny, and enduring what must have seemed like endless questions and requests for clarifications. Trust does not easily follow torture and persecution, but you trusted me with your stories, and for that I am very grateful.

Thanks also to Maher, for contributing such a powerful foreword, and for your important input throughout this project. That you and Monia have not just survived but somehow thrive and contribute so much to society, despite everything you have had to endure, never ceases to amaze me.

Alex Neve, Jeff Sallot, and Riad Saloojee, I am grateful for your inspiration and for encouraging me to take this on—you were right, it was hard work but was worth it! Alex, you've been especially supportive—thank you.

To the others who've had encouraging words and valuable insight: Paul Copeland, Breese Davies, Marlys Edwardh, Shirley Heafey, Hilary Homes, Barb Jackman, Jasminka Kalajdzic, Maria LaHood, Hadayt Nazami, John Norris, Gar Pardy, John Tackaberry, Roch Tassé, Lorne Waldman, Maureen Webb, and Sameer Zuberi—I am very appreciative.

To my agent, John Pearce at Westwood Creative Artists—you've been incredible, really. I am so lucky I had you to help me navigate through this process. Thanks for all you've taught me.

For Diane Turbide, editorial director at Penguin, a huge thanks for having faith in a first-time author, for your commitment to this story, and for your never-ending patience. You are a pleasure to work with. Thanks also to Sandra Tooze for pulling it all together, to Debbie Gaudet, Judy Bunting, Elizabeth McKay, and everyone else at Penguin; to Sandy Cooke for hunting down photos; and to my editors and proofreaders, Judy Phillips, Heather Sangster, and Suzanne Needs.

To Jim Turk and my colleagues at the Canadian Association of University Teachers—I am grateful for your support and that you granted me the time I needed to pursue this project.

Finally, I leaned heavily on my family and friends to get this done. To my mother, Dolly, my father, Roger, and my brothers, Richard and Jason—thanks, as always, for being so supportive of my all-consuming ventures. I hope the newest addition to our family, Quinlan, understands why his aunt Kerry missed so much of his visit. And to my very good friends—Joan, Mim, Jamie, Kerri, Geoff, Jen, Rosemary, Gina, and Erik—thanks for being there.

INDEX

Mannville Public Library